Child Behavior and Development: Training for Diversity

Joan H. Cantor
Charles C. Spiker
Lewis P. Lipsitt

Editors

ABLEX PUBLISHING CORPORATION
NORWOOD, NEW JERSEY

Printed in the United States of America

Library of Congress Cataloging-in-Publication Data

Child behavior and development : training for diversity / Joan H.
    Cantor, Charles C. Spiker, and Lewis P. Lipsitt, editors.
        p. cm.
    Includes bibliographical references and index.
    ISBN 0-89391-726-5
    1. Child psychology. 2. Psychologists—Training of. 3. Child
psychology—Study and teaching (Graduate) I. Cantor, Joan H.
II. Spiker, Charles C. III. Lipsitt, Lewis Paeff, 1929-
BF722.C48   1991
155.4'07—dc20   91-9095
                                                        CIP

Ablex Publishing Corporation
355 Chestnut St.
Norwood, NJ 07648

Table of Contents

Preface

The field of child development and experimental child psychology has seemed to us, for many years, to be a fruitful area of scientific investigation, intellectual discourse, and social attention. Yet, in recent years, there has been a real decline in human energy committed to the science of child development, not to mention the decline in government and foundation funds relative to expenditures in other scientific areas. We are not certain why this has happened. Surely our society is interested in its children, in how they develop, and in the conditions under which they grow and learn.

When we contemplate the special problems of maturing children, we are especially taken with the indisputable fact that large numbers of youngsters are beset by (a) sensory deficits, often due to perinatal hazards; (b) learning problems, which may relate both to congenital deficits and environmental insufficiencies; and (c) familial conditions that conduce to the acquisition of defeatist and despondent reflections on one's self-worth. Yet we know of no way better to understand the developmental destinies of humans than through the discovery of their antecedents. In short, what is required is a better scientific understanding of the ways in which developmental outcomes are achieved.

We are not naive in this conceptualization. We know that we can be led astray by some of our best predictive tools, such as developmental tests, and by some of our best-supported psychological laws, even those obtained from experimental manipulative studies. Indeed we have had to introduce into our scientific language special concepts to account for the developmental surprises in our midst that are not so easily accounted for by our "common" understanding of the way things are. Thus, we have the "vulnerable but invincible" child and the "resilient" adolescent who were predicted to come to a bad end, but who endured and even excelled because of conditions which in principle can be understood, and even predicted, but were not anticipated. We have the "underachiever," whose attainments simply have not met our expectations. We have the "superachiever," who has (presumably) conquered all the impediments to success and has, despite these handicaps, risen to a level not predicted by our assessments. We hear ourselves saying, "If we only knew more."

Knowing more: That is the issue. How do we know more? We, the editors, are convinced that knowledge comes from the judicious application of the best empirical technology available at the time the scientific work is done. This includes the "technology" of the philosophy of science, and particularly of logic, as much as it does the modern polygraph and computer. We are convinced, moreover, that much of the technology of science, available even now, remains to be appropriated by behavioral and developmental scientists. In particular, we are hoping that this volume will help to revitalize a field which seems sometimes to have lost its steam, not because there are not exciting problems to be solved but because there is insufficient recognition that *behavior* problems are amenable to solution.

It is obvious that behavior and behavior problems are at the root of many developmental issues that society wishes to resolve. Accidents, suicide, and homicide, for example, are the principal killers of children—and indeed of all young people up to age 34. These three sources of mortality exceed in their toll all diseases combined. If one adds excessive drinking, drug abuse, eating aberrations, dangerous sexual behavior, and aggressive behaviors leading to assault and injury, not to mention those hazardous conditions in our lives caused by the well-meaning behavioral misadventures of others, such as road engineers and playground designers, it is clear that behavioral factors are *the* most important determinants of adverse life outcomes. Surely, these "killer" behaviors should be accorded some sort of primacy in the hierarchy of the biomedical sciences. Yet diseases win the funds, and the awards are garnered by those who provide inroads into the scientific understanding of lethal and morbid infections.

Has our society put the behavioral and social sciences aside for some reason? We think so. Most people do not believe that behavior can be understood well enough to effect, through behavioral or environmental intervention, anything like what can be achieved by developing an immunization. There is in our midst a skepticism about what can be achieved by an application of the scientific method to behavioral processes. Given a choice of spending a million dollars on research into the viral origins of multiple sclerosis or the same amount on the experiential origins of aggressive behavior or of hyperactive impulse disorder, from which many more persons die, most people would opt for the expenditure for MS, even though this affliction affects only one one-thousandth the number of people who have behavior problems.

Why does our society have little confidence in the exploration of the origins of human behavior? Perhaps one of the best guesses is that we, the behavioral and developmental scientists, have not been sufficiently convincing about the efficacy of scientific explorations in revealing answers about the origins of human behavior. This state of affairs may be due, in part, to our having been rather ineffective to date in revealing such answers!

Our antidote is this: Our young developmental and behavioral scientists need to learn the methods of scientific investigation that will solve the problems or answer the questions that they wish to pose. We know of no better way to bring on the next generation of scholars in child development than to assure they will undertake the task of learning to construct fruitful theories, to predict statements of fact that can and will be subjected to empirical scrutiny, and to evaluate with skill the data that are harvested in support of their hypothetical pronouncements.

It is toward that end that we dedicate this volume.

May 1991

Joan H. Cantor
Charles C. Spiker
Lewis P. Lipsitt

Social Development and Social Psychology: Perspectives on Interpersonal Relationships*

Willard W. Hartup
University of Minnesota

INTRODUCTION

Social development consists of changes over time in the child's understanding of, attitudes toward, and actions with others. Relevant concerns include: (a) normative issues, that is, age-related changes in social activity that are characteristic of most children everywhere; and (b) individual differences, that is, differences among children that emerge as they grow older.

Social development circumscribes different subject matters from other domains in developmental psychology. Persons possess certain characteristics that other objects in the child's world do not. First, human beings have *intentions*. Second, persons have *feelings* and *emotions*—anger, happiness, sadness, and fear. Third, people *communicate* with one another. The mysteries and complexities of human communication have no clear counterpart in the manifestations to be understood about the physical world. Fourth, human beings have *cognitions* and *motives* unlike those characterizing other organisms. Deriving from these attributes, theories are constructed by human beings about *themselves* and *others* that are unlike their theories about other things in the universe (no other organism, for example, is known to

* Preparation of this chapter was facilitated by Grant No. RO1 MH 42888, National Institute of Mental Health. Author's address: Institute of Child Development, University of Minnesota, 51 E. River Road, Minneapolis, MN 55455.

appreciate its own mortality). *Relationships* formed by human beings with one another also have dimensions unlike the relationships existing among other entities in the natural world. Finally, *groups* and *institutions* have characteristics unlike other natural aggregations or "systems." Ontogenetic concomitants of these entities comprise the subject matter of social developmental psychology.

Along with the rest of developmental psychology, the study of social development is essentially a correlational endeavor. Experimental analysis is used to clarify many issues, but subjects cannot be assigned randomly to different age groups for purposes of investigation: observers must necessarily study the "natural" unfolding of social activity over time—its ontogenesis. The study of social development is essentially the study of time-dependencies, a "genetic" enterprise in the strict sense of the world (relating to the origin, development, or causal antecedents of something; *Webster's Ninth New Collegiate Dictionary*, 1983).

Because social development refers to the child's behavior with other individuals, the subfield connects to a number of other social sciences. One can cite connections to history (cf. Hareven, 1978), economics (Keniston, 1977), and political science (Hess & Torney, 1967). The disciplines which have generated the closest relations with developmental psychology, however, have been sociology and social psychology.

Developmental psychologists and sociologists share major interests in socialization (i.e., the processes leading to the integration of the individual into society) and the social context, especially cultural variations in the growth and development of children and institutions. Connections between sociology and child development have been evident since the early years of the century, when Cooley (1909) argued:

> that human nature is not something existing separately in the individual, but a group nature or primary phase of society. It is the nature which is developed and expressed in those simple, face-to-face groups of the family, the playground, and the neighborhood. In the essential similarity of these is to be found the basis, in experience, for similar ideas and sentiments in the human mind. In these, everywhere, human nature comes into existence. Man does not have it at birth; he cannot acquire it except through fellowship, and it decays in isolation. (pp. 29–30)

Developmental psychologists and social psychologists have had common interests—both substantive and methodological—for nearly a century. The first social psychological experiment was Tripplett's (1897) demonstration that school children were more energetic and performed better at winding fishing reels when they worked in groups than when they worked alone. And, over the years, several major advances in the technology of social psychology originated in work with children: child psychologists, for example, conducted the major benchwork leading to methods for systematically observing social interaction in situ (Thomas, 1929; Goodenough, 1928) and for studying group dynamics (Lewin, Lippitt, & White, 1938).

Nevertheless, social developmental psychology and social psychology have remained largely separate tracks or areas of specialization in graduate training, departmental tables of organization, and professional networking. Contemporary social developmental psychology thus does not represent a developmental *social psychology* much more than cognitive developmental psychology represents a developmental *cognitive psychology* (Masters, Yarkin-Levin, & Graziano, 1984).

Considerable activity, however, occurs in the interface between developmental and social psychology; this activity and its implications for graduate training bear examination and analysis. But this work does not define a subfield or even a specialization, and it is not my purpose to lament that fact. On the other hand, my purpose *is* to encourage work in this interface because of its importance in understanding both certain features of development and certain features of human social intercourse.

This chapter is divided into three main sections: First, the interface (i.e., "boundary area") between developmental and social psychology is described in terms of the contemporary work that goes on there. Historical considerations will be taken. Second, social and developmental work on close relationships will be described. In this section, I will attempt to view current research activity "from the bridge" between social and developmental psychology. Finally, training implications will be examined, including both changes we might make and changes that should not be made.

BOUNDARIES BETWEEN DEVELOPMENTAL AND SOCIAL PSYCHOLOGY

Historical considerations

Genetic themes were evident in many areas of philosophical and biological thought in the nineteenth century, and it is no great surprise that many of the early psychologists were interested in the ontogeny of behavior. Charles Darwin and Herbert Spencer were forerunners; Alfred Binet, Wilhelm Preyer, William Stern, James Mark Baldwin, Sigmund Freud, and G. Stanley Hall were early practitioners. The ontogenetic assumption guiding the work of these individuals can be stated relatively simply: "in order to understand man you have to understand the life history of his activities . . . psychology is a natural science—a definite part of biology" (Watson, 1926, p. 34). The mental and social lives of adults, then, were assumed to be best understood by analysis of the child's activities—the core concern of developmental psychology to this day—and by use of observational and correlational methods.

Other psychologists, including Wilhelm Wundt, took a different view concerning what the child can and cannot teach us, and what the methods of natural science can and cannot uncover. Using adults as both subjects and observers, Wundt (1907) and others argued that experimental methods were basic to understanding behavior. Brass instruments were required for both controlled presentation of stimuli and carefully calibrated measurement, although, to be sure, research instruments were not always made of brass (trait names on a piece of paper were sometimes the "brass instruments" of the early social psychologists, and check marks on a piece of paper were the responses to be calibrated). Hypothesis-testing rather than description became the defining activity of the discipline.

The division between developmental and experimental psychology occurred very early in the history of psychology and generated considerable debate (Cairns & Ornstein, 1979); moreover, the debate refuses to come to an end, although the role of experimental analysis in the study of developmental issues is widely appreciated (McCandless & Spiker, 1956). Some historians (Boring, 1950) have thought that ontogenetic views might actually have come to dominate psychology had these early debates gone differently, but this did not happen, and experimental psychology has largely prevailed. The Division on Developmental Psychology (Division 7) became a refuge for genetic psychologists in the 1940s, when the American Psychological Association became divisionally organized—a safe distance, speaking numerically, from the Division of Experimental Psychology (Division 3) but comfortably close to the Division of Comparative and Physiological Psychology (Division 6) and its comparative developmentalists.

The history of social psychology is closely associated with the history of experimental psychology (Allport, 1954), and its theories and methods clearly show that lineage. Whereas developmental psychologists have been concerned with *substantive* issues (What develops?) and with behavioral description, social psychologists have been mainly concerned with *process* issues (Why does an event occur or an effect come about?). Cause and effect in social psychology is studied in relation to both social understanding and social action; experimental methods have been dominant. Although children have found their way into experiments conducted by numerous social psychologists, this is usually because they have been convenient subjects or their naivete has been a methodological asset. Fortunately, this situation seems to be changing (see below).

Contemporary Differences

Not surprisingly, many topics interest both social psychologists and social developmental psychologists. Research workers in both areas study social attraction, close relationships, self-knowledge, social effectance, social motivation, emotions, the integration of social information, and many more. These subject matters are everyday concerns, and it is hardly surprising that they have become core issues in both subfields. It is also not surprising that different orientations to the same subject matter have emerged. Nor is it surprising that, over time, these differences have become institutionalized, that is, reflected in scientific networking. The distinctive orientations emerging in social and developmental psychology are exemplified in the next two subsections through some observations on research in impression formation and social attraction.

Impression formation: An example. Feldman and Ruble (1981) described the different orientations taken in these two subfields in work on person perception. According to these writers, social psychologists have been interested mainly in the *processes* by which impressions are formed (e.g., information integration) and the implications of such impressions for behavior (e.g., their impact on social interaction). Process issues drawing the attention of social psychologists have included the manner in which trait information combines in social perception (whether it is additive or averaged), primacy and recency effects, and the circumstances that bring about distortions in the way individuals perceive others. Major causal questions have been addressed, including the manner in which information is used by individuals to attribute particular motives or abilities to others, as well as the relation of these attributions to the categories individuals use in describing others, making social judgments, and making predictions about other persons. Finally, an extensive literature deals with the effects of these impressions on social interaction, for example, showing that one's behavior toward other individuals is congruent with the expectations one forms (e.g., Snyder & Swann, 1978).

Social developmentalists, on the other hand, have examined social understanding largely as an event constrained by cognitive development, and largely within the theoretical framework known as cognitive developmental theory (Shantz, 1983). Thus, children's understanding of other individuals is thought to reflect general changes in perspective-taking ability (Selman, 1980) that coincide with the shift from egocentric to decentered thinking or with changes in the child's theories about the way the mind works (Flavell, 1988). Not much attention has been given to the origins or beginnings of impression formation, although the early manifestations of self-knowledge and the early use of social attributions are increasingly studied (Bretherton, in press; Ruble & Rholes, 1981). Mostly, the developmental agenda has consisted of describing the *contents* of children's impressions rather than the manner in which these impressions are deduced and elicited. Much attention, for example, has been given to age changes in the differentiation, complexity, and organization of impressions (see Shantz, 1983).

Methods have been different in developmental and social psychological work in this area, too. The use of unstructured, free descriptions obviously fits the objectives of developmental researchers, whereas the process-oriented work of the social psychologists commonly requires the use of artificially constrained information. Exclusive use of either method carries certain risks, so that the methodological difference between fields is not especially desirable (Feldman & Ruble, 1981).

Social attraction: An example. Social (interpersonal) attraction has been a long-standing concern in both developmental and social psychology. Scholars in both fields were influenced by the early work of Moreno (1934), but empirical work has diverged in ways that resemble the divergence among studies of impression formation (see above). That is, social psychologists have concerned themselves with notions about the processes responsible for the emergence of interpersonal attraction, whereas developmentalists have been concerned primarily with identifying the characteristics of individuals (i.e., the behavioral content) that make them attractive or unattractive to others and their long-term implications.

Among the vast number of studies emerging from the social psychological laboratory have been results suggesting the relevance of similarity in attitudes and other personal characteristics to attraction, and demonstrations that this association depends on the degree to which similarity is positively reinforcing or instrumental in furthering the partners' goals. Still other investigations have concerned personal complementarities as determinants of attraction, although the idea that "opposites attract" turns out to be simplistic. Exchange theories have provided the most robust theoretical base for use in accounting for social attraction in numerous contexts—both its origins and its functions (Berscheid, 1985).

Developmentalists have been interested in attraction too, but surprisingly little attention has been paid to origins and to changes with age. Perhaps there is little reason to be interested in the origins of mother–child attraction, since both prenatal and perinatal propinquity are so obviously involved. Rather, developmentalists have been concerned with the personal qualities (in babies and mothers) that extend mutual attraction into a relationship, and especially into different kinds of relationships—for example, "secure" ones and "insecure" ones (Ainsworth, Blehar, Waters, & Wall, 1978). Once again, it is the content of the interactions comprising these relationships which is most interesting, as well as the classes of interactions that work best in predicting developmental outcomes.

Similar differences in emphasis on process and content are evident between social and developmental psychology in the treatment of peer attraction. Theodore Newcomb (1961) entitled his classic book *The Acquaintance Process* to signal an interest in the experiential determinants of social attraction. No comparable work exists in the developmental literature. Relevant developmental studies are mostly correlational investigations showing the advantages of possessing an attractive face, a beautiful body, an ordinary name (as opposed to an offbeat one), and a repertoire of friendly, prosocial, nonaggressive, and socially competent behaviors. Once again, it is the "contents" of social attraction that have interested developmental psychologists. And, once again, the empirical work consists mainly of descriptive studies in contrast to the experimental investigations that have typified the social psychological literature. The functional significance of social attraction (e.g., its significance in forming and maintaining close relationships and its significance in long-term prediction of individual outcome) interests both social and developmental psychologists, but almost everything else about their investment in this area is different (see Berscheid, 1985; Hartup, 1983).

Comment. Despite these traditional differences, considerable activity occurs in the "boundary area" separating developmental and social psychology. Studies of impression formation and social attraction are cases in point. The study of interpersonal relationships is another. Turning now to this area, I attempt to identify similarities and differences in the work that developmental and social psychologists do, but also to identify certain understudied issues in the psychology of interpersonal relationships. It is my contention that these issues are understudied partly because they lie in the boundary area between the two subdisciplines.

INTERPERSONAL RELATIONSHIPS

Relationships are more or less enduring ties or connections between individuals, manifested behaviorally as a series of interactions. Personal investment in these entities is strong, a mutual desire for social contact is usually evident, and interactions are maintained over a considerable period (Hinde, 1979; Kelly et al., 1983b).

Relationships and their significance in human affairs have interested many investigators in a number of disciplines, although a "science" of relationships is still emerging (Berscheid & Peplau, 1983). Progress has been slow for many reasons, not the least of which are the strong taboos in our society against systematic study of social intimacies like love and sex, and against outside intervention into these same intimacies. Nevertheless, no one disagrees about the importance of close relationships in everyday life. The centrality of close relationships in individual well-being was recognized very early by Freud (1957), Durkheim (1951), and Cooley (1909), among others, as was the importance of social support (i.e., networks of relationships) and the importance of relationships in childhood socialization. New evidence concerning close relationships and their implications for health and happiness accumulates steadily. Thus, the importance of these social entities is well-recognized. On the other hand, illuminating the manner in which relationships mediate these effects has been a long and arduous task. In this sense, mainly, it can be said that a science of relationships is emerging.

Family relationships are among the relationships most extensively studied by both social and developmental psychologists. The reasons are obvious: family relationships are the most ubiquitous relationships known, the most durable (including sibling relationships, the longest ones), the most important in socialization and the transmission of culture, the most central to the individual's sense of well-being, and the most significant as economic and societal units. Perturbations within the relationships comprising one's family elicit the most intense emotions many people encounter—both "highs" and "lows." Likewise, secular changes in families as institutions instigate heated and protracted debates among policy makers.

The interests of developmental psychologists in the family have been child centered: parent–child relationships, sibling relationships, and husband–wife relationships (as these bear on the well-being of the child). The interests of social psychologists have largely been directed at social attraction and mate selection as well as spousal satisfaction. Although certain topics, (e.g., spousal satisfaction) have interested investigators in both subdisciplines, objectives differ. Developmental psychologists, for example, are mainly interested in marital satisfaction as a mediator in childhood socialization (Belsky, 1981), whereas social psychologists are primarily interested in the implications of spousal satisfaction for the well-being of husbands and wives themselves.

Friendships have interested both social and developmental psychologists, too. Developmental psychologists, not surprisingly, more frequently ask questions concerning the developmental functions of these relationships, that is, the contributions they make to the adaptation of the individual child. Social psychologists are more likely to be interested in the functions of these relationships among adults. While the questions asked about friendships may also differ according to subdiscipline, investment in these relationships is strong in both developmental and social psychology (see Hartup & Rubin, 1986; Duck, 1988a). Other relationships draw attention differentially according to whether their functions are mainly related to socialization (e.g., teacher–child relationships) or to adult concerns (e.g., work relationships, sexual relationships).

Developmental Psychology

Two issues account for most developmental research on interpersonal relationships: (a) the manner in which relationships contribute to the child's development, and (b) the manner in which the child's development changes them. Both adult–child and child–child relationships have been studied vigorously.

Family relationships. The emergence and functioning of caregiver–child attachments in the first 2 years of life has dominated this area. Attachment qualities ("secure" versus "insecure") have been differentiated and demonstrated to be relatively stable, at least when family conditions are stable (Waters, Hay, & Richters, 1986). Moreover, attachment security is associated with more effective socioemotional functioning in the child than attachment insecurity—both concurrently and later (Renken, Egeland, Marvinney, Sroufe, & Mangelsdorf, 1989).

The nature of attachments between children and their parents is not well explored in middle childhood and adolescence, but conceptual and measurement work is under way (Main, Kaplan, & Cassidy, 1985). Retrospective accounts of the childhood attachments that existed between adults and *their* parents have begun to appear (Ricks, 1983; Main et al., 1985), but relatively little is known about the concurrent status of these relationships among older adults. Overall, the development of attachments beyond infancy is understudied.

Studies of father–child relationships have received considerable attention, although our understanding of these relationships lags considerably behind our understanding of mother–child relationships. Especially understudied are relationships involving fathers who are primary caregivers. Nevertheless, fathers have been found to be generally competent caregivers, and father–child relationships are now known to be similar to mother–child relationships in many ways (Lamb, Pleck, Charnov, & Levine, 1987). Some studies, however, have been directed at differences in these relationships. For example, fathers have been shown to conduct themselves differently from mothers when playing with their children; and, while mother–child and father–child interaction both encompass positive and negative affect, positive interactions with mothers are more likely to occur in caretaking, and those with fathers are more likely to occur in play (Collins & Gunnar, 1990). Role relations differ, too, and change with age. As compared to fathers, for example, mothers become increasingly involved in both intimate and conflictual interactions with their youngsters in late childhood and adolescence, especially during early adolescence (Collins & Russell, in press).

Studies of sibling relations have centered on conflict, reflecting the long-time interest in sibling rivalry, and these conflicts have been shown to be important in the emergence of social understanding among young children (Dunn, 1988). Status issues in sibling relations, however, have been shown to decline in importance during childhood, at least in the children's eyes (Furman & Buhrmester, 1985).

Children's friendships. The development and significance of children's friendships has attracted considerable attention among developmental psychologists. Observational studies show that behavioral reciprocities are among the earliest markers of friendship interaction, emerging among toddlers who are considered "friends" by their mothers (Howes, 1983). Cooperation and mutuality are further refined among preschool and elementary school children who are friends (Newcomb & Brady, 1982), social knowledge is shared more extensively than with nonfriends (Ladd & Emerson, 1984), and conflicts are resolved between friends differently from those arising between nonfriends (Hartup, Laursen, Stewart, & Eastenson, 1988). Beginning in early childhood, children also talk about their friends differently from other children, emphasizing the reciprocity and commitment that exists between them and, as time goes on, their intimacy (Buhrmester & Furman, 1987). Developmental studies also show that troubled children have difficulties in making and maintaining friendships. Indeed, a lack of close friendships is a risk factor in social and emotional development (Rutter & Garmezy, 1983).

Relations among relationships. Finally, developmental psychologists have been interested in relations among relationships. New work, for example, confirms that the quality of the marital relationship is, indeed, related to mother–child interaction in early childhood and beyond (Sroufe & Fleeson, 1986; Belsky, Rovine, & Fish, 1989) and to the intensity as well as the positivity of the father–child relationship (Lamb & Elster, 1985). Process considerations underlying these results have not yet been sorted out, although most investigators believe that these configurations indicate the occurrence of both direct effects (e.g., happy wives make happy mothers) and indirect ones (e.g., marital conflict is both a stress event for the child and a "background" condition providing the child with opportunities to learn aggressive modes of conflict resolution rather than nondestructive ones; Cummings, Vogel, Cummings, & El-Sheikh, in press).

In addition, family relationships are known to be associated with the quality of the child's relations with other children outside the family. Secure attachments are believed to provide: (a) an emotional base conducive to successful first encounters with other children (Sroufe & Fleeson, 1986); (b) the impetus for mothers to arrange these contacts (Ladd & Golter, 1988); and (c) social regulatory skills among young children that generalize to their interactions with other children (Parke, MacDonald, Burks, Carson, & Bhavnagri, 1989). Parent and peer relationships, then, are synergistic entities.

Comment. Taken together, developmental studies reflect considerable interest in describing the *content* and *qualities* of close relationships. Secure and insecure attachments have been described; mother–child relationships have been contrasted with father–child relationships in terms of constituent interactions; the stability of these relationships has been studied. In addition, developmental researchers have demonstrated strong interest in individual outcome, that is, the manner in which relationship histories are salient in childhood socialization and personality development. Surprisingly, relatively little attention has been given to relationship origins. Normative changes in parent–child relations beyond early childhood are just beginning to be charted (Collins & Gunnar, in press); normative changes in peer relations are not well documented (Hartup, 1983). Finally, causal mechanisms in attraction and relationship change in the short term (proximal causation) have received relatively little attention in spite of great interest among developmentalists in long term outcomes (distal causation).

Social Psychology

Social psychology has become the nexus through which the contributions of numerous disciplines to the study of relationships are channeled. Social psychologists arguably produce more work in the area than members of any other discipline and, in recent decades, have initiated most of the major volumes devoted to theoretical and methodological integration. By one count (Duck, 1988b), social psychologists account for more than 80% of the more than 25 volumes of this kind published in the last decade.

Sheer volume thus makes a brief synthesis of social psychological work on relationships impossible. The interested reader is referred to works by Kelley et al. (1983a), Duck (1988a), Argyle and Henderson (1985), and the forthcoming *Review of Personality and Social Psychology* (Vol. 10). Nevertheless, broad trends in this work can be identified, and historical changes noted.

Description. Everyone agrees that one urgent issue has been to find good ways of describing relationships. Consensus has emerged around the condition of *interdependence* in the social interaction between two individuals as the essential quality that distinguishes relationships from other social entities (Sears, 1951; Kelley et al., 1983b). Closeness, then, refers to *high* interdependence or impact, as indicated by the frequency, strength, diversity, and duration of the interconnected activity (Berscheid & Peplau, 1983). Not everyone is comfortable with this scheme, since metaphors ("ties," "bonds," "attachments") are still used to describe relationships in many literatures. But reducing relationships to specified dimensions has been a giant step toward a science of relationships, an objective espoused by most scholars.

a. The enduring nature of relationships. Encounters between strangers are not good models of relationships, except for studying the bases on which people sort themselves out and become acquaintances. Brief encounters between strangers don't provide sufficient information about the dimensions characterizing relationships to enable them to be classified and their development studied. Behavioral content, for example, is commonly used to describe relationships (i.e., what two individuals do together), but emotional qualities, the range of activities encompassed and their patterning, the symmetry of the interaction (i.e., who influences whom over time), and the duration of social contact are relevant dimensions, too (Hinde, 1979; Kelley et al., 1983b). While it may be possible to identify important dimensions in some close relationships by means of brief encounters (e.g., by watching mothers and infants in the 20-minute Strange Situation, Ainsworth et al., 1978, or by observing husbands and wives discussing how to spend their money or plan a vacation, Gottman, 1979), ongoing relationships can seldom be described except by aggregating observations over time. In addition, relationships are emergent phenomena: Whether examined in terms of "stages" that include "formation," "maintenance," and "termination" (Levinger & Levinger, 1986) or in some other manner, most relationships undergo major transformations over time. Obviously these transformations cannot be studied using brief encounters. Largely for these reasons, recent empirical studies show a shift among social psychologists from studying social attraction and acquaintanceship among comparative strangers to the dynamic, changing nature of relationships among individuals who know one another well (Duck, 1988a; Kelley et al., 1983a).

b. "Outsider" and "insider" methods. Two main strategies are used to study interpersonal relationships: (a) "outsider methods," that is, measuring the overt interactions between two individuals over time by means of outside observers; and (b) "insider methods," that is, measuring the perceptions and interpretations of the interactants, as these occur over time (McClintock, 1983; Furman, 1984).

Tremendous advances have been made in the recording, reduction, and statistical modeling of overt interaction. Through them, we have learned, for example, that satisfied married couples, as compared to dissatisfied couples, exhibit less patterning and structure in their interactions, are more positive and less negative toward one another (especially the latter), are less likely to exhibit reciprocity in negative behavior, and are more symmetrical in their predictions about one another (Gottman, 1979). Similarly, comparisons between children who are becoming friends and children who are not "hitting it off" show that: (a) communication clarity and connectedness in first encounters is the best predictor of hitting it off, and (b) communication clarity and connectedness are even more closely related to hitting if off when measured in subsequent sessions, and self-disclosure then appears on the roster of significant correlates along with information exchange, conflict management, and reaching common ground in activities (Gottman, 1983).

Relationships also need to be viewed from the "inside" in order to determine the manner in which their functions are understood by the interactants and the manner in which their actions are construed (and these construals used). Thus, adult–child relationships are known to be perceived by *both* parents and children as asymmetrical, "vertical" relationships in terms of power distribution and authority for controlling the child (Youniss, 1980; Furman & Buhrmester, 1985). Children quickly learn to interpret the actions of both their parents and themselves in terms of these understandings (e.g., giving in to a child is not always viewed by children as a kindness, Youniss, 1980), and to modulate their actions accordingly. Other studies show that children know that different provisions derive from their relationships with different individuals. Parents are regarded as major providers of affection, assistance, and ego support; grandparents are viewed as sources of affection and support, too, but not as sources of assistance; friends and siblings are understood to be providers of companionship and intimacy, but it is siblings, not friends, with whom one expects conflict (Furman & Buhrmester, 1985).

Finally, investigators have studied the means used by relationship members to create contexts that are consistent with interpretations of one another. Situations may be altered or structured by one member so that the other's actions confirm one's expectations (sometimes called "framing"). In other instances, attributional biases may be used by one member to clarify the ambiguous actions of the other. Thus, Dodge and Frame (1982) found that aggressive boys, as compared to nonaggressive ones, more readily perceive the actions of other children toward themselves as hostile, and behave accordingly. Such results are merely one indication that overt and covert events interconnect in determining the interaction that occurs within relationships.

Causation. The most extensive commitments among social psychologists interested in relationships have been to the study of causation, i.e., to the conditions which generate continuities in relationships, on the one hand, and changes in them, on the other. Causation is not a simple matter to construe but, generally, it refers to events and conditions that cooccur with the designated continuities or changes, and which are necessary for them to occur.

a. Causal events and conditions. One type of causal event occurs within social interaction, that is, in the relation between the actions of one individual and the actions of another. A second set of causal "conditions" consists of personal attributes and environmental characteristics that affect the interaction occurring between individuals (Kelley et al., 1983b).

Numerous studies demonstrate that causal chains exist in social interaction. Patterson (1982) and his colleagues, for example, identified a series of causal events occurring in family interaction that are called "coercive cycles." Briefly, one person behaves in a manner that is aversive to another, and the second is likely to be aversive in return, especially if the first person's aversive actions appear to be modifiable. These exchanges continue, and escalate, until one person ceases to behave aversively; usually, this stops the aversive behavior of the other individual. But the person who first forces his or her partner to stop behaving aversively is encouraged thereby to use aversive behaviors in the future (particularly toward the submitting individual). Empirical studies demonstrate that, through these coercive cycles, mothers and their children are both trained to become initiators and victims of aggression. Understanding these negative reinforcements (which are difficult to demonstrate with controlled laboratory experiments or in brief encounters) has been a breakthrough in understanding the family relationships of aggressive, antisocial boys and the manner in which close relationships are involved in the etiology of both adolescent and adult aggression (Patterson; 1982; Patterson & Bank, 1989).

Personal causes are "relatively enduring characteristics of the individuals, such as their personality traits or abilities" that bear on their interaction with one another (Berscheid & Peplau, 1983, p. 14). Relational causes refer to conditions in which either the *combination* of dispositions represented by two individuals or their previous interaction affects their behavior toward one another. Continuity and change in relationships thus derive from sources both within individuals and between them. For example, when two toddlers both have histories of secure attachments to their mothers, their interaction with one another tends to be harmonious and reciprocal. When a secure toddler interacts with another toddler who has a history of *anxious*-resistant attachment, there is also little strife. In fact, secure children are somewhat more sociable and constructive following object struggles with anxiously resistant associates than with securely attached associates. But interaction between secure toddlers and toddlers who are *avoidantly* resistant to their mothers is marked by relatively high aggression—to which both partners contribute (Pastor, 1981). Children thus behave differently depending on the developmental histories of their partners, and their relationships with different partners also vary.

Situational or environmental causes are "features of the social environment or of the physical environment within which the relationship is embedded" (Berscheid & Peplau, 1983). Social causes range from the societal norms that govern the interaction between two individuals in some way to the activities they engage in. Relevant environmental conditions range from weather conditions to toys and equipment, and include all of the elements comprising "behavior settings" (Barker, 1968). Thus, situational stress and scarce resources have been linked to conflict in relationships (Peterson, 1983), and the conditions commonly called "working class status" have been related to conflict as well (Rubin, 1976). Conflicts are also related to social norms as a function of the partner's identity: for example, adolescent conflicts with mothers and fathers are likely to involve norms relating to work and social obligations, whereas conflicts with friends more often concern activities and friendship obligations (Laursen, 1989). Social networks in the immediate environment are also related to relationships. Unstable network conditions, for example, are associated with lesser stability in the security of caregiver–infant attachment than stable ones are (Egeland & Farber, 1984), and social support compensates for environmental instabilities in promoting good caregiver–infant relationships involving teen mothers (Crockenberg, 1981).

b. Exchange (learning) theories. Among the many theories advanced within social psychology to account for continuity and change in relationships, the most widely known are the so-called *exchange theories* (see Burgess & Huston, 1979; Kelley & Thibault, 1978; Kelley et al., 1983a). Essentially, these theories are all based on the proposition that relationships emerge only to the extent that this is in the mutual interest of the individuals involved. Numerous variations on exchange theory exist, but they all reflect their origins in learning theory.

Many ambiguities exist in thinking about relationships in exchange terms. These ambiguities reflect our limited understanding of how persons evaluate what they "receive" from a social exchange; why human beings are so strongly motivated to make social comparisons and to concern themselves with "fairness"; how information about self and other is integrated in determining social interaction; and the significance of the actual commodities, resources, and rewards that are exchanged (see Hinde, 1979; Graziano, 1984). Answers to these questions may differ greatly when considered in relation to short-term and long-term exchanges. Within enduring relationships (the sort with which social psychologists are increasingly concerned), aggregates of exchanges, rather than single occurrences, are the dimensions to be understood (Kelley & Thibault, 1978).

c. *Cognitive theories.* Cognitive theories have contributed greatly to the study of relationships, most notably, dissonance and balance theories (Festinger, 1957; Heider, 1958; Newcomb, 1953). The general notion underlying these approaches (which are actually diverse) is that the feelings two individuals have about one another vary according to the extent they share opinions about themselves, others, and objects in the environment. When attitudes and beliefs about another person are consistent (e.g., another individual is liked and also believed to be similar to oneself), "balance" exists; inconsistencies are experienced as "dissonances" or "imbalances" that must be resolved in order for one to be comfortable. These notions have been useful in exploring the role of similarities and complementarities in social attraction, and a vast literature is based on them. Balance notions are flexible, having been successfully applied to many different situations and conditions bearing on relationships (Secord & Backman, 1974). These notions have not been as successful in accounting for disliking as for liking, though, and the assumption that inconsistencies are always aversive is questionable. Additionally, the use of these notions for studying long-term, ongoing relationships has been difficult.

Cognitive theories are, however, being elaborated to account for continuities and changes in relationships. In some instances (e.g., social comparison theory), cognitive dimensions are being incorporated into exchange theories (Kelley & Thibault, 1978). Still other theoretical advances offer new ways of thinking about relationships altogether.

Ginsburg (1988), for example, has attempted an integration of three viewpoints currently enjoying considerable vogue: rules, scripts, and prototypes. *Rules* apply to social exchanges both microanalytically (e.g., in turn taking) and macroanalytically (e.g., in establishing privacy conditions). Rules are known to constrain the expression of power in relationships—they govern autonomy and dependence; they apply to the manner in which social control is achieved and accounted for. *Scripts* are shared notions about "what happens" in different situations or, more precisely, stereotyped representations of the actions occurring in various situations (e.g., getting ready for bed or hosting a dinner party). Scripts serve as a basis for organizing social information in memory, and may have a bearing on social action. Presumably, relationship information as well as routine situations occurring within relationships are "scripted," but this notion has not been explored very extensively. *Prototypes* ("best exemplars") are believed to constrain the representations that people have about their relationships (e.g. their friendships or their romantic relationships), as well as other events in the world. That is, how we think and talk about our relationships may determine the kinds of relationships we produce. Overall, these notions are interesting, they have attracted wide attention, and little stands in the way of using them productively in relationships research. Demonstration of their utility, however, lies largely in the future.

d. Motivational theories. Motivational theories concerning relationship origins and functioning emerged from personality theory rather than from social psychology. The contributions of the psychoanalytic theorists (both Freudian and neo-Freudian) are well known. Revisions of these theories continue to be made, and certain revisionist positions have been enormously influential. Bowlby's (1969) attachment theory, for example, derives from psychoanalytic theory, even though its motivational aspects have been stripped away.

Essentially, motivational theories consider the origins and functions of interpersonal relationships to be rooted in conditions of personal need (McAdams, 1988). In some instances, a single, unitary need is regarded as the "theme" around which every significant element in an individual's relationships reverberates. In other instances, relationships are believed to resonate to more than one need: two needs, in some cases (e.g., sex and aggression, power and intimacy) and numerous needs, in others (see Murray, 1938). Not wishing to minimize the contributions of these theories to our causal understanding of relationships, it is nevertheless the case that these views are less central in social psychology today than once was the case.

Comment. Two issues dominate current work on interpersonal relationship in social psychology: (a) *description*, and (b) *causation*. Relationships are better specified than they used to be, both from the "outside" and from the "inside." The greatest contribution of the social psychologists, however, may be the elaboration of theories to account for the origins, maintenance, and changes that occur in close relationships.

Similarities and differences thus exist in the issues about relationships to which social and developmental psychologists have devoted themselves. Describing relationships is a major concern in both fields. Ontogenetic issues, not surprisingly, receive attention mostly from the developmentalists while the processes underlying both continuities and changes in relationships have been largely ignored by these psychologists. Causal theories, on the other hand, have burgeoned within social psychology.

Understudied Boundary Issues

The boundaries between developmental and social psychologists in studying interpersonal relationships have had some unfortunate consequences, among which are these: (a) First, the theories which have been used in developmental psychology to account for continuities and changes in relationships over time are weak, and interest in the causes of continuity and change in relationships is insufficient. Second, the developmental generalizability of our most widely used causal theories is largely untested. Developmental analysis has not been used, to the extent that it ought, to determine whether these theories are entirely correct. Third, the dialectics involving the development of individuals are mostly unstudied. Changing relationships impinge on changes in individual growth and development, but the individual's development unquestionably changes these same relationships. These dialectics are especially understudied as they involve children's cognitive development (Hartup, 1985).

Accounting for developmental change. Attachment theorists (Bowlby, 1969) have argued that the child's earliest relationships emerge on the basis of intermingled genetically determined "biases" in the infant and "pre-established" patterns of caregiving in the mother. "Given the biases in the infant's learning abilities, sensitive care acts like a catalyst (or a lubricant) to insure that components of the attachment control system . . . fall in place" (Waters, in press). These biases, however, are not well specified, are relatively weak explanations to account for the near-universal onset of attachment in the second 6 months, and are similarly weak in accounting for the irregularities with which secure base behavior is organized in different families and in different cultures.

Even if universal, wired-in characteristics account for the integration that occurs in mother–infant interaction, it is difficult to account for subsequent transformations in the same way. Secure-base behavior is not well organized at the outset, but, rather, children improve as they grow older (Waters, in press). Three-year-olds manifest an elaborate and *gradually* acquired relationship system which permits them to explore at greater distances from their mothers than 2-year-olds, and that doesn't require visual access to the mother. No one believes that these changes mark a waning of attachment; ordinarily, they are regarded as "transformations."

Earlier investigators (e.g., Gewirtz, 1976) described the origins of secure base activity and its subsequent transformations in terms of operant learning. Contiguity theories also have been used as explanations for attachment origins (Cairns, 1979). Relatively unexplored, however, are suggestions from Kelley (1983) and Graziano (1984) that social reciprocities (i.e., exchanges) may be involved, and that exchange theories may offer assistance in thinking about origins and transformations in infant–caregiver attachments.

Consider that "sensitive care," the major determinant of secure attachments according to Ainsworth et al. (1978), is comprised of: (a) contingent responsiveness to the baby's signals, (b) affection and warmth, and (c) stimulation of the baby (when the infant is receptive). Such exchanges are known to be in the interests of both mothers and babies. A "contingency bias" (i.e., a preference for stimulus changes that one controls) is characteristic of infants (Watson & Ramey, 1972) as well as adults (Seligman, 1975). The mother's investment in these exchanges may also be supported by extrinsic rewards from other individuals such as her mother, her husband, and her friends. In any event, the empirical evidence shows that caretakers learn quickly to anticipate crying and laughter in their infants, and that infants quickly gaze and reach selectively in ways that elicit caregiving (Brazelton, Koslowski, & Main, 1974; Kaye, 1977).

These observations suggest that the attachment between infants and their caregivers can be appropriately viewed as an evolving system of exchange and mutual accommodation. And, even if the organization of maternal care and genetically determined biases in the infant were to account for the origins of attachments, exchange processes may be better models for subsequent continuities and changes than constructs such as "internal working models" (Bowlby, 1973).

Early encounters of children with one another also show reciprocities to be involved in the beginnings of interpersonal relationships (friendships, in this case). Howes (1983) observed that toddlers and preschoolers whom their teachers considered to be friends could be distinguished behaviorally from nonfriends according to the extent that they engaged in positive affective exchanges and reciprocities in play. Both toddlers and preschoolers sorted themselves out initially on these grounds, and continued to prefer such play partners throughout the year. Objects were more important exchange commodities among the toddlers than among the older children; complementary and reciprocal play (and reciprocated vocalizations) were the commodities exchanged most frequently among older "friends."

Many observations could be used to document the versatility of exchange theory (and its variants) in accounting for relationship continuities and changes in child development. These observations are mentioned because they are not ordinarily cited in the literature on exchange processes and, moreover, were not intended to contribute to that literature. Especially noteworthy is the demonstration, in both mother–infant and child–child relations, that social exchanges have a bearing on the formation and maintenance of relationships at a time when children are usually assumed to be too young to engage in the kind of social evaluation necessary to their use in relationship formation. Close examination of these early relationships, then, may reveal ambiguities/deficiencies in the exchange theories themselves.

Developmental analysis and theoretical limitation. Developmental data should be used to a greater extent to demonstrate that basic theories about relationships are (or may not be) generalizable. Certain developmental results make it quite clear that young children utilize social information differently from adults. For example, young children's relationships seem not to require the causal attributions and cognitive evaluations characteristic of older children and adults. Not only do young children make social attributions using different principles at different ages (e.g., covariation or discounting), but this information seemingly is not required for certain exchanges to be maintained (Kassin, 1981).

Similarly, the emotional signaling of the infant seems not to be guided by the cognitive representations that serve as elicitors among adults (Saarni, 1978). In these instances, the results are revealing, not only because they demonstrate something that children don't do, but because children do some things differently from adults. Actually, affective expression among infants and among adults is similar in some ways (e.g., the expression of anger), and emotions are embedded in interpersonal relationships in both instances (Berscheid, 1986). On the other hand, emotional expression seems "biologically" driven among infants but "knowledge driven" to a great extent among adults (Saarni, 1978). Terwogt and Olthof (1989) point out that, while inconsistent with each other, the child data and the adult data are each consistent with *different* current theories of emotion. The child data, for example, are reminiscent of Zajonc's (1980) view that a relatively independent emotional system exists, not ordinarily affected by cognition. The adult data, on the other hand, are consistent with the notion that knowledge stored in long term memory affects emotional experience by means of "context evaluation" (Frijda, 1987). These age differences will take time to sort out, but the results should inform both our theories of emotion and our theories of relationships.

Overall, studies of developmental discontinuities most frequently concern cognitive development as a constraint on social relations. Consequently, more has been learned about cognitive development and the various consistency theories, for example, than about developmental changes in theories of relationships.

Developmental dialectics. Mother–child interaction (or the interaction between siblings or the interaction between classmates) depends on the developmental status of both individuals. A mother's interaction with her 2-year-old, for example, differs as a function of whether the mother is an early-timing mother (one whose child was born when the mother was in her early twenties) or a late-timing mother (one who was in her thirties when the child was born). Early-timing mothers have more difficulties with discipline and setting limits (Walter, 1986), suggesting that women who are at different stages of adult development bring different interpretive frameworks and social skills to their interactions with their children.

We know relatively little about the mechanisms through which the child's growth triggers relationship changes. For example, when their children are somewhere between the ages of 2 and 4, mothers stop cuddling them and reduce the frequency with which they take them on their laps. As suggested elsewhere (Hartup & Laursen, in press), the main determinants of this change include: (a) the child's increasing size, (b) the child's interest in exploring the environment, and (c) the child's increased understanding that the mother is a "secure base" even though she is not immediately available. Neither mothers nor children have to be told or taught to make these changes, although sanctions may be encountered should a mother continue to cuddle her 9- or 10-year-old in public. Nothing about these changes suggests that either children or their mothers have become less attached to one another. Nevertheless, the commodities supporting the exchange relation between mothers and their toddlers have clearly shifted.

To make matters more complicated, the mother–child relationship contributes its own variance to the transactions observed between them (see above). Thus, mother–child interactions involving early-timing and late-timing mothers may differ according to the developmental status of the mother, the developmental status of the child, *and* their relationship with one another. Much new work is directed toward a better understanding of the manner in which the development of children and adolescents changes their relationships with adults (see Collins & Gunnar, 1990). Nevertheless, this topic is understudied. And we know even less about maternal development as a source of change in mother–child relationships than about child development in this regard. Consider, too, that similar dialectics occur in father–child interaction, sibling interaction, and peer relations.

Close relationships are believed to bear on the child's development, as well as the reverse. The most studied outcomes identified with interpersonal relationships have to do with social and emotional functioning; the relevance of both family relationships and peer relationships has been established (see Hartup, 1989). The relevance of these relationships to the child's cognitive development, however, is not known. Almost everyone assumes that cognitive structures emerge from the child's commerce with the environment (including the late Jean Piaget). Nevertheless, most studies have not dealt with the social antecedents of these changes (Ruble, Higgins, & Hartup, 1983).

Certain evidence suggests, however, that the quality of a child's relationships may have something to do with the internalization of regulating and monitoring mechanisms in cognitive development (Hartup, 1985). For example, children who are "securely attached" to their mothers in early childhood have been shown to be more sophisticated at 2 years of age in negotiating coordinated problem solving with the mother (Matas, Arend, & Sroufe, 1978), and better at age 4 in exploratory tasks requiring social coordinations with the mother as well as in "academic" tasks in which the mother teaches the child a simple skill (Sroufe & Fleeson, 1986). The cognitive residuals of early relationships have not been demonstrated very consistently with intelligence tests, but many studies show that supportive mother–child relationships foster intellectual development and that this relation extends into middle childhood (Belsky, 1981).

Various theories have been advanced to account for the "socialization of cognition," including social interactive ones (Vygotsky, 1978). Accordingly, mothers are conceived as cultural agents, and important influences on the child's cognitive functioning. Little recognition, however, is given to qualitative differences in mother–child relationships as these relate to the child's cognitive development. Yet the shift from mother-guided action to child-guided action, as observed when mothers help their young children carry out simple tasks, should differ according to the quality of the relationship between them. Smooth, mutually regulated social interaction marks "secure relationships" between young children and their caretakers; one can guess that maternal instruction in such contexts should be regulated differently and should be associated with different outcomes than instruction occurring in the context of insecure relationships. Thus, no dearth of interesting developmental notions exists to implicate close relationships in the socialization of cognition. Nevertheless, empirical studies are very rare.

Much remains to be learned about the developmental dialectics involved in children's relationships. The issues involved require more than description and more than prediction-and-outcome studies. Process-oriented investigations are badly needed to come to grips with these dialectics; the full capabilities of developmental and social psychology are required.

BOUNDARIES: WHAT'S TO BE DONE? NOT DONE?

Boundaries in science act conservatively; they maintain the traditions responsible for their own existence. Boundaries, for example, assure that orthodox juries will be available, as needed, to select new faculty members and to select work for publication in the existing journals (Masters et al., 1984).

Boundaries are not always lamentable, since "core knowledge" needs continuous dissemination and a professional cadre committed to do this. In addition, resources need to be expended on the basis of focused priorities rather than too widely scattered. But unless boundaries are permeable, they retard rather than sustain the growth of new knowledge. Significant questions are overlooked, understudied, or never asked.

Until the early 1980s, common cause among social psychologists and social developmentalists was not very evident in professional networking. Most major psychology departments, even now, advertise separate graduate training programs in social and developmental psychology, and only a few universities (e.g., New York University) have mounted joint programs. Faculty positions are usually allocated to social and developmental programs separately, and it remains difficult for trainees with dual credentials to obtain positions without declaring primary allegiance to one or the other.

The American Psychological Association has encouraged its divisions to use program time jointly (and this has resulted in several notable "boundary area" gatherings) but relatively few individuals belong to both the developmental and social divisions. Moreover, as scientists have fallen away from active participation in the Association, social psychologists have gravitated to the Society for Experimental Social Psychology for networking purposes and social developmentalists have gravitated to the Society for Research in Child Development. For example, relatively few individuals who study "social cognition" or "social relationships" are active in both organizations, publish their work in both social and developmental journals, and serve on study sections serving both sub-fields.

What's to be done, then? What's not to be done?

Training

Reasonable arguments can be made in favor of joint training programs as one method of increasing the permeability of the boundaries between social and developmental psychology. Presumably, students who are trained in both subfields will be better equipped, both theoretically and methodologically, to address boundary issues in their future work and will be able to cross boundaries as needed in their professional networking.

There are certain difficulties with this argument, however. First, boundary research is not likely to be encouraged if students only take classes and seminars dealing separately with the core content of developmental and social psychology. Mastery of more than one subject matter does not assure mastery of border issues (Campbell, 1969). Second, given the sheer size of the knowledge base, even well-intentioned attempts to acquire expertise in both developmental and social psychology are likely to lead to shallowness rather than mastery. Third, most current researchers who operate successfully in border areas got there without formal training and by "discovering" the border issue(s) on their own. Indeed, it can be argued that whatever success most of these individuals have had derives from their mastery of one discipline or the other, rather than mastery of both:

> Boundary area researchers should not lose sight of their own special expertise from their own (sub)discipline while attempting to study a somewhat alien method in a creative way. It is this expertise that allows the proper creative selection of the construct or method under study, such that between the question and the method there is a complementarity that advances understanding in a new direction, rather than simply further along the same road. One might characterize boundary area research as providing disjunctive increments to knowledge, as contrasted to the conjunctive increments that occur from significant but mainline (sub)disciplinary research. (Masters et al., 1984, p. 7)

In my view, joint programs should be organized relatively rarely as a means of promoting border work between social and developmental psychology, and then only in institutions that are uniquely equipped to sustain them. One requirement, for example, is that mentors be available who themselves engage in border work, both in the classroom and in the laboratory.

Otherwise, the main training provisions needed for encouraging work in the boundary area between social and developmental psychology are traditional ones: intensive specialization through association with mentors who can both socialize students into the mainstream of one discipline and, at the same time, make common cause with researchers in the other. Minimally, reading lists and certain seminars should extend across literatures—in every institution. Good grounding in one subdiscipline, however, remains essential for every student.

Centers

One of the most effective ways to encourage "border work" between developmental and social psychology is the creation of research centers. Ordinarily, such centers are best located in universities and involve senior faculty, junior faculty, and graduate students. Staff members in "boundary centers," however, must have a strong sense of common cause. General cross-fertilization of ideas will not usually fulfill this function. Although cross-fertilization will support a center's activities in the short term, it seldom attracts the individual investment necessary for sustaining long term relationships.

Ordinarily, more concrete objectives must exist to support effective center work. One can envision well-functioning operations built around *issues* or *questions*, for example, "social cognition" or "interpersonal relationships." But issues and questions will not support a center by themselves. Committed individuals are also needed. A collective must exist as well as superordinate goals (Sherif, Harvey, White, Hood, & Sherif, 1961). Stated somewhat differently: Individual investment in center exchanges must be mutually strong for the relationships to emerge that are necessary to sustain the unit. Given these caveats, though, center structures can make the boundaries between social and developmental psychology more permeable than otherwise would be the case.

Organization, Conferences, Journals, and Volumes

Among the most common complaints among academicians is the flood of reading matter that threatens to inundate both mind and library. Other complaints concern the number of conventions and special meetings that one must attend. Nevertheless, new organizations and reading outlets are virtually inevitable when a boundary area becomes "hot."

Based on current activity, relatively little needs to be done to encourage networking among developmental and social psychologists. Organizations or quasiorganizations like the *International Society for the Study of Personal Relationships* and the *International Society for Research on Emotions* have already been established, each with schedules of conferences and publications. Special conferences and volumes have also appeared, dealing explicitly with boundary issues in social and developmental psychology: *Social developmental psychology*, edited by Brehm, Kassin, and Gibbons (1981); *Social cognition and social development*, edited by Higgins, Ruble, and Hartup (1983); *Boundary areas in social and developmental psychology*, edited by Masters and Levin-Yrakin (1984); and *Handbook of personal relationships*, edited by Duck (1988a). New journals include the *Journal of Personal and Social Relationships, Journal of Social and Clinical Psychology*, and *Social Cognition*, as well as a special issue of the latter on the topic of social cognitive development. Thus, organizational and editorial mechanisms already exist for disseminating boundary work, needing only the continuing support of their constituencies.

Comment

Carefully managed training adjustments are needed to advance border work between developmental and social psychology. Although mastery of both subfields is not a necessary objective, senior researchers working in border areas must be more effective as models and tutors. Research centers are good mechanisms for furthering border work between developmental and social psychology but, to be effective, they need focused objectives and committed members. Organizational structures already exist for dissemination of most border work in social developmental psychology.

CONCLUSION

Social and developmental psychologists share many interests: in social cognition, interpersonal relationships, social motivation, and intergroup relations. Different issues and different methods engage research workers in these subfields. Among those interested in interpersonal relationships, considerable effort is devoted in both subfields to describing these entities. Differences among individuals in their relationship histories are especially interesting to developmental psychologists as well as the manner in which these differences predict later functioning. Causal explanations for continuities and changes in relationships are not as well advanced in developmental psychology as in social psychology.

Scientific interest in interpersonal relationships is burgeoning. Many disciplines, including sociology, family and marital counseling, psychiatry, and ethology, are contributing to this effort. Social and developmental psychologists, it is argued in this chapter, should com-

mit more of their resources to integrated activities: general theories of relationships should be subjected to developmental analysis and theories of developmental change and continuity need strengthening. No one would seriously argue that identities be abandoned in this effort, or that students should not continue to identify themselves mainly as social psychologists or developmental psychologists. A new generation of researchers is needed, however, that thrives in the boundary area between these subdisciplines.

REFERENCES

Ainsworth, M. D. S., Blehar, M., Waters, E., & Wall, S. (1978). *Patterns of attachment*. Hillsdale, NJ: Erlbaum.

Allport, G. W. (1954). The historical background of modern social psychology. In G. Lindzey (Ed.), *Handbook of social psychology, Vol. 1, Theory and method* (pp. 3–56). Reading, MA: Addison-Wesley.

Argyle, M., & Henderson, M. (1984). *The anatomy of relationships*. London: Methuen.

Barker, R. G. (1968). *Ecological psychology*. Palo Alto, CA: Stanford University Press.

Belsky, J. (1981). Early human experience: A family perspective. *Developmental Psychology, 17*, 3–23.

Belsky, J., Rovine, M., & Fish, M. (1989). The developing family system. In M. Gunnar & E. Thelen (Eds.), *The Minnesota symposia on child psychology* (Vol. 22, pp. 119–166). Hillsdale, NJ: Erlbaum.

Berscheid, E. (1985). Interpersonal attraction. In G. Lindzey & E. Aronson (Eds.), *Handbook of social psychology* (3rd ed., Vol. 2, pp. 413–484). New York: Random House.

Berscheid, E. (1986). Emotional experience in close relationships: Some implications for child development. In W. W. Hartup & Z. Rubin (Eds.), *Relationships and development* (pp. 135–166). Hillsdale, NJ: Erlbaum.

Berscheid, E., & Peplau, L. A. (1983). The emerging science of relationships. In H. H. Kelley, E. Berscheid, A. Christensen, J. H. Harvey, T. L. Huston, G. Levinger, E. McClintock, L. A. Peplau, & D. R. Peterson (Eds.), *Close relationships* (pp. 1–19). New York: W. H. Freeman.

Boring, E. G. (1950). *A history of experimental psychology* (revised ed.). New York: Appleton Century.

Bowlby, J. (1969). *Attachment and loss, Vol. 1, Attachment*. New York: Basic Books.

Bowlby, J. (1973). *Attachment and loss, Vol. 2, Loss*. New York: Basic Books.

Brazelton, T. B., Koslowski, B., & Main, M. (1974). The origins of reciprocity: The early mother–infant interaction. In M. Lewis & L. A. Rosenblum (Eds.), *The effects of the infant on its caregiver* (pp. 49–76). New York: Wiley.

Brehm, S. S., Kassin, S. M., & Gibbons, F. X. (1981). *Developmental social psychology*. New York: Oxford University Press.

Bretherton, I. (in press). Pouring new wine into old bottles: The social self as internal working model. In M. Gunnar & L. A. Sroufe (Eds.), *The Minnesota symposia on child psychology* (Vol. 23). Hillsdale, NJ: Erlbaum.

Buhrmester, D., & Furman, W. (1987). The development of companionship and intimacy. *Child Development, 58*, 1101–1113.

Burgess, R. L., & Huston, T. L. (Eds.). (1979). *Social exchange in developing relationships.* New York: Academic Press.

Cairns, R. B. (1979). *Social development: The origins and plasticity of interchanges.* San Francisco: W. H. Freeman.

Cairns, R. B., & Ornstein, P. A. (1979). Developmental psychology. In E. Hearst (Ed.), *The first century of experimental psychology* (pp. 459–510). Hillsdale, NJ: Erlbaum.

Campbell, D. T. (1969). Ethnocentrism of disciplines and the fish-scale model of omniscience. In C. W. Sherif & M. Sherif (Eds.), *Interdisciplinary relationships in the social sciences* (pp. 328–348). Chicago: Aldine.

Collins, W. A., & Gunnar, M. (1990). Social and personality development. In M. R. Rosenzweig (Ed.), *Annual review of psychology* (Vol. 41, pp. 387–416). San Francisco: Annual Review Publications.

Collins, W. A., & Russell, G. (in press). Mother-child and father-child relationships in middle childhood and adolescence: A developmental analysis. *Developmental Review.*

Cooley, C. H. (1909). *Social organization.* New York: Scribners.

Crockenberg, S. (1981). Infant irritability, mother responsiveness and social support influences on the security of infant-mother attachment. *Child Development, 52*, 857–865.

Cummings, E. M., Vogel, D., Cummings, J. S., & El-Sheikh, M. (in press). Children's responses to different forms of expression of anger between adults. *Child Development.*

Dodge, K. A., & Frame, C. L. (1982). Social cognitive biases and deficits in aggressive boys. *Child Development, 53*, 620–635.

Duck, S. W. (Ed.). (1988a). *Handbook of personal relationships.* New York: Wiley.

Duck, S. W. (1988b). Introduction. In S. W. Duck (Ed.), *Handbook of personal relationships* (pp. xiii–xvii). New York: Wiley.

Dunn, J. (1988). *The beginnings of social understanding.* Cambridge, MA: Harvard University Press.

Durkheim, E. (1951). *Suicide.* New York: Free Press. (Original work published 1897).

Egeland, B., & Farber, E. A. (1984). Infant-mother attachment: Factors related to its development and changes over time. *Child Development, 55*, 753–771.

Feldman, N. S., & Ruble, D. N. (1981). The development of person perception: cognitive and social factors. In S. S. Brehm, S. M. Kassin, & F. X. Gibbons (Eds.), *Developmental social psychology* (pp. 191–206). New York: Oxford University Press.

Festinger, L. (1957). *A theory of cognitive dissonance.* Palo Alto, CA: Stanford University Press.

Flavell, J. H. (1988). The development of children's knowledge about the mind: From cognitive connections to mental representations. In J. W. Astington,

P. L. Harris, & D. Olson (Eds.), *Developing theories of mind* (pp. 244–267). New York: Cambridge University Press.

Freud, S. (1957). The interpretation of dreams. In J. Strachey (Ed.), *The complete psychological works of Sigmund Freud* (Vols. 4–5). London: Hogarth. (Original work published 1900).

Frijda, N. H. (1987). *The emotions.* New York: Cambridge University Press.

Furman, W. (1984). Some observations on the study of personal relationships. In J. C. Masters & K. Yarkin-Levin (Eds.), *Boundary areas in social and developmental psychology* (pp. 16–42). New York: Academic Press.

Furman, W., & Buhrmester, D. (1985). Children's perceptions of the personal relationships in their social networks. *Developmental Psychology, 21,* 1016–1024.

Gewirtz, J. L. (1976). The attachment acquisition process as evidenced in the maternal conditioning of cued infant responding (particularly crying). *Human Development, 19,* 143–155.

Ginsburg, G. P. (1988). Rules, scripts, and prototypes in personal relationships. In S. W. Duck (Ed.), *Handbook of personal relationships* (pp. 23–39). New York: Wiley.

Goodenough, F. L. (1928). Measuring behavior traits by means of repeated short samples. *Journal of Juvenile Research, 12,* 230–235.

Gottman, J. M. (1979). *Marital interaction: Experimental investigations.* New York: Academic Press.

Gottman, J. M. (1983). How children become friends. *Monographs of the Society for Research in Child Development, 48* (Serial No. 201).

Graziano, W. G. (1984). A developmental approach to social exchange processes. In J. C. Masters & K. Yarkin-Levin (Eds.), *Boundary areas in social and developmental psychology* (pp. 161–194). New York: Academic Press.

Hareven, T. K. (Ed.). (1978). *Transitions: The family and the life course in historical perspective.* New York: Academic Press.

Hartup, W. W. (1983). Peer relations. In P. H. Mussen (Ed.) & E. M. Hetherington (Vol. Ed.), *Handbook of child psychology, Vol. 4: Socialization, personality, and social development* (pp. 103–196). New York: Wiley.

Hartup, W. W. (1985). Relationships and their significance in cognitive development. In R. A. Hinde, A.-N. Perret-Clermont, & J. Stevenson-Hinde (Eds.), *Social relationships and cognitive development* (pp. 66–81). Oxford: Clarendon.

Hartup, W. W. (1989). Social relationships and their developmental significance. *American Psychologist, 44,* 120–126.

Hartup, W. W., & Laursen, B. (in press). Relationships as developmental contexts. In R. Cohen & A. W. Siegel (Eds.), *Context and development.* Hillsdale, NJ: Erlbaum.

Hartup, W. W., Laursen, B., Stewart, M. I., & Eastenson, A. (1988). Conflict and the friendship relations of young children. *Child Development, 59,* 1590–1600.

Hartup, W. W., & Rubin, Z. (Eds.). (1986). *Relationships and development.* Hillsdale, NJ: Erlbaum.

Heider, F. (1958). *The psychology of interpersonal relations.* New York: Wiley.

Hess, R. D., & Torney, J. V. (1967). *The development of political attitudes in children.* Chicago: Aldine.

Higgins, E. T., Ruble, D. N., & Hartup, W. W. (1983). *Social cognition and social development.* New York: Cambridge University Press.

Hinde, R. A. (1979). *Towards understanding relationships.* New York: Academic Press.

Howes, C. (1983). Patterns of friendship. *Child Development, 54,* 1041–1053.

Kassin, S. M. (1981). From laychild to "layman": Developmental causal attribution. In S. S. Brehm, S. M. Kassin, & F. X. Gibbons (Eds.), *Developmental social psychology* (pp. 169–190). New York: Oxford University Press.

Kaye, K. (1977). Toward the origin of dialogue. In H. R. Schaffer, (Ed.), *Studies in mother–infant interaction* (pp. 89–117). New York: Academic Press.

Kelley, H. H. (1983). Epilogue: An essential science. In H. H. Kelley, E. Berscheid, A. Christiansen, J. H. Harvey, T. L. Huston, G. Levinger, E. McClintock, L. A. Peplau, & D. R. Peterson (Eds.), *Close relationships* (pp. 486–503). New York: W. H. Freeman.

Kelley, H. H., Berscheid, E., Christensen, A., Harvey, J. H., Huston, T. L., Levinger, G., McClintock, E., Peplau, L. A., & Peterson, D. R. (Eds.). (1983a). *Close relationships.* New York: W. H. Freeman.

Kelley, H. H., Berscheid, E., Christensen, A., Harvey, J. H., Huston, T. L., Levinger, G., McClintock, E., Peplau, L. A., & Peterson, D. R. (1983b). Analyzing close relationships. In H. H. Kelley, E. Berscheid, A. Christensen, J. H. Harvey, T. L. Huston, G. Levinger, E. McClintock, L. A. Peplau, & D. R. Peterson (Eds.), *Close relationships* (pp. 20–67). New York: W. H. Freeman.

Kelley, H. H., & Thibault, J. W. (1978). *Interpersonal relations: A theory of interdependence.* New York: Wiley.

Keniston, K., and the Carnegie Council on Children. (1977). *All our children.* New York: Harcourt, Brace Jovanovich.

Ladd, G. W., & Emerson, E. S. (1984). Shared knowledge in children's friendships. *Developmental Psychology, 20,* 932–940.

Ladd, G. W., & Golter, B. S. (1988). Parents' management of preschoolers' peer relations: Is it related to social competence? *Developmental Psychology, 24,* 109–117.

Lamb, M. E., & Elster, A. B. (1985). Adolescent mother-infant-father relationships. *Developmental Psychology, 21,* 768–773.

Lamb, M. E., Pleck, J., Charnov, E., & Levine, J. (1987). A biosocial perspective on paternal behavior and involvement. In J. Lancaster, J. Altmann, A. Rossi, & L. Sherrod (Eds.), *Parenting across the life span: Biosocial dimensions* (pp. 111–142). New York: Aldine de Gruyter.

Laursen, B. P. (1989). *Relationships and conflict during adolescence.* Unpublished doctoral dissertation, University of Minnesota.

Levinger, G., & Levinger, A. C. (1986). The temporal course of close relationships: Some thoughts about the development of children's ties. In W. W. Hartup & Z. Rubin (Eds.), *Relationships and development* (pp. 111–133). Hillsdale, NJ: Erlbaum.

Lewin, K., Lippitt, R., & White, R. K. (1938). Patterns of aggressive behavior in experimentally created "social climates." *Journal of Social Psychology, 10,* 271–299.

Main, M., Kaplan, K., & Cassidy, J. (1985). Security in infancy, childhood, and adulthood: A move to the level of representation. In I. Bretherton & E. Waters (Eds.), *Growing points of attachment theory and research. Monographs of the Society for Research in Child Development, 50*(Serial No. 209).

Masters, J. C., & Yarkin-Levin, K. (Eds.). (1984). *Boundary areas in social and social psychology.* New York: Academic Press.

Masters, J. C., Yarkin-Levin, K., & Graziano, W. G. (1984). Boundary areas in psychology. In J. C. Masters & K. Yarkin-Levin (Eds.), *Boundary areas in social and developmental psychology* (pp. 1–14). New York: Academic Press.

Matas, L., Arend, R. A., & Sroufe, L. A. (1978). Continuity of adaptation in the second year. *Child Development, 49,* 547–556.

McAdams, D. P. (1988). Personal needs and personal relationships. In S. W. Duck (Ed.), *Handbook of personal relationships* (pp. 7–22). New York: Wiley.

McCandless, B. R., & Spiker, C. (1956). Experimental research in child psychology. *Child Development, 27,* 75–80.

McClintock, E. (1983). Interaction. In H. H. Kelley, E. Berscheid, A. Christensen, J. H. Harvey, T. L. Huston, G. Levinger, E. McClintock, L. A. Peplau, & D. R. Peterson (Eds.), *Close relationships* (pp. 68–109). New York: W. H. Freeman.

Moreno, J. L. (1934). *Who shall survive?* Washington, DC: Nervous and Mental Diseases Publishing Co.

Murray, H. A. (1938). *Explorations in personality.* New York: Oxford University Press.

Newcomb, A. F., & Brady, J. E. (1982). Mutuality in boys' friendship relations. *Child Development, 53,* 392–395.

Newcomb, T. M. (1953). An approach to the study of communicative acts. *Psychological Review, 60,* 393–404.

Newcomb, T. M. (1961). *The acquaintance process.* New York: Holt, Rinehart, & Winston.

Parke, R. D., MacDonald, K. B., Burks, V. M., Carson, J., & Bhavnagri, N. (1989). Family and peer systems: In search of linkages. In K. Kreppner & R. M. Lerner (Eds.), *Family systems in life span development* (pp. 65–92). Hillsdale, NJ: Erlbaum.

Pastor, D. (1981). The quality of mother-infant attachment and its relationship to toddlers' initial sociability with peers. *Developmental psychology, 17,* 326–335.

Patterson, G. R. (1982). *Coercive family process.* Eugene, OR: Castalia.

Patterson, G. R., & Bank, L. (1989). Some amplifier and dampening mechanisms for pathologic processes in families. In M. Gunnar & E. Thelen (Eds.), *Minnesota symposia on child psychology* (Vol. 22, pp. 167–209). Hillsdale, NJ: Erlbaum.

Peterson, D. R. (1983). Conflict. In H. H. Kelley, E. Berscheid, A. Christensen, J. H. Harvey, T. L. Huston, G. Levinger, E. McClintock, L. A. Peplau, & D. R. Peterson (Eds.), *Close relationships* (pp. 360–396). New York: W. H. Freeman.

Renken, B., Egeland, B., Marvinney, D., Sroufe, L. A., & Mangelsdorf, S. (1989). Early childhood antecedents of aggression and passive-withdrawal in early elementary school. *Journal of Personality, 57,* 257–281.

Ricks, M. (1983). *The origins of individual differences in competence: Attachment history and environmental support.* Unpublished doctoral dissertation, University of Massachusetts, Amherst.

Rubin, L. (1976). *Worlds of pain: Life in the working class family.* New York: Basic Books.

Ruble, D. N., Higgins, E. T., & Hartup, W. W. (1983). What's social about social-cognitive development? In E. T. Higgins, D. N. Ruble, & W. W. Hartup (Eds.), *Social cognition and social development* (pp. 3–12). New York: Cambridge University Press.

Ruble, D. N., & Rholes, W. S. (1981). The development of children's perceptions and attributions about their social world. In J. H. Harvey, W. Ickes, & R. Kidd (Eds.), *New directions in attribution research* (Vol. 3, pp. 3–36). Hillsdale, NJ: Erlbaum.

Rutter, M., & Garmezy, N. (1983). Developmental psychopathology. In P. H. Mussen (Series Ed.) & E. M. Hetherington (Vol. Ed.), *Handbook of child psychology, Vol. 4, Socialization, personality, and social development* (pp. 775–911). New York: Wiley.

Saarni, C. (1978). Cognitive and communicative features of emotional experience, or do you show what you think you feel? In M. Lewis & L. A. Rosenblum (Eds.), *The development of affect* (pp. 361–375). New York: Plenum.

Saarni, C. (1989). Children's understanding of strategic control of emotional experience in social transactions. In C. Saarni & P. L. Harris (Eds.), *Children's understanding of emotion* (pp. 181–208). New York: Cambridge University Press.

Sears, R. R. (1951). A theoretical framework for personality and social behavior. *American Psychologist, 6,* 476–483.

Secord, P. F., & Backman, C. W. (1974). *Social psychology.* New York: McGraw-Hill.

Seligman, M. E. P. (1975). *Helplessness: On depression, development, and death.* San Francisco: W. H. Freeman.

Selman, R. L. (1980). *The growth of interpersonal understanding.* New York: Academic Press.

Shantz, C. U. (1983). Social cognition. In P. H. Mussen (Ed.), J. H. Flavell & E. Markman (Vol. Eds.), *Handbook of child psychology, Vol. 3, Cognitive development* (pp. 495–555). New York: Wiley.

Sherif, M., Harvey, O. J., White, B. J., Hood, W. R., & Sherif, C. W. (1961). *Intergroup conflict and cooperation: The Robbers Cave experiment.* Norman, OK: University of Oklahoma Press.

Snyder, M., & Swann, W. B. (1978). Behavioral confirmation in social interaction: From social perception to social reality. *Journal of Experimental Social Psychology, 14,* 148–160.

Sroufe, L. A., & Fleeson, J. (1986). Attachment and the construction of relationships. In W. W. Hartup & Z. Rubin (Eds.), *Relationships and development* (pp. 51–72). Hillsdale, NJ: Erlbaum.

Terwogt, M. M., & Olthof, T. (1989). Awareness and self-regulation of emotion in young children. In C. Saarni & P. L. Harris (Eds.), *Children's understanding of emotion* (pp. 209–237). New York: Cambridge University Press.

Thomas, D. (1929). Some new techniques for studying social behavior. *Child Development Monographs* (No. 1). New York: Teachers College, Columbia University.

Triplett, N. (1897). The dynamogenic factors in pacemaking and competition. *American Journal of Psychology, 9,* 507–533.

Vygotsky, L. S. (1978). *Mind in society: The development of higher psychological processes* (M. Cole, V. John-Steiner, S. Scribner, & E. Souberman, Eds.). Cambridge, MA: Harvard University Press.

Walter, C. S. (1986). *The timing of motherhood: Is later better?* New York: Heath.

Waters, E. (in press). Attachment, identity, and identification: Milestones and mechanisms. In M. Gunnar & L. A. Sroufe (Eds.), *Minnesota symposia on child psychology* (Vol. 23). Hillsdale, NJ: Erlbaum.

Waters, E., Hay, D., & Richters, J. (1986). Infant-parent attachment and the origins of prosocial and antisocial behavior. In D. Olweus, J. Block, & M. Radke-Yarrow (Eds.), *Development of anti-social and prosocial behavior: Research, theories, and issues* (pp. 97–126). New York: Academic Press.

Watson, J. B. (1926). What the nursery has to say about instincts. In C. Murchison (Ed.), *Psychologies of 1925.* Worcester, MA: Clark University Press.

Watson, J. S., & Ramey, C. T. (1972). Reactions to responsive contingent stimulation in early infancy. *Merrill-Palmer Quarterly, 18,* 219–227.

Wundt, W. (1907). *Outlines of psychology.* New York: Stechert.

Youniss, J. (1980). *Parents and peers in social development: A Sullivan-Piaget perspective.* Chicago: University of Chicago Press.

Zajonc, R. B. (1980). Feeling and thinking: Preferences need no inferences. *American Psychologist, 35,* 151–173.

chapter 2

The Making of a Developmental Psychopathologist*

Dante Cicchetti
Departments of Psychology and Psychiatry
Director, Mt. Hope Family Center
University of Rochester

Sheree Toth
Department of Psychology
Associate Director, Mt. Hope Family Center
University of Rochester

INTRODUCTION

In this chapter we explore issues related to the training of developmental psychopathologists. When viewed in the context of what is known about the epidemiology of child, adolescent, and adult mental disorders, the urgency of such training and the development of training guidelines in developmental psychopathology becomes immediately evident. According to recent estimates provided by a report from the Institute of Medicine (IOM), the overall prevalence rates of mental

* The preparation of this chapter was supported, in part, by grants received from the John D. and Catherine T. MacArthur Foundation Network on Early Childhood, the A.L. Mailman Family Foundation, Inc., the National Institute of Mental Health, the Smith Richardson Foundation, Inc., and the Spunk Fund, Inc. We wish to acknowledge Thomas Achenbach, Norman Garmezy, Paul Meehl, Michael Rutter, Alan Sroufe, and Edward Zigler for their major contributions to the discipline of developmental psychopathology and to our professional development. The statements about clinical training expressed herein are ours and should not be construed as representing the views of the Clinical Psychology program at the University of Rochester. We thank Victoria Gill for typing this manuscript.

illness and addictive disorder are approximately 15 to 22.5 percent of the entire population (IOM, 1985). In a study completed as part of the National Institute of Mental Health's Epidemiologic Catchment Area Program (ECAP), Regier, Boyd, Burke, and their colleagues (1988) obtained results congruent with the IOM report. These investigators found that over 15 percent of the 18 and older population in the United States suffered from a mental disorder or substance abuse each month. A recent IOM report stated that of the 63 million children in the United States, at least 12 percent suffer from a mental disorder (IOM, 1989). Nearly half of these children are considered to be seriously disordered. The 1989 IOM report further stated that in children exposed to severe psychosocial adversity, such as inner-city children, the prevalence rates for mental disorder may exceed 20 percent (IOM, 1989). Furthermore, the ECAP study found that men had higher rates of antisocial personality disorders and substance abuse than women, while women manifested increased instances of mood, anxiety, and somatization disorders. When considered in tandem with earlier ECAP studies revealing that 33 percent of the population is likely to develop a mental illness or substance abuse disorder in their lifetime (Eaton & Kessler, 1985), these epidemiologic studies highlight that much basic and clinical research on psychopathology needs to be conducted.

As an illustration of the pervasiveness of these disorders across the life-span, it is important to point out that no age group escapes them. For example, there are approximately two million children with a serious mental disorder who are in need of immediate and intensive psychiatric care (Saxe, Cross, & Silverman, 1988). Likewise, 10 percent of all persons over age 65 develop some form of mental disorder, including severe motoric and cognitive impairment and dementia (such as Alzheimer's disease), alcoholism and alcohol abuse, and depression (IOM, 1985). It also needs to be noted that some individuals are counted on more than one occasion in these epidemiological estimates because persons often have more than one mental disorder. The existence of these co-morbid disorders is apparently quite common and is exemplified by such combinations as autism and mental retardation, conduct disorder and attention deficit disorder, childhood depression and conduct disorder, mood disorder and personality disorder, and major depression and alcoholism (American Psychiatric Association, 1980, 1987; Cantwell, 1986; Millon & Klerman, 1986; Puig-Antich, 1982).

To provide some specific information on these mental disorders, schizophrenia, one of the most serious of all psychopathologies, is present in 1 percent of the population, with approximately 300,000 such episodes occurring yearly in the United States (IOM, 1985). Likewise, the affective or mood disorders, another extremely serious type of

mental disorder, are among the most devastating in terms of prevalence, mortality, family functioning, and mental health costs (IOM,
1985).

For example, epidemiological studies estimate that 9 to 16 million
people currently have a mood disorder (i.e., manifest a unipolar depression or a bipolar manic-depressive episode). Additionally, 15 percent of the population, or roughly 30 million persons, experience a
minimum of one serious bout of clinical depression at some point in
their lives (IOM, 1985; Weissman & Boyd, 1984). Despite the fact that
approximately 80 percent of all persons with a mood disorder can be
helped by the appropriate use of drugs and/or psychotherapy, fewer
than one third of these afflicted individuals receive any form of treatment. Furthermore, approximately 5 to 10 percent of the general population and 20 percent of all psychiatric inpatients are estimated to have
a severe personality disorder (IOM, 1985).

In a related vein, based on data from the National Institute on
Alcoholism and Alcohol Abuse, 10 million adults and over 3 million
children and adolescents abuse alcohol, and an additional 30–40 million are affected either by virtue of their close relationship to the
alcoholic or to an individual injured or killed by a person under the
influence of alcohol (IOM, 1985). Similarly, many persons abuse serious drugs in this country. The National Institute of Drug Abuse reports
that there are over 5 million cocaine users, half a million heroine
addicts, and 7 million persons who use addictive prescription drugs
without proper medical supervision (IOM, 1985).

Similarly, 12 to 15 percent of all children, or nearly 10 million
children, require mental health interventions (Gilmore, Chang, &
Coron, 1984; Gould, Wunsch-Hitzig, & Dohrenwend, 1981). However,
fewer than 50 percent of these children receive any form of treatment
and many of those treated receive inappropriate services (Inouye, 1988;
Kazdin, 1988; Saxe et al., 1988). This situation is particularly distressing because problems in childhood often portend the appearance of
pathological problems in later years (Robins, 1966; Rutter, 1988; Sroufe
& Rutter, 1984).

A number of groups of children are at heightened risk for the devel-
opment of a psychopathological disorder, including the offspring of
parents with various forms of psychiatric disorder and substance abuse
(Beardslee, Bemporad, Keller, & Klerman, 1983; Beardslee, Son, &
Vaillant, 1986; Deykin, Levy, & Wells, 1987; Earls, Reich, Jung, &
Cloninger, 1988; Newcombe, Maddahian, & Bentler, 1986; Offord,
Boyle, & Racine, in press; Rutter, 1987; Weissman et al., 1987), children
who have been abused and neglected (Cicchetti, 1990b; Cicchetti &
Carlson, 1989; Kazdin, Moser, Colbus, & Bell, 1985), children from
socioeconomically deprived families (Aber, Allen, Carlson, & Cicchetti,

1989), children in foster care (Keane, 1983), incarcerated juveniles (Knitzer, 1982), and homeless children (Alperstein, Rappaport, & Flanigan, 1988).

As the IOM (1985) report highlights, the cost of these mental and addictive disorders to society is staggering. These investigators estimate that personal health care for such individuals exceeds 20 billion dollars yearly. Moreover, when one also considers the harm that mental and addictive disorders have on these patients' future productivity and the total economic costs of these disorders to society, estimates have been placed at 185 billion dollars per year (IOM, 1985).

Needless to say, given the preponderance and diversity of mental disorders across the life-span it is essential to have a critical mass of competently trained scientific investigators and practitioners if progress in the understanding and treatment of these disorders is to keep pace with their identification. Unfortunately, an examination of the ranks of the subdiscipline of psychology most directly relevant to the establishment of this goal, clinical psychology, reveals that, despite the growing number of doctorates awarded, the research personpower of this field is sorely lacking.

In 1984, Pion and Lipsey made an important observation:

> 1980 may have been a turning point for academic psychology . . . almost as many recipients of a new doctorate in the research specialties took positions outside academia as within it for perhaps the first time since World War II. At the same time, graduate training programs began to show evidence of a significant redirection towards applied research and preparation for nonacademic careers. (p. 753)

To provide several striking examples of this state of affairs, it is instructive to examine the employment choices of clinical psychologists as well as the percentage of their time that they spend involved in research activities.

Using information obtained from a new (1983–1986) sample of PhDs in clinical psychology conducted by the American Psychological Association, Pion (1988) reported that nearly two thirds (65%) were employed in a human services setting, while fewer than 20 percent held their primary positions as faculty members. Moreover, more than half of the recent doctoral recipients who responded to this survey spent none of their time conducting research. Additionally, nearly 85 percent of the respondents spent from zero to 20 percent of their time engaged in research. In contrast, only 4 percent spent over 50 percent of their time carrying out scientific investigations (Staff, VandenBos, & Tucker, 1985).

Furthermore, two disciplines closely allied to clinical psychology—

adult and child psychiatry—face similar personpower shortages in the scientific arena (Burke, Pincus, & Pardes, 1986; Haviland, Pincus, & Dial, 1987). Fewer than 5 percent of all medical students choose psychiatry as their profession. Estimates are that 20–30 percent of the latter group decide to enter child psychiatry as a profession (Weissman & Bashook, 1986).

Using Association of American Medical College survey data, Haviland and colleagues (1987) found that approximately one-third of graduating medical students planning to specialize in psychiatry professed the intent to engage in some form of research as they embarked upon their careers. However, the vast majority (76.9%) of those who stated that they had an interest in research wanted to be only "somewhat involved" or "involved in a limited way." Fewer than 20 percent of these potential psychiatrists planned to be "exclusively" (0.8%) or "significantly involved" (17.3%) in research. Moreover, as Burke and his collaborators noted, in comparison with physicians in other areas of specialization, academic psychiatrists have had less research training and devote less of their time to carrying it out. Not surprisingly then, a disproportionate amount of research funds appropriated by the National Institute of Mental Health are concentrated in a small number of the strongest medical school departments of psychiatry (Burke et al., 1986). In addition, far fewer full-time psychiatric faculty have had at least one year of postdoctoral research than their academic peers in other medical specialities (12% versus 34%, respectively—see Burke et al., 1986). Regardless of whether or not psychiatrists choose a research career track, unlike the discipline of clinical psychology, both adult and especially child psychiatry are experiencing severe personpower shortages (Funkenstein, 1978; Graduate Medical Education National advisory Committee, 1980; Haviland, Dial, & Pincus, 1988; Nielson, 1979; Silver, 1980; Tuma, Mitchell, & Brunstetter, 1987).

Taken in tandem, it is clear that both clinical psychology and psychiatry are at critical crossroads. Irrespective of the sheer numbers of clinical psychology PhDs, there continues to be a dearth of researchers involved in investigations of psychopathology. While clinical psychology PhDs continue to rise, approximately one-third of all new doctorates in clinical psychology in 1983 were awarded by practitioner programs (Pion, 1988). Significantly, the data reveal that the majority of the growth in new clinical psychologists can be accounted for by an increase in PhD graduates from unranked and low-ranked departments of psychology. Pion (1988) notes that 25 percent of psychology PhDs in the health services (clinical, counseling, and school psychology) received their PhDs from institutions at or below the 10th decile, while over 10 percent were awarded their degrees from unranked programs.

Likewise, grave concern has been expressed by the rising number of degrees awarded in clinical psychology to graduates of purely practitioner programs (Howard et al., 1986). As Howard and colleagues stated:

> The growth in the proportion of doctoral students graduating from practitioner programs in clinical counseling, and school psychology, coupled with evidence that individuals trained in these specialties tend to spend less time in research . . . suggests that psychology may be unable to respond optimally to national priorities and remain at the forefront of clinical research. (p. 1314)

Clearly, a consensus has emerged regarding the enormous burden associated with mental illness in terms of human suffering, as well as social and service costs. Unfortunately, a vast discrepancy exists between needs and resources available to address them. Even more severe shortages exist with regard to personnel trained to conduct research on psychopathological conditions from a developmental perspective (cf. Achenbach, 1990; Cicchetti, 1984; Selman & Yando, 1980; Zigler & Glick, 1986). It is critical that specialists be trained in methods of developmentally guided research which explore the interfaces among biological, psychological, and social aspects of functioning in conditions of psychopathology. Concomitantly, programs of training in which individuals learn to apply research knowledge to intervention strategies and likewise learn to utilize knowledge derived from the provision of service to improve programs of research hold great promise for addressing the critical needs which exist in areas associated with the social and behavioral sciences. It is this approach that holds promise for addressing the shortages of mental health researchers.

HISTORICAL PERSPECTIVES ON TRAINING IN CLINICAL PSYCHOLOGY

In conceptualizing training for a comparatively young discipline, it is essential to examine and learn from efforts which have been initiated previously. Therefore, before we discuss our explicit beliefs for training aspiring developmental psychopathologists, it is important to note that, throughout history, academicians and clinicians have grappled with similar issues pertaining to the matriculation of psychologists with basic and applied research as well as clinical interests. In particular, and most germane and instructive for our purposes here, much has been written about the education of clinical psychologists (see, for example, Cattell, 1954; Hoch, Ross, & Winder, 1966; Korchin, 1983; Korman, 1976; Leitenberg, 1974; Matarazzo, 1983; Meehl, 1964, 1971, 1972; Meltzoff, 1984; Peterson, 1966, 1985; Raimy, 1950; Reisman, 1976; Rogers, 1939; Ross, 1959; Routh, 1983; Shaffer, 1947; Shakow, 1938, 1939, 1942; Yerkes, 1941).

Writing over half a century ago, David Shakow (1938, 1939, 1942) discussed issues related to the training of clinical psychologists. Shakow argued that diagnosis, research, and therapy should be the major responsibilities of such professionals, and he delineated sample undergraduate, graduate, and postgraduate curricula. In addition, he discussed the importance of the internship experience in the training process and strongly urged that research opportunities become an integral part of this intensive clinical experience (Shakow, 1942, 1946).

Subsequent to Shakow's ideas, clinical psychology periodically has been depicted as a profession in search of an identity (see, for example, Blank & David, 1963; Garfield & Kurtz, 1976; Kahn & Santostefano, 1962; Meehl, 1954, 1957, 1964, 1972, 1987: Peterson, 1976a, 1976b, 1985; Sarason, 1981; Tryon, 1963). Several landmark conferences have been held in which the training of the clinical psychologist has been debated and the goals of such trainees and professionals have been formulated (Korman, 1976; Matarazzo, 1983; Peterson, 1985; Raimy, 1950; Strickland, 1988). Moreover, the discipline of clinical psychology also has been discussed at length during two national conferences on graduate education in psychology held in Miami, FL in 1958 (Roe, Gustad, Moore, Ross, & Skodak, 1959) and in Salt Lake City, UT in 1987 (Bickman, 1987; see also, Altman, 1987; Spence, 1987). A conference held at Hilton Head, SC in 1985 addressed clinical child psychology and also provided recommendations relevant to the development of training goals.

The first major conference held on training in clinical psychology took place in Boulder, CO during August, 1949 (see Raimy, 1950; also consult Matarazzo, 1983). Societal factors, specifically the large number of veterans returning from World War II in need of mental health services and the paucity of competently trained clinical psychologists, provided the major impetus for the Boulder meeting. The U.S. Public Health Service and the Veterans Administration requested the American Psychological Association to institute a training model for graduate students enrolled in university clinical psychology programs (Bickman, 1987; Strickland, 1988). In keeping with Shakow's viewpoint, the participants at the Boulder Conference recommended a scientist–practitioner model of training that continues to serve as the framework for the majority of clinical psychology programs in the United States. Henceforth, this approach to training clinical psychologists has been refereed to as the Boulder model.

Later conferences held at Stanford University in 1955 (Strother, 1956) and in Chicago in 1965 (Hoch et al., 1966) also suggested that training in clinical psychology integrate science and practice in the education of PhD students. However, once gain changes in American society (e.g., the civil rights movement, the Vietnam War) presented new concerns and challenges for the discipline of clinical psychology (Bickman, 1987). One of the prominent issues facing the discipline was whether it should retain the fee-for-service model developed at Boulder or adopt a potentially more cost-effective community perspective. While the Chicago conference participants primarily reaffirmed the conclusions of the Boulder meetings, the conference at Chicago nonetheless advocated far more diversification in the training of clinical psychologists. One possible alternative suggested was the implementation of more practitioner-oriented training programs leading to a Doctor of Psychology (PsyD) degree (see Bickman, 1987, and Peterson, 1985, for an elaboration).

In a related vein, in 1964 the American Psychological Association (APA) formed a special ad hoc committee, chaired by Kenneth E. Clark, on the Scientific and Professional Aims of Psychology. This committee advocated a two-track educational system for training clinical psychologists, one for researchers and one for practitioners (American Psychological Association, 1967). Paul Meehl, one of the most influential thinkers and systematizers in the history of clinical psychology, returned from these meetings and suggested to his colleagues at Minnesota that a practitioner training program be initiated as a complement to the existing Boulder-model clinical training program already offered (Meehl, 1964, 1971). While Meehl's proposal largely fell on deaf ears, conferences began to appear which strongly encouraged the development of practitioner programs. One of the most well known of these conferences was the one held at Vail in July, 1973 (Korman, 1976), during a period of great sociopolitical unrest (e.g., the disillusionment associated with the Watergate scandal). Though for many years well-known clinical psychologists had touted the benefits of practitioner-oriented or professional training programs (Derner, 1959; Meehl, 1964, 1971; Peterson, 1966; Rogers, 1939), the recognition which the Vail Conference provided for an educational and training model that placed far less emphasis on scientific training and more attention to training for clinical competence contributed to the proliferation of professional programs in clinical psychology (Strickland, 1988). These practitioner-oriented schools generally award either a doctor of psychology (PsyD) or a doctor of philosophy (PhD) degree and often are not located within major research universities (i.e., they are housed in freestanding professional schools—Peterson, 1985). Beginning with the establishment of the first practitioner program at Adelphi University in 1964, there now are approximately 50 such programs in the United States (Peterson, 1985).

The current zeitgeist appears to be somewhat more skeptical about the efficacy and wisdom of such nonscientific clinical training programs. In particular, in recent years increasing concern has been voiced about the quality of education received in the freestanding practitioner programs (Bickman, 1987; Peterson, 1985). Meehl, one of the earlier strong advocates of the practitioner model as a viable alternative to the Boulder model, has even gone so far as to argue that clinical psychology programs should focus exclusively on training researchers (Meehl, 1972). While few solely research clinical psychology programs exist in American universities, there is a renewed movement toward a rekindling of the Boulder-model approach.

Although held to address the concern that too few psychologists were prepared to meet the mental health needs of children and adolescents (Tuma, 1982), the 1985 Hilton Head Conference reached a number of conclusions relevant to training in clinical psychology as a whole (Johnson & Tuma, 1986). Specifically, the Boulder Scientist-Practitioner Model of training was endorsed at the graduate level. Interestingly, it also was recommended that internship training incorporate a research component into the placement rather than serving exclusively as a service-provision experience. The importance of ensuring that clinicians are well-versed in research is underscored by evidence derived from research studies on psychotherapy which support the utility of research findings for the provision of clinical services (Strupp, 1989). By incorporating a research component into clinical training, the likelihood that therapists will be privy to, as well as generate, data which can enhance clinical practice increases.

The APA report authored by Howard and colleagues (1986) entitled, "The Changing Face of American Psychology," highlighted the problems in the relation between graduate education and the future of psychology as a discipline. Spurred in part by the report's documentation of declining enrollments in research areas of the field, a state of affairs which many believed could bring about an erosion of the basic foundation of the discipline, a second conference on graduate education was convened in Salt Lake City, UT. This conference, the first national meeting which addressed the entire discipline of psychology in almost 30 years, focused on several themes. Specifically, disciplinary unity and diversity, or the centripetal and centrifugal trends in psychology, respectively (Altman, 1987; Spence, 1987), as well as quality of graduate education and responsiveness to societal needs and concerns, were among the major issues discussed (Bickman, 1987).

Regarding unity, attendees at the conference underscored that *all* psychologists should be trained in the conduct of scientific investigation. However, it was recognized that a unified discipline also must permit diversity of pathways to professional outcome. Consequently, the scientist–practitioner method of training was not viewed as the preferred or only way to educate future practitioners. As such, the legitimacy of the PsyD was substantiated. However, an important recommendation that was an outgrowth of the conference was that different and clearly specifiable criteria must be developed for clinical training programs with different emphases. Moreover, it was stipulated that quality standards become integral aspects of the diversity issue. As a further reaffirmation of the importance of unity for the discipline, it was recommended that scientific training become a part of *all* doctoral programs in psychology, PhD or otherwise. In an effort to impart uniform standards of quality, the conference exhorted the APA to require that by 1995 all freestanding professional schools must be university affiliated in order to receive accreditation.

THE INTEGRATIVE POWER OF THE DEVELOPMENTAL PERSPECTIVE FOR TRAINING

Clearly then, the objectives of unity, diversity, quality control, and responsiveness to societal needs which emerged from the Utah conference call for some modifications in our current approaches to training clinical psychologists. In view of these goals, we concur that training approaches can be unified by a renewed commitment to the incorporation of a research component into all clinical psychology programs. The inclusion of a mandatory scientific component not only fosters the cohesiveness of those trained, but also addresses societal needs for increased knowledge banks upon which to base clinical and social-policy decisions (see, for example, Aber et al., 1989; Goldstein, Freud, & Solnit, 1973; Melton, 1987; Wald, Carlsmith, & Leiderman, 1988). Even clinical psychologists who choose to become full-time practitioners must be well versed in theory and scientific data in order to provide their patients with the most informed treatments available for their problems.

Since its inception over four decades ago, the Boulder model of training clinical psychologists has sought to integrate research with service delivery. Unfortunately, current statistics seriously call into question the ability of the current scientist–practitioner model of training to meet its goals. In fact, in most academic departments, research and practice continue to coexist uncomfortably (Schneider, 1987). For example, the majority of the graduates of these programs fail to publish empirical work and rarely integrate research with clinical practice. Moreover, there is a paucity of job opportunities which afford graduates of scientist–practitioner programs the opportunity to utilize both of these skills. In essence, with the exception of the vague dictum of training scientist–practitioners, the Boulder model lacks an overarching concept and framework which can serve to unify training. We believe that the absence of such an integrative organizational approach results in a too diverse training philosophy which leaves only the most creative, diligent, and autonomous students properly prepared to embark on productive scientific careers. The developmental psychopathology approach to training which we advocate can be defined succinctly as the study of abnormal behavior through the measurement of the effects of genetic, ontogenetic, affective, social, or any other developmental influence on behavior (Rolf & Read, 1984). The developmental approach to psychopathology requires that equal attention be directed to biological, behavioral, and social factors and their interactions. In addition, central tenets of this approach include an analysis of risk and protective factors, the study of how the functions, competencies, and tasks of development modify the expression of a disorder, and the recognition that a given stress or underlying mechanism may lead to different behavioral difficulties at different times and in varied settings (Cicchetti, 1984, 1990a; Rutter & Garmezy, 1983). While the application of this approach to training is an outgrowth of the Boulder model, it differs in some important respects.

First and foremost, the utilization of the developmental approach as a unifying framework within training in this new discipline provides an important addition to traditional Boulder models. The importance of incorporating a life-span developmental approach to training was emphasized by Stanley Schneider in his discussion of the role of community psychology (Schneider, 1987). Typically, conventional scientist–practitioner programs involve an adult focus, and a variety of theoretical orientations may be incorporated into the program structure. We believe that training in developmental psychopathology departs from this approach and, as a "macroparadigm" (Achenbach, 1990), provides a cohesive way of conceptualizing and organizing a wide array of phenomena.

Our use of the term developmental is not meant to be viewed synonymously with the study of children, as it is possible to investigate normal and abnormal childhood issues from nondevelopmental perspectives. It is this perspective which serves to clearly distinguish developmental psychopathology from the field of child clinical psychology. The field of developmental psychopathology has emerged as a logical extension of the belief that the developmental approach can be applied to any unit of behavior, discipline, or population (Cicchetti, 1984; Kaplan, 1983; Werner, 1948). A developmental analysis is as amenable to the study of the gene or cell as it is to the investigation of the organism, family, or society. From this developmental "world view" (Pepper, 1942), *any* psychopathology can be conceived as a distortion in the normal ontogenetic process (see also Cicchetti, 1987). Thus, this view is at direct odds with the position espoused in the *Diagnostic and Statistical Manual of Mental Disorders* (American Psychiatric Association, 1987), which considers few disorders as developmental and includes only those which usually are first apparent during infancy, childhood, or adolescence (e.g., mental retardation, autism, academic skill disorders, language and speech disorders, and motor skills disorders).

The integrative potential of developmental psychopathology is summarized by Rutter (1980) who stated that the process of development

> constitutes the crucial link between genetic determinants and environmental variables, between sociology and individual psychology, and between physiogenic and psychogenic causes. Development thus encompasses not only the roots of behavior in prior maturation, in physical influences (both internal and external) and in the residues of earlier experiences, but also the modulations of that behavior by the circumstances of the present. (p. 1)

Given the paucity of competently trained researchers on clinical problems, we propose that training in developmental psychopathology emphasizes the acquisition of research skills within a program comprised of faculty unified by their commitment to the developmental perspective. While we think that developmental psychopathology programs should be housed within a clinical psychology program, faculty involved integrally in the process should also include those in developmental psychology, developmental psychobiology and psychophysiology, and, ideally, colleagues from scientific disciplines that have become increasingly central to mastering the corpus of knowledge required to conduct research in psychopathology (e.g., developmental molecular and behavioral genetics, the developmental neurosciences, advanced statistics and psychometric theory, etc.). We believe that psychology departments can be organized with this developmental perspective in mind. This state of affairs would result in increased communication among faculty members and students within the department, as well as in the facilitation of the multidisciplinary collaborations increasingly required to conduct investigations of the roots, course, sequelae, and treatment of psychopathology (see Cicchetti, 1984, 1990a, 1990b). Moreover, this approach would minimize a narrow, over-specialized focus (Schneider, 1987).

From the inception of their training, students will be taught that their primary task is to develop scientific skills and a mastery of the

broad-based developmental perspective necessary to embark on productive research and teaching careers (cf. Meehl's [1972] thoughts on
"second-order relevance"). They will be trained to carry out research in
a variety of contexts and to conduct their work in a number of settings,
including hospitals, day treatment programs, day care centers, and
schools, in addition to the usual academic institutions, such as departments of psychology or medicine. Because the number of available
academic research jobs in psychopathology fluctuates as a function of
economic and other factors, and because many settings which have
excellent access to clinical populations have no ongoing research programs, we believe that this breadth of perspective will ensure both that
there are enough jobs to accommodate these trained scientists and
guarantee that there will be increased communication between researchers and clinicians (cf. Achenbach, in press).

Even though we are advocating that prospective trainees in this new
discipline should be prepared to embark upon research careers, the
developmental approach also is useful in implementing clinical work.
Examples of the utility of a cohesive developmental perspective for
promoting the integration of research and practice already can be found
in the literature. For example, Selman and Demorest (1984) have employed structural developmental theory in their design of peer-pair
therapy for youngsters with interpersonal problems. Developmental
approaches to individual child therapy also have emerged in the writings of Harter (1983) who describes the importance of cognitive developmental considerations in play therapy, and of Santostefano (1978,
1985) whose cognitive control therapy is conceptualized within a developmental perspective. Likewise, the field of social-cognition, greatly
influenced by structural-developmental principles, has obvious implications for the understanding and treatment of childhood, adolescent,
and adult disorders (Damon & Hart, 1988; Kegan, 1982; Noam & Kegan,
1982; Selman, 1980). To provide a final exemplar, Guidano and Liotti
(1983; see also Guidano, 1987) and Greenberg and Mitchell (1983) both
illustrate how two related developmental orientations (i.e., attachment
and object relations theories, respectively) can be used to change the
poor quality of internal working models of a variety of psychiatric
patients (see also Egeland, Jacobvitz, & Sroufe, 1988, in this regard).

HISTORICAL ROOTS AND GENESIS OF
DEVELOPMENTAL PSYCHOPATHOLOGY

Now that we have discussed the utility of the developmental psychopathology approach and highlighted the integrative power of this perspective, we next explore its history and evolution in more depth.

Because the delineation of developmental psychopathology as a distinct scientific field did not occur until the 1970s (Cicchetti, 1984), formalized training for this discipline is in its infancy. Moreover, as a young field, theoreticians are continuing to define and clarify its parameters (Cicchetti, 1984, 1990a, 1990b; Rutter, 1988; Sroufe & Rutter, 1984; Zigler & Glick, 1986).

Historically, the roots of developmental psychopathology represent a wide range of disciplines and areas of inquiry. Prior to the 1970s, three major developmental theories were dominant within the behavioral sciences. These included the Wernerian organismic-developmental theory, the psychoanalytic developmental theory, and the Piagetian structural-developmental theory, all of which stress the "organismic" rather than "mechanistic" view of development (Reese & Overton, 1970). The organismic model emphasizes the dynamic role of the individual and defines the individual as an organized whole, very unlike the reactive organism portrayed by a mechanistic model of development (Overton, 1976, 1984).

Interestingly, the concepts central to the organismic model of development can be traced to the writings of Plato and Aristotle (Kaplan, 1967). In fact, it is with Plato that the idea of hierarchically integrated domains of functioning emerges. According to this principle, later adaptation builds upon the resolution of earlier developmental issues. Therefore, an early developmental failure increases the likelihood that future difficulties will occur. Similarly, successful task resolution facilitates future positive adaptation (Sroufe & Rutter, 1984). In fact, many prominent developmental theorists have espoused similar beliefs about the importance of hierarchical integration (cf. Erikson, 1950). Because an organism's early structures are not lost in development via hierarchic integration, integrity and continuity in the face of change, so rapid that it might otherwise cause problems for the sense of internal continuity, can be maintained (Block & Block, 1980; Cicchetti & Schneider-Rosen, 1986).

Important principles which have influenced the emergence of developmental psychopathology also can be seen in the writings of Aristotle, who was one of the first to argue that individuation, differentiation, and self-actualization were central aspects of developmental transformations, and that the interdependence between the individual and the environment was important. The genesis of the transactional approach, which emphasizes reciprocal interactions and the resultant reorganization which occur in both the individual and the environment, is central to developmental psychopathology (see Sameroff & Chandler, 1975).

Throughout time, these developmental principles have continued to emerge across disciplines and areas of inquiry that play integral roles in developmental psychopathology (Cicchetti, 1990a; Kaplan, 1967, 1983;

Overton, 1984). Working within diverse disciplines, including embryology, the neurosciences, clinical and experimental psychology and psychiatry, researchers have utilized high-risk, atypical, pathological, and psychopathological populations to elucidate, expand, and affirm further the basic underlying principles of their developmental theories. For example, the work of Jackson (1884/1958) and Sherrington (1906) in neurophysiology, of Waddington (1957, 1966) and Weiss (1961, 1969) in embryology, of Teitelbaum (1971, 1977) in psychobiology, and of Jacobson (1978) in neurobiology, all can be seen as influential in the genesis of developmental psychopathology. Contemporary theory and research in this discipline continue to emphasize the importance of the relation between normal and abnormal development and the multidisciplinary perspective. Historically, a number of eminent scientists, theoreticians, and clinicians have adopted the premise that knowledge about normal and abnormal development can inform each other (Cicchetti, 1984, 1990a; Rutter, 1988; Sroufe & Rutter, 1984). The principle of the interrelations of abnormal and normal functioning finds perhaps its clearest expression in the work of Sigmund Freud who indeed drew no sharp distinction between normal and abnormal functioning (Cicchetti, 1984). Freud's emphasis on the prime importance of irrationality highlighted the close connection between the normal and the abnormal. As Freud's ideas gradually permeated the substance of psychology proper, his thesis, that there was a normality/abnormality continuum, met with increasingly wide acceptance.

Most certainly, one of the major impetuses underlying the emergence of developmental psychopathology during the past two decades has been that the science of normal development has matured, acquiring a broader basis of firm knowledge in domains other than cognitive development (Cicchetti, 1990b, 1990c; Cicchetti & White, 1988; Hesse & Cicchetti, 1982). Consequently, researchers are in a much stronger position to draw conclusions about high-risk or pathological populations now that better information exists about the processes and products of normal ontogenesis.

DEFINITIONAL PARAMETERS OF DEVELOPMENTAL PSYCHOPATHOLOGY

In order to possess relevance for informing training needs, the parameters of developmental psychopathology must be defined clearly. While some definitional divergence exists, it is generally agreed that developmental psychopathology involves the study of functioning through the assessment of ontogenetic, biochemical/genetic, neurophysiological, cognitive/representational, socioemotional, social-cognitive, and environmental influences on behavior (Cicchetti, 1984, 1990a, 1990b; Cicchetti & Schneider-Rosen, 1986; Rolf & Read, 1984). Rather than limiting their attention to conditions of pathology, developmental psychopathologists also believe that knowledge of normal development is necessary in order to understand deviations from normality. Similarly, information obtained from studying pathology is utilized to enhance the understanding of normal development. As such, developmental psychopathologists may be as interested in high-risk individuals who, over time, do not manifest pathology as they are in individuals who develop an actual disorder (Sroufe & Rutter, 1984). Developmental psychopathologists also are dedicated to uncovering pathways to competent adaptation despite exposure to conditions of adversity (Garmezy & Rutter, 1983; Masten, in press; Rutter, 1985). A related component of the developmental psychopathology perspective involves an interest in mechanisms and processes which affect the ultimate outcome of risk factors (Cicchetti & Aber, 1986; Rutter, 1988). In order to obtain a comprehensive assessment of functioning, multidomain, multicontextual measurement strategies are necessary (Cicchetti & Todd-Manly, 1990; Cicchetti & Wagner, 1990). A final definitional element of developmental psychopathology which merits attention involves the population of interest. Specifically, we want to address what we consider to be an incorrect, but unfortunately somewhat widely held conception, that developmental psychopathology is concerned only with conditions of childhood. While many active researchers and theoreticians in developmental psychopathology have focused their efforts on childhood disorders, we believe that pathology calls for a life-span approach to understanding developmental processes (Cicchetti, 1984; Rutter & Garmezy, 1983; Zigler & Glick, 1986). It is only by exploring various conditions and populations from infancy through adulthood that developmental continuities and discontinuities can be elucidated fully.

Now that the parameters of developmental psychopathology have been defined, ways in which it differs from related fields of inquiry begin to emerge. Of course, similarities do exist among developmental psychopathology, clinical psychology, developmental psychology, and psychiatry. In many ways developmental psychopathology integrates components from various disciplines. It is this very integration which sets it apart as a unique approach. Moreover a developmental approach can enhance our understanding of psychopathology in ways that a nondevelopmental approach may overlook. For instance, in the absence of a developmental approach, one may focus on symptomatic continuity and fail to attend to age-specific manifestations of psychopathology (Cicchetti & Schneider-Rosen, 1986; Sroufe & Rutter, 1984). In addition, a focus on isolated experiments could fail to elucidate the processes which affect adaptation. Perhaps most importantly, developmental psychopathology strives to reduce the schism which so often separates scientific research from the application of knowledge to clinical populations (see also Santostefano, 1978). This last point serves as a major impetus behind our commitment to furthering the training of developmental psychopathologists.

The principles which guide the field of developmental psychopathology are not necessarily excluded from other fields of inquiry. Moreover, we are not suggesting that research and intervention guided by these principles must emanate exclusively from the discipline of developmental psychopathology. However, we are calling for the incorporation of these principles into training, and we believe that developmental psychopathology provides a necessary integrative framework. As Rolf and Read (1984) have noted, few existing training programs in developmental psychology, child (and adult) clinical psychology, or child (and adult) psychiatry encompass the diversity inherent in the field of developmental psychopathology. In addition, few researchers are sufficiently prepared to address developmental processes across the lifespan.

In developing an educational approach for aspiring developmental psychopathologists, the guiding principles of the discipline and their implications for the structure of a formalized training program need to be considered. These principles are important to keep in mind, as ideally, any training program will incorporate curriculum strategies which facilitate the attainment of these overarching integrative goals. In this chapter, we focus on training for students of psychology. While a similar approach can be applied across disciplines, members of specific fields will need to determine how best to incorporate these ideas into the structure of their respective training programs.

STRUCTURE OF A TRAINING PROGRAM IN DEVELOPMENTAL PSYCHOPATHOLOGY

Just as developmental psychopathologists emphasize the importance of multiple pathways to understanding adaptation/maladaptation, we believe that alternate pathways to training in the area of developmental psychopathology are necessary. For our initial curriculum, we address training for those individuals who determine, relatively early, that they wish to pursue a career in developmental psychopathology. In many ways, this is the ideal situation that enables the development of a relatively straightforward approach to training.

If possible, preparation as a developmental psychopathologist can begin at the undergraduate level with a major in psychology. To accomplish this, exposure to the discipline through the incorporation of undergraduate courses on developmental psychology and developmental psychopathology is important. The presence of faculty who are knowledgeable regarding the importance of developmental psychopathology and who are able to generate interest among students early in their education is necessary if the undergraduate experience is to serve as a legitimate component of training. Unfortunately, often undergraduate faculty, especially those with clinical degrees, deemphasize the value and importance of acquiring research expertise. Because faculty members may be invested in teaching or service provision, the potential breadth of a career as a developmental psychopathologist may be overlooked. While this scenario is less likely to occur in large universities where research is a priority, it is important that faculty at smaller universities and colleges be invested in conveying the presence of clinical research opportunities to their students. Unless this occurs, the personpower shortages described earlier are likely to persist.

Rather than limiting undergraduate study to clinical or developmental courses, we believe that a range of coursework in the psychological and biological sciences is most appropriate. This breadth of experience will serve as the foundation upon which increasingly specialized courses can be added. While it is unrealistic to expect undergraduate students of developmental psychopathology to master the span of topical areas relevant to the discipline, it is important that they possess a working knowledge of a range of areas of inquiry. By beginning to identify developmental psychopathology as a focus early in one's career, a greater number of options for specialization remain open. For example, if it is determined that the neurosciences are of interest, a sound grounding in biology prior to beginning graduate study would be beneficial. Again, however, we wish to stress the importance of a breadth of experience at this level. While the student may choose to focus on a certain area of specialization, this should not be pursued so zealously as to preclude exposure to other areas. In effect, we believe that the best preparation for a career as a developmental psychopathologist is exposure to diverse coursework within the behavioral and biological sciences taught from a developmental perspective.

Involvement in research and clinical work through participation in an undergraduate externship also could prove to be advantageous. This could occur during the academic year, or be offered as a summer option. Opportunities which integrate clinical and research components will be extremely valuable. For example, involvement as a counselor or research assistant in a summer camp designed to assess development in socioeconomically deprived and maltreated children affords exposure to children as well as to various methods of observational and questionnaire assessment (see, for example, Kaufman & Cicchetti, 1989). Participation in the development and evaluation of intervention strategies also provides rich opportunities for experiential learning (see, for example, Selman & Demorest, 1984).

Upon completion of undergraduate coursework, admission to a doctoral-level program in psychology is one possible pathway to follow. While, in time, a PhD in developmental psychopathology may become a reality, at present, no such degree award program exits. Therefore, as stated earlier, we believe that a training program in developmental psychopathology can best be subsumed within departments offering doctoral degrees in clinical psychology. Ideally, the training program should be housed within a university which is sufficiently large to offer continuing exposure to a range of courses within psychology. Clearly, a developmental focus must permeate all coursework and a strong division of developmental psychology also is a necessary component of training. In addition, interdepartmental collaboration in training is important so that trainees can continue to gain a breadth of knowledge from areas outside of the behavioral sciences. We wish to emphasize, however, that this suggested diversity of experience must not cause the central developmental focus to be compromised. In this regard, a core faculty available to serve as mentors to oversee individual training experiences is necessary. In fact, we consider the mentor system to be critical to the successful implementation of the training which we are describing. Significantly, we are not proposing that mentors be drawn exclusively from the ranks of psychology. It is more important that they are firmly grounded in developmental theory and utilize it as an integrative framework in which to conceptualize their work. Because developmental psychopathology is such a young science, this acceptance of the wealth of knowledge possessed by faculty outside of psychology proper increases the likelihood of a large enough number of individuals being available to serve as mentors. In essence, we advocate the involvement of academicians who have the necessary expertise, regardless of their area of specialization or of their particular degree.

As we mentioned, various pathways to training in developmental psychopathology are possible. Why then have we recommended that a degree in clinical psychology be awarded rather than a degree in developmental or some other subdiscipline of psychology? Because one of the goals of developmental psychopathology is bridging the separations that have existed for so long between research into psychopathology and the application of this knowledge to clinical disorders, we believe that training as a clinical psychologist may be a benefit to the attainment of this integration. Although we suggest that the primary function of developmental psychopathologists should be to conduct research into the precursors, manifestations, course, and sequelae of psychopathology across the life-course, we also maintain that a background in clinical psychology can enhance this pursuit. Specifically, exposure to various disorders may serve to guide the formulation of important programmatic research endeavors. Moreover, a working knowledge of theories of psychotherapy and the application of these principles to clinical populations may increase the reception that researchers receive when trying to gain access to clinical facilities. By being able to understand the experience of professionals who engage exclusively in the provision of treatment, developmental psychopathology researchers are more likely to be perceived as professional colleagues and collaborators. Finally, expertise in clinical psychology also may minimize the impediments toward the incorporation of research knowledge into clinical practice. By ensuring that clinicians who are treating patients also are knowledgeable consumers of and contributors to research knowledge, the quality of interventions being offered is likely to be enhanced. Clearly, this integration is an aspiration that can benefit the behavioral sciences in their entirety.

Now that we have presented our thoughts on the structure of a training program for developmental psychopathology, we address what we consider to be necessary curriculum components at the graduate level. To begin, the core course requirements of a clinical track must be fulfilled. Thus, for example, courses or seminars in assessment and diagnosis, personality theory, research design and methodology, statistics, psychometric theory, history and systems, psychobiology, ethics, and principles of psychotherapy must be taken. In efforts to address the marginal growth of knowledge in statistics and psychometric theory which has occurred in the past two decades (Aiken et al., 1990), a strong focus on these areas will be important (see Meehl, 1990, as an exemplar of the integration of this knowledge). In order to attain the necessary grounding in developmental psychology, we also recommend that courses in developmental theory and methodology and lifespan developmental psychopathology be required, and suggest that several advanced seminars on specialized areas of development also be taken (e.g., cognitive, socioemotional, social-cognitive, linguistic, and perceptual development). Regardless of area of specialization, we believe that courses in developmental neuropsychology and developmental behavioral genetics are needed to provide the desired breadth of knowledge. This core set of courses can be completed during the first three years of the five-year graduate PhD program. While it may be argued that this results in an excessively didactic curriculum, we believe that it is critical to attain a well-rounded knowledge of these areas. The curriculum is rigorous, but it is necessary if the core of requisite knowledge is to be obtained.

In addition to formal coursework, graduate training for developmental psychopathologists must include both clinical and research practicum experiences. We recommend that this begin with a 10–15 hour-per-week research apprenticeship during the student's first year. As one component of this, exposure to nondisordered individuals, either through research or observation of various populations, is important (e.g., observing children in day care centers, studying peer relations at a summer camp setting, etc.). It is only through a sound acquisition of the development of normally functioning children and adults that abnormal development can be comprehended adequately. All too often clinicians begin to work with populations before having this necessary baseline knowledge and may interpret a normative developmental process as aberrant. While initially it is recommended that students be involved in the ongoing research of their mentor(s), more independent research should be expected as the student develops increasing skill and self-sufficiency, most likely during the third year of training. In order to facilitate the acquisition of increased autonomy in the area of research, we also recommend that a required independent research project (possibly a Master's thesis) be conducted and completed by the end of the student's second year of graduate study. This may be an outgrowth of the mentor's area of research, but should constitute an addition to scientific knowledge with the potential for publication. Because we hope to train individuals who will become engaged in investigative research, we feel that positive experiences early in training are needed. In fact, we believe that students who publish early during their training will be far more likely to continue to engage in research activities after graduation. Upon completion of the independent research project, the student will be eligible to sit for qualifying/preliminary examinations.

During the second semester of the second year, we also recommend a 10 hour-per-week placement in a clinical facility where the student can engage in the provision of direct service to clinical populations. A minimum of two such placements are necessary prior to the internship, and ideally they should occur with a range of patient types. Because we are departing from the more traditional approach, in which child or adult clinical specialization is elected, and are opting instead for a life-span approach, exposure to different age groups is necessary. For example, one placement may occur in a child-focused facility, while the second may involve working primarily with adults.

In addition to breadth with respect to the developmental level of clients being served, we also recommend diversity with regard to the severity of problems observed. For example, if one placement occurs in a community-based or outpatient setting, we strongly urge that experience with more severely disordered populations be obtained subsequently through inpatient or residential placements. Knowledge of patients from a variety of ethnic backgrounds and socioeconomic levels also is necessary; in the absence of such knowledge an incomplete view of functioning and utilization of therapeutic techniques effective for only a segment of the population may result. Ideally, the trainee should be exposed to and interface with various community resources as a function of these clinical placements. For instance, if conducting outpatient therapy with a child, liaison work with school personnel and familiarity with services available through the local school district should occur. Similarly, if working in inpatient settings, exploration of community supports and aftercare services will be an integral aspect of the educational process.

As can be seen, we are advocating an intense, broad-based approach that incorporates ongoing research involvement and at least two semesters of 10 hours-per-week clinical placements. By the end of the third year of training, all core coursework as well as the required research project will have been completed, and students will then be able to cultivate their chosen area of specialization. Developmental subspecialities may include areas such as neuropsychology, psychophysiology, neurophysiology, epidemiology, linguistic and representational processes, or socioemotional development. Because even departments known for their excellence with regard to subspecialties of psychology are unlikely to offer more than two or three advanced courses per area, students will necessarily need to acquire knowledge through reading and independent studies courses, guided by a knowledgeable mentor.

Following completion of all core and subspeciality requirements, but prior to the award of the degree, we recommend that a year-long full-time internship be completed, normally during the fifth year of graduate school. The dissertation proposal must minimally have been approved prior to internship placement. Because completion of a doctoral dissertation is a stressful process which may interfere with the student's capacity to become immersed in the internship, ideally the dissertation should be well on the way to completion prior to internship placement (i.e., data should be collected and analyzed). In keeping with the goal of integrating research and clinical experience, the internship site should enable students to continue with their research pursuits while developing clinical expertise (cf. Shakow, 1942, 1946). In fact, even though recent guidelines developed by the APA Section 1 Task Force on Internship Training (Elbert, Abidin, Finch, Sigman, & Walker, 1988) acknowledge that the primary function of the internship is the enhancement of clinical skills, participation in research during the internship was advocated.

Because our goal in training developmental psychopathologists is to stem the flow of PhDs who are involved exclusively in service delivery, we are advocating a modification of the dictum that the purpose of internships is to train clinicians. It is this very belief which has resulted in a decrease of productive researchers in the area of psychopathology, thereby markedly compromising our understanding and treatment of disordered populations. Because, currently, so many internship sites focus on clinical work to the exclusion of research involvement, it is important to ensure a 50–50 time allocation of research and clinical responsibilities for students being trained as developmental psychopathologists. To attain this balance, departments invested in training developmental psychopathologists may need to advocate increased availability of sites which are committed to this dual focus. It may be useful and necessary for psychology faculty to gain appointments in affiliated medical centers to facilitate this internship training capability. In addition, the development and expansion of centers committed to the attainment of the goals of developmental psychopathology is recommended. Specifically, those settings providing clinical services that maintain an equal commitment to conducting developmental research with various populations are a very viable option for internship training in developmental psychopathology. We strongly frown upon the completion of an internship in a setting that discourages research involvement, as the result may be a loss of the momentum which the aspiring developmental psychopathologist has gained during graduate training. Moreover, an intern attempting to integrate research into a setting that is not supportive of these interests may receive censure from both supervisors and fellow interns.

In view of the importance of the internship site for fostering the acquisition of necessary clinical and research skills, we next describe internship training opportunities in more detail. The clinical experience itself should build upon the foundation developed through the graduate school clinical practicum placements. To this end, we continue to advocate exposure to populations that vary with respect to developmental level, severity, and chronicity of symptomatalogy, ethnic background, and socioeconomic status. Because two practicum experiences cannot supply the breadth of experience that we are recommending, it is important that mentors help their students to evaluate areas of relative deficit and encourage application to internships which can broaden their experience base. The internship year provides an opportunity to apply therapeutic techniques that were learned during graduate training. To facilitate the likelihood of utilizing a range of approaches, the availability of clinical supervisors with diverse areas of expertise is important. This broad experience will enable the intern to begin to acquire an orientation that is consistent with his or her emerging philosophy of treatment.

The research experience during the internship promises to be most successful if the intern is able to utilize the resources available at the internship site. For example, becoming involved in an ongoing staff research project, examining clinical records to assess the feasibility of incorporating them into an archival project, or designing a treatment evaluation study all are feasible undertakings which are likely to be supported by internship facilities. If the intern finds that the internship faculty are not actively pursuing research, creativity around research involvement will be necessary. In those instances, promising alternatives include conducting a comprehensive literature search on an identified area with the intention of submitting a review article for publication or designing a single-subject study of a patient in treatment. We want to emphasize that if graduate training has been successful, students of developmental psychopathology will be as invested in sharpening these skills as they are in developing their clinical capabilities.

In addition to involvement in clinical and research activities, we consider attendance at seminars and case conferences to hold considerable potential for achieving the integration between clinical practice and academic inquiry which we are seeking for the intern in developmental psychopathology. Clinical case conferences can be organized around a theoretical stance supported by research knowledge (see Meehl, 1973, in this regard).Rather than focusing on descriptive presentations which chronicle the course of treatment, the incorporation and critical evaluation of research related to the clinical condition being presented is recommended. Journal clubs designed to explore topical areas and to cull readings from the current literature also provide a valuable forum for the integration of clinical and research pursuits. Finally, seminars on therapy and assessment can incorporate relevant studies on etiology and intervention outcome. Overall we are underscoring that even clinical activities can be conducted within a developmental and theoretical research-driven framework.

While this approach to internship training is not a radical departure from previous training philosophies, we believe that increased communication between academic graduate programs and training sites is necessary if the goals of integration of clinical and research activities during internship training are to be achieved. The objectives of the graduate program as well as the needs and philosophies of internship sites must be clearly communicated. In order to ensure the attainment of the articulated goals of training, we also suggest that internships be approved by the student's department of origin before an application is submitted. While this will reduce the number of training sites available, it is unrealistic to expect all current sites to be receptive to the needs of developmental psychopathologists. Therefore, as long as expectations are recognized by the student and by potential training sites, the probability of a successful internship experience will be enhanced.

Upon completion of the internship and pending completion of the doctoral dissertation, the PhD will be awarded. For purposes of illustration, a sample curriculum is presented in Table 3.1.

POSTDOCTORAL TRAINING

While thus far we have presented a rather straightforward "main effects" approach to training, we have alluded to the existence of "alternate pathways" to the attainment of expertise in developmental psychopathology. One such divergent mechanism involves meeting the needs of individuals who have completed their graduate training prior to the ascendance of programs designed to address the tenets of developmental psychopathology. Obviously, a basic core of knowledge in the behavioral and biological sciences is necessary if specialization in developmental psychopathology is to be gained. Therefore, we address the training specialization needs of those individuals who already have attained doctoral degrees in clinical and developmental psychology. This postdegree approach also could be modified to meet the needs of individuals who have been trained in other disciplines, including psychiatry, psychiatric nursing, pediatrics, and social work.

We see two major routes through which training may be completed at this point. One mechanism for respecialization would involve enrolling for a one- or two-year full-time postdoctoral degree program in developmental psychopathology. The nature of the training should be tailored to the areas which have been omitted during prior educational experiences. If, for example, a professional has a solid grounding in developmental theory, coursework, and research, the respecialization will need to address more clinically specific training and enhanced knowledge about psychopathology. Similarly, individuals with considerable prior background in coursework and service provision in psychopathology will need to focus on cultivating research expertise within a developmental perspective. Involvement of a mentor skilled in developmental psychopathology is again critical, as this will ensure a customized stance on training designed to meet the individual needs of the student.

Although this approach provides an intensive educational experience, it is infeasible for established professionals; therefore, alternate mechanisms for acquiring expertise in developmental psychopathology are necessary. One possible alternative is the use of externships designed to involve the aspiring developmental psychopathologist in supplemental educational experiences. Initially, seminars and didactic readings are likely to be necessary. Involvement in research and in clinical practica also is considered to be an important aspect of training. Most often, the professional will have a firm base in one of these

Table 2.1. Sample Curriculum

Year 1	
Fall Semester	**Spring Semester**
Personality Theory	Assessment and Diagnosis
Statistics	Research Design and Computer Methods
Developmental Theory and Methodology	History and Systems
Developmental Child and Adolescent	Socioemotional Development (Elective)
Psychopathology	Research Practicum (15 hours/week)
Research Practicum (15 hours/week)	

Year 2	
Fall Semester	**Spring Semester**
Developmental Adult Psychopathology	Principles of Psychotherapy
Cognitive and Social Cognitive	Psychometric Theory
Development (Elective)	Linguistic and Perceptual Development
Psychobiology	(Elective)
Advanced Statistics	Research Practicum (10 hours/week)
Research Practicum (15 hours/week)	(Required second-year research project
	completed)
	Clinical Placement (10–15 hours/week)
	Seminar on Ethical Principles for
	Psychologists

Year 3	
Fall Semester	**Spring Semester**
Qualifying/Preliminary Examinations	2 courses in area of specialization (may
Behavioral Genetics	occur outside of Department of
Neuropsychology	Psychology)
Dissertation	Dissertation
Clinical Placement (10–15 hours/week)	

Year 4	
Fall Semester	**Spring Semester**
2 courses in area of specialization (may	2 courses in area of specialization (may
occur outside of Department of	occur outside of Department of
Psychology)	Psychology)
Dissertation	Dissertation

Year 5	
Internship	
Dissertation Completed	

areas and specialization will only need to focus on imparting a developmental perspective to the individual's knowledge base.

Another possible training experience for professionals could be provided through involvement in summer institutes. An interdisciplinary team of professionals involved in research in developmental psychopathology would be available to provide an intensive, one-month training program with the goal of integrating knowledge and research strategies from clinical and developmental areas of inquiry. Over time, more specialized, thematic institutes also could be offered. For example, a month-long gathering of leading attachment theorists could be cultivated wherein seminars and exemplary research programs could be presented. This would afford professionals with considerable expertise in their fields the opportunity to acquire knowledge relevant to the goals of developmental psychopathology. This is especially important for the advancement of developmental psychopathology as it enables continued multidisciplinary collaboration and allows an influx of new information into the discipline. Additional opportunities for communication regarding advances in the area of developmental psychopathology also can be afforded through the institution of conferences and publications devoted to this goal. Currently, an annual conference on developmental psychopathology is held at Mt. Hope Family Center, University of Rochester, and the proceedings are published in an edited volume (see, for example, Cicchetti, 1989). In addition, a journal entitled *Development and Psychopathology* was initiated in 1989 and serves as a vehicle for publishing material in the field of developmental psychopathology. It is only through a commitment to interdisciplinary training that the goals of developmental psychopathology can truly be achieved.

CREDENTIALING IN DEVELOPMENTAL PSYCHOPATHOLOGY

Historically, the development of uniform guidelines for training in clinical psychology has been problematic. Confusion regarding requirements and internship structure has been further exacerbated by the influx of areas of specialization. In fact, the Hilton Head Conference was held to develop recommendations for training specifically in child clinical psychology (Elbert, 1985; Johnson, 1985; Tuma, 1985). This conference was spawned by the recognition of the importance for establishing criteria for training in an exciting and new area of specialization. Not surprisingly then, an emerging field, such as developmental psychopathology, will face similar challenges requiring resolution.

At this point, we recommend that training in developmental psychopathology be limited to inclusion in APA-approved departments of psychology which are housed within research-oriented universities. While ideally internship sites also should be APA accredited, we believe that some flexibility may be necessary regarding this requirement during the formative stages of establishing training in developmental psychopathology. Because we are advocating an innovative approach to training, internship facilities not currently credentialed through the APA may offer excellent training opportunities and should not be eliminated due to the absence of accreditation. Rather, the university should assess the quality of various sites with regard to their ability to meet the student's identified needs.

As the discipline of developmental psychopathology continues to grow, leaders in the field may wish to advocate the inclusion of a division to be housed within the APA. This division, then, would provide increased structure and a forum in which to explore and recommend restrictions on training and practice. Currently, however, quality control specific to developmental psychopathology awaits increased formalization and structure in the discipline. In the interim, while PhDs in clinical psychology with a specialization in developmental psychopathology are being awarded, adherence to the credentialing requirements of clinical psychology are recommended.

CONCLUSION AND FUTURE PERSPECTIVES

Clearly a dearth of individuals trained to conduct research in the area of psychopathology exists. There is an even greater shortage of scientists able to conduct such research from a developmental perspective. In view of the extensive needs which are present, an examination of the reasons underlying the paucity of trained researchers may be helpful in the alleviation of such needs.

The genesis of the current status of research personpower in psychopathology can be traced to problems inherent in academic institutions, as well as in society itself. Unfortunately, we have failed to educate society as to the importance of conducting research in the area of mental health. It is therefore critical that we begin to convey the benefits which will be derived from improving the quantity and quality of developmental research that is being conducted on conditions of psychopathology.

In many ways, investigations in the area of mental disorders are shunned by both clinicians and researchers. Academic departments in major universities often consider studies of psychopathology to be "soft science" and therefore a less prestigious area of endeavor. Unfortunately, this may impact upon tenure decisions and monetary recompense, thereby discouraging aspiring developmental psychopathologists from pursuing this pathway. In addition, clinicians can earn significantly higher incomes in purely service provision positions than is possible within the ranks of academia. Given these considerations, it becomes easier to understand why so few professionals are opting for major research involvement. To further compound the problem, many training options involve added time for the development of research competence. For example, following the completion of an internship experience which currently accompanies the Boulder-model of training, aspiring academicians often must complete a one-or two-year postdoctoral position that focuses on research before they can realistically expect to obtain a university faculty appointment. As the future earning potential of academic positions is not even comparable with that of clinical positions, students may be reluctant to invest more time and money to acquire training that has few future concrete benefits. In a related vein, Pion (1988) reports that students who received financial support from university or federal sources during training were more likely to be involved in research. This statistic is especially distressing, as financial support for graduate study in psychology has been reduced over the years. In fact, since 1981, the number of predoctoral awards from NIMH have decreased by 63 percent (Pion, 1988). Additionally, the lag time between degree completion and the attainment of research grant money also is quite long. Because monies for psychopathology research are especially scarce (IOM, 1985), the young researcher's ability to acquire funding necessary for the completion of this laborintensive work is hampered. This lack of research funding, in turn, further limits the likelihood that tenure will be awarded.

While these facts present a rather bleak scenario, they underscore the importance of providing positive research experiences early in training. We believe that the area of developmental psychopathology promises to address many of these impediments. By facilitating the interplay between clinical and academic pursuits, it will be increasingly possible to communicate the utility of the research which is being conducted. These arguments may then be presented to legislators and other officials who determine the allocation of governmental funds. Not surprisingly, the availability of increased funding and a concomitant recognition of the importance of supporting work in developmental psychopathology will serve to facilitate an influx of individuals committed to developing skills in this area.

In this chapter we have discussed the pervasiveness of mental disorders and the extensive need for researchers as well as practitioners trained to address these needs. We have proposed the field of developmental psychopathology as an integrative framework which may serve to link historically diverse value systems associated with clinical and research endeavors. We also have described the principles underlying the discipline of developmental psychopathology and explored their implications for training. This has been a challenging undertaking for several reasons. Because it is a relative newcomer, the core of the discipline is continuing to evolve. Therefore, a danger in writing a chapter such as this may be the implication that the developmental process of the discipline has been completed. With regard to developmental psychopathology, nothing could be more incorrect. In fact, the very enthusiasm generated by this field of inquiry can be attributed to its receptivity to new ideas and the incorporation of this input into its development. To suggest that the training approach which we have presented should remain static is antithetical to the developmental "world view" of the discipline. Rather, we have addressed those elements which we see as reflecting the needs of the discipline as it now stands, while recognizing that these factors will require modification in accordance with the continued growth of the field.

Yet another consideration in writing a training chapter for developmental psychopathology lies in the field's commitment to interdisciplinary relevance and collaboration. By focusing on training for psychologists, we are singling out one component of the discipline. While the suggestions for training are relevant to other professions, we wish to stress the importance of maintaining those elements which comprise profession-specific identities. The discipline of developmental psychopathology is greater than the sum of its parts and any reduction in its breadth will minimize one of its most valuable assets.

A final area to address in this chapter involves the current status of funding in training. Rather than belabor what we all know to be a rather dismal state of affairs, we suggest advocacy and creative efforts to generate necessary support. Much of what we have presented can be incorporated into existing departmental structures with minimal added expense. For example, faculty from other departments might agree to participate in training efforts if psychology staff were willing to lecture in their departments. Similarly, contractual arrangements for student participation in classes could be established. In addition, collaborative work on large research projects between faculty of psychology and disciplines outside of psychology holds great promise. To provide an illustration, a developmental neuroscientist knowledgeable in brain imaging techniques and a developmental psychopathologist interested in brain/behavior interfaces could initiate collaborations that also could benefit students of both disciplines. This is but one example of a cross-departmental arrangement; many opportunities for undertakings such as this exist both within and between departments. In cases such as these, convincing the department of the importance of providing training in developmental psychopathology will present the major challenge. For postdoctoral training and respecialization, cooperative efforts among those professionals established as developmental psychopathologists are likely to be necessary. Educating legislators as to the benefits of training professionals in this area and stressing the costs associated with failure to learn more about psychopathology and its effective treatment will be important avenues to pursue. In addition, generating support from private sectors is a viable alternative to federal funding. Because developmental psychopathology can extend the understanding of psychopathology beyond that of nondevelopmental approaches, effective communication of these merits can enhance the availability of support for training.

As progress in ontogenetic approaches to the various disciplines of developmental psychopathology continues, the common theoretical and empirical threads running through this work will come together in a foundation upon which an increasingly sophisticated discipline of developmental psychopathology can be built. If this growth is to be fostered, theoretically grounded training programs must be developed.

REFERENCES

Aber, J. L., Allen, J., Carlson, V., & Cicchetti, D. (1989). The effects of maltreatment on development during early childhood: Recent studies and their theoretical, clinical, and policy implications. In D. Cicchetti & V. Carlson (Eds.), *Child maltreatment: Theory and research on the causes and consequences of child abuse and neglect* (pp. 579–619) New York: Cambridge University Press.

Achenbach, T. (1990). What is "developmental" about developmental psychopathology? In J. Rolf, A Masten, D. Cicchetti, K. Neuchterlein, & S. Weintraub (Eds.), *Risk and protective factors in the development of psychopathology* (pp. 29–48). New York: Cambridge University Press.

Aiken, L., West S., Sechrest, L., Reno, R., Roediger, H., Scarr, S., Kazdin, A., & Sherman, S. (1990). Graduate training in statistics, methodology, and measurement in psychology. *American Psychologist, 45,* 721–734.

Alperstein, G., Rappaport, C., & Flanigan, J. (1988). Health problems of homeless children in New York City. *American Journal of Public Health, 78,* 1232–1233.

Altman, I. (1987). Centripetal and centrifugal trends in psychology. *American Psychologist, 42,* 1058–1069.

American Psychiatric Association Committee on Nomenclature. (1980). *Diagnostic and Statistical Manual of Mental Disorders, III.* Washington, DC: American Psychiatric Association.

American Psychiatric Association Committee on Nomenclature. (1987). *Diagnostic and Statistical Manual of Mental Disorders, III (Revised).* Washington, DC: American Psychiatric Association.

American Psychological Association, Committee on the Scientific and Professional Aims of Psychology. (1967). The scientific and professional aims of psychology. *American Psychologist, 22,* 49–76.

Beardslee, W. R., Bemporad, J., Keller, M. D., & Klerman, G. L. (1983). Children of parents with major affective disorder: A review. *American Journal of Psychiatry, 140,* 825–832.

Beardslee, W., Son, L., & Vaillant, G. (1986). Exposure to parental alcoholism during childhood and outcome in adulthood: A prospective longitudinal study. *British Journal of Psychiatry, 149,* 584–591.

Bickman, L. (1987). Graduate education in psychology. *American Psychologist, 42,* 1041–1047.

Blank, L., & David, H. P. (1963). The crisis in clinical psychology training. *American Psychologist, 18,* 216–219.

Block, J. H., & Block, J. (1980). The role of ego-control and ego resiliency in the organization of behavior. In W. A. Collins (Ed.), *Minnesota symposium on child psychology* (Vol. 13). Hillsdale, NJ: Erlbaum.

Burke, J., Pincus, H., & Pardes, H. (1986). The clinician-researcher in psychiatry. *American Journal of Psychiatry, 143,* 968–975.

Cantwell, D. (1986). Attention deficit and associated childhood disorder. In T. Millon & G. Klerman (Eds.), *Contemporary directions in psychopathology* (pp. 403–427). New York: Guilford Press.

Cattell, R. (1954). The meaning of clinical psychology. In L. A. Pennington & I. A. Berg (Eds.), *An introduction to clinical psychology* (pp. 3–25). New York: Ronald.

Cicchetti, D. (1984). The emergence of developmental psychopathology. *Child Development, 55,* 1–7.

Cicchetti, D. (1987). Developmental psychopathology in infancy: Illustration from the study of maltreated youngsters. *Journal of Consulting and Clinical Psychology, 55,* 837–845.

Cicchetti, D. (Ed.). (1989). *Rochester symposium on developmental psychopathology* (Vol. 1). Hillsdale, NJ: Erlbaum Associates.

Cicchetti, D. (1990a). An historical perspective on the discipline of developmental psychopathology. In J. Rolf, A. Masten, D. Cicchetti, K. Neuchterlein, & S. Weintraub (Eds.), *Risk and protective factors in the development of psychopathology* (pp 2–28). New York: Cambridge University Press.

Cicchetti, D. (1990b). The organization and coherence of socioemotional, cognitive, and representational development: Illustrations through a developmental psychopathology perspective on Down syndrome and child maltreatment. In R. Thompson (Ed.), *Nebraska symposium on motivation. Vol. 36. Socioemotional development* (pp. 259–366). Lincoln, NE: University of Nebraska Press.

Cicchetti, D., & Aber, J. L. (1986). Early precursors to later depression: An organizational perspective. In L. Lipsitt & C. Rovee-Collier (Eds.), *Advances in infancy research* (Vol. 4, pp. 81–137). Norwood, NJ: Ablex.

Cicchetti, D., & Carlson V. (Eds.) (1989). *Child maltreatment: Theory and research on the causes and consequences of child abuse and neglect.* New York: Cambridge University Press.

Cicchetti, D., & Schneider-Rosen, K. (1986). An organizational approach to childhood depression. In M. Rutter, C. Izard, & P. Read (Eds.), *Depression in young people, clinical and developmental perspectives* (pp. 71–134). New York: Guilford.

Cicchetti, D., & Todd Manly, J. (1990). A personal perspective on conducting research with maltreating families: Problems and Solutions. In E. Brody & I. Sigel (Eds.), *Family research journeys: Volume 2: Families at risk* (pp. 87–133). New York: Academic Press.

Cicchetti, D., & Wagner, S. (1990). Alternative assessment strategies for the evaluation of infants and toddlers: An organizational perspective. In S. Meisels & J. Shonkoff (Eds.), *Handbook of early intervention* (pp. 246–277). New York: Cambridge University Press.

Cicchetti, D., & White, J. (1988). Emotional development and the affective disorders. In W. Damon (Ed.), *Child development: Today and tomorrow* (pp. 177–198). San Francisco: Jossey-Bass.

Damon, W., & Hart, D. (1988). *Self-understanding in childhood and adolescence.* New York: Cambridge University Press.

Derner, G. F. (1959). The university and clinical psychology training. In M. H. P. Finn & F. Brown (Eds.), *Training for clinical psychology.* New York: International Universities Press.

Deykin, E. Y., Levy, J. C., & Wells, V. (1987). Adolescent depression, alcohol and drug use. *American Journal of Public Health, 77,* 178–182.

Earls, F., Reich, W., Jung, K. G., & Cloninger, C. R. (1988). Psychopathology in children of alcoholic and antisocial parents. *Alcoholism: Clinical and Experimental Research, 12,* 481–487.

Eaton, W., & Kessler, L. (Eds.). (1985). *Epidemiologic field methods in psychopathology: The NIMH Epidemiologic Catchment Area Program.* Orlando, FL: Academic Press.

Egeland, B., Jacobvitz, D., & Sroufe, L. A. (1988). Breaking the cycle of abuse. *Child Development, 59,* 1080–1088.

Elbert, J. C. (1985). Current trends and future needs in the training of child diagnostic assessment. In J. M. Tuma (Ed.), *Proceedings: Conference on training clinical child psychologists* (pp. 82–87). Washington, DC: Section on Clinical Child Psychology.

Elbert, J., Abidin, R., Finch, A., Sigman, M., & Walker, C. E. (1988, January 13). *Guidelines for clinical child psychology internship training.* (Official report of the American Psychological Association Section on Clinical Child Psychology Task Force on Internship Training.) Washington, DC: American Psychological Association.

Erikson, E. (1950). *Childhood and society.* New York: Norton.

Funkenstein, D. H. (1978). *Medical students, medical schools and society during five eras: Factors affecting the career choices of physicians 1958–1976.* Cambridge, MA: Ballinger.

Garfield, S. L., & Kurtz, R. (1976). Clinical psychologists in the 1970s. *American Psychologist, 31,* 1–9.

Garmezy, N., & Rutter, M. (Eds.). (1983). *Stress, coping and development in children.* New York: McGraw-Hill.

Gilmore, L. M., Chang, C., & Coron, D. (1984). Defining and counting mentally ill children and adolescents. In *A technical assistance package for the Child and Adolescent Service System Program* (Vol. 2). Rockville, MD: National Institute of Mental Health.

Goldstein, J., Freud, A., & Solnit, A. (1973). *Beyond the best interests of the child.* New York: Free Press.

Gould, M. S., Wunsch-Hitzig, R., & Dohrenwend, B. (1981). Estimating the prevalence of childhood psychopathology: A critical review. *Journal of the American Academy of Child Psychiatry, 20,* 462–476.

Graduate Medical Education National Advisory Committee. (1980). *Summary report of the Graduate Medical Education National Advisory Committee* (Vol. 1, U.S. Department of Health and Human Services publication (HRA) 81-651). Washington, DC: Office of Graduate Medical Education, Health Resources Administration.

Greenberg, J., & Mitchell, S. (1983). *Object relations in psychoanalytic theory.* Cambridge, MA: Howard University Press.

Guidano, V. F. (1987). *Complexity of the self.* New York: Guilford.

Guidano, V. F., & Liotti, G. (1983). *Cognitive processes and emotional disorders: A structural approach to psychotherapy.* New York: The Guilford Press.

Harter, S. (1983). Cognitive-developmental considerations in the conduct of play therapy. In C. Schaefer & K. O'Connor (Eds.), *Handbook of play therapy* (pp. 95–127). New York: Wiley.

Haviland, M., Dial, T., & Pincus, H. (1988). Characteristics of senior medical students planning to subspecialize in child psychiatry. *American Academy of Child and Adolescent Psychiatry, 27,* 404–407.

Haviland, M., Pincus, H., & Dial, T. (1987). Career research involvement, and research fellowship plans of potential psychiatrists. *Archives of General Psychiatry, 44,* 493–496.

Hesse, P., & Cicchetti, D. (1982). Toward an integrative theory of emotional development. *New Directions for Child Development, 16,* 3–48.

Hoch, E. L., Ross, A. O., & Winder, C. L. (Eds.). (1966). *Professional preparation of clinical psychologists.* Washington, DC: American Psychological Association.

Howard, A., Pion, G. M., Gottfredson, G. D., Flattau, P. E., Oskamp, S., Pfafflin, S. M., Bray, D. W. & Burstein, A. G. (1986). The changing face of American psychology: A report from the Committee on Employment and Human Resources. *American Psychologist, 41,* 1311–1327.

Institute of Medicine. (1985). Research on mental illness and addictive disorders: Progress and prospects. [Supplement to] *The American Journal of Psychiatry, 1142,* 1–41.

Institute of Medicine. (1989). *Research on children and adolescents with mental behavioral, and developmental disorders.* Washington, DC: National Academy Press.

Inouye, D. K. (1988). Children's mental health issues. *American Psychologist, 43,* 813–816.

Jackson, J. H. (1958). Evolution and dissolution of the nervous system. In J. Taylor (Ed.), *The selected writings of John Hughlings Jackson* (Vol. 2). New York: Basis Books. (From the Crooniam Lectures, originally published in 1884).

Jacobson, M. (1978). *Developmental neurobiology.* New York: Plenum.

Johnson, J. H. (1985). Providing clinical training experiences in child treatment: Recommendations for the clinical child psychology specialty curriculum. In J. M. Tuma (Ed.), *Proceedings: Conference on Training Clinical Child Psychologists* (pp. 88–90). Washington, DC: Section on Clinical Child Psychology.

Johnson, J. H., & Tuma, J. (1986). The Hilton Head Conference: Recommendations for clinical child psychology training. *The Clinical Psychologist, 39*, 9–11.

Kahn, M. W., & Santostefano, S. (1962). The case of clinical psychology: A search for identity. *American Psychologist, 17*, 185–190.

Kaplan, B. (1967). Meditations on genesis. *Human Development, 10*, 65–87.

Kaplan, B. (1983). Genetic-dramatism: Old wine in new bottles. In S. Wapner & B. Kaplan (Eds.), *Toward a holistic developmental psychology*. Hillsdale, NJ: Erlbaum Associates.

Kaufman, J., & Cicchetti, D. (1989). The effects of maltreatment on school-aged children's socioemotional development: Assessments in a day camp setting. *Developmental Psychology, 25*(4), 516–524.

Kazdin, A. E. (1988). *Child psychotherapy: Developing and identifying effective treatments*. New York: Pergamon.

Kazdin, A. E., Moser, J., Colbus, D., & Bell, R. (1985). Depressive symptoms among physically abused and psychiatrically disturbed children. *Journal of Abnormal Psychology, 94*, 298–307.

Keane, A. (1983). Behavior problems among long-term foster children. *Adoption and Fostering, 7*, 53–62.

Kegan, R. (1982). *The evolving self*. Cambridge, MA: Harvard University Press.

Knitzer, J. (1982). *Unclaimed children*. Washington, DC: Children's Defense Fund.

Korchin, S. (1983). The history of clinical psychology: Some personal views. In M. Hersen, A. Kazdin, & A. Bellack (Eds.), *The clinical psychology handbook* (pp. 5–19). New York: Pergamon Press.

Korman, M. (1976). *Levels and patterns of professional training in psychology*. Washington, DC: American Psychological Association.

Leitenberg, H. (1974). Training clinical researchers in psychology. *Professional Psychology, 5*, 59–69.

Masten, A. (1989). Resilience in development: Implications of the study of successful adaptation for developmental psychopathology. In D. Cicchetti (Ed.), *Rochester symposium on developmental psychopathology* (Vol. 1, pp. 261–294). Hillsdale, NJ: Erlbaum Associates.

Matarazzo, J. D. (1983). Education and training in health psychology: Boulder or bolder? *Health Psychology, 2*(1), 73–113.

Meehl, P. E. (1954). *Clinical versus statistical prediction: A theoretical analysis and a review of the evidence*. Minneapolis: University of Minnesota Press.

Meehl, P. E. (1957). When shall we use our heads instead of the formula? *Journal of Consulting Psychology, 4*, 268–273.

Meehl, P. E. (1964, October). *Let's quit kidding ourselves about the training of clinical psychologists*. Paper presented at the Conference on Professional

Education in Clinical Psychology sponsored by the Graduate School of the University of Minnesota, Stillwater, MN.

Meehl, P. E. (1971). A scientific, scholarly, nonresearch doctorate for clinical practitioners: Arguments pro and con. In R. R. Holt (Ed.), *New horizons for psychotherapy: Autonomy as a profession.* New York: International Universities Press.

Meehl, P. E. (1972). Second-order relevance. *American Psychology, 27,* 932–940.

Meehl, P. E. (1973). Why I do not attend case conferences. In P. E. Meehl (Ed.), *Psychodiagnosis: Selected papers* (pp. 225–302). Minneapolis: University of Minnesota Press.

Meehl, P. E. (1987). Theory and practice: Reflections of an academic clinician. In E. F. Bourg, R. J. Bent, J. E. Callan, N. F. Jones, J. McHolland, & G. Stricker (Eds.), *Standards and evaluation in the education and training of professional psychologists* (pp. 7–23). Norman, OK: Transcript Press.

Meehl, P. E. (1990). Appraising and amending theories: The strategy of Lakatosian defense and two principles that warrant it. *Psychological Inquiry, 1,* 108–141.

Melton, G. (Ed.). (1987). *Reforming the law: Impact of child development research.* New York: Guilford Press.

Meltzoff, J. (1984). Research training for clinical psychologists: Point-counterpoint. *Professional Psychology: Research and Practice, 15,* 203–209.

Millon, T., & Klerman, G. (Eds.). (1986). *Contemporary directions in psychopathology* (pp. 403–427). New York: Guilford Press.

Newcombe, M. D., Maddahian, E., & Bentler, P. M. (1986). Risk factors for drug use among adolescents: Concurrent and longitudinal analyses. *American Journal of Public Health, 76,* 525–531.

Nielson, A. C. (1979). The magnitude of declining psychiatric career choice. *Journal of Medical Education, 54,* 632–637.

Noam, G., & Kegan, R. (1982). Social cognition and psychodynamics: Towards a clinical-developmental psychology. In W. Edelstein & M. Keller (Eds.), *Perspektivitat und interpretation.* Frankfurt: Suhrkamp.

Offord, D. R., Boyle, M. H., & Racine, Y. (in press). Ontario child health study: Correlates of disorders. *Journal of the American Academy of Child and Adolescent Psychiatry.*

Overton, W. (1976). The active organism in structuralism. *Human Development, 19,* 71–86.

Overton, W. (1984). World views and their influence on psychological theory and research: Kuhn-Lakatos-Laudan. In H. Reese (Ed.), *Advances in child development and behavior* (Vol. 18, pp. 191–226). New York: Academic Press.

Pepper, S. (1942). *World hypotheses.* Berkeley, CA: University of California Press.

Peterson, D. R. (1966). Professional program in an academic psychology department. In E. L. Hoch, A. O. Ross, & C. L. Winder (Eds.), *Professional preparation of clinical psychologists.* Washington DC: American Psychological Association.

Peterson, D. R. (1976a). Is psychology a profession? *American Psychologist, 31,* 572–581.

Peterson, D. R. (1976b). Need for the Doctor of Psychology degree in professional psychology. *American Psychologist, 31,* 792–798.

Peterson, D. R. (1985). Twenty years of practitioner training in psychology. *American Psychologist, 40,* 441–451.

Pion, G. (1988). *Clinical and development psychology: A preliminary overview of human resources.* Unpublished manuscript, American Psychological Association.

Pion, G. M., & Lipsey, M. W. (1984). Psychology and society: The challenge of change. *American Psychology, 39,* 739–754.

Puig-Antich, J. (1982). Major depression and conduct disorder in prepuberty. *Journal of the American Academy of Child Psychiatry, 21,* 118–128.

Raimy, V. (Ed.). (1950). *Training in clinical psychology.* Englewood Cliffs, NJ: Prentice-Hall.

Reiger, D. A., Boyd, J. H., Burke, J. D., Rae, D. S., Myers, J. K., Kramer, M., Robins, L. N., George, L. K., Karno, M., & Locke, B. Z. (1988). One-month prevalence of mental disorders in the United States. *Archives of General Psychiatry, 45,* 977–986.

Reisman, J. M. (1976). *A history of clinical psychology.* New York: Irvington.

Robins, L. (1966). *Deviant children grown up.* Baltimore, MD: Williams & Wilkins.

Roe, A., Gustad, J. W., Moore, B. V., Ross, S., & Skodak, M. (Eds.). (1959). *Graduate education in psychology.* Washington, DC: American Psychological Association.

Rogers, C. (1939). Needed emphasis in the training of clinical psychologists. *Journal of Consulting Psychology, 3,* 141–143.

Rolf, J., & Read, P. (1984). Programs advancing developmental psychopathology. *Child Development, 55,* 8–16.

Ross, A. O. (1959). *The practice of clinical child psychology.* New York: Grune & Stratton.

Routh, D. (1983). Training clinical child psychologists. In B. Lahey & A. Kazdin (Eds.), *Advances in child clinical psychology* (Vol. 8, pp. 309–324). New York: Plenum Press.

Rutter, M. (1980). Introduction. In M. Rutter (Ed.), *Scientific foundations of developmental psychiatry* (pp. 1–7). London: Heinemann.

Rutter, M. (1985). Resilience in the face of adversity: Protective factors and resistance to psychiatric disorder. *British Journal of Psychiatry, 128,* 493–509.

Rutter, M. (1987). Parental mental disorder as a psychiatric risk factor. In R. Hales & A. Frances (Eds.), *American Psychiatric Association Annual Review* (Vol. 6, pp. 647–663). Washington, DC: American Psychiatric Press, Inc.

Rutter, M. (1988). Epidemiological approaches to developmental psychopathology. *Archives of General Psychiatry, 45,* 486–495.

Rutter, M., & Garmezy, N. (1983). Developmental psychopathology. In P. Mussen (Ed.), *Handbook of child psychology* (pp. 775–911). New York: Wiley & Sons.

Sameroff, A., & Chandler, M. (1975). Reproductive risk and the continuum of caretaking casualty. In F. Horowitz, M. Hetherington, S. Scarr-Salapatek, & G. Siegel (Eds.), Review of child development research (Vol. 4, pp. 187–244). Chicago: University of Chicago Press.

Santostefano, S. (1978). A bio-developmental approach to clinical child psychology. New York: Wiley.

Santostefano, S. (1985). Cognitive control therapy with children and adolescents. Elmsford, NY: Pergamon Press.

Sarason, S. B. (1981). An asocial psychology and a misdirected clinical psychology. American Psychologist, 36, 827–836.

Saxe, L., Cross, T., & Silverman, N. (1988). Children's mental health: The gap between what we know and what we do. American Psychologist, 43, 800–807.

Schneider, S. (1987). Meanwhile, back at the ranch . . . (Can Community Psychology save Psychology?). American Journal of Community Psychology, 15, 591–601.

Selman, R. (1980). The growth of interpersonal understanding. New York: Academic Press.

Selman, R., & Demorest, A. (1984). Observing troubled children's interpersonal negotiation strategies: Implications of and for a developmental model. Child Development, 55, 288–304.

Selman, R., & Yando, R. (Eds.). (1980). Clinical developmental psychology. San Francisco: Jossey-Bass.

Shaffer, L. F. (Ed.). (1947). Fifty years of clinical psychology. [Special issue of] Journal of Consulting Psychology, 11, 1–54.

Shakow, D. (1938). An internship year for psychologists with special reference to psychiatric hospitals. Journal of Consulting Psychology, 2(3), 73–76.

Shakow, D. (1939). The functions of the psychologist in the state hospital. Journal of Consulting Psychology, 3(1), 20–23.

Shakow, D. (1942). Training of the clinical psychologist. Journal of Consulting Psychology, 6(6), 277–288.

Shakow, D. (1946). The Worcester internship program. Journal of Consulting Psychology, 10, 191–200.

Sherrington, C. (1906). The integrative action of the nervous system. New York: Scribners.

Silver, L. B. (1980). The crisis in child psychiatry recruitment in the United States—circa 1980. Journal of the American Academy of Child and Adolescent Psychiatry, 19, 711–719.

Spence, J. T. (1987). Centrifugal verus centripetal tendencies in psychology: Will the center hold? American Psychologist, 42, 1052–1054.

Sroufe, L. A., & Rutter, M. (1984). The domain of developmental psychopathology. Child Development, 83, 173–189.

Stapp, J., VandenBos, G., & Tucker, A. (1985). Census of psychological personnel. American Psychologist, 42, 1317–1351.

Strickland, B. R. (1988). Clinical psychology comes of age. American Psychologist, 43, 104–107.

Strother, C. R. (1956). Psychology and mental health. Washington, DC: American Psychological Association.

Strupp, H. (1989). Psychotherapy: Can the practitioner learn from the researcher? *American Psychologist, 44*, 717–724.

Teitelbaum, P. (1971). The encephalization of hunger. In E. Stellar & J. Sprague (Eds.), *Progress in physiological psychology* (Vol. 4). New York: Academic press.

Teitelbaum, P. (1977). Levels of integration of the operant. In W. K. Honig & J. Staddon (Eds.), *Handbook of operant behavior.* Englewood Cliffs, NJ: Prentice-Hall.

Tryon, R. C. (1963). Psychology in flux: The academic-professional bipolarity. *American Psychologist, 18*, 134–143.

Tuma, J. H. (Ed.). (1985). *Proceedings: Conference on Training Clinical Child Psychologists.* Washington, DC: Section on Clinical Child Psychology.

Tuma, A. H., Mitchell, W., & Brunstetter, R. W. (1987). Toward a manpower base for research in child psychiatry: Report of three National Institute of Mental Health workshops. *Journal of the American Academy of Child and Adolescent Psychiatry, 26*, 281–285.

Waddington, C. H. (1957). *The strategy of the genes.* London: Allen & Unwin.

Waddington, C. H. (1966). *Principles of development and differentiation.* New York: Macmillan.

Wald, M., Carlsmith, J., & Leiderman, P. H. (Eds.). (1988). *Protecting abused/ neglected children: A comparison of home and foster placement.* Stanford, CA: Stanford University Press.

Weiss, P. (1961). Deformities as cues to understanding development of form. *Perspectives in Biology and Medicine, 4*, 133–151.

Weiss, P. (1969). *Principles of development.* New York: Hafner.

Weissman, S. H., & Bashook, P. G. (1986). A view of the prospective child psychiatrist. *American Journal of Psychiatry, 143*, 722–727.

Weissman, M., & Boyd, J. (1984). The epidemiology of affective disorders. In R. Post & J. Ballenger (Eds.), *Neurobiology of mood disorders* (pp. 60–75). Baltimore, MD: Williams and Wilkins.

Weissman, M., Gammon, G., John, K., Merikangas, K., Warner, V., Prusoff, B., & Sholomskas, D. (1987). Children of depressed parents. *Archives of General Psychiatry, 44*, 847–853.

Werner, H. (1948). *Comparative psychology of mental development.* New York: International Universities Press.

Werner, H. (1957). The concept of development from a comparative and organismic point of view. In D. Harris (Ed.), *The concept of development.* Minneapolis: University of Minnesota Press.

Yerkes, R. M. (1941). Psychology and defense. *Proceedings of the American Philosophical Society, 84*, 1–16.

Zigler, E., & Glick, M. (1986). *A developmental approach to adult psychopathology.* New York: John Wiley & Sons.

chapter 3

Designing A Graduate Training Curriculum To Meet The Challenges of a Nonacademic Career

Victor Alan Spiker
Principal Scientist
Anacapa Sciences, Inc.
Santa Barbara, CA

INTRODUCTION

During the past 10 years, there has developed a growing awareness that the traditional curriculum offered by most graduate psychology departments is no longer sufficient to prepare its students for the changing job market they now face (Klatzky, Alluisi, Cook, Forehand, & Howell, 1985a). While calls to reexamine the content, scope, and orientation of graduate training have been heard for some time (e.g., Sternberg & Keppel, 1979; Stapp, Fulcher, Nelson, Pallak, & Wicherski, 1981), only recently have concerns over the poor match between training and employment received national recognition. These concerns are most clearly evident in such recent APA-sponsored actions as the 1987 National Conference on Graduate Education in Psychology (Bickman, 1987) and the Task Force on the Employment of Experimental Psychologists in Industry (Klatzky et al., 1985a).

These and other analyses have produced a host of statistics depicting changes in the distribution of Ph.D. recipients by subdiscipline and institution (Howard et al., 1986), an increased awareness among students of the importance of taking coursework in disciplines outside psychology (Geyer, Laughery, & Schwartz, 1984), and recommendations for developing educational guidelines in specific subdisciplines (e.g., Howell, Colle, Kantowitz, & Wiener, 1987). But of the many statistics that have been cited, certainly the most significant one is that fewer than half of all PhDs in experimental psychology—broadly defined to include all research-oriented subdisciplines—now obtain academic jobs following graduation (Klatzky et al., 1985a). This shift away from academic employment has been evident since the late 1970s (Stapp & Fulcher, 1982), though recent surveys show that the percentage of Ph.D.'s who find nonacademic employment has begun to stabilize (Stapp, Fulcher, & Wicherski, 1984).

More telling than the numbers, though, are the comments from graduates of experimental psychology programs newly employed in nonacademic settings who were recently surveyed by the APA Task Force on Employment (Klatzky, Alluisi, Cook, Forehand, & Howell, 1985b). Many of those surveyed criticized the lack of exposure to much-needed technical areas during their graduate training, leaving them without needed skills which then had to be acquired quickly once on the job. Besides gaps in coursework and relevant work experience, many respondents also complained of a lack of faculty support and encouragement for pursuing nonacademic careers. These individual comments, rather than the quantitative results of large-scale surveys, are perhaps the best indications of the need to revise the focus of graduate training so that psychology departments offer curricula that better prepare their students for what an increasing proportion of them will in fact be doing during their postgraduate careers.

OBJECTIVES OF CHAPTER

The primary objective of this chapter is to describe, in modest detail, a series of course offerings that would substantively prepare students for the unique challenges posed by a nonacademic career. In proposing this curriculum, the author will not be concerned with the cosmetic changes that departments might make in order to enhance their students' employment prospects. While ensuring the employability of its students is certainly one of the most important responsibilities of a psychology department, this issue has been discussed extensively (American Psychologist, 1987) and need not be repeated here. Instead, this chapter will outline a rigorous curriculum of study to supplement traditional graduate training in areas where it has been historically weak, so that new PhDs can make significant contributions from their first days on the job.

This chapter has been written from the perspective of one who has spent the better part of a 10-year postgraduate career working in a nonacademic setting, and who has on numerous occasions witnessed the unfortunate consequences of promising graduates failing to perform effectively in this demanding environment. Perhaps surprising to some, many of those who failed were students who were considered very promising scientists within their own graduate departments. In other words, these individuals were considered quite well trained *in the traditional sense*, and yet the nonacademic environment proved to be an unusually difficult one. As will be suggested below, the outcome could have been far more successful had each department included in its training appropriate content, analytic tools, and work habits.

In proposing this curriculum, it is not the author's intent to suggest that a complete revamping of training programs is required. As reflected in the survey comments of recent doctorate recipients, much of the graduate training that is presently provided is quite useful for both nonacademic and academic endeavors, suggesting that the revisions be supplemental, rather than fundamental, in scope.

The comments offered here should not be construed as resulting from a formal, systematic study of the lost opportunities of graduate training. This presentation is by its nature a personal one, based on the author's own experiences and observations, plus various insights provided by his colleagues. However, after reviewing hundreds of resumes and conducting numerous job interviews for nonacademic positions over the past few years, the author has noted a number of the strengths and weaknesses present in traditional graduate programs that are likely to be representative of the field in general.

At the outset, it should be noted that this chapter will focus on training issues whose implications are broader than preparing for a career in child behavior and development. As the subsequent text will undoubtedly show, the author's own background and professional experience lie outside the domain of child psychology, residing primarily in the area of applied experimental psychology. Nevertheless, the requirements for graduate training, the lessons learned, and the necessity for a job-oriented curriculum are particularly applicable to the employment opportunities that presently await doctorates in child behavior and development.

Organization of Chapter

This chapter is presented in four parts. The first section briefly describes the demographics of the changing job market, defines what is meant by a "nonacademic" career, and discusses four alternative courses of action that are available to graduate training departments in response to these changes. The second section describes three of the major challenges posed by the nonacademic environment, challenges that should certainly be addressed during graduate training.

The third section proposes a 12-course curriculum to improve students' preparation for nonacademic jobs of all types. The objectives and orientation of each course are discussed, as is the importance of the information and how it would be used on the job. The fourth section concludes with a summary of eight important lessons that the author has learned from working in the nonacademic world. This knowledge, often acquired through unnecessarily painful experience, could be incorporated into curriculum development to spare future graduates the same fate.

BACKGROUND

Overview of the Nonacademic Job Market

Employment Patterns for New PhDs. It is certainly no coincidence that the increased interest in nonacademic career prospects has paralleled the general decline in the number of university positions that are available, particularly to students in experimental psychology. Between 1975 and 1983, the percentage of new doctorate recipients who received employment in an academic setting declined markedly, from 50% to 31%. During this same period, overall unemployment of new PhDs hovered around its traditional rate of 2% (Stapp & Fulcher, 1982), suggesting that the decline in academic jobs was offset by an increasing number and diversity of nonacademic positions.

When employment patterns are examined by specific areas, the shifts during the past 10 years are equally dramatic. For example, between 1975 and 1983, the percentage of developmental PhDs employed in an academic setting decreased from 77% to 51%. Similarly, the corresponding percentages for experimental, comparative, and physiological psychologists declined from 69% to 49% (Howard et al., 1986).

In concert with these changing employment patterns, there has also been a major shift in the distribution of subspecialties represented by doctorate recipients. For example, of the 2,883 PhDs awarded in 1976, approximately one-fourth were in experimental psychology, including developmental, comparative, and physiological psychology. Fully one-half of all PhDs awarded that same year went to students in the clinical, counseling, school, and educational subareas (Howard et al., 1986). In contrast, by 1984, only 14% of the 3,223 PhDs awarded were in the experimental psychology subdisciplines, compared to 60% for the clinical and school specialties. During the past 10 years, not only has the relative contribution of experimental psychology to the total pool of psychology PhDs decreased, but the absolute number of degrees annually awarded in this subspecialty has declined by 300 on average.

Interestingly, the drop in the number of new experimental PhDs has been consistent across universities with varying reputations for scholarly quality. Using standard measures of departmental reputation, such as the mean rating of the scholarly output of its faculty, the percentage of experimental PhDs awarded by departments in the upper 25% of reputational status stayed at or near 50% between 1975 and 1983. During that same period, the corresponding percentage for clinical and counseling PhDs declined from 37% to 23%, in part reflecting the growing numbers of professional schools that award the nonresearch alternative degree, the PsyD.

A major result of the declining numbers of new experimental PhDs has been the increased proportion of the field that is now comprised by health-service providers, primarily clinicians. The field's shift away from an emphasis on experimental specialties can actually be traced back to the 1940s, in which the percentage of doctorates awarded to experimental students declined from 70% in 1940 to only 25% by 1960. A major impact of this demographic shift has been on the constituency of APA, where the percentage of APA members employed in private practice has grown from 12% in 1976 to 22% in 1985 (Stapp & Fulcher, 1982). Not surprisingly, there have been recent calls to reorganize APA into separate divisions to better represent the divergent, and apparently incompatible, interests of clinical health-care providers and the more scientific-minded experimental psychologists (Goodstein, 1987).

The decrease in the absolute number of new experimental PhDs has definitely improved the employment prospects for those still pursuing this endeavor. Even while the supply of psychologists trained in the experimental method has declined dramatically, the demand for individuals with this knowledge and expertise continues to grow. As discussed below, the nonacademic settings in which experimental psychologists can now work are quite diverse, while the scopes of these jobs are expanding in ever more challenging directions.

Employment prospects for new PhDs. As defined here, a nonacademic position refers to work that experimental psychologists would perform in virtually any setting outside the university. Four major types of employment settings can generally be identified: private industry, health service organizations, schools, and the government. While the physical environment and organizational structure associated with these four settings vary considerably, the requisite skills and job requirements overlap to a large extent.

The APA Task Force on the Employment of Experimental Psychologists reported that a broad range of employment opportunities are presently available in industry, which they defined to include firms or agencies involved in the areas of technology, testing, and consumer service (Klatzky et al., 1985a). Their survey showed that psychologists who were trained as traditional experimental psychologists can be found working for either large or small companies as human factors engineers, applied cognitive analysts, test and measurement specialists, and personnel selection analysts. Students specializing in the psychological applications of computer technology are employed by computer companies to design and evaluate the human-machine interface of new systems; they also work for software companies to evaluate the usability of new programs. Developmental psychologists use their knowledge of children's learning capacity to help toy manufacturers design and test new toys. They also write promotional literature that summarize the child's developmental stages for a new generation of better educated and more demanding parents. Physiological psychologists can be found conducting research for pharmaceutical firms, tobacco companies, and other industries whose products directly or indirectly influence the health of consumers.

Health service organizations, including hospitals, HMOs, and mental health clinics, have traditionally used experimental psychologists in a variety of roles. Some of the major duties include (a) program evaluation, in which the impact of behavior-oriented programs (e.g., maternal prenatal care) on health outcome is examined; (b) conducting studies of consumer acceptance of health procedures and policies, such as copayment insurance and Medicaid; and (c) analyses of physician behavior, in which quasiexperimental methodologies are used to identify areas where physician diagnoses and health care practices influence patterns of hospital utilization. Experimental psychologists also contribute to the mental health field through the application of behavior modification techniques and evaluation of alternative therapeutic approaches.

Within the school system, there are also opportunities for experimental psychologists beyond the roles traditionally prescribed for school psychologists. Some of these include the design and evaluation of remedial programs in reading and mathematics, quasiexperimental assessments of mainstreaming practices, and investigations into the distribution and uses of computers as a supplemental teaching resource.

Not surprisingly, the federal government is one of the largest employers of experimental psychologists in nonacademic positions. As the APA Task Force recently discovered, a large segment of government-employed psychologists work for the research laboratories of the three military departments, represented by the Army Research

Institute, the Navy Personnel Research and Development Center, and the Air Force Human Resources Laboratory. The job duties encompassed by these departments are quite diverse, and include test and evaluation, assessment of training effectiveness, management of ongoing research and development contracts, and providing on-site support to operations at various military installations.

There are also job opportunities for experimental psychologists within a number of the other government agencies, including the National Highway Traffic and Safety Administration, Health and Human Services Department (which oversees Medicare and Medicaid), and the Department of Energy, to name just a few. Basic knowledge of human behavior and the ability to apply experimental methodologies in creative ways are two areas of expertise attributed to experimental psychologists that are especially valued by government employers.

Despite the ample opportunities for employment that await new doctorates in experimental psychology, they must compete for these positions with individuals trained in other fields. For example, human factors specialists must compete with engineers and others having degrees in one of the applied sciences. Psychologists seeking market research and human resource positions have to vie with MBAs and others having specific business degrees. Psychologists' positions in health care settings will also be challenged by individuals whose degrees are in health and medicine, such as MDs, RNs, MSWs, and DSWs. Jobs in the school systems will be sought by individuals having EdD degrees, teacher certificates, and school credentials. Depending on the specific agency, psychologists seeking positions in the government will face keen competition from individuals having degrees in military science or prior military service, students with degrees in one of the physical sciences (e.g., physics, chemistry), as well as computer scientists, educational specialists, "media" technologists, plus representatives from a host of other disciplines.

Partly in response to this conflicting mix of employment opportunities and challenges, the 1987 APA National Conference on Graduate Education was held at Salt Lake City to consider a number of critical issues concerning the recruitment, training, and employment of graduate students in psychology (Bickman, 1987). Of the 11 major issues that were considered, four are most relevant to the present discussion. These include (a) the tradeoffs between having a core vs. individualized curriculum, (b) the structure and content of graduate education, (c) the appropriateness of training and education outside the domain of psychology, and (d) the responsibility of graduate departments for the marketability of their graduates. Some 17 recommendations resulted from a "resolution" of these four issues, with a total of 65 recommendations coming from the conference as a whole (American Psychologist, 1987).

Despite the good intentions of the attendees, the conference's recommendations for training and education were unfortunately quite vague and will no doubt be quite difficult to implement. From the standpoint of promoting nonacademic careers, the lack of specificity concerning the appropriate content of a core curriculum was particularly disappointing. While the conference report stated that "the responsibility for specifying core content of graduate education for all psychologists rests with departments and schools for psychology" (p. 1071), it made no further attempt to identify the core elements of a program that would transcend the confines of an individual institution. Even when discussing the nature of the content of graduate education, the conference recommended that "doctoral education should include both broad education in the field of psychology and specialization appropriate to the students' career goals" (p. 1072). Yet, the resolution failed to define the type of coursework that would qualify as either "broad" or "specialized" education.

Some of the conference's most specific directions were in the area of student marketability, where it recommended that the APA "study psychologists' effectiveness in their various capacities, in order to provide information on the successful elements of educational programs in various settings" (p. 1076). It further recommended that the individual departments "recognize and discourage attitudes and behaviors that appear to disparage work in nonacademic settings" (p. 1077). Nevertheless, the conference's resolutions did not specify any formal mechanism for ensuring that the results of an effectiveness evaluation are fed back into the curriculum development process for individual departments.

Alternative Training Strategies

There are at least four alternative training strategies that can be adopted by experimental psychology programs to face the challenges and exploit the opportunities for employment for their students. One of the simplest options open to a department is to expand its course offerings to include those from other disciplines. Indeed, this is one of the major recommendations for training that was made by the 1987 National Conference on Graduate Education (Resolution 2.4). Such an approach is used frequently within the area of human factors, in which students take courses in engineering, as well as computer science, mathematics, aviation, and so forth (Geyer, Pond, & Smith, 1986). In some cases, students may even graduate with a joint degree in psychology and engineering. A similar tack can also be taken in child development, with students taking formal minors in related areas that will help their subsequent marketability (e.g., market research, special education).

This approach is clearly useful when the type of nonacademic position awaiting the student is known, as when human factors students are being trained for employment in an aerospace or military research laboratory. Unfortunately, this state of affairs does not characterize the vast majority of experimental students for whom the postgraduate position is completely unknown. For these students, it is difficult to anticipate the outside disciplines, let alone the specific coursework, that will ultimately prove useful. While it may be possible to obtain a broad overview of areas such as health care, business, communications, and computer science, this would do little more than provide a survey-level exposure to selected topics within each field. This strategy would not provide students with substantive knowledge that could be used on the job, nor would it do much to enhance their chances of obtaining employment in a given nonacademic area.

A second, and related, strategy is to actually hire individuals from nonacademic settings to teach courses in their area of expertise, serving either as full-time faculty members or in an adjunct capacity. This approach differs from the first in that the department would be able to exert some control over the nature of the courses offered, and could in fact tailor them to better reflect and capitalize on the psychological background of the students. While this strategy is preferable in many ways to the first, it is still based on the assumption that experimental students should be devoting their energies to acquiring more of the *content* that is relevant to subsequent nonacademic positions.

It has been this author's experience, however, that the lack of applied content knowledge has not been, for the most part, a significant obstacle for experimental students, either in functioning in a nonacademic position or in obtaining one in the first place. As we shall see later, it is typically the case that much greater demands will be placed on their methodological and psychology-specific skills than on any presumed knowledge of the content associated with the business or industry in question. Consequently, sacrificing training in the methodological realm for a hit-or-miss sampling of potentially relevant coursework would seem to be a very poor tradeoff.

As a third option, the department can promote summer or year-long internships whereby students work on-site for some industry or government agency. This approach basically conforms to the scientist-practitioner model used in clinical psychology, in which coursework, laboratory experimentation, and practical experience receive equal emphasis. Not surprisingly, the establishment of research apprenticeships for students in experimental psychology was also recommended by the 1987 National Conference on Graduate Education (Resolution 5.3b).

In this author's experience, the research apprenticeship, while serving as an effective screening tool to identify those individuals who really do want to work outside academia, does not guarantee that students will receive the focused training required to hone their methodological skills to real-world problems. A major reason for this concern is that students are not used in the same capacity as they will be when they are hired as new Ph.D.'s; instead, students work primarily at a research assistant level rather than as a Ph.D. research analyst or associate. There is, of course, a major difference between these two levels, both in the expectations of employers and in the job demands placed on the individual.

The apprentice program is certainly a good model for clinical students, since they are learning vital diagnostic and therapy skills that they will later use as licensed, practicing clinicians. This model is less valid for experimental psychologists, however, as they are not acquiring specific research skills but rather generic skills pertaining to business conduct, dress, and work habits. While these activities provide good experience, they do not necessarily constitute good training and should probably not be considered as a substitute for structured coursework in experimental methodology.

A fourth course of action, and the one endorsed here, is to respond to these challenges by making significant, structural changes to the training curriculum. The recommended course offerings that should comprise the revised curriculum are described in a later section. But implicit in this curriculum revision are some fundamental changes in the methods by which graduate departments promote training. For example, the policy of having a student work in the same professor's laboratory for many years, to acquire highly specialized technical skills, does little to enhance productivity in a nonacademic position and should be discouraged.

In addition, departments need to downplay the emphasis on requiring students to publish extensively during their tenure, and return to the pre-1960 policy of having students devote the bulk of their time to taking coursework (Altman, 1987). The primary research products by the students would be their master's and doctoral dissertations, preferably in two markedly different areas. Publications count for less in the nonacademic market anyway, as there is a greater emphasis on "what the person can do" once he or she is on the job. An additional by-product of this revision would be a return to the policy of having students complete their degree work by the end of their fourth year. This would definitely enhance students' job prospects, as most employers in nonacademic settings look favorably on students who graduate within 4 to 5 years as a sign of an organized personality and a desire to "return to the real world" as quickly as possible.

Within the human factors area, recommended guidelines have already been proposed to develop a core curriculum that would prepare students for productive employment in selected nonacademic settings (Howell, et al., 1987). These guidelines are quite laudable in their specificity concerning the type of coursework that human factors students should receive. Recommended courses in the "core skills" area include research, statistics and quantitative methods, computer techniques, and communication. Five core content areas are also specified, including human information processing, human-machine integration, environmental factors, biological bases of behavior, and simulation and training. Courses are also recommended in areas referred to as "other psychological knowledge," such as history and systems and personality theory, as well as an extensive listing of fields outside psychology whose content would complement those of the human factors specialist.

In considering these guidelines, it should be recognized that the human factors area has historically been highly oriented toward applied work, as most human factors programs have developed curricula specifically designed to facilitate the employment prospects of their students (Geyer, 1983). Of course, the well-defined scope of candidate positions permits a human factors program to designate a realistic number of relevant courses that will ensure the student sufficient familiarity with practical knowledge upon taking his or her first job. While this option is generally not open to the more mainstream experimental psychology programs, where the targeted nonacademic position might be found in multiple settings, there is nevertheless much that could be gained by considering the human factors guidelines as a starting point for specifying the curriculum of study for general experimental psychologists. This issue will be discussed further in the third section of this chapter.

THREE MAJOR CHALLENGES IN A NONACADEMIC SETTING

A major problem in training students for today's job market is that many of the skills associated with a competent academic do not ensure success in the nonacademic realm. By their nature, most graduate programs are designed to promote skills that are highly valued in an academic setting, most notably scholarship, facility in interpreting abstract theoretical concepts, ability to conduct well-controlled experimental research, and focused attention toward methodological detail.

Within limits, these features are certainly exemplary training goals and their attainment should, of course, be strongly encouraged. Yet when rigidly adhered to and taken to extremes, these attributes can easily become liabilities for the newly graduated experimental psychologist who has opted for nonacademic employment as his or her first position.

A whole host of dimensions could be identified that would distinguish the type of activities that are performed in an academic setting from their nonacademic counterparts. However, three factors that characterize the nonacademic setting seem most important and encompass many of the other dimensions that might be identified. These include lack of experimental control, lack of time, and lack of information. As discussed below, these constraints pose significant challenges to experimental psychologists who have been trained in a tradition for which a high degree of experimental control, adequate time, and extensive information are the norm. But despite these major differences, one can nevertheless acquire a core set of skills and knowledge in graduate school to combat the myriad challenges that await the applied psychologist. Those issues will be taken up in the next section.

Lack of Experimental Control

A characteristic common to most applied problems is that the experimental psychologist will typically have only limited control over the extraneous factors that can intrude on the integrity of the research setting. These intruding factors correspond to the "threats to validity" that characterize applied research (Cook & Campbell, 1979). Some of the major threats include the intervening effects of history, differential maturation, and statistical regression artifacts, as well as the most damaging of all, lack of random assignment of subjects to treatment conditions. Whereas the academic trained in traditional experimental methods is apt to walk away from such poorly controlled settings, such an option is not open to the applied psychologist. Indeed, the psychologist will be expected to conduct such quasiexperimental research in a technically competent matter, coming up with interpretable results that can be defended using scientifically acceptable criteria.

When faced with a lack of experimental control, the applied psychologist must often customize research designs for a given application. This will sometimes require that the researcher deviate from conventional methodological approaches. As an example, the author recently conducted a field research study designed to quantify the impact of job experience on the maintenance proficiency of Army tank mechanics (Spiker, Wotkyns, & Lueb, 1982). Paradoxically, prior re-

search had failed to produce solid evidence showing that a tank mechanic's repair proficiency increases with the number of times he has
previously performed the repair. Failures to find a direct experience-
performance relationship contradict traditional learning theory, and
were interpreted by some to suggest that the Army was providing
inadequate on-the-job training (Schurman & Porsche, 1980).

In approaching this problem, we had to address two major problems
that plagued prior research in the area. The first was to find a way to
control the difficulty of the repair task. Specifically, we suspected that
prior studies, which used direct observations of maintenance performance in the motor pool area, failed to find a positive impact of job
experience on proficiency because the more proficient mechanics were
always assigned the more difficult repair tasks. To control for task
difficulty, we arranged to have proficiency testing be performed on
identical equipment, in which a tank engine was removed and placed
on a test stand.

We then developed a standard test of tank generator replacement
that was administered by a trained mechanic, a retired warrant officer
with more than 20 years of Army maintenance experience. During the
test, all required tools and training manuals were organized in a stan-
dardized layout, thus allowing time-to-complete the repair to be a valid
indicant of performance. As it turned out, repair speed served as a
highly reliable discriminator among different experience levels.

The second problem involved the choice of a suitable experimental
design. A traditional learning approach would have the same individual take the test multiple times, with successive measurements assessing
the amount of performance improvement accruing with each administration. While such within-subject manipulations are the most sensitive designs for studying learning effects, they are not very practical for
military research due to high levels of personnel turnover. Indeed,
because of frequent transfers, temporary duty assignments, and various
other interventions, intertest delays as short as a few weeks can produce subject losses as high as 33%–50%.

We therefore opted to use a between-subject design, in which subjects of different task experience levels were recruited (i.e., 0 prior
repair experiences, 1 repair experience, 2, 3, etc.), with each subject
being tested only once. While this method is less powerful than a
repeated measures design and requires more subjects overall, it did
allow us to obtain a quantitative estimate of proficiency at each experience level without suffering any differential loss of subjects or test-
retest effects. We were then able to demonstrate that repair proficiency,
as measured by both accuracy and time to remove a tank generator,
improves monotonically as a function of prior task experiences until
reaching an asymptote of six to seven times. After that, proficiency

declines somewhat, reflecting a slight deterioration in skills for the most highly experienced mechanics who have less recent hands-on experience as a result of their greater supervisory duties (Spiker, Harper, & Hayes, 1985).

When considering the issue of experimental control, it is important to realize that "control" is often viewed more broadly in applied research settings. A weak form of control may be imposed on a research topic by making some common sense assumptions about the behavior of those individuals who are in fact in control of the setting. In the case of military research, for example, this would entail tracking the timecourse and operating tempo of a given unit's training cycle, as this will dictate the degree of access we will have to that unit's personnel and resources. Similar strategies can be followed when planning research in the industrial sector.

Control may also be exercised by specifying an objective measure of performance that different observers can agree upon. Indeed, it is through such measurement specification that experimental psychologists will often make their most significant contributions to an applied research project. Delineating a suitable figure of merit is a fundamental activity for applied research, without which one cannot attempt any type of causal inference no matter how well controlled the experimental setting might be.

For example, in evaluating the impact of an integrated database management system on the proficiency of an Army maintenance unit, some objective index of unit performance was required. Based on a review of existing maintenance records, we developed a measure of "repeat" repairs, in which any repair task that had to be repeated on the same tank within a specified amount of time was defined as a repeat task. Superior unit performance would thus be associated with a lower incidence of such repeat repairs. The criteria used to define the time interval within which a repair task was counted as a "repeat," as distinct from normal breakage, were developed in conjunction with technical experts on automotive tank maintenance (Harper, 1984).

Lack of Time

In a nonacademic environment, research solutions must be arrived at "on time and within budget." This basic tenet holds whether one is working for profit or for a nonprofit agency. Since project deadlines are usually unreasonably stringent, the experimental psychologist must learn to determine the scope of a research problem in order to match the limited time and fiscal resources that are available. The ability to accurately "scope" the required level of effort demands, in turn, skills in estimating one's own productivity to determine how long it will take to complete a given piece of work. If these productivity estimates reveal that the work cannot be completed in the allotted time, then the proposed effort must be scaled back accordingly. Not only must this productivity estimate be determined for oneself, but estimates must also be obtained for any additional researchers or support staff who will be involved in the project.

Unfortunately, project scoping and productivity projections are not skills that are acquired in graduate school, an environment in which time is plentiful and one can work in bursts to complete research. This latter option is not always available to the applied psychologist, particularly where other people are involved, such as support staff who are paid on an hourly basis. Instead, nonacademic employment usually demands that every hour worked be accounted for. When working as a government contractor, for example, this accountability will even extend to annual audits of project labor charges. Such contingencies clearly place much greater demands on organization, efficiency, and accountability than exist in academia.

One cannot overstate the importance of having accurate information concerning the amount of time, figured in number of labor hours, a given project will take to complete. These data are essential in estimating budgets, developing project timeliness, and requesting resource allocations, as well as making decisions on whether to pursue a proposed project or to hire additional staff. Whether one is working at a technical or managerial level, the ability to accurately estimate one's own level of productivity (and that of others) is the one available hedge against the unreasonable time demands placed on the conduct of applied behavioral research.

In considering the feasibility of a proposed work plan, the applied researcher must continually balance the tradeoffs associated with maintaining high technical standards and completing the work in a timely, fiscally sound manner. For example, in a recent proposal to a government agency, the author's company offered to develop, implement, and evaluate a prototype maintenance proficiency evaluation system over an 18-month period in three nuclear power plants for approximately $345,000.

However, when the company was informed that only $150,000 of funding could be approved for the project, the proposed level of effort was scaled back to include the development, implementation, and evaluation of an integrated system at two plants. Furthermore, the evaluation was restricted to a 12-month period, where one of the candidate sites would be specifically chosen to be within driving distance of the company's home office. Importantly, even with the reduced funding, adequate data on system implementation and evaluation could still be obtained, with the bulk of the cost savings coming from reduced logistics requirements and a shorter monitoring period.

Lack of Information

While it may seem surprising to some, it is lack of information, rather than lack of experimental control or time, that often poses the stiffest challenge in a nonacademic setting. Indeed, experimental psychologists will often find themselves working on a problem that has been poorly defined and whose objectives are ambiguous. Such circumstances are almost always true of consulting work, but they also characterize much of the research that is conducted in support of government and industry. This ambiguity forces the applied psychologist to make critical assumptions about the nature and scope of the research question, as these assumptions may have to be defended later on.

Beginning psychologists are often quite shocked when they are first asked to investigate a research topic by an individual, such as a department supervisor or outside client, who has only the vaguest notions of what the topic of interest entails. Yet that same individual is, in turn, usually working from a set of equally vague instructions in which the final research product is completely unspecified. By default, then, it becomes the responsibility of the experimental psychologist to determine the form this research product should take, the level of effort to be expended, and the way the final results should be presented to the department or agency sponsoring the research.

Given the highly specified nature of research issues in academic settings, the ambiguity inherent in many applied problems may seem rather unsettling. Yet it must be recognized that these problems often stem from "uneasy feelings" at high levels of management, where the managers may not be able to articulate the reasons for these feelings or have a clear picture of the answers they seek. The key point is that applied research projects are not spawned by well-developed theories, nor are they spin-offs from prior research. Instead, proposed research topics mostly come from *people* who are not technically well-versed in the domain of interest. Quite often, these people are managers who were hired because of their skills in directing others to do the work rather than their technical acumen. Despite this ambiguity, the applied psychologist must sift through the set of conflicting requirements, identify a clear problem focus, develop and implement a research strategy, and "come up with a good story" for why the work was done in the first place.

The ability to tolerate such fuzzy thinking and work under ambiguous conditions is certainly not taught in graduate school, nor is it actively encouraged by faculty. But it is a skill that applied psychologists must quickly acquire if they are to be able to work within the constraints imposed by the nonacademic environment.

An as example, the author's company was hired to perform research in embedded training (ET), a recent technological initiative that promotes the incorporation of training-oriented software and/or hardware into operational equipment (Warm, Roth, & Sullivan, 1987). ET is presently a popular area within the military, as it is seen as a low-cost alternative to the expensive simulators now being used to train pilots, gunners, and vehicle operators. Our customer was specifically interested in pursuing applications of ET to Army armored vehicles, such as tanks. As a manufacturer of military hardware and software, the sponsor wanted to know where it should allocate its resources to profit from the current popularity of ET. Beyond this general aim, though, the sponsor provided little guidance in scoping the problem or in developing a plan of work.

As applied psychologists, our focus was on the behavioral implications of ET for improving the performance of tank crewmen. Accordingly, we defined the project scope to be the determination of high-payoff applications for ET in future armored vehicles. The overall project objective was to describe current methods used to train Army armor units and to identify those armor tasks most in need of improvement through application of ET technologies. The primary product of the project would be the development of several sample armor ET modules (Rogers & Spiker, 1987).

In approaching the problem, we took advantage of the free hand given by the sponsor to structure the project in a way that was consistent with our interests and with the limited time that was available (3 months). First, we reviewed the literature on ET to come up with an objective, working definition of ET. Second, we developed a set of guidelines for applying ET, where the guidelines were stated in terms of the task characteristics that would be most amenable to enhancement through ET (e.g., ET is appropriate for difficult tasks whose skill must be "honed" until mastery). Third, we reviewed army training manuals to identify a candidate set of operator tasks that would benefit from ET application (e.g., Direct Platoon Fires, Engage Targets with the Main Gun). Fourth, we interviewed expert armor officers and tank crewmen to reduce this list of candidate tasks by identifying the "high-payoff" tasks for ET application, that is, those tasks currently viewed as posing the most problems using existing training methods (e.g., Select Fire Positions, Recognize Friendly and Threat Armored Vehicles).

Finally, we developed the format and content for three sample ET modules. These modules were designed to address several of the key operational problem areas identified by the armored community, including vehicle identification, target prioritization, and calling for artillery fire. The sponsor was then able to incorporate these module specifications into software and hardware upgrades for their tank demonstrator. Because of our extensive front-end analyses directed toward clarifying the goals of the project, the information content and format of the ET displays were designed to be consistent with Army requirements and were well accepted by military personnel during demonstrations of the sponsor's training system.

PROPOSED TRAINING CURRICULUM

Overview

To meet the challenges of a nonacademic career, it is imperative that graduate training provide students in experimental psychology with the fundamental quantitative, methodological, and analytic tools that are required to solve real-world problems outside the laboratory. Graduate programs should also strive to prepare their students for the different goals and values of nonacademic environments by instilling critical business-oriented "metaskills" that transcend those required for traditional academic employment in psychology.

A 12-course curriculum that would help meet many of these challenges is depicted in Figure 3.1. This curriculum would divide coursework into three major categories, corresponding to a quantitative/methodology, metaskill, and applied psychology tier. It should be noted that these courses are intended to supplement, not replace, a program's existing core curriculum. The latter would most likely include training in such areas as basic statistics, experimental design, and history and systems, along with the various content courses in a student's particular area of specialization, most notably learning, perception, cognition, developmental, physiological, and biopsychology. As such, these courses would be integrated into each department's ongoing training program rather than serving as a specialized, separate curriculum for applied experimental psychology.

The quantitative/methodology tier lays the foundation for the curriculum by providing coursework in multivariate statistics, psychometrics and survey techniques, evaluation methodology, and philosophy of science. The four courses in the metaskill tier are intended to foster development of the tools needed to function effectively in the business world, including technical writing, presentation methods, accounting procedures, and business conduct. The applied psychology tier would emphasize the basic behavioral principles that can be ex-

TIER 1: QUANTITATIVE/METHODOLOGY COURSES

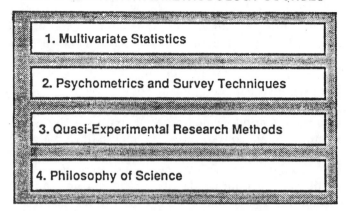

1. Multivariate Statistics

2. Psychometrics and Survey Techniques

3. Quasi-Experimental Research Methods

4. Philosophy of Science

TIER 2: META-SKILL COURSES

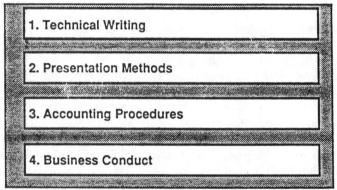

1. Technical Writing

2. Presentation Methods

3. Accounting Procedures

4. Business Conduct

TIER 3: APPLIED PSYCHOLOGY COURSES

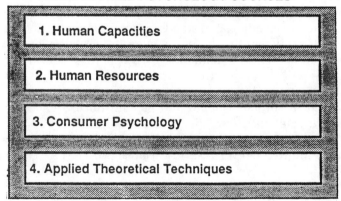

1. Human Capacities

2. Human Resources

3. Consumer Psychology

4. Applied Theoretical Techniques

Figure 3.1. A proposed 3-tier, 12-course curriculum of study to prepare students for nonacademic employment.

ploited outside the laboratory, including human capacities, human resources, consumer psychology, and applied theoretical techniques.

Depending on the scope and orientation of a program's existing core curriculum, students might either take these courses at a constant rate of three per year or perhaps complete the bulk of the coursework during the last several years of graduate school. In general, it would be advisable to take the quantitative/methodology courses early in a graduate student's tenure, while concentrating the metaskill courses during the latter stages of graduate training. The following subsections discuss each of the 12 courses in modest detail, describing the major course objectives, the specific topics and tools to be taught, and illustrating the ways in which the course information would prove useful to the student who later on works in a nonacademic capacity.

Quantitative/Methodology Courses

For the experimental psychology student who is planning on a non-academic career, the courses in this tier will be among the most important taken in graduate school. On the one hand, the development of sharply honed quantitative skills will make the applied experimental psychologist a valuable company asset from the first day on the job, giving him or her a powerful edge in solving applied problems using highly precise mathematical and statistical tools. Moreover, the ability to apply quantitative analyses in creative ways will make the psychologist's technical products that much more distinctive and highly valued.

On the other hand, the methodological courses in this tier provide the basic foundation upon which subsequent content knowledge may be added. Importantly, this methodological foundation will permit the experimental psychologist to standout from the nonpsychologists who lack similar skills and tools. While quantitative skills may be considered an "added bonus," methodological expertise is a skill that many employers will certainly expect experimental psychologists to bring to the job. Thus, it is all the more important that such critical information be covered in sufficient depth and breadth during graduate training.

Multivariate statistics. This course would teach students the fundamental principles that underly the major multivariate techniques, including multivariate analysis of variance (MANOVA), canonical correlation, factor analysis, discriminant analysis, principal component analysis, cluster analysis, and multidimensional scaling (MDS). As part of this training, students would become familiar with the basic operations of matrix algebra, the various test statistics generated by these techniques (e.g., Wilks' lambda, greatest characteristic roots, communalities, etc.), as well as the advantages of using multivariate statistics compared to their univariate counterparts.

To be useful for applied research, though, the course should address many of the practical problems that plague those who must apply multivariate statistics to research designs implemented outside the laboratory. Unfortunately, many of the topics of most concern to the applied analyst are not covered in an academic curriculum. Some of the key problem areas that should be addressed are: (a) determining which multivariate techniques are most appropriate for what type of data; (b) identifying the tradeoffs associated with using one technique versus another, particularly with regard to minimum sample size requirements; (c) specifying the data formats required for each technique; and (d) interpreting the results of the statistical tests in terms that the statistically uninitiated can readily understand.

For example, an issue that frequently arises when applying multidimensional scaling (MDS) is determining the type of data that can be accepted. While MDS is readily amenable to analysis of pairwise similarity judgments (A is similar to B, B is dissimilar to C), it can also be applied, under certain conditions, to rank order data (Shepard, 1972). In addition, many other critical practical issues must be resolved by the applied analyst, such as determining the number of factors to retain in a factor analysis or the number of dimensions to use in an MDS analysis, interpreting (i.e., applying a verbal label to) the factor structure in a factor analysis or the dimension space in an MDS analysis, and selecting the distance metric to use in cluster analysis.

While it is a good idea to cover the procedures needed to implement these techniques on mainframe and microcomputer software packages, it is more important that students be able to interpret the resulting printouts. The greater emphasis on interpretation is recommended because, in applied settings, it is often the case that some lesser trained individual, such as a research analyst, will have the responsibility for data entry, database management, and creation of the required program code. It will be the psychologist's job, on the other hand, to ensure that the data analyst has been given proper guidance regarding selection of the appropriate analytic technique and associated test statistics, formatting of the data structure, and interpretation of the statistical output.

There are several reasons why it is particularly important that the applied experimental psychologist have a thorough understanding of the fundamentals of multivariate statistics. First, these techniques are becoming increasingly more prevalent in field research, particularly in market research, opinion surveys, and behavioral observations settings. As a result, there will be greater expectations that psychologists understand these techniques and be able to use them effectively and creatively.

Second, most of the settings to be studied by the experimental psychologist will involve little or no experimental control. A by-product of this lack of control is that a single, important response measure may not be specifiable in advance. Consequently, multiple sets of measures will be collected, something akin to a "shotgun" approach, to ensure that at least one useful index of behavior is obtained. Multivariate techniques will be required to generate test statistics that take intro account this multiple comparison problem, by adjusting for the inflation of the experimentwise alpha level (Harris, 1975).

Third, and most important, multivariate techniques serve as a powerful tool for data reduction and organization. Whether the application involves multiple items on a paper-and-pencil questionnaire, a group of comments from a consumer focus group session, or different indices of behavior sampled in an observational setting, some type of multivariate statistic will be needed to reduce the initially large number of responses to a smaller, conceptually organized set. If the experimental psychologist is well versed in the different statistical techniques that can be applied, he or she will be able to impose a meaningful structure even on data collected under poorly controlled conditions.

Psychometrics and survey techniques. This course would cover the fundamental principles underlying test construction theory and introduce students to the major analytic techniques required to conduct large- and small-scale opinion surveys. For the psychometrics portion of the course, some of the major topics would include item analysis and rules for good test item design, alternative statistical methods for computing internal consistency (e.g., Spearman-Brown, Cronbach's alpha, analysis of variance, etc.), techniques for scaling rank-order data and deriving interval-scale metrics (e.g., the different Thurstonian scaling cases), the relative merits associated with different metrics of statistical reliability, and the various definitions, strategies, and uses behind the concepts of test validity (e.g., internal, external, construct, discriminant, etc.). The latter part of the course would address the issues associated with the design and conduct of opinion surveys, and include such topics as construction of questionnaires, techniques for identifying respondent segments and developing stratified sampling plans, methods for contacting potential survey respondents, and ways of ensuring high return rates when conducting surveys by mail (e.g., monetary inducements attached to postcards).

One need not look very hard in the nonacademic arena for reasons to justify such a course. Indeed, as one of their initial job duties, many applied psychologists are called upon to construct some type of "test."

While the information content of these tests will undoubtedly vary with the particular requirements of the job, they all demand that the psychologist engage in various psychometric activities that entail item review and analysis, internal consistency assessment, reliability computation or estimation, and some inference as to the test's overall validity. Unfortunately, despite the often meager methodological demands of such efforts, it has been this writer's experience that many beginning psychologists have been brought up short because they simply do not have the necessary background to begin the systematic activities required to develop a test or conduct a survey in a timely and efficient manner.

In part, this problem reflects a lack of emphasis on test construction in graduate education in recent years, with much of the instruction having been relegated to education psychology or other education-oriented departments. As chronicled in their recent review of graduate training, Davison, Damarin, and Drasgow (1986) cited a dramatic decline in the proportion of programs granting a specific psychometric degree (now less than 11%), as well as a reduced emphasis on measurement and scaling included as part of the overall quantitative training in many programs. Consequently, many psychologists are now graduating without having been exposed to even the most rudimentary principles of test construction theory, thereby mitigating their effectiveness in an area that many employers have always delegated to psychologists. The lack of attention to psychometrics is also evident in the difficulty of many recent PhDs in passing the national test for licensing accreditation, a test that contains a heavy concentration of questions on test construction and measurement theory (Examination for Professional Practice in Psychology, 1984).

A related problem is that many useful aspects of test construction are considered outmoded and are no longer taught within graduate psychology departments, even those that nominally have a strong emphasis on quantitative methods. For example, the computations required to convert rank order, similarity, or paired comparison data to an interval scale can be traced to Thurstone (1925, 1928), and comprise an extremely useful technique that applied psychologists should have in their bag of tricks. Yet such scaling procedures are rarely included in modern text books, and even ones where they are covered in great detail, such as Guilford (1954), are difficult to find or are out of print. Rather than requiring the beginning psychologist to discover these hidden treasures on his or her own, graduate departments should return to the basics and include these valuable skills as part of their standard curriculum.

Quasiexperimental research methods. This course would cover the basic principles underlying the application of quasiexperimental research techniques to nonlaboratory settings. Many of the techniques associated with quasiexperimental research stem directly from the program evaluation area, established by D. T. Campbell and his disciples (e.g., Campbell & Stanley, 1966; Cook & Campbell, 1979) in the early 1960s. Program evaluation began as a formal method for applying the principles of experimental design to infer the causal impact of large-scale social programs, such as Project Head Start. During the past 20 years, the field's scope has expanded enormously to include such diverse disciplines as political science, military training, judicial reform, and health care, to name just a few (Boruch, 1987). To extent that nonacademic psychologists can use these methodological tools in creative ways, they will become a valued asset even during the initial months on the job when job-specific content knowledge is still being acquired.

This course would be organized into two major sections. The first section would cover the philosophy behind the use of quasiexperimental methods, noting their primary goals and limitations. Major topics would include the strategy of ruling out competing hypotheses in lieu of making strict causal inferences, as well as elucidating the major threats to validity (e.g., nonrandom assignment of subjects to groups, historical effects, maturation, etc.) and the conditions under which each threat is most likely to occur. The second section would present the major statistical techniques that can be used in support of quasiexperimental field research. These would include stepwise and pre-planned multiple regression, interrupted time series, path analysis, and causal factor analysis.

For the applied psychologist who must interpret data collected in the absence of experimental controls, quasiexperimental research techniques will quickly pay for themselves. A common example is the iterative application of multiple regression analysis to quantify the impact of treatment on subjects who have not been randomly assigned to groups. The lack of random assignment typifies most health care or social programs where subjects/patients have selected themselves into treatment or control conditions. In such cases, the analyst must attempt to rule out as many competing hypotheses as possible that might provide alternative explanations for a significant treatment effect.

The most likely competing explanation is the possibility that substantial differences between the treatment and control groups existed along key demographic or personality characteristics prior to implementing the treatment. These alternative explanations may be examined, and hopefully ruled out, by repeatedly applying regression analyses in which the various group-difference variables (e.g., age, sex, income, education level, etc.) are stepped into the regression equation first, followed by membership in the treatment or control condition

(Judd, 1987). To the extent that any effect of treatment remains after adjusting for differences in other characteristics (e.g., age, sex, etc.), the researcher may conclude that the data are "at least consistent with" the presence of a significant treatment effect.

Alternatively, the analyst might attempt to recruit control subjects who are as much like the treatment group as possible. A common example is the use of people who are on the waiting list to receive health care services that comprise the treatment in question, such as a group of elderly who have applied to receive in-home nursing care, but who have yet to receive any visits from the medical staff (e.g., Hughes, Cordray, & Spiker, 1981). One must be careful, though, in interpreting the findings from such designs as there may still be important differences between the groups prior to initiation of services to the treatment group. Moreover, the researcher must ensure that the control group remains "pure" throughout the study and does not receive any spill-over effects from services provided in nearby or adjacent areas (Cook & Campbell, 1979). While the waiting group technique does not permit the unequivocal causal inference that is possible from random assignment of subjects to treatments, it is nevertheless a viable and ethically feasible methodology that can be used effectively in field settings. Such creative alternatives to traditional experimental control would provide much of the meat of this course, giving the nonacademician the methodological "street smarts" he or she will need.

Philosophy of science. This course would cover the basic principles underlying the logic of science, including such essential topics as the nature of scientific definitions, distinctions between inductive and deductive inference, formulation of laws, the role of axioms in theory development, and the interplay between laws and definitions within a well-organized scientific theory (Bergmann, 1957; C. C. Spiker, 1986). Unlikely many of the currently taught courses which bear the same name, there would be little emphasis on History and Systems, particularly as it relates to the different types of psychological theories. Rather, the primary focus would be on the successful theories in the physical sciences, such as Galileo's laws of motion, Newton's integration of celestial and terrestrial mechanics, and Einstein's theory of relativity.

It is interesting to note that within academia, PhD psychologists often credit the philosophy of science as being one of the most influential courses in their career, yet many have difficulty in citing specific examples of where or how the information actually helped them. The inability to articulate the benefits of this course is really not surprising, however, when it is realized that most academic research questions come from a well-defined body of literature where the corresponding theoretical work has at least been organized through comprehensive review papers and metaanalyses. Under such established groundrules, researchers can readily make transitions between questions, designing experiments to test each one, without necessarily understanding why certain issues are more important than others or why particular concepts seem to lead to more fruitful areas of research.

Outside of academia, though, there is no such ambiguity regarding the benefits of a firm grounding in the philosophy of science. Indeed, applied psychologists who lack the basic concepts are easy to spot. These are the ones whose test concepts are ill defined or fuzzy, whose research questions are untestable, and whose results are unanalyzable or uninterpretable. Not having a firm understanding of the nature of scientific knowledge, these unfortunate individuals are always failing to distinguish between induction and deduction, never knowing when an issue is to be settled through the collection of additional empirical data versus a redefinition of terms.

But perhaps the biggest disadvantage of poor training in the philosophy of science is that the ill-prepared psychologist will lack the essential skills to serve as a translator between scientists from different disciplines. Indeed, by properly using the tenets of philosophy of science, applied psychologists will be able to distinguish the content knowledge in a given scientific area (derived through induction) from its deductive elements (e.g., differentiating axiomatic principles from testable theorems). Once these latter, core logical concepts have been identified, they may then be conveyed to scientists from any background, regardless of their knowledge of the area's technical content.

Metaskill Courses

The four courses in this second tier have been labeled as *metaskill* to highlight the fact that they transcend any particular content area of methodological technique. These courses are usually not part of a graduate training program, and if they are offered at all, it is through another department in which much of the information is irrelevant to the types of employment that psychologists are likely to find.

Yet it is a lack of such courses that put psychologists at a distinct disadvantage relative to their MBA or market-research counterparts. Lacking even rudimentary business skills, the psychologist must pick them up on a catch-as-catch-can basis during the initial period on the job, clearly not an optimal time to acquire such information. Nevertheless, it is this writer's opinion that these courses can be taught within most departments without imposing any undue burden on students whose major interests in graduate school are understandably directed toward acquiring the content knowledge in their primary field of interest, passing comprehensive exams, and generating a research topic for the dissertation. Under such demands, it is the responsibility of each department and its faculty to convince students that the information in the metaskill courses should be acquired as a formal part of doctoral training, even though the benefits will not be realized until after graduation.

Technical writing. This course would provide students with practical information and useful tips on the proper methods for writing and organizing technical reports, monographs, letter reports, briefing summaries, and other written material intended for a nontechnical audience. In contrast to academic writing, which presumes a fairly high level of sophistication, interest, and background knowledge from the reader, truly effective writing in the applied world makes fewer assumptions about its audience.

It has been this writer's experience that many psychologists who enter the applied job market from academia are quite shocked to learn that their academic style of writing, a style which they may have suffered long and hard to develop under the tutelage of a major professor, is considered completely unacceptable to the applied community. Unfortunately, the problems with the writing style are usually not stated explicitly, with the disappointed new hiree merely told that his or her writing is "too academic." In the face of this ambiguous but clearly negative feedback, applied psychologists are left to discover for themselves the particular problem areas and appropriate remedies. However, this search can be quite time-consuming and damaging to the ego, and often the answers come too late to be of much help.

Given such common occurrences, the purpose of this course would be to teach students the fundamentals of good technical writing so they will not have to learn them from bitter experience. While there is no single set of rules that will ensure successful writing, there are a number of helpful tips that can be followed to help the academically trained writer "break set" and reach the desired result sooner. The course would be organized around a core set of these stylistic guidelines.

Some of the major rules include making extensive use of graphics to illustrate key points, using shorter paragraphs and smaller words to create a succinct style, employing a consistent format to help readers identify the key points more readily, summarizing lengthy reports with an executive summary, and placing greater reliance on summary descriptions. An example of the latter point would entail presenting the study's major findings as a list of one-sentence, bulleted highlights. In contrast to academic writing, effective technical writing will downplay the methods that were used to collect the data, and emphasize the importance of the results and their utility to the reader. As part of this material, the student would be exposed to techniques that are differentially effective depending on whether the primary objective is to persuade, impress, or educate the reader.

Presentation methods. This course would provide students with practical information concerning the most effective ways to present technical material verbally to an audience. As such, this course would be the oral counterpart to the technical writing course, and would follow a parallel organization and orientation.

While the need to develop an effective style of oral presentation is often less critical than for writing, there are nevertheless many instances in which the failure to communicate adequately at a meeting or a briefing can have disastrous consequences for the speaker. For example, although academia often tolerates poor speaking performances at national meetings, the applied world is much less forgiving. As with writing, there are some fundamental tips that can greatly improve the quality of one's presentation, even for individuals who are not blessed with a particularly compelling oratory style.

The basic principles of effective verbal presentation are similar regardless of the nature of the meeting, size of audience, or its background knowledge. Some of the most critical guidelines entail making effective use of visual aids, including slides, viewgraphs, and figures; reducing the length and complexity of each speaking point, to make it more compatible with the imperfect process of listening; using redundancy, highlighting, and rephrasing to emphasize major points; and making frequent eye contact with audience members to gauge their overall understanding and acceptance of the material. As part of this skill, students must learn how much detail they will require of their notes when speaking in front of an audience. In this regard, people vary in the amount of detail they both want and need from their notes when speaking. But in any case, the student's goal is to develop a verbal style that avoids the extremes of extemporaneous freewheeling and rote reading, finding instead a happy medium that ensures an even flow of presented information while maintaining the appearance of being in total command of the material.

Accounting procedures. This course would provide students with the fundamentals of fiscal management that are required to function effectively in a business environment. Even in nonprofit settings, the basic concepts of accounting can prove invaluable. Of course, such information is not normally part of the standard academic curriculum, as it is viewed as lying totally within the domain of applied research. This reputed lack of overlap is not surprising when one considers that the traditional academic model calls for professors to delegate many fiscal management decisions (e.g., administration of grant monies) to the university's business office, focusing their energies on the performance of the technical work.

On the other hand, the applied psychologist will, in many environments, be required to learn the fundamentals of fiscal management very quickly or may even be expected to know them prior to starting the job. Acquiring these basics in graduate school would give psychologists a valuable head start, reducing their disadvantage relative to their counterparts from the professional schools.

The basic principles are really quite straightforward, and do not require an accountant to teach them. Some of the key topic areas would include calculating overhead, direct labor, and burdened labor rates; specifying the components of indirect labor; examining the various classes of service contracts (e.g., fixed price, cost plus fixed fee, time and materials, etc.); reviewing the principles of invoicing; learning the tricks to pricing different types of service products; and noting the differences between government and commercial contracting rules and regulations. The course would also cover some of the traditional accounting principles that psychologists never seem to acquire but always need to know, such as accounts payable vs. accounts receivable, double ledger entries, and invoicing practices.

Besides basic accounting principles, the course would also introduce students to the different types of organizations within which applied work may be carried out. This would include a description of the major branches of government that sponsor psychological research and the intricate hierarchical relationships that exist. For example, in detailing the types of Army sponsors for behavioral research, the Department of Defense can be broken down into the Department of Army, Army Research Institute, Behavioral Systems Laboratory, particular field offices, and so forth. A similar description would be provided on the private industry side, where the major objective will be to give the student the "big picture" concerning the sources, routes, and types of funding that are available for applied psychological research.

Business conduct. This fourth course in the metaskill tier would expose students to a potpourri of knowledge and skills that are often expected of the applied psychologist in a business setting but are rarely taught in a formal way. Some of the major topic areas to be covered in this course would be the development of personal filing systems, handling and cultivating of customer relations, ethical issues involved in advertising, and general expectations for one's own personal conduct. In contrast to traditional courses, which emphasize factual knowledge and basic concepts, the Business Conduct course would be oriented toward teaching graduate students "the facts of life" in applied settings. While some may question whether such a nonintellectual orientation properly belongs in a graduate curriculum, a closer look at the differences between the academic and applied realms would strongly suggest the need for such a course.

To begin with, there are marked differences in personal styles between the academic and his or her applied counterpart. For example, within many academic departments, emotional conflicts over conceptual issues are often tolerated, and even expected. Heated outbursts, door-slamming, and name calling are certainly not uncommon among students or faculty. While tenure and a condition of mutual dependence are no doubt partly responsible for this social pattern, there is also the realization that the importance of intellectual truth and academic freedom should transcend standard conventions of politeness. This general acceptance of extreme behavior extends to other domains of conduct as well, of course, such as dress, manners, speech, correspondence, and organization. Regarding the latter issue, it is not uncommon for students or faculty to spend considerable time waiting for a colleague (or themselves) find a much-needed journal article or piece of data that has been buried under mounds of disheveled papers in an office or laboratory.

The situation in most business settings is markedly different, and students should be keenly aware of this before embarking on an applied career. In the applied world, emotional extremes are rarely tolerated, no matter how important the issue or one's degree of commitment to it. Indeed, door-slamming in a business setting tends to lose jobs rather than make debating points. Moreover, eccentricities in dress, grooming, manners, and filing are not viewed with mild amusement, but are instead taken as a sign of that individual's lack of professional competence. In this regard, it should be realized that aversions to extreme behaviors are not the same as requiring a completely homogeneous demeanor, the academic stereotype of the three-piece business-suit mentality not withstanding. Yet, it is important that beginning applied psychologists be educated in the *range* of behaviors that are considered acceptable in a variety of domains, so they may develop their own style of conduct that falls within these bounds.

Applied Psychology Courses

The courses in this third tier would focus on developing techniques for applying specific principles, methodologies, and theories of psychology to practical problem areas. For an applied psychologist to be worthy of the name, he or she must have some content knowledge that can be applied. As such, the four courses in this tier are intended to serve as the empirical adjunct to the methodological and metaskill courses discussed in the first two tiers. A primary objective of these courses would be to familiarize students with behavioral principles, sub-disciplines, and theories that their nonpsychologist counterparts in the business world might expect them to know, thus enhancing their credibility as a psychologist during the initial stages of their employment.

A secondary objective of these courses would be to expose students to some of the most useful areas of psychology from an applied standpoint. While no curriculum can claim to cover all the content information that a psychologist will need to know on the job, there are a number of well-established techniques and theories that have, for various reasons, been successfully applied to diverse behavioral areas over the last several years. The ultimate function of this tier, then, would be to provide training in these successfully applied techniques, ensuring that the graduating psychologist is current on the relevant applied literatures, knows the most useful reference sources and influential studies, and is very familiar with the key contributors in each of these content areas.

Human capacities. This course will cover the fundamental principles in a host of psychological areas that provide useful information concerning limits on human capacities to perform specific behaviors. The topics in the course would be organized along traditional lines, ranging from the basic sensory (e.g., visual, auditory, tactile) and physical (e.g., psychomotor, anthropometric) capacities, progressing to the more complex cognitive processing capacities (e.g., short- and long-term memory, speech and language acquisition, etc.), and culminating in the higher mental functions (e.g., decision making, reasoning, problem solving, inference, etc.).

The material itself would highlight the current state of knowledge concerning the limits of performance in each domain, along with a consideration of the conditions that bring about maximum and minimum performance. For example, the section on sensory limits would cover the maximum number of visual signals that can be distinguished at one time, how many sounds can be uniquely identified and localized from behind the head, and what areas of the skin are most sensitive to pressure and pain. Topics on human physical capacity would emphasize current knowledge in the areas of anthropometric design of workstations (e.g., optimal lighting conditions, furniture geometry, etc.) as well as reliability limitations on performing sequences of psychomotor actions. In the cognitive realm, the course would focus on what is currently known about the number of items that can be held in working memory as a function of different intervening events, as well as ways that an individual's long-term memory can be extended through judicious use of rehearsal and retrieval cues. Material on higher order mental processes would emphasize areas of psychology that concern the distribution of functions between machines and humans, noting areas where humans are both superior to (e.g., interpretation of imperfect, multisensory stimuli) and inferior to (e.g., rapid processing of repetitive events) automated systems.

The need for such information on human limitations arises with surprising frequency in the applied realm. Indeed, applied psychologists are all too often called upon to determine why a particular child is not able to be integrated into a day-care program, a certain individual is not able to function effectively in his or her job, or some organization or unit is performing at substandard levels. Armed with knowledge of the upper limits on human performance, the psychologist will be better able to systematically examine each potential domain (sensory, physical, cognitive, higher-order) and ascertain whether the conditions in each one are conducive to achieving performance that is at or near capacity.

Human resources. This course would provide students with a broad overview of the fundamentals in personnel management and productivity enhancement. In many ways, the material in this course can be considered the "soft" counterpart to that in the Human Capacities course. Some of the topics to be covered would include a comparison of the various techniques for job selection, such as aptitude test batteries, interest inventories, interviews, testing centers, and screening tests; alternative methods for enhancing job performance, such as job performance aids, job appraisals, quality circles, and peer reviews; and different strategies for training, such as embedded training, on-the-job training, refresher training, computer-aided instruction, self-paced instruction, and requalification programs.

If applied psychologists are often called upon to identify why performance deficiencies occur within an organization, they are just as likely to be asked to rectify the deficiency once it has been diagnosed. A thorough knowledge of the human resource area will prove invaluable for the psychologist who must consider alternative ways to improve performance in a complex, multivariable setting. By knowing which approaches have worked in the past under different conditions, and having some knowledge about why specific failures occurred, the applied psychologist will be in a much stronger position to recommend specific courses of action and estimate their probable impact on cost, worker morale, and overall productivity of the organization.

Consumer psychology. This course would cover a wide range of content areas in which people behave as consumers of some commodity. For the purposes of this course, *consumer* would be broadly defined to include such diverse situations as children's toy-buying preferences and the purchasing of medical care insurance by the elderly. The course would focus on the techniques and methods that have proven successful in inferring the physical, social, and environmental factors which control people's decision-making strategies under different behavioral conditions. Some topics would naturally be drawn from traditional courses in advertising and market research, such as the most effective techniques for attracting attention, enhancing memory, changing attitudes, and influencing buying decisions. Other parts of the course would cover less traditional areas of research, by focusing on the consumption of items other than products. As much as possible, these topics would come from the more popular issues of the day, such as decisions regarding the use of medical care, the relative risk of contracting AIDS, and the selection of political candidates.

When engaged in applied research, psychologists will often be required to examine and infer the causal factors underlying human behavior in complex settings. Sometimes these complexities stem from the ambiguities in the behavior itself, as in the public misperceptions of how viruses are contracted. Other times, the difficulty lies in the overwhelming number of candidate causal factors, as in examining the antecedents to the crash of a large airliner.

But whatever the source of the complexity, the applied psychologist must be able to draw upon some body of organized knowledge to help untangle these factors and implement some effective strategy for analyzing the evidence. Simply relying on the experimental method, and its one-variable-at-a-time analysis, will often prove unacceptably slow and cumbersome in coming up with potential solutions and tentative recommendations. To the extent that the psychologist is familiar with small pockets of empirical research (e.g., effects of copayments on the types and amounts of medical insurance purchases) and theoretical work (e.g., causal analyses of bicycle accidents) in complex decision domains, he or she will be able to use analogous strategies to eliminate untenable explanations more efficiently.

Applied theoretical techniques. The final course in the curriculum would cover the psychological theories, paradigms, and principles that have been successfully applied to solving problems outside the laboratory. For whatever reason, certain areas in psychology have simply proven more amenable to practical application than others. A number of notable examples come to mind in this regard, such as Sternberg's (1969) memory-scanning paradigm, Herrnstein's (1961) matching law, Green and Swets's (1966) theory of signal detection, Piaget's (1960) principle of volume conservation, Kohlberg's (1973) moral hierarchy, Rouse's (Rouse & Morris, 1986) development of mental models, and Spence's (1936) theory of discrimination learning, to name just a few.

The Applied Theoretical Techniques course would organize these various "success stories" along common lines (e.g., quantitative vs. qualitative analyses), introduce each technique by means of a specific practical example (e.g., using Sternberg's scanning paradigm to measure an aircraft pilot's cognitive workload), and attempt to summarize the factors that contribute to a given technique's practical utility. Regarding this latter topic, candidate factors might be: making minimal demands on the analyst's background knowledge, requiring little input data, having an organized hierarchy of the controlling variables, and having been derived from a well-established empirical database.

Understanding a set of behavioral principles in the abstract is not equivalent to applying them in a practical setting, and the component skills required for each are vastly different. Whereas one can undoubtedly teach bright students the science of principle development, there are fewer guarantees that the art of principle application can be successfully conveyed. Nevertheless, there is much to be gained from exposing students to concrete examples of how principles, methods, and theories can be applied to answer real-world questions. Even though no two practical problems are ever alike, problems often share common elements, and solutions found in one domain can be applied, with some modification, to others. For an academic program that is truly serious about fostering training for the applied job market, providing the advanced graduate student with the practical tools and information to tackle these demanding issues is one of the most valuable legacies that it can bestow.

EIGHT IMPORTANT LESSONS
FOR THE APPLIED JOB MARKET

The preceding pages have attempted to demonstrate that the presentation of information in an organized, focused curriculum can advance students' understanding of fundamental concepts and hone critical skills in a host of applied research areas. Nevertheless, there are a number of important lessons that are perhaps best acquired, and indeed in many cases may only be learned, through the stern teachings of hands-on experience. Accordingly, the chapter concludes with a brief discussion of eight lessons that the author has learned while working in applied settings over the past 10 years. These lessons are by no means intended as a systematic or exhaustive account of everything the applied psychologist needs to know in order to function effectively. Rather, they are offered to illustrate some of the insights that may be gained, particularly as they contrast with the requirements for academic employment.

Lesson 1: Importance of Methodology as a Stopgap Skill

Many applied psychologists report having felt very uncomfortable with their lack of job-specific content knowledge during their first few months of employment. Whether one works in a business, service, or government setting, it is a basic fact of life that graduate training in psychology offers only hit-and-miss preparation for many of the disciplines in which its students may be called upon to work. However, having well-developed skills in the methodological areas described in Tier 1 of the proposed curriculum, and being proficient in their implementation, will permit the beginning applied psychologist to use this methodological expertise as a stopgap skill until he or she has had sufficient time to acquire the job-specific information ultimately required to advance in the position.

Lesson 2: Importance of Writing Skills

If the inability to structure one's time effectively is the number one cause of job failure in the applied sector, then poor writing skills must surely be number two. Stated bluntly, the ability to write in clear, concise prose will make or break psychologists in many of the nonacademic positions for which they will be vying. In many cases, employers recognize that prospective applicants will come from divergent backgrounds and orientations, bringing with them a set of unique analytic skills in such areas as computers, statistics, business, and engineering. While it is difficult to compare employees' productivity along such diverse lines, it is much easier to evaluate their writing, be it in the form of a technical report, product specification, training manual, or annual company summary. Written products will serve as a common benchmark for productivity in many applied areas, regardless of whether one is working with engineers, manufacturers, doctors, or computer programmers. The applied psychologist whose ideas follow a logical flow, and who can put these ideas to paper quickly, will have already overcome a major stumbling block to the successful transition to the nonacademic world.

Lesson 3: Importance of Understanding the PhD Myth

Whether embarking on a new nonacademic career or seeking to leave academia for an applied position, it is important that psychologists be aware of the stereotype that many of their prospective employers will have about PhDs. While there are many facets to this myth that could be discussed, the most important one for our purposes concerns the fear that Ph.D. psychologists will want to do dissertation-length work on every project they are assigned. Unlike academia, where compulsive attention to detail is rewarded and even expected, the luxury of spending inordinate amounts of time on methodological details and technical issues simply does not exist in the applied sector. Whether in business or nonprofit settings, the watchword is that projects be finished "on time and within budget." Regardless of the technical quality of an individual's work, if it takes too long or costs too much money, then his or her professional competence will be impugned.

As a corollary to this point, applied psychologists are also expected to be an accurate judge of their own productivity. That is, the researcher must be able to predict how long it will take to write a report or manual, conduct a study, develop a computer program, and so forth. Often, these projections must be estimated to the nearest week or day, so that realistic budgets and timelines can be drafted. Only in this way can applied research be carried out under the severe constraints that typically exist.

Lesson 4: Importance of Personal Work Habits

A related lesson concerns the importance of developing personal work habits that are compatible with the standards expected in applied settings. As noted previously, there is simply much less tolerance for eccentric or unpredictable behavior upon leaving the confines of academia. Maintaining sloppy written correspondence, having disorganized files, or keeping poor records of telephone contacts is not acceptable in applied work. In the applied sector, time truly is money, and having rapid access to information is mandatory. Consequently, the applied psychologist will be expected to have, from Day One, a personal work style that meets the standards of his or her chosen field. In short, there simply is no on-the-job training offered for work habits, and researchers will be evaluated on this dimension before they even receive their first paycheck.

Lesson 5: Importance of High-Quality Technical Work

A common misperception within academia is that the quality of the technical products in the applied sector, particularly when working for-profit, is vastly inferior to that found in higher education. While it is the case that the lack of laboratory control over situational variables forces some compromises in the types of studies that can be conducted and the types of inferences that are permitted, these differences should not be mistaken for work of inferior quality. Indeed, one of the greatest disservices that faculty members can do is instill in their students the erroneous belief that applied research is necessarily of poor caliber. To the contrary, it has been this writer's experience that the need for high-quality research is equally important in the applied realm. Hence, the beginning applied psychologist should not go into his or her first job with the misguided expectation that there will be few demands placed on his or her technical competence.

There are three basic reasons why applied research must be technically sound. First, at some level or another, there is always an identifiable sponsor who has paid for the research that has been conducted. Not surprisingly, such individuals or organizations will need to be convinced that the work they have funded is of high quality to ensure that they are "getting their money's worth." Second, in the applied domain, an individual's professional reputation means everything. Since most applied research communities are like small towns, the "word gets out fast" when shoddy research has been conducted or an inferior technical product is released. Moreover, it is simply much easier to market one's services as an applied researcher if they are backed up with a solid reputation for consistently turning out high-quality technical products.

Third, even more than in academia, the work that is performed in the applied sector is an individual's professional legacy. Since applied researchers do not train students or supervise doctoral candidates, their primary products are the technical reports, user manuals, computer programs, and the like that were produced during their careers. Like any dedicated professional, the applied researcher is motivated by the desire to reflect back on this activity with a genuine sense of pride.

Lesson 6: Importance of Knowing One's Target Audience

This lesson is one of the hardest for applied psychologists to learn, yet it is one of the most important. In contrast to academia, where research is judged against archival standards of excellence, applied work is almost always performed for some end user who is often the judge of that product's overall merit. It therefore behooves the researcher to know who the audience for his or her work is, be it a specific individual, such as a department head or manager, or a group of people, such as an entire department or project team. The astute researcher will spend almost as much time investigating the target audience as the topic itself. Such a strategy will usually pay for itself, though, as it helps the researcher select the appropriate level of detail, terminology, technique, and choice among alternative methods of presentation.

Not only must the product satisfy the criteria for technical excellence discussed in the previous lesson, the research must also be viewed as having met the needs of the target audience. Since the publication lag of applied research is on the order of weeks rather than months, the feedback one receives is more rapid than in academia. Importantly, there is usually less chance for arbitration compared to academia. That is, while the academic has the option to resubmit a rejected paper to another journal, no such recourse is available to the applied researcher, who typically has one and only one source for the work. Given these high stakes, it is all the more reason why a thorough study of the target audience should always be undertaken in advance of any project.

Lesson 7: Importance of Maintaining Current Sources of Information

It comes as a surprise to many beginning applied psychologists that the primary sources of information to be used on their new job will not be the traditional journals and textbooks they have grown accustomed to in graduate school. To be sure, some applied areas do have their own journals, yet these usually play only a minor role in helping professionals stay abreast of current developments in their field. Instead, the much-sought-after information that applied professionals so diligently hoard comes from a broad range of sources that defy simple description. Depending on the area, these might include trade publications, newsletters, newspapers, magazines, industry reviews, conference proceedings, occasional books, handbooks, and monographs.

While busily acquiring the requisite content knowledge during their first few months on the job, applied psychologists must also be learning how their colleagues acquire their information. The psychologist should keep a watchful eye on the publications that his or her co-workers and supervisors subscribe to, as well as the in-house publications that are routinely circulated. The criteria for scholarship within the applied sector are much more pragmatic than in academia, and the need for up-to-date information on various topics is usually paramount. It is therefore essential that the applied psychologist first identify, and then acquire, these sources of information as soon as possible.

Lesson 8: Importance of Planning for Managerial Responsibilities

For psychologists who plan to devote their entire careers to applied work, this final lesson is in many ways the most important, as graduate training offers little preparation for performing managerial duties. The lack of emphasis upon management skills is not surprising when one considers that the basic duties of faculty members change little throughout their careers. Indeed, unless a professor actively seeks an administrative position, such as chairperson or dean, his or her job duties will primarily entail teaching classes, conducting research, and training students.

On the other hand, the situation is very different in the applied domain, where one's "technical half-life" is at most 10 to 15 years. That is, by the time a researcher has worked in an applied area for the better part of a decade, he or she must be ready to assume more supervisory duties, leaving the technical work to younger colleagues who are recipients of more recent training and education. The transition to management duties can be traumatic, and ultimately unsuccessful, if one has failed to acquire the requisite skills to function in this very different capacity.

In particular, the successful manager of applied research will have developed highly effective interpersonal skills, the ability to communicate clearly both orally and in writing, the capability to make tough choices under intense time constraints, and the strength to implement difficult decisions under strong negative social pressure. Whether one likes it or not, the advancement to managerial responsibilities is inevitable for most applied psychologists, and, like any challenge, the likelihood of a successful transition will be a direct result of the amount of prior planning and advance preparation that has taken place.

REFERENCES

Altman, I. (1987). Centripetal and centrifugal trends in psychology. *American Psychologist, 42*, 1058–1069.

American Psychologist. (1987). Resolutions approved by the national conference on graduate education in psychology. 42, 1070–1084.

Bergman, G. V. (1957). *The philosophy of science.* Madison, WI: University of Wisconsin Press.

Bickman, L. (1987). Graduate education in psychology. *American Psychologist, 42*, 1041–1047.

Boruch, R. F. (1987). Conducting social experiments. In D. S. Cordray, H. S. Bloom, & R. J. Light (Eds.), *Evaluation practice in review.* San Francisco, CA: Jossey-Bass, Inc.

Campbell, D. T., & Stanley, J. C. (1966). *Experimental and quasi-experimental designs for research.* Chicago: Rand-McNally.

Cook, T. D., & Campbell, D. T. (1979). *Quasi-experimentation: Design and analysis issues for field settings.* Chicago: Rand-McNally.

Davison, M. L., Damarin, F., & Drasgow, F. (1986). Psychometrics and graduate education. *American Psychologist, 41*, 584–586.

Geyer, L. H. (1983). A survey of recent human factors graduates. *Bulletin of the Human Factors Society, 29*, 1–3.

Geyer, L. H., Laughery, K. R., & Schwartz, D. R. (1984). Report of the 1983 survey of human factors students. *Bulletin of the Human Factors Society, 27*, 1–3.

Geyer, L. H., Pond, D. J., & Smith, D. D. B. (1986). A summary of the proposal for accreditation of graduate programs in human factors. *Bulletin of the Human Factors Society, 29*, 1–3.

Goodstein, L. D. (1987). Opening remarks to the national conference on graduate education in psychology. *American Psychologist, 42*, 1057.

Green, D. M., & Swets, J. A. (1966). *Signal detection theory and psychophysics.* New York: Wiley.

Guilford, J. P. (1954). *Psychometric methods.* New York, New York: McGraw-Hill.

Harper, W. R. (1984, August). *Final report on the development, implementation, and evaluation of a maintenance proficiency evaluation system* (Tech. Rep. No. 465–44). Santa Barbara, CA: Anacapa Sciences, Inc.

Harris, R. J. (1975). *A primer of multivariate statistics.* New York: Academic Press.

Herrnstein, R. J. (1961). Relative and absolute strength of response as a function of frequency of reinforcement. *Journal of the Experimental Analysis of Behavior, 4*, 267–272.

Howard, A., Pion, G. M., Gottfredson, G. D., Flattau, P. E., Oskamp, S., Pfafflin, S. M., Bray, D. W., & Burstein, A. G. (1986). The changing face of American psychology: A report from the committee on employment and human resources. *American Psychologist, 41*, 1311–1327.

Howell, W. C., Colle, H. A., Kantowitz, B. H., & Wiener, E. L. (1987). Guidelines for education and training in engineering and psychology. *American Psychologist, 41*, 602–604.

Hughes, S. L., Cordray, D. S., & Spiker, V. A. (1981). Combining process with impact evaluation: A long-term program for the elderly. In R. F. Conner (Ed.), *Methodological advances in evaluation research* (Vol. 10). Beverly Hills, CA: Sage Publications.

Judd, C. M. (1987). Combining process and outcome evaluation. In M. M. Mark & R. L. Shotland (Eds.), *Multiple methods in program evaluation.* San Francisco: Jossey-Bass.

Klatzky, R. L., Alluisi, E. A., Cook, W. A., Forehand, G. A., & Howell, W. C. (1985a). Experimental psychologists in industry: Perspectives of employers, employees, and educators. *American Psychologist, 40*, 1031–1037.

Klatzky, R. L., Alluisi, E. A., Cook, W. A., Forehand, G. A., & Howell, W. C. (1985b, May). *Final report of the task force on the employment of experimental psychologists in industry.* Washington, DC: American Psychological Association.

Kohlberg, L. (1973). Implications of developmental psychology for education: Examples from moral development. *Educational Psychologist, 10*, 2–14.

Piaget, J. (1960). *The psychology of intelligence.* Totowa, NJ: Littlefield, Adams, & Co.

Rogers, S. P., & Spiker, V. A. (1987, August). *Fundamental requirements for applying embedded training to future armored vehicles* (Tech. Rep. No. 714–5). Santa Barbara, CA: Anacapa Sciences, Inc.

Rouse, W. B., & Morris, N. M. (1986). On looking into the black box: Prospects and limits in the search for mental models. *Psychological Bulletin, 100,* 349–363.

Schurman, D. L., & Porsche, A. J. (1980). *Mean frequency for types of information-seeking or error events occurring under each type of task conditions* (Tech. Rep. No. 82–11). Valencia, PA: Applied Sciences Associates, Inc.

Shepard, R. N. (1972). Introduction to Volume 1. In R. N. Shepard, A. K. Romeny, & S. B. Nerlove (Eds.), *Multidimensional scaling: Volume 1, theory.* New York: Seminar Press.

Spence, K. W. (1936). The nature of discrimination learning in animals. *Psychological Review, 43,* 427–449.

Spiker, C. C. (1986). Principles in the philosophy of science: Applications to psychology. In L. P. Lipsitt & J. H. Cantor (Eds.), *Experimental child psychologist: Essays and experiments in honor of Charles C. Spiker.* Hillsdale, NJ: Erlbaum.

Spiker, V. A., Harper, W. R., & Hayes, J. F. (1985). The effect of job experience on the maintenance proficiency of Army automotive mechanics. *Human Factors, 27,* 301–311.

Spiker, V. A., Wotkyns, A. L., & Lueb, W. (1982, November). *Maintenance proficiency systems (organizational). The effect of job exposure on maintenance proficiency: Test results for the automotive tank mechanic (63N)* (Tech. Rep. No. 465–27). Santa Barbara, CA: Anacapa Sciences, Inc.

Stapp, J., & Fulcher, R. (1982). The employment of 1979 and 1980 doctorate recipients in psychology. *American Psychologist, 37,* 1159–1185.

Stapp, J., Fulcher, R., & Wicherski, M. (1984). The employment of 1981 and 1982 doctorate recipients in psychology. *American Psychologist, 39,* 1408–1423.

Stapp, J., Fulcher, R., Nelson, S. D., Pallak, M. S., & Wicherski, M. (1981) The employment of recent doctorate recipients in psychology. *American Psychologist, 36,* 1211–1254.

Sternberg, S. (1969). The discovery of processing stages: Extensions of Donders' method. *Acta Psychologica, 30,* 276–315.

Steinberg, S., & Keppel, G. (1979). *Some suggestions for making academic experimental psychology more effective in industry.* Unpublished manuscript.

Thurstone, L. L. (1925). A method of scaling psychological and educational tests. *Journal of Educational Psychology, 16,* 433–451.

Thurstone, L. L. (1928). Scale construction with weighted observations. *Journal of Educational Psychology, 19,* 441–453.

Warm, R. E., Roth, J. T., & Sullivan, G. K. (1987). *Tri-service review of existing system embedded training (ET) components.* Butler, PA: Applied Sciences Associates, Inc.

chapter 4

It is What You Know That Lets You Grow: Looking to the Future of Language and Cognitive Development

David S. Palermo
The Pennsylvania State University

> During human development, from infancy to maturity, the relations be-
> tween the linguistic and the nonlinguistic elements in cognition change
> very markedly. What precise combination, or balance, of linguistic and
> nonlinguistic skills we can properly demand at any particular stage of
> development before agreeing to say that a child "recognizes" or "knows"
> or "perceives" something, can be decided only when we understand
> better how these two allied types of cognitive skill *come to be related.*
> (Toulmin, 1971, p. 46, author's emphasis)

In considering what the future might hold, I am always inclined, before
looking ahead, to explore the past, which is the foundation on which
the future is built. In the areas of language development, or developmental psycholinguistics, and cognitive development, there have been
incredible changes since the early 1950s, when I did my graduate work
in the Iowa Child Welfare Research Station at the University of Iowa. In
fact, the term *cognitive development* was seldom used then and *psycholinguistics* did not exist, although the word had been introduced
earlier (Kantor, 1935). While I was interested in *language behavior* (to
use terminology more attuned to that era) and I wanted to do my
dissertation on some aspect of children's language acquisition, I was
advised that I would have a great deal of difficulty doing so because it
would be hard to arrange a task that children could learn on a memory
drum. In those days, the study of language acquisition implied the
study of serial and paired-associates learning of words and that required a memory drum. Without the proper equipment I could not

investigate language acquisition, and, as a result, I did my dissertation on a different topic. A brief look at what was happening in child psychology at the time may help explain the context and, at the same time, make clear the dramatic changes which have occurred in the field since that time.

A HISTORICAL PERSPECTIVE

I finished my doctoral work in 1955, which was a time of great excitement in the field of child psychology. The excitement was created by the faculty at Iowa who were beginning to have some success in convincing the rest of the field that a new experimental approach to the study of development would be more fruitful than the traditional developmental perspective (McCandless & Spiker, 1956). The "experimental child psychology" movement emphasized theory and experimental research in the tradition of the neobehavioristic learning theoretical approach taken by the broader field of experimental psychology and exemplified at Iowa by Spence, who was an advocate of and major contributor to Hull's learning theory (cf. Spence, 1956). The crusade initiated by McCandless, Castaneda, and Spiker at Iowa in the 1950s was designed to build an experimental child psychology on what were considered, at the time, the soft foundations laid by the child developmentalists who had dominated the field for the preceding decades. The precipitating factor for this movement was a major concern within the field that developmental psychologists were collecting an overwhelming number of descriptive facts about children none of which were being integrated into any kind of encompassing theoretical framework (cf. Nowlis & Nowlis, 1952). The accumulation of theoretically unrelated observations tied together by no more than the thread of age, it was forcefully argued, would never give us a deep understanding of the processes by which the child emerges as an adult. Researchers interested in human development needed theory, and theory in the early 1950s meant learning theory.

While my graduate professors never implied that Spence's version of Hullian learning theory (Spence, 1960) was the only acceptable theory, there was no other theory given any serious consideration. Eclecticism was not a part of the Iowa tradition at that time. Students were taught one theory within the framework of a logical positivist philosophical framework, and they learned it well. From a historical perspective, there may have been some cracks showing at other places in the neobehavioristic paradigm at the time, but Iowa was a stronghold of learning theory, and the empiricist, if not "dustbowl" empiricist, tradition of psychology was as strong as ever there. The important thing, however, was that we budding child psychologists could not take an atheoretical approach to our subject matter as exemplified by the descriptive work of Dorothea McCarthy (1954), Arthur Jersild (Jersild & Holmes, 1936), and Arnold Gesell (Gesell & Thompson, 1943), whose papers we were assigned to read to be sure we understood. Our interests, in contrast, lay in experimental research with children which explored the dimensions of classical conditioning, generalization, discrimination, and transposition within a learning theory framework (cf. Palermo & Lipsitt, 1963). While we know from our current historical vantage point that learning theory was not to hold center stage for much longer, we embraced it as the saving grace for child psychology at the time.

The focus upon Hull-Spence theory had the effect of creating a group of students who were skilled at conceptualizing problems within that theoretical framework and who could generate sound experimental tests which extended the theory well beyond the scope initially envisioned by Hull or Spence. On the other hand, the same focus closed the door to two well-articulated developmental theories available at the time, those of Lewin and of Piaget. Piaget, who had been publishing research and theoretical papers in Geneva since 1921 and published his first book in English in 1926 (Piaget, 1926), was never even mentioned in my graduate career. To be fair, however, Piaget was being studiously avoided by most of American psychology at the time.

Lewin, who had been a professor at Iowa from 1935 to 1944, could not be as easily ignored in that context. His theory was, however, presented in an ambivalent way, reflecting an admiration for his experimental contributions and his theoretical scope but a perplexed dismay with the phenomenological nature of his theorizing. Lewin, after all, had done some very clever research on the relations between frustration and regression, leadership and children's group behavior, level of aspiration, and the Zeigarnik effect, among other things (cf. Lewin, 1935, 1951). The relation between his theory and the research generated within the framework of that theory, however, was not always clear. More important, if behavior was, as Lewin argued, a function of the person and the environment *as viewed by the person*, it seemed impossible to us at the time to gain any purchase on what the perspective of the person might be. Constructing a theoretical model of what was going on in the child's mind was not even conceivable at that point. The time was not ripe for Lewinian theory in child psychology, not at Iowa and, despite the importance of Lewin's influences in social psychology, not anywhere else.[1]

---

[1] I am ignoring the small enclave led by Barker at the University of Kansas which continued to be productive long after Lewin died in 1947.

On the other hand, the acceptance of neobehaviorism and the learning theory which was dominant at the time, along with the failure to fully understand Lewin and the framework within which his theory was conceptualized, may have left us less well prepared for the new wave of interest in Piagetian theory which swept the field shortly thereafter. In the period roughly from 1963, when Flavell published his classic volume (Flavell, 1963) communicating most effectively what Piaget was all about, to the time of Piaget's death in 1980, Piagetian theory became the centerpiece of theorizing in child psychology. At the same time, the influence of Chomsky's theorizing in the field of linguistics began to be felt in psychology (e.g., Chomsky, 1957, 1959), first in the areas of language acquisition and language processing and gradually spreading more broadly to influence all of the thinking in cognitive psychology. While Piaget and Chomsky did not agree on everything (cf. Piattelli-Palmarini, 1980), their approaches to theorizing are not incompatible, in the sense that both are concerned with accounting for behavior in terms of an underlying mental competence model, a model much more compatible with Lewinan theory than with learning theory. The acceptance of such a model, of course, involves the acceptance of an entirely different perspective on the field whether one wishes to describe the acceptance as a scientific revolution, paradigm shift (Kuhn, 1962), change in research program (Lakatos, 1970), or change in world view (Pepper, 1970).

The difference between a cognitive approach and a neobehavioristic learning theory approach to the study of cognitive and psycholinguistic topics involves a difference in what is meant by a theory of mind. When I was a graduate student, Spence told me that he was trying to develop a theory of the mind and believed that Hull-Spence theory was such a theory. He suggested in another place (Spence, 1956) that verbal responses might be used "as a base from which to make inferences concerning hypothetical, covert psychological processes" (p. 15). But Spence was an ardent neobehaviorist, and, as a result of the logical empiricist philosophy to which he adhered, his theory of mind was constrained so that it remained very close to the surface structure manifestations of mind. This constraint meant that all of his theoretical constructs had to be reducible to the physicalistic level of stimuli and responses. As he put it, "all terms employed by the scientist, no matter how abstract, must ultimately be referrable back to some primitive or basic set of terms that have direct experiential reference" (Spence, 1956, p. 13).

While it is necessary for the purposes of communication about one's research to use a language which allows for minimal ambiguity about the observations made and the categories into which those observations have been placed, it is not required that every theoretical term be so defined. To require that every theoretical term be operationally defined, as Spence and other behaviorists did, is to impose constraints upon theorists which are much too restrictive. One of the confusions here is between the need to communicate clearly, for replication purposes, what was observed in an experiment, and what may be advanced as a theoretical account of the universe in which any particular operationally defined observation plays a very small part. Theoretical constructs are much more encompassing than the referential specifics of any particular operationally defined set of variables in an experiment. The relationship is much the same as the relationship between sense and reference in semantics which we will discuss later in this chapter. One knows the sense of the word *dog*, for example, if one can identify Chihuahuas and Saint Bernards as referential members of the class of dogs, as well as any other kind of dog one may encounter in the future regardless of the characteristics of the particular dog observed. The knowledge one has that allows classification of never-before-experienced new exemplars of dogs seems extraordinarily abstract and must go beyond the physicalistically constrained artificial language the logical empiricists assumed would objectify science.

The change which is taking place under the banner of cognitive psychology, and I do not think that it *has* taken place, involves a change in the theoretical account of mind (Weimer, 197) and not a change in the observational procedures used in research. Scientists will continue to make use of operational definitions in research, but such constraints on the language of theory defeat the purposes of theory. Operational definitions pertain to surface forms, that is, the observations, while theory pertains to the abstract structures underlying those surface forms. The same language is not required of the two, because the observational data are ambiguous in the sense that they may be attributable to more than one underlying abstract structure just as one underlying abstract structure may be manifest in more than one observable form. The cognitive revolution pertains to the metatheoretical or paradigmatic orientation that identifies the permissible classes of theories that will be acceptable, and it does not pertain to research. The content of the latter may change, but it is the theories that dictate which observations will be made. How one may use those observations with respect to the theory is yet another matter (Weimer, 1979).

I will assume for the purposes of the arguments to be advanced in the remainder of this paper that the shift to a cognitive psychology will take place. My reasons for questioning that assumption relate to the fact that there seem to be large numbers of psychologists, both developmental and otherwise, who call themselves cognitive psychologists but who have not recognized, or at least have not acted upon, the change in orientation required by the description I have presented. There are, it seems to me, a significant number of individuals who have done no more than shift their terminology from learning theory habits to cognitive rules, forgetting to memory, and associationism to connectionism, while adding terms such as *strategy*, *information processing*, *knowledge*, and *meaning* without the accompanying conceptual reorganization at the theoretical and metatheoretical levels required to move out of the neobehavioristic and into the cognitive perspective toward the field. Merely changing what is observed with an accompanying change in description to use the "in" terms of the cognitive psychologist does not make for a paradigm shift.

LANGUAGE AND COGNITIVE DEVELOPMENT

While language acquisition was not being studied in the early 1950s, other than in a descriptive manner, there was a strong interest in the influence of words on learning in various kinds of tasks. The experimental child psychologists saw the influence of language upon learning as a particularly important area in which they could make a contribution to learning theory. The child, after all, begins as an animal with no language and, eventually, learns a language that changes, in turn, the child's ability to learn other things. Following the lead provided by the dissertations of Birge (1941) at Yale and Kuenne (1946) at Iowa, Spiker and his students (e.g., Norcross, 1958) and the Kendlers (Kendler & Kendler, 1959) pursued the facilitating and interfering influences of words on learning in a variety of tasks in addition to the changes which occur in learning as a function of having language available. These studies focused on the acquired distinctiveness and the acquired equivalence of stimuli resulting from learning names for stimuli, and the influence of names on the transfer of learning from one task to another through verbal mediation. The concept of verbal mediation developed through this and other research (Jenkins, 1963) was the basis of at least one of the theoretical accounts of language acquisition offered during this period (Jenkins & Palermo, 1964).

In 1963, however, three different research teams began publishing the results of similar research programs which suddenly changed the direction of language research by developmental psychologists. All three reported some interesting and very similar results pertaining to children's acquisition of language. The first into print was Braine (1963), followed by Brown and his colleagues (Brown, Fraser, & Bellugi, 1964) and Ervin and her colleagues (Miller & Ervin, 1964). Each of these groups decided to follow a small group of children from their first efforts to put two words together through their early period of sentence construction. All three groups reported that their observations revealed the children to have a grammar for their constructions from the very beginning. It was an extremely important set of observations at the time, because this group of researchers, as well as others, had recently become aware of the new approach to grammar being advanced by Chomsky (1957, 1959) at that time. Chomsky's new linguistics appeared to focus primarily upon syntax, and the observations made by these researchers were interpreted to mean that the child had a syntactic system in the very first multiple word utterances produced. While these early results were based upon only two to five children in each case, the children appeared so consistent in their language constructions that a great deal of attention was drawn to the study of the acquisition process and how one might account for it. The early theoretical accounts of those data ranged from those based upon classical and operant conditioning principles, through those based upon verbal mediation theory, information processing, and intentionality of the speaker, to those which argued that the child is endowed with innate linguistic capacities that interact with linguistic experience allowing language to develop automatically, naturally and with unusual speed relative to other kinds of cognitive abilities (see Slobin, 1971, for representative examples of these various positions).

In a matter of a few years, the pendulum of thought about language acquisition swung from an atheoretical disinterest, through an assumption that language was learned as almost any other kind of behavior, to a position that language is basically an innately given property of the species that appears naturally when the child is in the presence of other persons who use the language. While the argument about how the child manages to acquire the language continues, a considerable amount of research and additional theoretical effort has been devoted to the issue since those heady days when the old-fashioned learning theorists and the new-look mentalistic, rationalistic, innatists squared off for theoretical debates. As is so often the case in such arguments, it would appear that both sides had something going for them but that both were overstating their case. An overview of what has been learned during this period will provide some insight about where we have progressed, and a background for predicting the directions to be taken by the developmental psycholinguists who will contribute to building the future theoretical and empirical knowledge about language acquisition and the cognitive development which inevitably accompanies it.

LANGUAGE ACQUISITION: A BRIEF OVERVIEW

Biological bases of language. Since the time of the Greeks we have known that the left and right hemispheres of the brain have different functional relationships to language. Broca, in 1861 (Kann, 1950), and, a few years later, Wernicke (1874), provided experimental evidence to support the relationship between brain damage and language impairment. More recently, Lenneberg (1967) summarized the biological bases of language, which, in turn, stimulated a great deal of research that has not only improved our understanding of the relation between the brain and language (e.g., Gazzaniga, 1983) but has also explored the relation between the characteristics of the vocal tract and language production in the context of trying to understand the evolution of language (cf. Lieberman, 1977).

Developmentally we know that the left and right hemispheres of the infant are differentially responsive to language and nonlanguage stimuli prior to birth (Molfese & Molfese, 1980). Furthermore, auditory evoked responses recorded from the brain at birth appear to be predictive of later language development at three years of age (Molfese & Molfese, 1985). Molfese (1985) has also reported that auditory evoked responses of the brain differentiate positive and negative semantic features of words. In addition, it is known that the superlaryngeal vocal tract must assume a particular position in the young child before language production is possible (Lieberman, 1977). In short, language is a biologically based function of our species. The behavioral manifestations of that function are created as the organism develops from the time of conception through the end of the life span as the biological structure matures and changes. Insults to the biological system affect the functions of that system, including the acquisition and use of language. Clearly, a full understanding of the acquisition process requires knowledge of the biological bases upon which language depends (cf. Segalowitz & Molfese, 1987).

Linguistic components of language. Broadly speaking, the linguist views the grammar of a language as comprised of three components: phonology, syntax, and semantics. Taking the sentence as the basic unit of analysis, one may analyze the sentence into the sound components and the relations among those components which specify the words and the word components and their relationships which specify the syntactic unit, as well as the meaning of the sentence. As indicated earlier, the earliest work on language acquisition that was influenced by Chomsky's linguistics focused upon syntax, at least in part, because that is where Chomsky seemed to place his emphasis. While there was and remains an interest in the acquisition of the phonological system (Locke, 1983; Mehler, Jusczyk, Lambertz, Halsted, Bertoncini, & Amiel-Tison, 1988; Werker, 1989), the resurgence of interest in language acquisition in the past 30 years has grown out of the study of syntax.

The initial focus upon syntax allowed the early researchers to maintain the assumption that language develops as an independent system unrelated to the rest of cognitive development (cf. McNeill, 1970, for a discussion of the issues here). As the research progressed, however, it became clear that what the child was trying to communicate was at least as important as how the child was constructing any particular utterance syntactically. Bloom (1970) was the first to clearly make the point that the semantic system should be examined as seriously as the syntactic or phonological system. Bever (1970) provided the first theoretical effort to cast language acquisition within a larger cognitive framework. Slobin (1973) expanded upon that theme, and, more recently, he (Slobin, 1985) has developed his position more clearly as a function of having studied language acquisition in 15 to 20 different languages. Despite the increased information available, Slobin notes that "we do not know enough yet about . . . [the language acquisition process] . . . to be very clear about the extent to which it is specifically tuned to the acquisition of language as opposed to other cognitive systems, or the degree to which . . . [the language acquisition process] . . . is specified at birth—prior to experience with the world of people and things, and prior to interaction with other developing cognitive systems" (Slobin, 1985, pp. 1158–1159).

Language and cognitive development. As soon as the possibility was considered that language and cognitive development might be intimately related, it was natural for developmental psycholinguists to turn to Piagetian theory. Piaget, of course, had a well-developed theory of cognitive development, and some of his colleagues and students had already begun to examine the relationships between language and cognitive development. Sinclair (1975), for example, suggested that language is just one manifestation of the child's capacity for representing things and begins at about the same time as other representational systems such as gesturing, drawing, mental imagery, and dramatic or symbolic play. On this account, the capacity to represent, in the sense of creation, regardless of the form, depends upon the development of knowledge about what the symbols represent and a differentiation of action and representational thought. While Sinclair's position emphasizes the dependence of language development upon cognitive development, Karmiloff-Smith (1978, 1988) presents data which she interprets as suggesting that the relation between language and cognitive development is a two-way street in the sense that language influences the development of categories as well as the reverse.

The incorporation of cognitive development as necessary to any account of language acquisition expanded research and theory in several directions. Kessen and Nelson (1978), for example, pointed out that infants, prior to language, seek regularities and ignore exceptions in their environmental interactions. Classes of objects and events are created from particulars which are subsequently fit together in categories because they relate functionally to the infant and to other objects and events in space and time. It is this process of categorization, well developed in early infancy (cf. Cohen & Younger, 1983; Quinn, 1987), which, when language emerges, is the basic cognitive skill that enables the child to learn language as well as to organize thought. Thus, the prerequisites of language have been formed long before language appears, as revealed, for example, in the infant's ability in the first few days after birth to discriminate utterances in their own language from those of another language, apparently on the basis of characteristic prosodic differences (Mehler et al. 1988). The latter is one example of the strategies for acquiring language carried from infancy into the language acquisition period. The infant comes equipped at birth with inherited categories or, at least, predispositions thereto, and strategies for acquiring other categories, although those strategies often are context determined.

Recognition that children develop hypotheses or strategies in their efforts to break the language code, and the investigation of the nature of those strategies, has led to the recognition that there are individual differences in the strategies used. Evidence is now available to make it clear that there is more than one way for children to learn their first language. The product may be essentially the same, and it may be achieved at roughly the same age, but the route may differ from child to child (Bloom, Lightbown & Hood, 1975; Nelson, 1981). Prior to this attention to individual differences in language acquisition, most researchers focused upon how children were building syntactic structures as they moved from one to several word constructions in what was assumed to be a uniform, systematic manner. It has become clear at this point that children use all the tools available to them to solve the puzzle of language. They are engaged in synthetic and analytic processes at all levels at different times. They may categorize and label all things as *it*, or be very specific with names; they may build syntactic structures a unit at a time or start with a sentence and subsequently analyze it into units; they may use language as a cognitive tool or as a social instrument; and they may use some of thee strategies in one context and others in another context. In the process of using the tools available to them, children may show evidence in their performance of moving from apparent incompetence to apparent competence, or they may show evidence that could be interpreted as moving from apparent competence to apparent incompetence (Bowerman, 1985b). They may show evidence of comprehending a particular syntactic structure with one set of words but reveal incompetence with another set of words (e.g., Sudhalter & Braine, 1985). The particular words with which children succeed often appear to be prototypical of their class in the sense of having semantic and distributional properties which are more common than those of other members of the class (e.g., deVilliers 1980; Maratsos & Chalkley, 1980).

It has become abundantly clear in the process of examining how children go about acquiring their first language that they are processing phonological, syntactic, semantic, and pragmatic characteristics of the language all at the same time—all of this while applying analytic, synthetic, general and specific, and social and cognitive strategies to the comprehension and production processes required for acquiring the language. The children are doing all of this while, at the same time, they are being socialized to share, develop empathy, acquire control of excretory processes, and eat with the proper utensils, to mention only a few examples of the physical, cognitive, and emotive abilities that this supposedly cognitively confused preoperational child achieves between the time of birth and four or five years of age. All normal children do it, and each succeeds to the extent that he or she can carry on a relatively sophisticated level of communication with an adult by that age. There is, of course, more to be acquired (Palermo & Molfese, 1972; Palermo, 1984) but the 5-year-old has achieved a monumental success in light of the relative paucity of knowledge at his or her command relative to the linguist and psychologist still trying to understand the process.

LANGUAGE AND KNOWLEDGE

It does not seem to matter, however, whether we examine the child's acquisition of phonology (e.g., Macken & Ferguson, 1983; Pye, Ingram & List, 1988), syntax (e.g., Bever, 1970; Valian, 1986), semantics (e.g., Keil, 1979; Kuczaj & Barrett, 1986), or any other aspect of language acquisition—we are continually confronted with the fact that the child's knowledge plays an important part in the acquisition process. Lack of knowledge constrains the process, and available knowledge facilitates the process. One might have expected Piaget to have contributed to our understanding of the interaction of knowledge and language, but his theory fails us in this respect. The reason for this deficiency in Piagetian theory is not immediately obvious. Piaget, after all, spent nearly his entire life trying to account for how the human comes to transcend its biological limitations through the intellect; how the human comes to know and thereby possess the means to go beyond the constraints of the biological system (Piaget, 1971). Since the human comes into this world without those capacities and emerges as an adult with those capacities, Piaget focused upon the developmental processes which produced those changes. Yet, except for his early book (Piaget, 1926), he did not focus upon the function of language in those processes.

Piaget is primarily known as a structuralist in the sense that, until the last few years of his life, his developmental theory was concerned with building the formal operational mental structures (defined in terms of the characteristics of logical-mathematical groups), characteristic of adult cognitive processing, from the primitive sensory motor intelligence developed in infancy. Thus, the newborn infant exercises its reflexive behavioral repertoire in response to stimulation, internal and external, and gradually modifies that behavior as he or she comes to know the world through sensory-motor schemata. The sensory-motor knowledge eventually becomes internalized via images and, subsequently, other representational systems of which language is the most obvious exemplar. Again, through social interchange, by which Piaget meant environmental interactions not just personal interactions, the internal cognitive structures evolve through stages of relative disorganization in the preoperational period, to the stable concrete operations and, finally, the more abstract formal operations when the mind is capable of operating on abstract operations independently of external stimulation. All of these transitions in cognitive structures take place as a result of the processes of assimilation of stimulation to the current structures and accommodation of the structures to the new aspects of the stimulation. In short, Piaget argued that the child constructs meaning for environmental events in terms of the structures available to it at the time of the events.

The structures themselves are adjusted to give meanings to new events as they come along. Thus, the equilibration process is one of constructing structures, or abstract models, which allow the developing child to give meanings to events in the environment. How the child interprets the environment at any point in time and, therefore, what the child does in response to the environment is a function of the mental structures available to the child at that moment. Other than at times when the child is at an equilibrated plateau in development at the end of one of the developmental stages, the structure available for interpreting the events of the world may change at any moment. The changes are not likely to be dramatic from moment to moment but, nevertheless, changes take place with each new experience. In this sense, Piagetian theory and Lewinian theory are not that much different. Both theorists argued that the child responds to the events in the environment in terms of the interpretation constructed for those events at the moment, and both agreed that the interpretation might change at a later time, depending upon the mental structure available at that later time.

Piaget shifted the emphasis of his theorizing away from the structuralist components and more toward a functionalist position in his later years (Beilin, 1984, 1987; Chapman, 1988). In Overton's terminology (Overton, In press), this shift may be described as a change in emphasis from pattern conservative to pattern progressive explanations. Such a shift in emphasis does not mean that Piaget gave up his structuralist position, but that he changed his focus of attention from concern with structural characteristics of mental capacities at points in the developmental process to a concern with the pattern or process of progression from one developmental point to another. This shift in emphasis is reminiscent of the distinction the French linguist de Saussure made when discussing the focus of linguistics on synchronic or diachronic aspects of language. In the first case the focus is upon the structure of a language at a point in time, while the latter is a concern with the historical changes in a language over time. Synchronic analyses are static in the sense of attempting to capture the nature of language as it exists at a particular moment, while diachronic analyses are dynamic in attempting to account for the processes of change from one moment to another.

As Beilin (1984) has pointed out, however, the concept of stage remains an integral part of the theory regardless of the shift in emphasis designed, in part, to reduce the importance of stages in the theory. Intimately related to the idea of stages is the notion of the structure d'ensemble, that is, that the structure achieved at a particular stage reflects a unified abstract entity that functions across cognitive domains. Thus, as everyone is aware at this point, conservation of mass, weight, volume, and area are acquired at different developmental times, but by the end of the concrete operational period all have been integrated into one structure d'ensemble which operates across all the content areas in which conservation may be said to take place.

Stage theory and the structure d'ensemble have long been theoretical problems for Piagetian theory. Piaget was aware of it as well as were his critics. I do not wish to get into a review of the nature of the issues and the empirical evidence which has been used to argue for the abandonment of the stage-related structuralism with which Piaget is associated. These matters have been well aired in other places (e.g., Flavell, 1971; Flavell & Wohlwill, 1969; Brainerd, 1978; Beilin, 1984).

Piaget's concern with structure, however, was a concern with how we know, the structures which make it possible for us to know at each developmental level. He was much less concerned with what we know, that is, the content of knowledge. His theory was constructed in an effort to account for the assumed changes in knowing how to know, with little attention to the issue of knowing that. While it may be the case that we know some things in a sensory-motor manner and other things in terms of concrete operations or formal operations, there is increasing evidence that the content of knowledge, knowledge that, is much more important than Piaget had assumed. It appears to be the case that, in many areas, the manner in which one conceives a problem depends upon the nature of the problem and the knowledge that one has accumulated and can bring to bear on the content of that problem area.

There is now a considerable body of recent evidence that may be interpreted as indicating that structure, in the Piagetian sense, does not change developmentally over the life span from birth to adulthood. While it may be the case that the organization of the content of knowledge changes at any time within the life span as one learns more about a particular content area, the evidence now suggests that there is little or no difference in the manner in which children and adults approach an intellectual problem. Here I am referring, for example, to the research reported by Langer (1980, 1986), which he interprets to mean that the cognitive processes for logic and mathematics are available to the infant long before the representational system and various other cognitive developments usually associated with them have been acquired (see also Sinclair, Stambak, Lézine, Rayna, & Verba, 1989). As will be discussed later in the chapter, Langer shows that there are developmental steps in the building of protological operations which anticipate further development when representational systems, in this case the metalanguage of formal logic, are acquired. Langer's work may be interpreted to indicate that the infant has the necessary logical processes but not the knowledge base of an adult to which the processes may be applied.

Gelman's (1977) work on the child's concept of number suggests that children may have abilities comparable to those of an adult in reasoning about numbers if the child is able to obtain a specific numerical representation, that is, if the child has the knowledge of the number set with which he or she is asked to reason. Cohen, in his research on early infant categorization, has commented that "The processes . . . infants use to generate categories seem quite similar to those used by older children and adults . . . the mechanism they use to form categories is quite sophisticated. . . . They are . . . capable of using multiple attributes to form categories and even of taking the correlations among these attributes into account" (Cohen & Younger, 1983, p. 216).

There are a number of other researchers working on other problems who have come to similar conclusions. In the area of language, for example, Hardy and Braine (1981) conclude, after several studies of the case system of 4- and 5-year-old children, that "the adults' case system is remarkably similar to the children's . . . the definition of the case roles, and the way in which they are organized, probably remain unchanged . . . What changes during development after five years . . . is the knowledge that these roles can at times be reassigned to the syntactic categories of sentence subject, object, and prepositional phrase . . . Thus, while we learn more about exceptions during development, and the basic system may become amplified and refined, it is probably not fundamentally reorganized" (pp. 220–221).

Macnamara (1982), in his book concerned with how children are able to learn the names for things, comes to the conclusion that he "knows of no evidence that the minds of children and adults differ structurally" (p. 236). He goes on to state that, in the course of reviewing the evidence, "we have seen considerable evidence that even to learn names for things, a modest part of what the very young child learns even in language, they [children and adults] must be structurally equivalent" (p. 236). Macnamara came to these conclusions because a child who learns names for things must know how to comprehend three-place predicates of referring, many-place predicates relating to truth, and the relation between referring predicates and truth judging predicates, as well as a powerful propositional logic, among other things (Macnamara, 1986). Note that Langer's work suggests that the logic Macnamara indicates is required is available to the child learning language.

In the area of conceptual development, Keil (1979, 1981) has argued and presented data to support the contention that there are constraints on the learnability of natural classes and relations among classes. These constraints on class formation are both universal and invariant throughout development. To put it in Keil's terms, "Although a child's knowledge in a particular domain may be less differentiated than an adult's, it is systematically related to the latter, for structures at all ages share many formal properties . . . What knowledge children do have conforms to the same formal constraints as adult knowledge, but it is less elaborated" (Keil, 1981, p. 202).

In the area of memory there are similar arguments being made. Chi (1978), for example, on the basis of research on memory for the places of chess pieces on a board, argues that the knowledge base of the individual determines the memory performance. She demonstrated that 10-year-old chess experts could remember chess piece placement much better than adult chess novices. The adults, on the other hand, showed better recall of 10 digits. More recently, Kail and Nippold (1984) have reported a developmental study of retrieval from semantic memory. The results indicated that the older the subjects, the greater the total number of items retrieved, but the form of the retrieval curve over time was the same for all ages, the number of clusters of items was constant across ages, and at all ages the prototypic category members were recalled first, followed by typical and atypical members. They argue that the amount of knowledge the child has changes with age, but that the processes used to retrieve that knowledge are the same at all ages.

Similarly, in a recent paper on hypothesis testing by Cantor and Spiker (1982), the authors concluded that "there is mounting evidence that children as young as kindergarten age, and probably younger, are capable of using quite sophisticated strategies if the appropriate conditions are carefully arranged" (p. 523). In this case, if the child knows what to attend to and knows that there are multiple options for solution which must be sought out to find the correct solution, the young child solves multidimensional discrimination learning problems much as do older children.

Finally, the research my students and I have been doing on children's comprehension of metaphor suggests that 3- and 4-year-old children comprehend metaphor in the same manner as do adults, if the metaphors pertain to issues about which they know (e.g., Palermo, 1986; Waggoner, Messe, & Palermo, 1985). Children of this age understand the emotional reactions of happiness, sadness, anger, and fear. They are, therefore, able to understand that, if you are a "bouncing bubble" or a "silver minute," you are happy, but that, if you are a "sinking boat" or a "used joke," you are sad (Waggoner & Palermo, 1989).

In summary, the conclusions of these authors working with rather diverse age groups and diverse cognitive tasks suggest that the cognitive structures may be in place from the very beginning. Whether we are talking about concept formation, language acquisition, logical reasoning, arithmetic skills, hypothesis testing, metaphor, or chess, it appears that the structure and the processes assumed to be associated with the structure are constants across the age span. Infants, 5-, 10-, and

20-year-olds all appear to process those cognitive tasks in the same way based upon what are the same, presumably inherent, structures. As Mandler (1983) notes in a discussion of the Piagetian concept of schema, a cognitive structure she considers universal, "in spite of the differences in complexity of the child's and adult's knowledge, the format of the representations and the manner in which processing takes place appear to be similar in the two cases" (p. 119). She continues, "In Piagetian theory . . . the structures that result from these modes of processing [assimilation and accommodation] are thought to differ qualitatively at different stages. But as we look more closely at the schemata that are formed by these processes, it appears that at least some of them remain structurally invariant as well . . . [and] . . . provide more continuity from childhood to adulthood than we have often admitted" (p. 121).

What appears to change as the child develops is not structure, as Piaget would have it, but knowledge. By *knowledge* I mean the set of facts and relations among facts that the child believes to be true of the world or of some cognitive domain within his or her conception of the world—or *life space*, to use Lewin's terminology. For infants, the facts may relate to no more than states of comfort and discomfort. Gradually, the facts are differentiated into states of comfort in relation to feeding, dry diapers, or being held by an adult, and states of discomfort in relation to different sets of circumstances. As the baby continues interacting with the environment, the accumulation of facts, or differentiation of the life space, continues. The baby, however, cannot merely accumulate lists of facts, no more than developmental psychologists can accumulate lists of facts. Facts are meaningful only insofar as they are a part of a theoretical framework. Thus, a complete definition of knowledge must include the schema or, more broadly, the theory or theoretical model of the world that organizes the facts and schemata that the child believes to be true of the world, or cognitive domains constructed by the child within the world. The theory is, so to speak, the glue which holds the world together—at least the child's conception of the world. Piaget's efforts, as well as those of other developmental theorists, are directed toward describing the structure of the child's theory and the processes by which it develops from infancy to adulthood.

THE DOMAIN OF NUMBERS

For illustrative purposes, let us consider the development of the operations associated with knowledge in the logical and mathematical content areas applied so widely by adults, especially in literate societies. It might be anticipated that the child would be late in acquiring this cognitive domain, because it is much more abstract and involves systems in which the symbols have no particular referents. As Langer (1986) points out, "Language remains the most abstract, powerful, and flexible symbolic medium available to children until their cognitive development enables them to begin to acquire mathematical forms of notation. . . . Mathematical notation completes the detachment of symbols from their objects of reference" (p. 393).

Langer's research, however, suggests that knowledge in this content area begins to develop long before the abstract symbolic system of language and mathematical notation has been acquired. His careful observations of 6- to 12-month-old children (Langer, 1980), and his subsequent work with 1- to 2-year-olds (Langer, 1986), reveal what he interprets as the precursors of logicomathematical operations. These proto-operations are inferrable from the spontaneous behavior he has observed when infants are presented with objects such as square and round rings, wooden cars, Play-Doh, and other manipulable objects. He reports that the infants exhibit what he calls first-order proto-operations consisting of correspondences, substitutions, and classifications to construct equivalence, nonequivalence, and reversibility with the items presented. These part–whole transformations which occur in the first year of life are inferred from the activities of picking up, combining, rearranging, banging, and otherwise exploring the objects presented to them.

The behaviors Langer describes are not only systematic, but show a nonlinear developmental progression within the recursive model of development Langer proposes. The recursive aspect of the model may be seen in the second year of the child's life, when development continues both in terms of continued advances in the individual proto-operations begun in the first year but where, in addition, the child begins to combine these individual activities into routines that involve doing two things at once or in a coordinated sequence. For example, the child may pick up an object with one hand and, while holding the object in that hand, use the other to set another object in an upright position to be knocked over by the object held in the other hand. This sequence or routine may be repeated several times with or without variations, and it may be interrupted and returned to without disruption. The individual parts which occurred separately in the first year are referred to as unileveled first-order operations, and the sequence is a second-order operation, because it involves the coordination into a cohesive unit of the first-order operations.

The whole developmental process is recursive in the sense that development continues at the first-order level even as the second-order level progresses, although not necessarily continuously, nor at the same time or rate. Langer notes that the higher level whole, composed of the unilevel parts, has its own emergent properties determined, not just by the parts, but by their relations within the second-order structure. The process of moving from one level to another takes time. Observations reveal that the more highly developed first-order processes may yield more efficient performance than second-order processes at some developmental periods until the higher-level processes develop to a point that is beyond what is possible for processes of the lower level. Thus, we may observe in the child's behavior continuities in cognitive development, but, in addition, we may observe discontinuities and regressions as the child is observed to move through the cognitive developmental processes associated with a knowledge domain. On one hand, the observations in this domain are reminiscent of Bowerman's (1985b) observations with respect to the progressions, regressions, and progressions in language acquisition. On the other hand, Langer's theoretical proposal of a multilevel progression of development is similar in many ways to Beilin's description of the spiral development proposed by Piaget toward the end of his life (Beilin, 1987)

In any case, Langer's observations suggest that the child moves from grouping small numbers of objects on the basis of similarity, to enlarging those groupings and enlarging the numbers of groupings. At the same time, the child exchanges objects between groups to maintain equivalence, adds to and subtracts from groups, combines groups, and separates groups in observably systematic ways. It is these manipulations of objects that reveal for Langer the logicomathematical cognition evident in the child well before the language system is established.

It is these same logicomathematical cognitive structures which surely form the foundation for development of the child's concept of number as studied, for example, by Gelman and her associates (e.g., Gelman & Meck, 1986). Gelman assumes that the initial competence 3- to 5-year-old children bring to the task when acquiring the skill of counting includes at least the following five principles: (a) one-to-one correspondence, that is, each item in a set must have a unique tag; (b) stable order principle, that is, the tags must come from a stably ordered list; (c) the cardinal principle, that is, the last tag assigned in counting has the special status of designating the cardinal value of the set; (d) the item-indifference principle, that is, the tags may be assigned to any collection of items; and (e) order-indifference principle, that is, the order of tagging is irrelevant and may be changed as may the order of the items to be tagged. Gelman appears safe in making these assumptions about the competence of the child in light of the analyses by

Langer of the performance of 1- to 2-year-old children prior to the emergence of the language required for counting.

Gelman and her colleagues (e.g., Gelman & Gallistel, 1978; Gelman & Meck, 1986; Greeno, Riley, & Gelman, 1984) assume the same kind of competence-performance distinction in connection with the acquisition of counting, and presumably other arithmetic abilities, as others have assumed in connection with language. In the case of counting, she and her co-workers argue that there are three interacting kinds of competence or knowledge required to count: conceptual, procedural, and utilization knowledge. The conceptual knowledge consists of implicit counting principles, such as those five listed above, that presumably derive from innate characteristics of the organism and such prior experiences as described in elegant detail by Langer. Conceptual knowledge, consisting of these principles, is basic to the other kinds of knowledge but, by itself, does not guarantee appropriate counting performance. The latter requires procedural and utilization knowledge.

Procedural knowledge consists of planning solutions within the constraints of conceptual knowledge. For example, to demonstrate understanding of the conceptual principle of one-to-one correspondence, the child must also plan his or her counting such that it begins at one end of an array and ends at the other without skipping or double counting an item within the set. The principle and the knowledge of how to apply the principle are two different kinds of knowledge. Utilization knowledge, the third kind postulated by Gelman and her associates, concerns proper assessment of the task to implement the procedural knowledge. In this case, for example, the child must be able to recognize that if a set of items is in a random array, some system of arranging the array or keeping track of the items counted must be implemented in order to assure the proper application of the procedural knowledge and the conceptual principles.

Gelman's group has provided a variety of empirical data which they interpret as support for this theoretical account (e.g., Gelman & Meck, 1983). More important, perhaps, are the experiments which they interpret to show the interrelations among the three kinds of knowledge and how each feeds the other in the acquisition or development of the system of knowledge pertaining to counting. Thus, for example, Gelman, Meck, and Merkin (1986) report a set of experiments in which they found that 3- and 4-year-old preschool children appeared to be acquiring the knowledge that if a set of items in a linear array were counted, the number associated with an item also identifies its spatial location in the array. This appears to be a case in which conceptual knowledge develops through the implementation of procedural knowledge. The child learns something about the spatial domain and the relation of the numerical and spatial domains from the procedure developed to deal with counting. This seems to be a very nice indication of the emergent properties of conceptual knowledge resulting from the social interaction of the child on which Piaget placed so much emphasis. The interdependency among these knowledge domains may not be simple, however; as suggested by Miura, Kim, Chang, and Okamoto (1988) in connection with their cross-cultural observations, the structure of the language used by children may influence their cognitive representation of number.

This example of the child's acquisition of the knowledge domain pertaining to number is only illustrative. Parallel results are being reported for early cognitive development in other domains. For example, Flavell and his collaborators have focused recently on the child's ability to distinguish between the subjective and objective dimensions or, as he has tended to examine it, the appearance-reality distinction and the comprehension of the difference between the perspectives of self and other with respect to appearance (Flavell, Flavell, & Green, 1983). The recent finding that these distinctions are acquired earlier in the tactile than in the visual mode speaks to the issues of the conceptual knowledge-procedural knowledge distinctions, the independent development of knowledge domains, and/or a recursive model of cognitive development depending upon theoretical developments and further experimental exploration of these results (Flavell, Green, & Flavell, 1989). Similarly, the work of Perner and his associates (e.g., Perner & Ogden, 1988) on children's ability to imput mental states, Wellman's work on young children's ability to reason about beliefs (e.g., Wellman & Bartsch, 1988) and a variety of other approaches to the child's developing theory of mind (cf. Leslie, 1987), are interrelated and bear on the larger issues indicated above. There are at least some indications that children have a much higher degree of conceptual knowledge than anticipated on the received view and, if that is the case, it may be that cognitive development reflects the development of procedural and utilizational knowledge more than the development of conceptual knowledge.

KNOWLEDGE AND THE FUTURE
OF CHILD PSYCHOLOGY

The future of child psychology, on this account, lies in the exploration of the acquisition of knowledge of all kinds and the nature of the mental model or models that the child constructs to organize his or her knowledge about specific content areas, as well as the relationships among the models created for different content areas. As I see it, we will be working at two levels of analysis. First, at the abstract level where the concern will be with concepts and relations among concepts which are a part of the child's mental model or theory of the world. How does the child establish abstract categories and relate them to each other? For example, how does the child come to know what Rosch (Rosch, Mervis, Gray, Johnson, & Boyes-Braem, 1976) has called basic level concepts such as fish, bird, or mammal, their relations to each other at one level, to the concept of animal, living thing, and object at a more encompassing or more abstract level, and to the concepts of trout, robin, and cow at a more specific or lower level of abstraction.

Regardless of level, all of these words pertain to abstract classes, each of which has a meaning or sense. I use *sense* as the linguist or philosopher uses the term. The sense of the term *bird*, for example, is that knowledge we have of the concept bird which allows us to classify each of the indefinite number of birds that we could happen upon in our lives within the class of birds, while at the same time excluding all of the nonbirds. The sense of the concept of bird is not a list of features describing the concept bird, for the features must be in just the proper relationships to make a bird. Nor is the concept of bird a particular bird, it is an abstraction which makes it possible to know a bird when we see one—it is the sense of birdiness, if you will. Any particular bird to which we may apply the term is a referent of the concept bird, as opposed to the sense of the concept bird. The sense of the concept encompasses all the birds, while any particular referent bird may fail to fulfill all of the characteristics which are possible for members identified by the concept.

Interesting questions for child psychologists of the future relate to the source of concepts. Some surely are innate—that is to say, some of the concepts of humans are determined by the hard wiring which comes with each individual as a function of being a member of the species Homo sapiens as opposed to species of birds, cows, or fish. Thus, it is natural for each of these species to acquire those attributes, modes of conceptualizing, and behaviors characteristic of that species. Among birds, for example, it is natural for members of the species to produce a species-specific song. In the case of some species, the young must hear the song during a critical period to be able to produce the song; others can produce their song without such input. Almost no bird acquires the song of another species, even when exposed only to the song of the other species.

Members of the species Homo sapiens are predisposed to acquire language instead of song. As in the case of birds, however, humans appear to be innately predisposed to categorize speech sounds and separate them from other kinds of sounds such as music (Molfese, Freeman, & Palermo, 1975). Individuals of the species acquire the particular language or languages to which they happen to be exposed. As in the case of birds acquiring song, no explicit teaching is required for the human to acquire language. Regardless of the language, however, children acquire the language at about the same age and at the same rate.

The concept of naturalness, as used here, refers to the innate characteristics of the species which predispose its members to respond in characteristic ways, given some context. It is a slippery concept, because the predisposition and the context interact in all situations, forcing a consideration of relative influences in all cases. In extreme examples, the concept is clear; birds acquire songs and humans language. Neither acquires the other naturally. Furthermore, it is not only unnatural but impossible for birds to acquire language. In the human case, the child has the innate predisposition to make a conceptual distinction between, for example, the phoneme /p/ and the phoneme /b/. That being the case, he or she merely needs to be exposed to the two speech sounds, and the classification will be made. The infant, in this case, will treat them differently in the sense of putting them in two different categories and, in turn, responding to them differently. The phonemes /p/ and /b/ will have two different meanings for the infant the very first time the child encounters exemplars of those concepts.

We are likely to spend some time in the future establishing what is natural and what is not, that is, what children are innately predisposed to use as a basis for their concepts and how they acquire concepts that are based upon unnatural distinctions. While language as a cognitive content area seems to involve a large number of innate predispositions, the closely related content area of reading does not (Stuart & Colheart, 1988). It is natural to talk, it is unnatural to read. Thus, although it is natural for the human child to make the distinction between the phonemes /p/ and /b/, the distinction between the letters p and b, as teachers of reading well know, may be treated as equivalent by the same child. The two letters are treated as members of the same concept and, therefore, responded to as if they had the same meaning. Not until the child is forced to make an unnatural distinction can the two letters be differentiated and thereby given different meanings and, as a result, responded to differently.

In the case of the phonemes, a conceptual distinction may be identified on the basis of a single referential example, while in the letter case hundreds of examples may be required before a conceptual distinction can be established. An interesting question arises in the first case. Is the conceptual distinction possible without the referential instantiation; that is, can the child create the exemplars through knowledge of the abstract concept alone or must the exemplars impinge on the sensory apparatus before such differentiations are made?

Given that we do develop concepts and models of cognitive domains on the basis of our social interactions with events in our world, the second level of analysis will relate to how we construct models on the basis of singular referents, that is, on the basis of single exemplars or events instantiating those models. Since one interaction with a single event can not inform us about all the information we might expect to know about that event, models of the event must be constructed with default values, inferences, implications, and presuppositions which extend the models beyond the particulars of the event. At the same time, the particular model constructed is constrained to one of an infinite number of possible models for a particular exemplar or life event.

Let me present an example to illustrate some of the points I wish to make. The following is a simple and very short story to illustrate the idea I have in mind.

> Gene and Mary were invited to Fred's party. Not long after they arrived, Mary fell into Fred's lap. Gene, watching from the other side of the room, turned to Louise, who was pulling her hand out of the punch bowl, and said "My sister loves Fred but she is a jerk." On their way home from the party, Gene told his mom that Mary would never forget Fred's eighth birthday.

As you read this story, you constructed a model of a world populated by people including Gene, Mary, Fred, and Louise. Now, if I am not mistaken, the model you constructed had to be drastically revised upon reading the last sentence. Prior to the last sentence, I suspect that among other assumptions you made in constructing a model to give meaning to these verbally described events was the assumption that Gene, Mary, and Fred were adults, or at least beyond the age of puberty. You probably had an alcoholic drink in the punch bowl, some assumptions about the relation between alcohol and Mary's falling, and some assumptions about the relationship between Gene and Mary. In fact, my guess is that you would be quite likely to say that Mary is Gene's sister, although you might not be quite so sure that Gene is Mary's brother. Neither relationship is specified in the story, and Gene's name is, of course, deliberately ambiguous regarding sex (at least in the oral version) until the last sentence. Finally, you probably filled in the default values for the people such that they had clothes on, arms, legs, noses and so on.

The point of this exercise is to make clear the fact that we construct mental models, minitheories of what events in our world are all about and what the meaning of those events is for us. Johnson-Laird (1983) has recently presented a convincing case for the construction of mental models in his book by that name (but see Rips, 1986, for a critical analysis). We constantly are constructing such mental models, and I have argued elsewhere (e.g., Palermo, 1986) that we each have our own personal theory of the world, that is, a more general model, within which such minimodels or schemata are constructed. The theory, and the models within the theory, are not limited to linguistic input; we regularly construct models of what we see, hear, taste, etc. We construct models of what happened in the past and will happen in the future. As Lewin (1946) pointed out, we can even construct models of what we wish would have happened in the past and what we hope will happen in the future. Somewhat paradoxically, it is easier to comprehend that we can construct models of what could have been and what might be than of what is, what was, and what will be.

In any case, the models and the more general theory are based upon what we know. It's what we know that lets us grow. What we know, however, is a complicated issue which implies an exciting future for child psychologists. As we have already noted, what we know is already partially wired into the system, because we are members of a particular biological species that knows different things and in different ways than other biological species. We know the difference between speech and nonspeech, or /p/ and /b/, in a way unknown to the clam or the dog, for example. The clam cannot know these distinctions for lack of an auditory system, and the dog for lack of an auditory system for which those distinctions are categorically separated. The dog, of course, can know other distinctions, in the higher frequencies for example, which humans cannot know (without mechanical aid). Furthermore, the dog can learn some of the distinctions humans know naturally, while the clam can never know any of them.

The question of what infants know by virtue of their species characteristics is an interesting developmental question. Perhaps more interesting is the question of the constraints upon human knowledge. What is not natural but can be learned, and what is both unnatural and unlearnable? As with any other psychological question, we need to know about individual differences. What variations in the biological system allow for knowledge, force knowledge to be learned, or prevent knowledge from being acquired? Study of the learning-disabled child may give us some clues here.

More interesting to me are questions related to model or theory building per se. In the construction of a model or a theory the child, as the adult, cannot know everything to make the theory complete. Both child and adult must and do construct their theory on the basis of what they know and what they presuppose, assume, and infer—in a sense, on what they think they know. Thus the question of what we know and what we think we know often gets confused. In the case of the story I presented earlier, until the last sentence most likely you thought you knew that the story was about adults, and that Mary was Gene's sister, but neither of those bits of knowledge were ever given in the story. You made them up as a part of the coherent model you created and from which you would draw at a future time if you were to discuss or answer questions about the story. Note that, if I were to change only the names of the characters in the story, I could change what you assume you know about the story event. If I had named the people Suzie, Jeanie, and Bobby, you might have constructed a story about children at the beginning, since we use those kinds of names for children but less often for adults. If I had instead named the three main characters Martha-Jean, Sarah-Jane, and Billy-Bob, you might have been convinced that the party took place south of the Mason-Dixon line. The point is that the child, as the adult, uses all of the knowledge at his or her disposal for constructing a model of the domain under consideration at any point in time.

Let me emphasize that I am not limiting this type of construction to verbal materials. We do this type of filling in to complete our model in all situations. If we enter a room which has another door in it, we assume another room beyond the door. If I indicate that I will sign my student's dissertation with my pen, the student assumes I will use an instrument about six inches long and an inch or so in circumference; furthermore, he or she assumes that there will be an ink in that pen which will last at least until the graduate school approves the dissertation. While I have never used disappearing ink for such important occasions, I have noticed quite remarkable reactions from my students when I pull out a pen for signing such documents which is three inches in circumference and eleven inches long.

Most of the time, however, we have no problems with the assumptions, inferences, and presuppositions that we make in constructing theories or models of our world. Most of the time we don't even distinguish between what we assume, infer, and presume and what we actually know. Furthermore, we seldom realize that many other models would be consistent with what we know. We rarely notice the ambiguity of events, that is, the multiple meanings which could be given to those events. We act on the basis of our theory and successfully keep out of trouble with the world, because, most of the time, our theory is close enough to what does happen in the world that we have no problems. If there is not a room beyond the door in the room we enter, either the door is locked, boarded up on the other side, or a part of a Marx brother's movie in which our assumption is made fun of in a humorous way. Note that our knowledge is incorporated in a model about how we think the world ought to be and not about how the world actually is. It is a theory of how we understand the world to be at any particular moment, and, as a theory, it is subject to error.

Child psychologists, however, will spend some time in the future figuring out what children know, what they assume, presuppose, infer, and how they put it all together in their developing theory of the world. It will not be an easy task, because it will continue to be necessary to construct convergent forms of evidence on which to base theoretical inferences about mind. We have come a long way from the early experiments showing that imitation, comprehension, and production yield different results leaving the researcher in a quandary regarding what the child knows (Fraser, Bellugi, & Brown, 1963). It has become clear, as I have suggested in another paper on this general topic (Palermo, 1983), that children's comprehension and production of language is a complex interaction among such factors as the way the particular referents are used in the task, the way they are referred to, the syntax of the instructions, the contextual situation in which linguistic and referential objects are presented, and the knowledge the child has of the referents and their relationships. Often an experimental situation leads to an underestimation of the child's knowledge because that context is unfamiliar. Sometimes an experimenter will note that the child uses the same forms outside the experiment which seem to be totally bewildering in the experimental context that may seem very strange to the child. Sensitivity to these issues combined with ingenious experimental procedures can usually solve these kinds of difficulties.

More serious problems have been raised recently by Bowerman (1985a), who has noted what she calls "late errors" in the acquisition process. She has suggested that such late errors may involve spontaneous reorganizations of semantic knowledge that occur 2 or 3 years after the child has been credited with knowledge of particular language forms. Almost everyone is familiar with this phenomenon in connection with the order in which past tense inflectional forms in English are acquired. Children acquire some of the irregular forms first, followed by learning the regular forms, overgeneralization of the regular to the irregular forms and, finally, both regular and irregular forms are used correctly. Bowerman has found many other instances of this type of phenomenon, except that, in some cases, the shift in performance from correct to error may be a year, or sometimes as much as 3 years, later followed by recorrection at a new level of knowledge. Bowerman has been able to note these kinds of semantic reorganizational events through careful observations of small numbers of children. Such observations have always been fruitful additions to our understanding of children and often have provided the stimulant to experiments designed to test the hypotheses which come from the initial natural observations. Experimental explorations of related mental reorganizations taking place over 1- to 3-year periods will, however, take considerable creativity on the part of future researchers. The work of Nelson and his collaborators (e.g., Baker & Nelson, 1984) on the influence of input targeted to specific structures may provide useful hints toward an approach that would show the relationships between input forms and the shifting organization of the child's mental knowledge of representational systems.

Other efforts in the near future will try to establish specific models of particular language or cognitive domains followed by attention to the transfer dilemma, as Diana Kuhn (1986a) calls it. The transfer dilemma refers to the ability to recognize and use the relevant aspects of a model developed in one domain to apply to a new and/or different domain. Her question, thus, becomes one of determining under what circumstances a structure d'ensemble is possible.

Kuhn is also interested in the conditions under which data influence the formulation or modification of the child's model or theory. We are aware that scientists do not consider all of the data in formulating theories; they attend to and incorporate only those data they feel are relevant. Kuhn has begun to explore similar cases with children (Kuhn, 1986b). Her findings suggest that there is a complex interaction between incoming information and one's changing model of the domain in both child and adult groups. On one hand, new data contrary to the theory held by an individual are unlikely to be viewed as contradicting the theory and, therefore, do not necessitate a theory revision. On the other hand, new data that are not only partially supportive of the theory, but also partially contradictory to the theory, are viewed as supportive of the theory. These data indicate that establishing how mental models and theories are created, and how they may be modified as the child engages his or her environment, promises to be no simple task. It looks to be a scientific problem well worth the attention of future child psychologists, both in terms of the intellectual challenges it poses as well as the payoff in our understanding of the mind of the developing child.

A recent volume edited by Gentner and Stevens (1983; see also Chi, Glaser, & Farr, 1988) is devoted to efforts to understand how individuals move from novice theories to expert theories of pocket calculators, space and motion, physics problems, heat and temperature relations, among other kinds of problems about which each of us has a theory at a more or less advanced level. Most of the researchers who contributed to this volume are looking at the models of adults. All of us know that looking at the developing child will give us the answers they seek.

Let me close this crystal-ball-gazing effort with one more reference to Lewin. It seems to me that, today, we are in a much better position to understand Lewin's theory. His phenomenologically oriented theory was a predecessor of today's mental model theories. He understood that the child's conception of the world needs to be understood if we are to understand the behavior or, more important, the mind that governs that behavior. Yesterday he had difficulty explicating how one could go about establishing the child's theory of the world, model of the task, or structure of the life space, to use his term. Today, after our experience with Piaget and Chomsky, perhaps it is time to reevaluate the formula that behavior is a function of the person and the environment as viewed by the person. Perhaps, it is time to explore Lewin's theory of how the child's life space expands on the dimensions of reality and irreality, past and future, and the differentiation of knowledge areas, as well as the constructs of force, valence, and personal goals. Now we can not only understand the theory but have the research sophistication to test the ideas implicit within the theory. Let's reread his work before we reinvent his ideas. Dressed up in the terminology of mental models, Kurt Lewin may look very handsome to those who will plot the future of child psychology.

CONCLUSIONS

Whether we are directing our attentions to language and cognitive development or to any other aspect of developmental psychology, we begin with a biological organism. Piaget, a biologist by training, was concerned about the manner in which the child comes to transcend the biological limits through the development of cognitive structures. The present chapter has suggested that the structures do not change, but, rather, that changes occur in the amount of knowledge the child constructs within the framework of the child's conceptualization of the world and how it works. As Piaget suggested, those changes occur as a function of the processes of assimilation and accommodation to the theory the child has developed at any particular moment. Regardless of which of these proposals is correct, any theory of child development must take into account the biological structure of the child and the constraints placed upon development in other areas by that biological structure.

If we are to study the child's acquisition of language, we certainly need to have some understanding of the structure of language. Psychologists must make the effort to explore the field of linguistics for at least two reasons. First, the obvious need to understand the complexities involved in the language a child seems to master with such relative ease. In the past, psychologists paid little attention to linguistics until Chomsky became critical of psychologists for their ignorance. Psychologists took up the challenge in the late 1950s and in the 1960s, but the linguistics they learned soon changed and psychologists became disillusioned with the fact that they always seemed to be working with an outdated set of linguistic information in their research. Many gave up on what they considered a fickle or, at best, an unstable field. Although it may have been the case that the field of linguistics was in rapid transition at that time, it remains necessary to understand the nature of language if psychologists are to pursue the psychology of language and the acquisition process. In addition, it is of value to study linguistics to become familiar with the critical and theoretical processes linguists employ in the pursuit of their subject matter. Psychologists are well trained in empirical approaches to obtaining critical observations relevant to hypotheses they may develop, but they are not as sophisticated in the development of theory and the critical evaluation of theories once they are proposed. The study of linguistics is well worth the effort from that perspective.

Epistemology is another area into which psychologists, particularly psychologists in the psycholinguistic and cognitive fields, need to delve. While many psychologists agree that knowledge plays an important part in the acquisition of language as well as in cognitive development, few have a deep knowledge of what philosophers have discovered about that topic. Psychologists often make statements about knowledge that might seem quite naive, at best, from the perspective of anyone familiar with the vast writings in the philosophical literature since the time of Plato. Matters pertaining to the differences between knowledge that and knowledge how, knowledge by acquaintance and knowledge by description, knowledge and belief, knowledge and truth, and evidence which may be taken as supportive of knowledge have all received extensive attention from philosophers and should be familiar to psychologists who wish to investigate the acquisition of knowledge or invoke knowledge as an explanation of other phenomena (see Palermo, 1989, for a discussion of these matters).

In short, there is no short-cut to an understanding of the child's acquisition of language and a cognitive theory of the domains of knowledge which occupy the human mind. One needs a familiarity with biology, developmental psychology, linguistics, epistemology, convergent research methods, the nature of theory, and the relation of theory to critical evaluation by rational and empirical methods. Nobody said it would be easy, but the excitement of reaching into the area and discovering the answers to Toulmin's challenge about what it means to say that the child "recognizes" or "knows" or "perceives" something should make the future of the field attractive to the finest minds.

REFERENCES

Baker, N. D., & Nelson, K. E. (1984). Recasting and related conversational techniques for triggering syntactic advances by young children. *First Language, 5,* 51–62.

Beilin, H. (1984). Dispensable and core elements in Piaget's research program. *The Genetic Epistemologist, 13*(3), 1–16.

Beilin, H. (1987). Current trends in cognitive development research: Towards a new synthesis. In B. Inhelder, D. de Caprona, & A. Cornu-Wells (Eds.), *Piaget today.* Hillsdale, NJ: Erlbaum.

Bever, T. G. (1970). The cognitive basis for linguistic structures. In J. R. Hayes (Ed.), *Cognition and the development of language* (pp. 279–352). New York: Wiley.

Birge, J. (1941). *The role of verbal responses in transfer.* Unpublished doctoral dissertation, Yale University, New Haven, CT.

Bloom, L. (1970). *Language development.* Cambridge, MA: MIT Press.

Bloom, L., Lightbown, P., & Hood, L. (1975). Structure and variation in child language. *Monographs of the Society for Research in Child Development, 40* (1), Serial No. 160.

Bowerman, M. (1985a). Beyond communicative adequacy: From piecemeal knowledge to an integrated system in the child's acquisition of language. In K. E. Nelson (Ed.), *Children's language* (Vol. 5, pp. 369–398). Hillsdale, NJ: Erlbaum.

Bowerman, M. (1985b). What shapes children's grammars? In D. I. Slobin (Ed.), *The crosslinguistic study of language acquisition. Vol. 2: Theoretical issues* (pp. 1257–1319). Hillsdale, NJ: Erlbaum.

Braine, M. D. S. (1963). The ontogeny of English phrase structure: The first phase. *Language, 39,* 1–13.

Brainerd, C. J. (1978). The stage question in cognitive-developmental theory. *Behavioral and Brain Sciences, 1,* 171–213.

Brown, R., Fraser, C., & Bellugi, U. (1964). Explorations in grammar evaluation. In U. Bellugi & R. Brown (Eds.), *The acquisition of language. Monographs of the Society for Research in Child Development,* Serial No. 92, *29*(1), 79–92.

Cantor, J. H., & Spiker, C. C. (1982). The effect of the temporal locus of the introtract probe on the hypothesis-testing strategies of kindergarten children. *Journal of Experimental Child Psychology, 34,* 510–525.

Chapman, M. (1988). *Constructive evolution: Origins and development of Piaget's thought.* Cambridge, UK: Cambridge University Press.

Chi, M. T. H. (1978). Knowledge structures and memory development. In R. Siegler (Ed.), *Children's thinking: What develops?* (pp. 73–96). Hillsdale, NJ: Erlbaum.

Chi, M. T. H., Glaser, R., & Farr, M. J. (1988). *The nature of expertise.* Hillsdale, NJ: Erlbaum.

Chomsky, N. (1957). *Syntactic structures.* The Hague: Mouton.

Chomsky, N. (1959). Review of *Verbal behavior* by B. F. Skinner. *Language, 35,* 26–58.

Cohen, L. B., & Younger, B. A. (1983). Perceptual categorization in the infant. In E. K. Scholnick (Ed.), *New trends in conceptual representation: Changes in Piaget's theory* (pp. 197–220). Hillsdale, NJ: Erlbaum.

deVilliers, J. G. (1980). The process of rule learning in child speech: A new look. In K. E. Nelson (Ed.), *Children's language* (Vol. 2, pp. 1–44). New York: Gardner Press.

Flavell, J. H. (1963). *The developmental psychology of Jean Piaget.* New York: Van Nostrand Reinhold.

Flavell, J. H. (1971). Stage-related properties of cognitive development. *Cognitive Psychology, 2,* 421–453.

Flavell, J. H., Flavell, E. R., & Green, F. L. (1983). Development of the appearance-reality distinction. *Cognitive Psychology, 15,* 95–120.

Flavell, J. H., Green, F. L. & Flavell, E. R. (1989). Young children's ability to differentiate appearance-reality and level 2 perspective in the tactile modality. *Child Development, 60,* 201–213.

Flavell, J. H., & Wohlwill, J. F. (1969). Formal and functional aspects of cognitive development. In D. Elkind & J. H. Flavell (Eds.), *Studies in cognitive development: Essays in honor of Jean Piaget* (pp. 69–120). New York: Oxford University Press.

Fraser, C., Bellugi, U., & Brown, R. (1963). Control of grammar in imitation, comprehension, and production. *Journal of Verbal Learning and Verbal Behavior, 2,* 121–135.

Gazzaniga, M. S. (1983). Right hemisphere language following brain bisection: A 20-year perspective. *American Psychologist, 38,* 525–537.

Gelman, R. (1977). How young children reason about small numbers. In N. J. Castellan, D. P. Pisoni, & C. R. Potts (Eds.), *Cognitive theory* (Vol. 2, pp. 219–238). Hillsdale, NJ: Erlbaum.

Gelman, R., & Gallistel, C. R. (1978). *The child's understanding of number.* Cambridge, MA: Harvard University Press.

Gelman, R., & Meck, E. (1983). Preschoolers' counting: Principles before skill. *Cognition, 13,* 343–359.

Gelman, R., & Meck, E. (1986). The notion of principle: The case of counting. In J. Hiebert (Ed.), *Conceptual and procedural knowledge: The case of mathematics* (pp. 29–57). Hillsdale, NJ: Erlbaum.

Gelman, R., Meck, E., & Merkin, S. (1986). Young children's numerical competence. *Cognitive Development, 1,* 1–29.

Gentner, D., & Stevens, A. L. (1983). *Mental models.* Hillsdale, NJ: Erlbaum.

Gesell, A., & Thompson, H. (1943). Learning and maturation in identical twins. In R. G. Barker, J. S. Kounin, & H. F. Wright (Eds.), *Child behavior and development* (pp. 209–228). New York: McGraw-Hill.

Greeno, J. G., Riley, M. S., & Gelman, R. (1984) Conceptual competence and children's counting. *Cognitive Psychology, 16,* 94–143.

Hardy, J. A., & Braine, M. D. S. (1981). Categories that bridge between meaning and syntax in five-year-olds. In W. Deutsch (Ed.), *The child's construction of language* (pp. 201–222). New York: Academic Press.

Jenkins, J. J. (1963). Mediated associations: Paradigms and situations. In C. N. Cofer & B. S. Musgrave (Eds.), *Verbal behavior and learning: Problems and processes* (pp. 210–244). New York: McGraw-Hill.

Jenkins, J. J., & Palermo, D. S. (1964). Mediation processes and the acquisition of linguistic structure. In U. Bellugi & R. Brown (Eds.), *The acquisition of language. Monographs of the Society for Research in Child Development, 29*(1), Serial No. 92., 141–169.

Jersild, A. T., & Holmes, F. B. (1936). Children's fears. *Child Development Monographs* (No. 20). New York: Teacher's College, Columbia University.

Johnson-Laird, P. N. (1983). *Mental models.* Cambridge, MA: Harvard University Press.

Kail, R., & Nippold, M. A. (1984). Unconstrained retrieval from semantic memory. *Child Development, 55,* 944–951.

Kann, J. (1950). A translation of Broca's original article on the location of speech centers. *Journal of Speech and Hearing Disorders, 15,* 16–20.

Kantor, J. R. (1935). *An objective psychology of grammar.* Bloomington, IN: Principia Press.

Karmiloff-Smith, A. (1978). The interplay between syntax, semantics, and phonology in language acquisition processes. In R. N. Campbell & P. T. Smith (Ed.), *Recent advances in the psychology of language* (Vol. 4a, pp. 1–24). New York: Plenum.

Karmiloff-Smith, A. (1988, June). *Beyond modularity: Innate constraints and developmental change.* Keynote presentation, Eighteenth Annual Symposium of the Jean Piaget Society.

Keil, F. C. (1979). *Semantic and conceptual development: An ontological perspective.* Cambridge, MA: Harvard University Press.

Keil, F. C. (1981). Constraints on knowledge and cognitive development. *Psychological Review, 88,* 197–227.

Kendler, T. S., & Kendler, H. H. (1959). Reversal and nonreversal shifts in kindergarten children. *Journal of Experimental Psychology, 58,* 56–60.

Kessen, W., & Nelson, K. (1978). What the child brings to language. In B. Z. Presseisen, D. Goldstein, & M. H. Appel (Eds.), *Topics in cognitive development* (pp. 17–30). New York: Plenum.

Kuczaj, S. A., & Barrett, M. D. (Eds.). (1986). *The development of word meaning: Progress in cognitive development research.* New York: Springer Verlag.

Kuenne, M. R. (1946). Experimental investigation of the relation of language to transposition behavior in young children. *Journal of Experimental Psychology, 36,* 471–490.

Kuhn, D. (1986a). Education for thinking. *Teachers College Record, 87,* 495–512.

Kuhn, D. (1986b, June). *Coordinating theory and evidence in reasoning.* Invited address to the Jean Piaget Society Symposium, Philadelphia, PA.

Kuhn, T. S. (1962). *The structure of scientific revolutions.* Chicago: University of Chicago Press.

Lakatos, I. (1970). Falsification and the methodology of scientific research programs. In I. Lakatos & A. Musgrave (Eds.), *Criticism and the growth of knowledge* (pp. 91–195). London: Cambridge University Press.

Langer, J. (1980). *The origins of logic: Six to twelve months.* New York: Academic Press.

Langer, J. (1986). *The origins of logic: One to two years.* New York: Academic Press.

Lenneberg, E. H. (1967). *Biological foundations of language.* New York: Wiley.

Leslie, A. M. (1987). Pretense and representation: The origins of "Theory of Mind." *Psychological Review, 94,* 412–426.

Lewin, K. (1935). *A dynamic theory of personality: Selected papers.* New York: McGraw-Hill.

Lewin, K. (1946). Behavior and development as a function of the total situation. In L. Carmichael (Ed.), *Manual of child psychology* (pp. 791–844). New York: Wiley.

Lewin, K. (1951). *Field theory in social science: Selected theoretical papers* (D. Cartwright, Ed.). New York: Harper & Bros.

Lieberman, P. (1977). *Speech physiology and acoustic phonetics.* New York: Macmillan.

Locke, J. L. (1983). *Phonological acquisition and change.* New York: Academic Press.

Macken, M. S., & Ferguson, C. S. (1983). Cognitive aspects of phonological development: Model, evidence, and issues. In K. E. Nelson (Ed.), *Children's language* (Vol. 4, pp. 256–282). Hillsdale, NJ: Erlbaum.

Macnamara, J. (1982). *Names for things.* Cambridge, MA: MIT Press.

Macnamara, J. (1986). *Border dispute: The place of logic in psychology.* Cambridge, MA: Bradford/MIT Press.

Mandler, J. M. (1983). Structural invariants in development. In L. S. Liben (Ed.), *Piaget and the foundations of knowledge* (pp. 97–124) Hillsdale, NJ: Erlbaum.

Maratsos, M. P., & Chalkley, M. A. (1980). The internal language of children's syntax: The ontogenesis and representation of syntactic categories. In K. E. Nelson (Ed.), *Children's language* (Vol. 2, pp. 127–214). New York: Gardner Press.

McCandless, B. R., & Spiker, C. C. (1956). Experimental research in child psychology. *Child Development, 27,* 75–80.

McCarthy, D. (1954). Language development in children. In L. Carmichael

(Ed.), *Manual of child psychology* (2nd ed., pp. 492–630). New York: Wiley.

McNeill, D. (1970). *The acquisition of language: The study of developmental psycholinguistics.* New York: Harper & Row.

Mehler, J., Jusczyk, P., Lambertz, G., Halsted, N., Bertoncini, J., & Amiel-Tison, C. (1988). A precursor of language acquisition in young infants. *Cognition, 29,* 143–178.

Miller, W., & Ervin, S. (1964). The development of grammar in child language. In U. Bellugi & R. Brown (Eds.), *Monographs of the Society for Research in Child Development, 29*(1), Serial No. 92, 9–34.

Miura, I. T., Kim, C. C., Chang, C., & Okamoto, Y. (1988). Effects of language characteristics on children's cognitive representation of number: Cross-national comparisons. *Child Development, 59,* 1445–1450.

Molfese, D. L. (1985). Electrophysiological correlates of semantic features. *Journal of Psycholinguistic Research, 14,* 289–299.

Molfese, D. L., Freeman, R. B., Jr., & Palermo, D. S. (1975). The ontogeny of brain lateralization for speech and non-speech stimuli. *Brain and Language, 2,* 356–368.

Molfese, D. L., & Molfese, V. J. (1980). Cortical responses of preterm infants to phonetic and nonphonetic speech stimuli. *Developmental Psychology, 16,* 574–581.

Molfese, D. L., & Molfese, V. J. (1985). Electrophysiological indices of auditory discrimination in newborn infants: The bases for predicting later language development? *Infant Behavior and Development, 8,* 197–211.

Nelson, K. (1981). Individual differences in language development: Implications for development and language. *Developmental Psychology, 17,* 170–187.

Norcross, K. J. (1958). Effects on discrimination performance of similarity of previously acquired stimulus names. *Journal of Experimental Psychology, 56,* 305–309.

Nowlis, V., & Nowlis, H. H. (1952). Child psychology. *Annual review of psychology* (pp. 1–28). Palo Alto, CA: Annual Reviews, Inc.

Overton, W. F. (In Press). The structure of developmental theory. In P. van Geert & L. P. Mos (Eds.), *Annals of theoretical psychology* (Vol. 7).

Palermo, D. S. (1983). Looking to the future: Theory and research in language and cognitive development. In Th. B. Seiler & W. Wannenmacher (Eds.), *Concept development and the development of word meaning* (pp. 297–319). New York: Springer-Verlag.

Palermo, D. S. (1984). Cognition and language development. In M. D. Levine & P. Satz (Eds.), *Middle childhood: Development and dysfunction* (pp. 3–29). Baltimore: University Park Press.

Palermo, D. S. (1986). From the marble mass of language, a view of the developing mind. *Metaphor and symbolic activity, 1,* 5–23.

Palermo, D. S. (1989). Knowledge and the child's developing theory of the world. In H. Reese (Ed.), *Advances in child behavior and development* (Vol. 21, pp. 269–295). New York: Academic Press.

Palermo, D. S., & Lipsitt, L. P. (1963). Research readings in child psychology. New York: Holt, Rinehart & Winston.

Palermo, D. S., & Molfese, D. (1972). Language acquisition from age five onward. Psychological Bulletin, 78, 409–428.

Pepper, S. C. (1970). World hypotheses: A study in evidence. Berkeley, CA: University of California Press.

Perner, J., & Ogden, J. E. (1988). Knowledge for hunger: Children's problem with representation in imputing mental states. Cognition, 29, 47–61.

Piaget, J. (1926). The language and thought of the child. New York: Harcourt, Brace.

Piaget, J. (1970). Piaget's theory. In P. H. Mussen (Ed.), Manual of child psychology (Vol. 1, pp. 703–732). New York: Wiley.

Piaget, J. (1971). Biology and knowledge. Chicago: University of Chicago Press.

Piattelli-Palmarini, M. (1980). Language and learning: The debate between Jean Piaget and Norm Chomsky. Cambridge, MA: Harvard University Press.

Pye, C., Ingram, D., & List, H. (1988). A comparison of initial consonant acquisition in English and Quiche. In K. E. Nelson & A. Van Kleeck (Eds.), Children's language (Vol. 6, pp. 175–190). Hillsdale, NJ: Erlbaum.

Quinn, P. C. (1987). The categorical representation of visual pattern information by young infants. Cognition, 27, 145–179.

Rips, L. J. (1986). Mental muddles. In M. Brand & R. M. Harnish (Eds.), The representation of knowledge and belief (pp. 258–286) Tucson, AZ: University of Arizona Press.

Rosch, E., Mervis, C. B., Gray, W. D., Johnson, D. M., & Boyes-Braem, P. (1976). Basic objects in natural categories. Cognitive Psychology, 8, 382–439.

Segalowitz, S., & Molfese, D. (1987). Developmental implications of brain lateralization. New York: Guilford Press.

Sinclair, H. J. (1975). The role of cognitive structures in language acquisition. In E. H. Lenneberg & E. Lenneberg (Eds.), Foundations of language development (Vol. 1). New York: Academic Press.

Sinclair, H. J., Stambak, M., Lézine, I., Rayna, S., & Verba, M. (1989). Infants and objects: The creativity of cognitive development. New York: Academic Press.

Slobin, D. I. (1971). The ontogenesis of grammar. New York: Academic Press.

Slobin, D. I. (1973). Cognitive prerequisites for the development of grammar. In C. A. Ferguson & D. I. Slobin (Eds.), Studies of child language development (pp. 175–208). New York: Holt, Rinehart & Winston.

Slobin, D. I. (1985). Crosslinguistic evidence for the language-making capacity. In D. I. Slobin (Ed.), The crosslinguistic study of language acquisition. Vol. 2: Theoretical issues (pp. 1157–1256). Hillsdale, NJ: Erlbaum.

Spence, K. W. (1956). Behavior theory and conditioning. New Haven, CT: Yale University Press.

Spence, K. W. (1960). Behavior theory and learning. Englewood Cliffs, NJ: Prentice-Hall.

Stuart, M., & Colheart, M. (1988). Does reading develop in a sequence of stages? Cognition, 30, 139–181.

Sudhalter, V., & Braine, M. D. S. (1985). How does comprehension of passives develop? A comparison of actional and experiential verbs. *Journal of Child Language, 12,* 455–470.

Toulmin, S. (1971). The concept of "stages" is psychological development. In T. Mischel (Ed.), *Cognitive development and epistemology* (pp. 25–60). New York: Academic Press.

Valian, V. (1986). Syntactic categories in the speech of young children. *Developmental Psychology, 22,* 562–579.

Waggoner, J. E., Messe, M. J., & Palermo, D. S. (1985). Grasping the meaning of metaphor: Story recall and comprehension. *Child Development, 56,* 1156–1166.

Waggoner, J. E., & Palermo, D. S. (1989). Betty is a bouncing bubble: Children's comprehension of emotion-descriptive metaphors. *Developmental Psychology, 25,* 152–163.

Weimer, W. B. (1977). A conceptual framework for cognitive psychology: Motor theories of the mind. In R. E. Shaw & J. D. Bransford (Eds.), *Perceiving, acting, and knowing: Toward an ecological psychology* (pp. 267–311). Hillsdale, NJ: Erlbaum.

Weimer, W. B. (1979). *Notes on the methodology of scientific research.* Hillsdale, NJ: Erlbaum.

Wellman, H. M., & Bartsch, K. (1988). Young children's reasoning about beliefs. *Cognition, 30,* 239–277.

Werker, J. F. (1989). Becoming a native listener. *American Scientist, 77,* 54–59.

Wernicke, C. (1874). Der aphasische symptomencomplex. *Eine psychologische studie auf anatomischer basis.* Breslau: Cohen & Weigert.

chapter 5

Behavioral Development: Universals and Nonuniversals Training for a Universalized Developmental Perspective*

Frances Degen Horowitz
The University of Kansas

Physicists, biologists, and chemists often express bewilderment at the issues that bedevil behavioral scientists. Unlike the older, more codified, sciences, behavior science can appear to be in disarray with respect to methodology, theory, and even the acceptance of the elemental laws. Although there seems to be agreement in the commonality of the contents of the basic textbooks in the field, the fact is that there is no strong consensus on such fundamental issues as whether the simple laws of conditioning can significantly influence the behavioral repertoire of the normal human organism.

Nowhere are these issues more commonly focused than in the area of child psychology, child development, and developmental psychology. Where behaviorism once held sway, organismic theory took over. Where Freud's psychodynamic view was previously dominant, no overall theoretical view or solid, widely accepted empirical body of

* Most of the content of this chapter was originally presented as an invited address at the International Society for the Study of Behavioral Development meeting in Tours, France, in July 1985, and again at the conference on Future Directions in Child Psychology at the University of Iowa in 1986. The ideas presented here represent a kind of precis of the main themes in the author's book *Exploring Developmental Theories: Toward a Structural/Behavioral Model of Development*, published by Erlbaum in 1987. The author acknowledges the helpfulness of John Colombo for his critical reading of the initial draft of this chapter and of Lew Lipsitt's assiduous editing contributions.

data has been substituted. Yet we all study behavior. But how we pose our questions and organize our interpretations reflects, I think, differing emphases in relation to the nature of the phenomena we hope to codify in the form of laws.

The diversity of our enterprise is everywhere apparent. Some of us catalog behaviors at different ages and call that development. Some of us describe the conditions that result in the occurrence of children's behavior and that exert control over behavior; we identify such activity as doing child psychology. When we chart the course of the appearance of behavior, its metamorphosis and its elaboration, we emphasize development as our domain of interest and refer to ourselves as developmentalists. We may invoke principles of learning in the study of behavior, and principles of development, without inquiring into the unity of these two sets of principles in a presumably single human organism.

The potential for the unity of these two sets of principles, and the implications for training the students who will be the future scientific leaders of the field, are the focal points for this chapter. The primary question is whether a theoretical and empirical integration is possible such that essentially separate arenas of thinking and research might be joined into a more comprehensive, universal account of behavioral development (Horowitz, 1987). If the structural/behavioral model proposed here succeeds in this integration, there are implications for a universalized developmental and child psychology and, in turn, for graduate programs in developmental and child psychology.

HISTORICAL BACKGROUND

Our theoretical roots all find their historical base in the early part of this century, with differential emphasis upon development and behavior, depending upon the theory. Arnold Gesell (Gesell, Amatruda, Castner, & Thompson, 1939; Gesell, 1954), James Mark Baldwin (1906) and Jean Piaget (1926, 1983) emphasized sequential events, which were believed to reflect the strong influence of the evolutionary history of the human species. Sequential events were regarded as demonstrating an inevitable unfolding of the human behavioral repertoire. Piaget took this point of view but emphasized an active interplay of the organism and the environment as responsible for the behavioral unfolding. Gesell focused more on sequences, emphasizing innate developmental growth principles to account for the phenomena described.

Piaget's and Gesell's data were persuasive because they appeared to represent a universality of organized and structured behavioral development. Such an emphasis fits well with Waddington's ideas about a highly probable predetermined general course of development (Waddington, 1966). This is reflected in Waddington's concept of canalization: Deviance or variations from the normal course in most normal organisms are but temporary phenomena. The inherent "righting" forces will, under normal environmental circumstances, exert strong influence in bringing the organism back onto the normal track of development because of the deeply wrought grooves of evolutionary history which predispose the organism to a given developmental course.

The analogical example for canalization is represented by a ball rolling down a deep valley. Its individual journey may take it up onto one side of the valley and perhaps over onto the other side. Ultimately, it will find its basic course reestablished as it comes back to the central groove and moves along a highly probable path to a highly probable outcome. Thus, all normal human infants will eventually smile, will gain increasingly sophisticated motoric control, will move through a series of cognitive stages, and will develop the capacity to communicate—despite temporary delays or deviant byways, despite vastly different environments and child-rearing conditions. In Waddington's view, normality is destined to prevail, and the normal developmental course of the typical human organism will occur.

What processes may be invoked to account for these normative human characteristics? According to Piaget, there is an interplay between an active organism and a rather universal basic environment. Through the processes of assimilation and accommodation by which the organism interacts with the environment, there will be an inevitable construction of behavioral structures in an organized sequence of stages. Piagetians acknowledge that the child must "learn" the behaviors through reciprocal relationships with the environment for behavioral development to occur. The processes by which learning is thought to occur, however, have been of lesser interest, generally, than the unfolding story of the sequential laws that describe behavioral development. The mechanisms of assimilation and accommodation are embedded in analogies tucked far away from the experimental knife. These processes cannot be dissected for component parts and are not necessarily related to the known laws of learning. Learning is, in this view, generally regarded as almost trivial and hardly worth elevation to the role of central processes involved in behavioral development.

A quite other point of view prevails among those most interested in learning processes themselves. The study of learning has been largely in the province of behaviorists, who trace their historical roots to John B. Watson (Watson & Rayner, 1920; Watson, 1924), Pavlov (1960), Hull (1943), and Skinner (1938, 1953). In the behavioristic perspective there are a few innate responses to particular stimulus conditions. All other responses are thought to be acquired as a function of contingent relationships between responses and stimuli. In the behavioristic view development is represented by the cumulative acquisition of a response repertoire. Structure, and structural changes, stages, and sequences, have no inherent functional role in behavioral development. At best, they are merely convenient descriptors for groups of responses that bunch together in the course of the acquisition of responses. These entities—stages, structures, sequences—have no role as principles in guiding the developmental course or in affecting the topography of developmental outcome.

The traditional radical behavioristic account pays little theoretical attention to the age of the individual. Time or age is of no consequence in itself. It simply represents the accrual of a response repertoire without concern for the regularities to be found in the course of behavioral development or the qualitative, topographical differences in behavior at different ages. If the correct response involves choosing a particular stimulus, one child age 4, and another age 10, may both make the same response. A developmentalist with a Piagetian or other cognitive orientation will see these seemingly similar behaviors as quite different. The behaviorist will view these as objectively similar disregarding developmental context. The behaviorist is not being simplistic, however; what is demanded is a description of the context, the history of the learned behavior and its relationship to the remainder of the behavioral repertoire. As long as these can be objectively described, the behaviorist sees no need to invoke cognitive structures or stages of development.

SOME CURRENT THEORETICAL PERSPECTIVES
LEARNING AND COGNITION

This has been the traditional opposition of behaviorist and cognitivist positions regarding development. However, it has become increasingly difficult to attach oneself to one developmental theory or even to a specific research paradigm especially suited to developmental or behavioral studies. The data have not been cooperative in making dogmatism easy. Nevertheless, various pronouncements appear to ignore this fact. For example, the dominance of behaviorism and stimulus–response (S-R) psychology in North America is said to have waned. Indeed, a paradigmatic revolution in the Kuhnian sense (Kuhn, 1970) has been proclaimed recently. It has been said that S-R psychology has now been overthrown (Stevenson, 1983). This is, of course, not the case. There continues to be a productive and vigorous enterprise in the study of learning and conditioning and in the application of many of these principles to the modification of behaviors in a vast array of different settings with many different populations (Martin & Pear, 1978). Further, numerous miniliaisons between cognitive psychology and behavior modification have been forged in such enterprises as cognitive behavior modification. Concepts once thought of as contestants from opposing camps are being discussed in relation to one another.

On the cognitive side, recent reviews of Piagetian concepts and of the research that was heavily influenced by Piaget's theory have yielded conclusions that question the universal existence of many of the tightly structured sequences and stages posited by Piaget (Harris, 1983; Gelman & Ballargeon, 1983). It has been suggested that the stages and sequences may not be organismically based but embedded in learning the developmental tasks that the human organism is required to master in order to function in the normal environment and in the particular culture or social setting in which the individual is developing (Feldman, 1980).

Thus we see a moving out from previously rigid theoretical boundaries. In his discussion of the contributions of ethology to the study of child development, the ethologist Hinde (1983) cited processes of operant conditioning as being involved in the development of the attachment of the young to the parent. The basic ethological point of view recognizes that there are species characteristics in species-related constraints on what is to be learned and when it is to be learned but also that the processes of learning are essential to the acquisition of behavior.

To achieve an integrated view of behavioral development we need to take cognizance of a number of problems and issues. They can be summarized as follows: (a) a shift to a psychobiological view requires a reformulation of our questions; (b) Our research is largely nondevelopmental in nature; (c) We must become more sensitive to the role of culture as a pervasive organizer of environmental stimulation; and (d) We must determine whether the question of continuities and discontinuities in behavioral development should be phrased in terms of the consistency and inconsistency across time in specific behaviors or in terms of the processes that underlie behavioral development.

A PSYCHOBIOLOGICAL PERSPECTIVE

We now find increasing attention to the psychobiological perspective, especially in the study of infant behavior and organizational restructuring, so that the role of saliency of particular environmental stimuli for the infant or child changes with a concomitant change in the qualitative dimension of the response repertoire of the individual (Emde, Gaensbauer & Harmon, 1976; Gottlieb, 1983). Similarly, there is an emphasis upon "biological boundaries of learning" (Seligman & Hagar, 1972) and upon the notion of an evolutionary legacy that produces different levels of neurological plasticity for different kinds of learning (Rozin, 1976; Rozin & Kalat, 1972).

An additional perspective is to be found in the proposal that biological constraints, however long their evolutionary history, are not necessarily immutable. Z-Y, Kuo's ingenious program of experimental research, carried out largely in China, provides compelling evidence about behavior potentials. He claimed that even seemingly innate behavioral dispositions could be altered given sufficiently strong counterconditioning environmental arrangements (Kuo, 1967). Kuo showed that hungry dogs could be taught to avoid food, and that innate enmities could be modified substantially. He further demonstrated that immediate environmental factors during the embryonic stage engender prenatal behavioral conditioning of a species-specific nature. Gottlieb has experimentally demonstrated the influence of various prenatal conditioning on postnatal learning in a number of species. He, along with Schneirla (1959, 1966), emphasized the importance of "describing the contributions of environmental experience to species-typical development." Thus, a number of theoretical points of view about behavior development have converged. Perhaps it is possible to combine developmental principles and the principles governing the acquisition of specific behaviors or classes of behaviors toward the goal of a unified and universalized theory. A key to the reformulation of our questions about development might be found.

ADEVELOPMENTAL RESEARCH

The study of children's behavior is not necessarily the study of the development of behavior. This has been observed, for example, about the information processing literature (Siegler, 1983). Much of the recent work on intelligence, moreover, has been concerned with redefining intelligence and fashioning new measures of intelligence rather than of its *developmental* characteristics (Gardner, 1983; Sternberg, 1985). Indeed, Benigni and Valsiner (1985) broadened these observations when they noted that much of the recent empirical research in developmental psychology has been relatively nondevelopmental in its orientation. Even a casual perusal of our major journals will reveal a large number of articles that study behavioral phenomenon at only one point in time.

CULTURE AND DEVELOPMENT

A critical analysis of the current circumstances in which we find ourselves as developmental scientists demands yet another perspective. One has only to travel about this planet to sense the wide range of experiences associated with different cultural contexts. Yet much research in developmental psychology is unicultural, with little recognition that published findings may not generalize beyond the cultural context in which the data were collected. A small cadre of psychologists has been sensitive to this issue, although our anthropological colleagues have long been critical of the lack of a comparative cultural perspective in much of the work in behavioral development.

Berland's (1982) anthropological study of cultural influences on cognition in his book *No Five Fingers Are Alike* stresses the idea that cultural and contextual factors act as cognitive amplifiers, directing perception and cognitive systems. Michael Cole and his colleagues (Laboratory of Comparative Human Cognition, 1983) have worried about the degree to which most of our published findings about cognitive development can be generalized beyond the cultural context in which the data were collected. David Feldman (1980) has suggested that environments condition for the universals as well as the nonuniversals in development. He has proposed that there is a continuum of developmental domains from the universal to the unique. The universals are found everywhere and in all normal human organisms; the nonuniversals are of various kinds. One involves the development of behaviors as a function of the particular culture in which one is reared, such as reading, writing, and arithmetic in most postindustrial societies. Another involves development of behaviors based in a particular discipline—such as music or science. Another involves behaviors related to a particular specialization. Finally, he posits a developmental domain that covers the unique, creative developmental characteristics of a particular individual such as one might find in a gifted and talented person who invents new domains of knowledge or achieves what has not been achieved before.

The issue of universals has nowhere been more debated than in relation to infant behavior and development. Some observers have become so impressed with the presumably universal characteristics of development in the first 2 years of life that they have declared these early years to be essentially buffered, highly canalized, highly overdetermined, and thus little influenced by environmental variations with respect to the basic template of the developmental course (Kagan, Kearsley, & Zelazo, 1978; Scarr-Salapatek, 1976).

A more considered view, however, appears to be in order. It is obvious that all normal infants in all normal environments will go through a developmental course marked by the behavioral milestones that have been so fully documented. But we also know a great deal about the active learning, information processing, and perceptual capabilities of the infant. The human infant is at birth a learning organism (Lipsitt, 1977, 1979; Lipsitt & Werner, 1981). The newborn infant comes into the world equipped to discriminate stimuli in every stimulus modality (Horowitz, 1984). Increasingly, we discover that the human newborn's information-processing capacities are more sophisticated than we heretofore expected. For example, Antell and Caron (1985) reported the newborn's ability to discriminate spatial relationships and to extract from stimulus displays informative invariant information.

The data on the human infant's information-processing and learning capabilities make it possible to propose that learning–information-processing activities guide the infant's interaction with environmental stimulation. These interactions are, in turn, constrained and guided by the highly predisposed human developmental course. Neal Miller, many years ago, observed that it was possible to load onto the mechanisms of learning a great deal of responsibility for behavioral acquisition in the human organism, because the human organism came into the world so fully prepared as a learning organism (Miller, 1959).

If this is the case then we must take a hard look at the parameter of culture and the role of cultural variations in behavioral development. Culture has been defined in various ways, but the all-inclusive approach adopted by Kroeber and Kluckhohn (1952) requires us to consider that culture functions as an overriding variable, exerting a profound and pervasive influence on the manner in which the environment is organized and on the patterns of behavior to be acquired. We should therefore expect to see the influence of culture in the very earliest patterns of infant interactions with caregivers, and recent reports suggest this is so (Field, Sostek, Vietze, & Leiderman, 1981; Leiderman, Tulkin, & Rosenfeld, 1977).

There exists a universal core of behavioral commonalities in infant development. This does not contradict the notion that there are environmental variations in response to these behaviors determining the way the infant is joined to the social context of its rearing (Super, 1981). That these environmental variations begin in the very earliest moments of life, and are continuing and powerful factors fashioning the acquisition of the specific behavioral repertoire for each individual, is a viable hypothesis, not only with respect to sensorimotor development in infancy, but in relation to language development, cognitive development, social-emotional development, and personality development throughout the life span. Vygotsky (1962, 1978) saw this most clearly as a theorist.

CONTINUITIES AND DISCONTINUITIES

In the effort to map development and to understand the processes that underlie behavioral development, it has not always been clear whether the questions relate to particular behaviors in a system, such as object permanence as a phenomenon in cognitive development, or to the basic processes that account for the development of the phenomena. Similarly, clear distinctions have not been drawn between the universals in the behavioral repertoire and the nonuniversals. As a result, oversimplified models have been employed and oversimplified debates have been tolerated. When the data did not support the idea that early existence was linearly related to later developmental status, the belief in developmental continuity was sorely tested and, in some instances, recanted (Kagan et al., 1978). The infancy period was characterized, subsequently, as being so predetermined in its nature and so impervious to environmental variation that, if we were going to search for continuities, that was better begun after 2 years of age. Recently, more sophisticated views have begun to emerge, fueled in part by advances in biology and genetics and by a number of thoughtful discussions and reviews of the continuity–discontinuity literature (Emde & Harmon, 1984).

How one approaches the question of continuity and discontinuity in development is dependent upon the nature of the developmental model one uses. A dynamic, biological system is partly characterized by nonlinear characteristics. As von Bertalanffy (1968, 1975) repeatedly stressed in his general systems theory discussions, such systems are open systems wherein it is possible for different sets of conditions following different pathways to produce similar outcomes. Developing open systems periodically undergo metamorphical changes, with emergent qualities and dimensions that were not in evidence prior to the transition.

Despite the foregoing argument, open systems also contain subsystems that are analogous to closed or routinized systems which can be described by input–output models of a rather precise nature. Thus stimulus–response pairings occur with a certain degree of uniformity and predictability in a closed system. Indeed, as the open system develops, larger and larger portions of the system are organized in closed subsystems, lending a high level of functional stability to the basic operation of a complex open system. This analogy for the behavioral system is very attractive but must be taken in its entirety: dynamic open systems contain within them routinized closed subsystems. In other words, while there are multiple pathways possible in behavioral development, over time larger and larger portions of the behavioral repertoire involve routine S-R pairings that are cumulative, stable and repetitive, reflecting a depiction of the role of learning and experience that is compatible with the S-R linear model of development.

In the headlong rush to see a paradigmatic revolution in psychology from the linear, S-R model to a complex organic model, general systems theory has been embraced enthusiastically (Sameroff, 1983). Nonetheless, a tendency has existed to tout only the open, "dynamic" concepts of the theory and to forget the importance of the closed linear S-R model subsystems dimensions of the theory. Indeed, some of the most significant behaviors that children and adults must acquire in each of our cultures may best be described as obeying closed-system laws and may best be facilitated by employing an input–output model of learning. For example, the acquisition and maintenance of arithmetic skills are best understood as representing successful S-R learning—a closed system routine, an input–output analogy.

The existence of both open and closed systems in the behavioral domain complicates the discussion of continuities and discontinuities. The more sophisticated view referred to here involves the recognition that, when we seek for continuities, we are searching for "meaningful links over the course of development—not a lack of change" (Rutter, 1984, p. 62). Such a meaningful link orientation means, in my frame of reference, that structural reorganizations common to open systems may introduce *discontinuities* or may set the occasion for discontinuities; normative and nonnormative transitions may do likewise. On the other hand, if the functional equation of organism–environment interaction has a particular transformational characteristic, transitions and reorganizations may yield *continuities*.

These observations lead to the conclusion that the continuity–discontinuity debate, especially in the recent past, has been somewhat off the mark. Take the case of a biological cell unit. At one point in time a cell or group of cells in the body is functioning normally; at a later point in time these cells, unpredictably, may behave abnormally and can be found to be cancerous. In looking at the functioning of the cell over the two periods of time, do we declare for discontinuity? In finding the discontinuity, do we choose to assert that there is a lack of continuity in development, because we cannot predict early to later relationships? Obviously not. Any sensible scientist and educated layperson realizes that something changed in the functioning of the processes affecting the cell, and that the clue to making the prediction lies in understanding those processes and specifying the conditions under which the processes will be affected. Rutter's notion of meaningful links over the course of development is more likely to yield to our understanding if we focus on processes and the conditions that affect the processes rather than being concerned exclusively with developmental phenomena in and of themselves. In other words, we ought not to be looking for continuity in the phenomena of development but in the processes of development. Nature abounds with examples where morphological structure changes dramatically over time: for example, the pollywog to the frog, the caterpillar to the butterfly. The focus on understanding the continuities in development in these examples is on the processes that account for the changes, not the changes themselves.

A STRUCTURAL/BEHAVIORAL MODEL
OF DEVELOPMENT

It is time to turn to the structural/behavioral model of development and its potential. The model must be inordinately complex, and it must incorporate a broad array of elements and processes, to have any chance of accounting for the laws of behavior and the laws of development. Figure 5.1 (from Horowitz, 1987) provides a schematic for the basis of this discussion. Its shape is purposely amorphous and abstract, though one may read into its outline whatever association one chooses.

The elements in the schematic and the interactions described encompass the conglomerate of the ingredients necessary and functional in behavioral development. First, there are the general domains of universals and nonuniversals. Two kinds of universals are posited. Universal I behaviors are those that are deeply indebted to our evolutionary history as a species and are the givens of our most rudimentary behavioral system. All that is required for their function is a normal ambient environment. They are the behaviors that are the least amenable to environmental manipulation, are the most deeply embedded in our organismic functioning, and undergo little in the way of a developmental course. Some of the most basic behaviors associated with species-typical physiological and perceptual functioning are of this kind. They are closely linked to the physiological and biological characteristics of our organism. The main continuum of variability in these behaviors results from individual constitutional differences.

The Universal II behaviors suggested here are the kind we typically think of when we talk about universals. They are the highly probable behaviors which appear in the course of the normal development of all normal human beings. Their appearance in gross topography is roughly similar from child to child; their expression is probably highly overdetermined. However, they are on a continuum different from Universal I type behaviors in that they are subject to environmental variations in the rate of their development and in the manner in which they are connected to the social context of experience and become functional

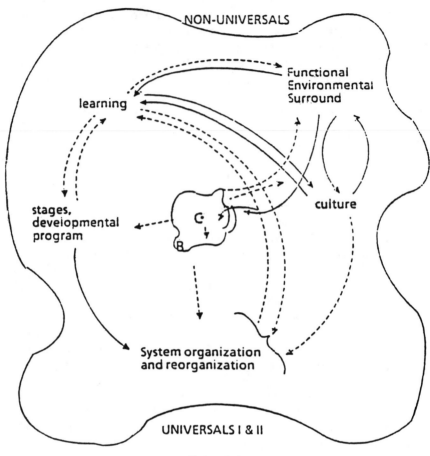

Figure 5-1.

elements in the overall behavioral repertoire of the organism. For example, all normal children acquire the ability to speak and communicate.
Language capability is thus a universal. Nevertheless, the specific
language acquired is a function of the language community in which
the child is being reared. Additionally, the manner in which language
is used, its role in social reciprocity, its extensivity in communication
patterns, and its generalizability to nonverbal patterns are all subject to
environmental experience and to the shaping of the behavior as the
individual organism (with its own range of individual differences)
interacts with the environment.

The internal elements in the figure have more or less relationship
with the universal and nonuniversal borders. Stages and developmen-

tal programs and the system organization and reorganization of behavior have some universal components, while other aspects are influenced by opportunities to learn, by the functional environmental surround and by the manner in which the culture organizes the environment. Culture in this schematic is an overriding, pervasive, and, in many instances, extremely subtle, factor influencing how the environment is organized. This, in turn, influences learning opportunities and the manner in which the universal behaviors are woven into the fabric of the behavioral repertoire.

At the center of the schematic is the event of conception, and the internal figure represents the 9 months of gestation during which the developing fetus is influenced, not only by its genetic background, but by maternal behavior and environmental elements. The double line at one portion of the inset represents the perinatal period—a particularly critical point in the organism's development when events such as oxygen deprivation can drastically alter an otherwise normal developmental potential. The "B," and the line it intersects, represents birth, the passage from the uterine to the extra-uterine environment and all the attendant readjustment that is entailed.

This schematic is primarily designed to set out the basic components of what a universalized theory of behavioral development needs to encompass. In Figure 5.2 is a working, structural/behavioral model that could serve as a guide to developmentally oriented research (Horowitz, 1987). It was adapted from a model used by Gowen (1952, 1962) to describe the interaction of host susceptibility and bacterial virulence for predicting infection. The adaptation of this model for behavioral development is based upon the notion that developmental status or outcome at any point in time can be represented by an equation made up of the variables associated with the organism and the variables associated with the environment. Further, these equations will differ at different periods of development, and the specific equation for an individual may well be different for different domains of development. This is not a formal theory of development. It is not a model to be tested as a model. Rather, it is a schematic designed to diagram sources of influence on development and to stimulate developmental questions in the form of equations for predicting developmental status or outcome in which variables are specified, weighted, and described as a set of functional relationships with given weights.

The top surface of the figure represents the level of adequacy of developmental status in a given behavioral domain. An inset can be superimposed on the top surface of the figure to convey the notion of system organization within a domain. Its breadth, and the thickness of its boundaries, could describe the dispersion of developmental out-

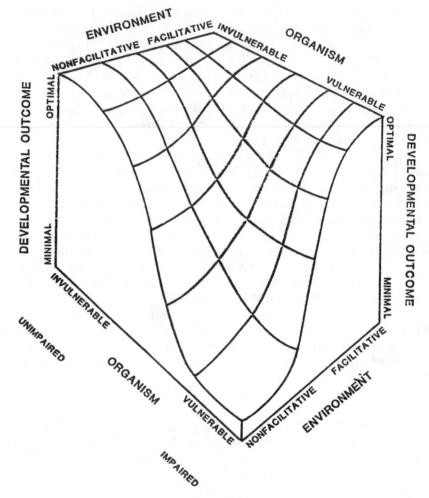

Figure 5-2.

come in that domain and its relative level or organization and permeability with respect to organizational stability. That is a complicating dimension discussed in more detail elsewhere (Horowitz, 1987).

There are two major dimensions that contribute elements to the equation. They are familiar to us all. One is environment external to the individual; the other is the individual organism. The environment is shown as ranging on a continuum that goes from highly facilitative of development to relatively nonfacilitative of development. In certain cultures we have begun to describe what constitutes "facilitative of development," but my hunch is that this dimension is highly culture specific in some of its particular parameters. The organismic dimension is represented along two continua. One relates to degree of impairment—mainly physical impairment. The other relates to organismic resiliency or vulnerability.

Some oversimplified examples will be useful here. The child who has cerebral palsy is physically impaired with respect to motor development. At the present time there is no known environmental circumstance that will produce normal motor development in a CP individual. Hence, by definition, there is no environment that will be facilitative of normal motor development, and the developmental outcome in the motor area will inevitably put the individual in the lower near quadrant of our figure. This fate, however, may someday be overcome by either preventive strategies or by discoveries of effective environmental manipulations that facilitate normal motor development. Such was the case with PKU, the metabolic disorder that prevents the metabolism of phenylalanine. Fifty years ago a child with PKU was destined for the lower near quadrant of this figure in the area of mental development, because there was no knowledge that permitted the creation of a facilitative environment to overcome the effects of the PKU disorder. However, with the discovery of the chemical basis of the disorder and the environmental intervention that alters the initial diet so that it is free of the offending substance, children with PKU can now be helped to achieve a higher level of mental development. In terms of this figure, they were moved up on the surface of the development outcome from the poor lower quadrant to more nearly the middle of the surface (Berman, Waisman, & Graham, 1966). Some day, intervention tools may accomplish the same thing for the cerebral-palsied individual in the realm of motor development. Much successful work in behavior modification with retarded and otherwise handicapped individuals can be represented as creating more facilitative environments and helping the individuals attain a higher level of functioning or developmental outcome—moving them up along the surface of this figure. Impairment in one domain, such as motor for the CP child, does not necessarily mean impairment in another domain. The motorically impaired CP child may achieve a cognitive developmental capacity in the mid-range of IQ, for example.

On the other organismic dimension shown in this figure, we can think about individual differences along a continuum labeled in terms of vulnerability. The relatively invulnerable individual, as Garmezy (1974; Garmezy & Neuchterlein, 1972) has discussed, is one whose developmental potential is not tied inextricably to a highly facilitative environment. The more vulnerable individual is more dependent upon a facilitative environment for a similar level of developmental outcome.

A concrete example may be helpful. In cognitive development we know that children acquire a number of cognitive skills. For instance, there is a very high probability that all normal children will acquire the ability to classify along multiple dimensions, will be able to acquire the concept of number, and can be taught arithmetic. Classification thus has some universality borne in the evolutionary history of the organism and in the high probability influence of learning opportunities in the normal environment, given normal organismic structural brain characteristics. What the child learns to classify, and whether, for instance, the child learns arithmetic skills, is entirely a function of environmental input. How *well* the child learns such skills is a further qualification. It depends upon the interaction between the individual organismic characteristics and the environment. Thus, children learn arithmetic in environments that teach these skills. In such environments some children will learn to do arithmetic at a high level of skill in part because the instruction provided by the environment was very facilitative of such learning. However, there is a wide range of individual difference in relation to the need for good environmental input to attain a certain level of skill. Some children may be less dependent upon environmental variation than others. They will learn whether or not the instructional experience is good. There are the resilient, relatively invulnerable children. Their placement in the upper quadrant of this figure will occur whether or not the environment is particularly facilitative of good developmental outcome or of learning. Even under relatively adverse environmental circumstances, they often give evidence of good development and good learning.

Other children are much more dependent upon a facilitative environmental experience to acquire the same level of skill. They will be in the upper quadrant under conditions of a good environmental experience, and further down on the surface when the environment is not facilitative. These are the children most "at risk," because the presence of a facilitative environment is critical to good developmental outcome. This characteristic of vulnerability may or may not be true for a child in all his or her behavioral domains. A child whose cognitive development is relatively independent of the quality or quantity of environmental input may be much more dependent upon environmental input in the domain of emotion/social development, and vice versa. Gardner's "frames of mind" areas for different kinds of intelligence may offer a way in which to split out the domains for looking at relative dependence upon environmental input (Gardner, 1983).

Now an additional level of complexity needs to be introduced. To the extent that there are "periods of development" or "stages of development," we may find that the combinatorial relationship of organism vulnerability and environmental facilitation which holds in one period of development may not hold in another period of development. In fact, we may be able to arrive at a functional empirical definition of stage that is derived from knowledge about the transitional points at which the combinatorial relationship is labile and thus *subject* to change—though not necessarily changing. This conceptualization of the notion of stage appears to hold promise for looking at stages or periods in terms of combinatorial transition points (Horowitz, 1987).

It is important to emphasize that, in all domains and in relation to all skills, the role of culture in organizing environmental input is critical, including the particular elements that determine what constitutes a facilitative or a nonfacilitative environment. A number of years ago Gerald Lesser and his colleagues (Lesser, Fifer, & Clark, 1965) published a monograph reporting on the mental abilities of lower- and middle-class Jewish, Black, and Puerto Rican children in the United States. He reported that the lower- and middle-class children from each cultural group tended to excel in the same areas. However, the strongest areas were different in the cultural groups. Thus, the Jewish-American children had their highest performance in verbal areas and poorest performance on spatial concepts, with the middle-class children doing generally better than the lower-class children. Black-American children showed stronger performance on spatial concepts than on verbal skills with the middle-class children doing better than the lower-class children within the cultural group.

It would be interesting to see if this finding would be replicated now, and to do a concomitant observation of the environment. My hypothesis would be that the emphasis on and reinforcement for verbal behavior in the Jewish homes far exceeded the reinforcement for behavior involving spatial skills, while, in the Black homes, the reverse ought to be found to be true. The point here is self-evident: Each cultural environment shapes the peaks and valleys of the behavioral profile of its young by the values it holds and the patterns of behavior it expects, and by the contingencies it sets to reinforce those values and expectations. As cultural environments change and evolve, the peaks and valleys of the patterns of behavior shaped in the young should also change.

SOME IMPLICATIONS FOR UNIVERSALIZING
THE DEVELOPMENTAL PERSPECTIVE

It should be clear by now from the issues discussed here, and from the model suggested, that the developmental enterprise is a complex one. The laws of behavioral acquisition will be found in the laws of learning *and* in laws of development. The laws of learning appear to be best accounted for in the traditional S-R (mechanistic, if you will) paradigm; the laws of development may well follow a descriptive analog related to the Universal Type II behaviors—the broad parameters of these behaviors are sequenced as a result of the shaping of the human behavioral repertoire in the evolutionary history of our species. But the behavioral repertoire which develops around these core developmental characteristics is subject to acquisition according to laws of behavior (i.e., laws of learning) which, in turn, are influenced by the values each culture transposes to apply to the rearing of its young. The organismic model of an open and dynamic system relates both to the Universal II type behaviors and to the creative edge of individual and species development. Hence, human development proceeds according to a mixed model, neither wholly mechanistic nor wholly organismic in character.

This point of view is not particularly controversial now but its implications are not always taken seriously. We are not yet at the point of studying behavioral phenomena and behavioral processes where we incorporate distinctions related to universals and nonuniversals and where we employ models that accept both linear and nonlinear elements. Developmentalists have not been vigilant in pursuing the systematic accumulation and evaluation of knowledge in these terms. Science proceeds most effectively by carefully stacking the building blocks of knowledge. As behavioral scientists we are not good block stackers—we don't replicate enough or build systematically across knowledge bases. There have been few 'integrations" of lower-level laws into higher order accounts. The blinders that shield us from the cultural variations and the practicalities that mitigate against longitudinal investigations contribute to slowing our progress.

The implications of the model we have described for achieving a universalized developmental psychology are not specific in their guarantees of success. Rather, they offer a guide to a kind of research agenda that takes into account individual differences and environmental variables. The focus of this research agenda ought to be on the combinatorial possibilities leading to developmental outcomes and on how different basic processes and mechanisms function in the developmental equations. Robert Cairns (1983) concluded his chapter on the emergence of developmental psychology in the recent Mussen *Handbook* by noting that our current scientific task is "(1) to state models with greater precision than has been done up to this point and (2) to determine their limits in integrating (and predicting) the diverse features of sensory, cognitive, and social development" (p. 90). The structural/behavioral model is a modest entry as far as a model goes. The effort to determine its utility could be a fruitful enterprise for our science.

IMPLICATIONS FOR TRAINING FOR DIVERSITY

If the structural/behavioral model of development is thought to offer a way to unify diverse points of view, then it may seem paradoxical to suggest that the future direction for the training of developmental and child psychologists involves training for diversity. This paradox need not trouble us if we take the point of view that such unification in fact frees us to pursue a diversity of phenomena without involving ourselves in chaotic controversy over what constitutes the basic elements of our discipline.

If the structural/behavioral model serves as the basic developmental prototype, then it becomes possible to identify phenomena in terms of their components as involving universal and nonuniversal characteristics and structural and behavioral or learning characteristics. The methodology for pursuing investigations of universal and nonuniversal characteristics and of pursuing structural and behavioral processes may be different. However, the results of these diverse investigations should be seen in relation to an overall model and in relation to a goal of determining how much of the developmental puzzle we have described. Such a perspective could go a long way toward rooting our scientific enterprise in a unified base.

There is a certain obviousness to the point of view taken in this chapter. Few would argue against the basic premises. Yet, paradoxically, much current research is carried out without attempting to cast results in the context of the complexities that are implied. For example, we have the development of a new infant test of intelligence that predicts later intelligence better than the Bayley and Gesell scales (Fagan & Singer, 1983). We have early classifications of attachment predicting later attachment behavior (Bretherton & Waters, 1985). While the predictions, in and of themselves, are informative, they emphasize a point of view that focuses on continuities between early and later assessments of behavior rather than on the processes that account for the continuities and the discontinuities. The *significant* correlations in these studies typically account for less than half the variance. The importance of understanding what is responsible for the stabilities *and* the instabilities is obvious but rarely given much attention in the discussion of results involving significant correlation over time.

The value of the traditional S-R research strategies as one approach to understanding the nonuniversal aspects of behavioral development receives scant attention in much of the traditional development literature and in many traditional child psychology and developmental training programs. Yet the application of S-R psychology in the use of behavior modification in classrooms and with special populations has resulted in impressive behavioral and developmental gains. On the other hand, few training programs that emphasize behaviorism, especially the now traditional behavior modification approaches, provide good grounding in the standard developmental literature that focuses upon cognitive, social, and emotional development.

It would be advantageous to the field of child psychology if the operant principles that appear to account for response acquisition were incorporated into effort to analyze and explain cognitive development or attachment behavior. Similarly, benefits would be realized if the accounts of developmental changes observed in these domains were included in trying to understand how operant principles are affected or made irrelevant at particular points in development. Some attempts along these lines are to be found in Fischer's description of skill theory (Fischer, 1980) and Hinde's discussion of ethological approaches to child development (Hinde, 1983).

Ultimately the fullest account of child behavior and development will require an understanding of the processes of development of the universal and the nonuniversal behavioral repertoires. Cognitive-developmental, organismic concepts, and behavioral, mechanistic concepts will have to be brought to bear upon theory and research. To that end, the training of child psychologists will need to include both traditions.

REFERENCES

Antell, S. E. G., & Caron, A. J. (1985). Neonatal perception of spatial relationships. *Infant behavior and development, 8,* 15–23.

Baldwin, J. M. (1906). *Mental development in the child and the race.* New York: Macmillan.

Berland, J. C. (1982). *No five fingers are alike.* Cambridge, MA: Harvard University Press.

Benigni, L., & Valsiner, J. (1985). Developmental psychology without the study of developmental processes. *ISSBD Newsletter, 1* (Serial No. 7), 1–13.

Berman, P. W., Waisman, H. A., & Graham, F. K. (1966). Intelligence in treated phenylketonuric children: A developmental study. *Child Development, 37,* 731–747.

Bretherton, I., & Waters, E. (Eds.). (1985). Growing points of attachment theory and research. *Monographs of the Society for Research in Child Development, 50* (1–2), (Serial No. 209).

Cairns, R. B. (1983). The emergence of developmental psychology. In P. H. Mussen (Ed.) & W. Kessen (Vol. Ed.), *Handbook of child psychology: Vol. 1: History, theory and methods* (pp. 41–102). New York: Wiley.

Emde, R. N., Gaensbauer, T. J., & Harmon, R. J. (1976). Emotional expression in infancy: A biobehavioral study. *Psychological Issues, Monograph, Series* 10 (37).

Emde, R. N., & Harmon, R. J. (Eds.). (1984). *Continuities and discontinuities in development.* New York: Plenum Press.

Fagan, J. F., & Singer, L. T. (1983). Infant recognition memory as a measure of infant intelligence. In L. P. Lipsitt & C. K. Rovee-Collier (Eds.), *Advances in infancy research* (Vol. 2, pp. 31–78). Norwood, NJ: Ablex Publishing Corp.

Feldman, D. H. (1980). *Beyond universals in cognitive development.* Norwood, NJ: Ablex Publishing Corp.

Field, T. M., Sostek, A. M., Vietze, P., & Leiderman, P. H. (1981). *Culture and early interactions.* Hillsdale, NJ: Erlbaum.

Fischer, K. W. (1980). A theory of cognitive development: The control and construction of hierarchies of skills. *Psychological Review, 87*, 477–531.

Gardner, H. (1983). *Frames of mind: The theory of multiple intelligences.* New York: Basic Books.

Garmezy, N., (1974). The study of competence in children at risk for severe psychopathology. In E. J. Anthony & C. Koupernik (Eds.), *The child in his family: Children at psychiatric risk* (Vol. 3, pp. 77–98). New York: Wiley.

Garmezy, N., & Neuchterlein, K. H. (1972). Invulnerable children: The fact and fiction of competence and disadvantage. *American Journal of Orthopsychiatry* (abstract), *77*, 328–329.

Gelman, R., & Baillargeon, R. (1983). A review of some Piagetian concepts. In P. H. Mussen (Ed.) & J. H. Flavell & E. M. Markman (Vol. Eds.), *Handbook of child psychology, Vol. 3: Cognitive development* (pp. 167–230). New York: Wiley.

Gesell, A., Amatruda, C., Castner, B. M., & Thompson, H. (1939). *Biographies of child development.* New York: Paul B. Hoeber.

Gesell, A. (1954). The ontogenesis of infant behavior. In L. Carmichael (Ed.), *Manual of child psychology.* New York: Wiley.

Gollin, E. (Ed.). (1981). *Developmental plasticity.* New York: Academic Press.

Gottlieb, G. (1983). The psychobiological approach to developmental issues. In P. H. Mussen (Ed.), & M. M. Haith & J. J. Campos (Vol. Eds.), *Handbook of child psychology, Vol. 2: Infancy & Developmental psychobiology* (pp. 1–26). New York: Wiley.

Gowen, J. W. (1952). Humoral and cellular elements in natural and acquired resistance to typhoid. *American Journal of Human Genetics, 4* (4), 285–302.

Gowen, J. W. (1962). Genetic patterns in senescence and infection. *Journal of the American Geriatrics Society, 10* (2), 107–124.

Harris, P. L. (1983). Infant cognition. In P. H. Mussen (Ed.), & M. M. Haith & J. J. Campos (Vol. Eds.), *Handbook of child psychology, Vol. 2: Infancy and psychobiology* (pp. 689–782). New York: Wiley.

Hinde, R. A. (1983). Ethnology and child development. In P. H. Mussen (Ed.), & M. M. Haith & J. J. Campos (Vol. Eds.), *Handbook of child psychology,*

Vol. 2: Infancy & developmental psychobiology (pp. 27–93). New York: Wiley.

Horowitz, F. D. (1984). The psychobiology of parent-offspring relations in high-risk situations. In L. P. Lipsitt & C. Rovee-Collier (Eds.), *Advances in infancy research* (Vol. 3, pp. 1–22). Norwood, NJ: Ablex Publishing Corp.

Horowitz, F. D. (1987). *Exploring developmental theories: Toward a structural/ behavioral model of development.* Hillsdale, NJ: Erlbaum.

Hull, C. L. (1943). *Principles of behavior.* New York: Appleton-Century-Crofts.

Kagan, J., Kearsley, R. B., & Zelazo, P. R. (1978). *Infancy: Its place in human development.* Cambridge, MA: Harvard University Press.

Kroeber, A. L., & Kluckholn, C. (1952). *Culture: A critical review of concepts and definitions.* Papers of the Peabody Museum of Archaeology & Ethnology (Vol. 47, No. 1). Cambridge, MA: Harvard University.

Kuhn, T. (1970). *The structure of scientific revolutions.* Chicago: University of Chicago Press.

Kuo, Z. Y. (1967). *The dynamics of behavioral development.* New York: Random House.

Laboratory of Comparative Human Cognition. (1983). Culture and cognitive development. In P. H. Mussen (Ed.), & W. Kessen (Vol. Ed.), *Handbook of child psychology, Vol. 1: History, theory and methods* (pp. 295–356). New York: Wiley.

Leiderman, P. H., Tulken, S. R., & Rosenfeld, A. (Eds.). (1977). *Culture and infancy: Variations in the human experience.* New York: Academic Press.

Lesser, G. S., Fifer, G., & Clark, D. H. (1965). Mental abilities of children from different social-class and cultural groups. *Monographs of the Society for Research in Child Development, 30* (4, Serial No. 102).

Lipsitt, L. P. (1977). The study of sensory and learning processes of the newborn. *Clinics in Perinatology, 4* (4), 163–186.

Lipsitt, L. P. (1979). The newborn as informant. In R. B. Kearsley & I. Sigel (Eds.), *Infants at risk: Assessment of cognitive functioning* (pp. 1–22). Hillsdale, NJ: Erlbaum.

Lipsitt, L. P., & Werner, J. (1976). The infancy of human learning processes. In E. Gollin (Ed.), *Developmental plasticity.* New York: Academic Press.

Luria, A. R. (1976). *Cognitive development. Its cultural and social foundations.* Cambridge, MA: Harvard University Press.

Martin, G., & Pear, J. (1978). *Behavior modification.* Englewood Cliffs, NJ: Prentice-Hall.

Miller, N. E. (1959). Liberalizations of basic S-R concepts: Extensions to conflict behavior, motivation and social learning. In S. Koch (Ed.), *Psychology, a study of a science* (Vol. 2). New York: McGraw-Hill.

Pavlov, I. P. (1960). *Conditioned reflexes.* New York: Dover Edition. (Original work published 1927).

Piaget, J. (1926). *The language and thought of the child.* New York: Harcourt, Brace.

Piaget, J. (1983). Piaget's theory. In P. H. Mussen (Ed.), & W. Kessen (Vol. Ed.),

Handbook of child psychology, Vol. I: History, theory and method (pp. 101–128). New York: Wiley. (Original work published 1970).

Rozin, P. (1976). The evolution of intelligence and access to the cognitive unconscious. In J. M. Sprague & A. N. Epstein (Eds.), *Progress in psychobiology and physiological psychology* (pp. 245–279). New York: Academic Press.

Rozin, P., & Kalat, J. W. (1972). Learning as a situation-specific adaptation. In M. E. P. Seligman & J. L. Hagar (Eds.), *Biological boundaries of learning* (pp. 66–96). Englewood Cliffs, NJ: Prentice-Hall.

Rutter, M. (1984). Continuities and discontinuities in socio-emotional development. In R. N. Emde & R. J. Harmon (Eds.), *Continuities and discontinuities in development* (pp. 41–68). New York: Plenum Press.

Sameroff, A. J. (1983). Developmental systems: Contexts and evolution. In P. H. Mussen (Ed.), & W. Kessen (Vol. Ed.), *Handbook of child psychology, Vol. 1: History, theory and methods* (pp. 273–294). New York: Wiley.

Scarr-Salapatek, S. (1976). An evolutionary perspective on infant intelligence. In M. Lewis (Ed.), *Origins of intelligence: Infancy and early childhood* (pp. 165–197). New York: Plenum.

Schneirla, T. C. (1959). An evolutionary and developmental theory of biphasic processes underlying approach and withdrawal. In M. Jones (Ed.), *Nebraska symposium on motivation* (pp. 1–42). Lincoln, NE: University of Nebraska Press.

Schneirla, T. C. (1966). Behavioral development and comparative psychology. *The Quarterly Review of Biology, 41*, 283–302.

Seligman, M. E. P., & Hagar, J. L. (1972). *Biological boundaries of learning.* Englewood Cliffs, NJ: Prentice-Hall.

Siegler, R. S. (1983). Information processing approaches to development. In P. H. Mussen (Ed.), & W. Kessen (Vol. Ed.), *Handbook of child psychology Vol 1: History, theory & methods* (pp. 129–212). New York: Wiley.

Skinner, B. F. (1938). *The behavior of organisms: An experimental analysis.* New York: Appleton-Century-Crofts.

Skinner, B. F. (1953). *Science and human behavior.* New York: Macmillan.

Skinner, B. F. (1974). *About behaviorism.* New York: Knoff.

Sternberg, R. J. (1985). *Beyond I.Q.* Cambridge, UK: Cambridge University Press.

Stevenson, H. (1983). How children learn—the quest for a theory. In P. H. Mussen (Ed.), & W. Kessen (Vol. Eds.), *Handbook of child psychology, Vol. I: History, theory and methods* (pp. 213–236). New York: Wiley.

Super, C. M. (1981). Cross-cultural research on infancy. In H. C. Triandis & A. Heron (Eds.), *Handbook of cross-cultural psychology, Developmental psychology* (Vol. 4, pp. 17–53). Boston: Allyn & Bacon.

von Bertalanffy, L. (1968). *General system theory* (rev. ed.). New York: Braziller.

von Bertalanffy, L. (1975). *Perspectives on general system theory.* New York: Braziller.

Vygotsky, L. S. (1962). *Thought and language.* Cambridge, MA: M. I. T. Press.

Vygotsky, L. S. (1978). *Mind in society*. Cambridge, MA: Harvard University Press.

Waddington, C. H. (1966). *Principles of development and differentiation*. New York: Macmillan.

Watson, J. B. (1924). *Behaviorism*. New York: W. W. Norton.

Watson, J. B., & Rayner, R. (1920). Conditioned emotional reactions. *Journal of Experimental Psychology, 3,* 1–14.

chapter 6

Graduate Training in the Fourth Establishment: Tradition and Change in the Study of Human Development

Sheldon H. White
Harvard University

Developmental psychologists are members of a research tradition that can be traced back to the 1890s, with the first programmatic explorations of child development by G. Stanley Hall and his students at Clark University (Sears, 1975; Siegel & White, 1982; White, 1985, 1990). A stream of philosophical writings about human development became joined, at the turn of this century, to new questions arising from enlargements of public participation in education and socialization, and to an emerging body of methods for the scientific study of mind and behavior. People had drawn upon traditional philosophy to suggest values and ideals for programs for children. Beginning in the 1890s, they turned towards a new kind of corrigible philosophy, developmental theory. Developmental theories were used to suggest "philosophies" for new education and service programs. But the theories themselves were not fixed and dogmatic ideologies; they were subject to exploration, elaboration, and challenge by new bodies of research. A triadic relationship of philosophy, science, and social practice arose; one sees this very clearly in the case of early education (White & Buka, 1987).

The research tradition has lived for about a century, waxing and waning from time to time. The tradition has been elaborated in three cooperative research programs: the child study movement with its central effort at Clark University between 1894 and 1904; the child development movement in the 1920s and 1930s; and the developmental psychology that rose to prominence in the 1950s and continues today. The lines between these eras are not absolutely hard and clear. Selected people, research issues, and ideas have moved from one era to the next. But there are enough differences between periods, and there is enough of a rising and falling pattern, to warrant the conclusion that there have been three historic waves of work. The developmental psychology of the present resembles the program of the child development period only in certain respects, and that, in turn, differed substantially from the earlier child study questionnaire work. By looking at what has been relatively continuous and discontinuous in the past, we may get a better sense of what might move forward from the present towards the future.

THREE ESTABLISHMENTS

Developmental psychology is a rich and complicated enterprise, with surprising subtleties, overtones, and hidden depths. It is, on the surface, child psychology—a scientific mapping of what happens to children over the course of time, and as such, as scientific colleagues point out from time to time, not very interesting in principle. Time doesn't cause anything. But some in the community of developmental psychologists have large visions of the enterprise. They see the study of the child as an occasion for the study of all psychology or, occasionally, of evolution in general or cosmology. Some see the study of children and work with children as a point of entry for fundamental questions of social design and social policy. We need to consider three aspects of contemporary developmental psychology: "developmental theory," "basic research," and "applied developmental psychology."

Much of what we talk about as "developmental theory" has grown out of a preexisting German philosophical tradition of nature philosophy and idealism, alive and well in the midst of 20th-century research procedures, adapted to live with them and to grow and change by means of dialogue with them. Piaget's stage theory elaborates late 19th-century theories of cognitive development (White, 1983); those grew out of an earlier tradition of "universal histories" (White, 1976), and such theories, in turn, are situated in a 2000-year-old lineage of Great-Chain-of-Being theories (Lovejoy, 1936).

The establishment of developmental psychology was part of a broad pattern of establishment of all the social and behavioral sciences near the turn of this century, accompanied by efforts to use them as instruments of social planning and design. We commonly think about Sir

Francis Bacon as an early philosopher of science, but the full range of the man's writings were directed towards the reconstitution of society and governance on the basis of scientific and technological development. To an interesting extent, the developments in Western societies at the turn of this century look like a fulfillment of the utopian vision sketched out in his "New Atlantis" (Bacon, 1627/1909). What seems to have caused this philosophical tradition to develop an empirical arm was the fact that a new class of social and institutional structures came into existence; the fundamental logic of that new movement entailed an obligation to seek practical elaborations of developmental ideas.

Developmental psychologists were part of a new class in American society, concerned to bring scattered localities into an integrated, patterned, ordered national system (Wiebe, 1967). Developmental philosophy and the affairs of children were of great concern. Society, it was thought, develops:

> The major theme in this phase of dissent was an historically rooted sense of progress by stages. Blending organicism and idealism, these theories described how society as an entity had evolved step by step from lower, simpler forms to higher and more complex ones. In each succeeding stage Intellect, or Rationality, exercised greater dominance over the material, an Idea came increasingly to control the involvements of the workaday world. (Wiebe, 1967, pp. 140–141)

To help beneficial social change to happen, one must improve the education and socialization of children:

> If humanitarian progressivism had a central theme, it was the child. He united the campaigns for health, education, and a richer city environment, and he dominated much of the interest in labor legislation. Female wage earners—mothers in absentia—received far closer attention than male movements for industrial safety and workmen's compensation invariably raised the specter of the unprotected young, and child labor laws drew the progressives' unanimous support. The most popular versions of legal and penal reform also emphasized the needs of youth. . . . Here was a dream utterly alien to the late nineteenth century. Instead of molding youth in a slightly improved pattern of their fathers, like cyclically reproducing like, the new reformers thought in terms of fluid progress, a process of growth that demanded constant vigilance. (Wiebe, 1967, p. 169)

We have to see three historic streams as flowing together at the turn of this century: a tradition of developmental philosophies, a movement towards the rational design and management of social and political institutions, and a stream of late 19th-century science. The man who began child study, G. Stanley Hall, did not see his genetic psychology as a freestanding science. He knew the variety of psychologically relevant science that lay outside psychology and, in the first numbers of his *American Journal of Psychology*, had catalogued their work (Reynolds & White, 1990). Hall (1904) pulled together his scientific vision of the development of the child through a remarkable compilation of the data of 19th-century work in anthropometry, medicine, biology, physiology, linguistics, and other disciplines. The "scholarship" that reduces Hall's 1,200 pages of literature reviews to an essay on recapitulationism is, simply, an evasion. Hall's developmental psychology was a substantial piece of scholarship. In spirit, it was an effort to respond to the knowledges, issues, imperatives, and demands of the philosophical, practical, and scientific streams.

Developmental psychologists today swim in the confluence of the three streams, though the conceptual frameworks we use are borrowed from science and engineering and give us only a limited ability to grasp the fact that we are working within social and intellectual traditions.

As developmental inquiry has been established in one way and then another, there have been changes in who studied children, where research was housed, how it was funded, what people hoped to achieve by such research, and what the prominent scientific paradigms were. During the 20th century, there have been three periods of heightened research on developmental psychology, and in each period, research was organized in a slightly different way.

The Child Study Movement

A first American effort to elaborate a systematic developmental psychology was led by G. Stanley Hall at Clark University, with his journal, *The Pedagogical Seminary*, serving as its central scientific forum (White, 1990). Questionnaire studies undertaken at Clark, Stanford, and a few other university centers explored children's emotional and social development; the studies in the universities were a part of something much broader. Beginning in October, 1894, the series of Clark questionnaires asked about "Anger," "Dolls," "Crying and Laughing," "Toys and Playthings," "Folk-Lore Among Children," "Early Forms of Vocal Expression," "The Early Sense of Self," and so on. One or two hundred research publications came out of the Clark questionnaire inquiries (White, 1990, 1991). In the same period, Louis B. Wilson, Clark's Librarian, put together bibliographies of child study writings with over 4,000 titles (Wilson, 1975). While the Clark studies elaborated an evolutionary vision of child development, other contemporary writings discussed "The moral instruction of children," "Child study and religious education," "Tests for defective vision in school children," "Manual training: Its educational value," "Memoir upon the formation of a deaf variety of the human race," "The wee ones of Japan," and so on.

The larger body of child study writings expressed the cares and problems of those dealing with children. There were many new services, occupations, and institutions. People had new experiences in dealing with children and they wrote about the new puzzles, problems, and solutions they were finding. Some looked more broadly; educators, social workers, physicians, parents, philosophers, ministers, scientists, politicians, teachers of the handicapped, early educators, social reformers, and do-gooders wrote about schemes for larger and smaller reconstructions of social arrangements for the care, protection, and education of children. New legislation, agencies, and interlacing social arrangements for children were being created (Belden, 1965; Hendricks, 1968; Ross, 1972; Siegel & White, 1982). The child's path to adulthood—customs, facilities, expectations, options, ideals, and choices—was slowly redesigned. With the redesign of society's 12-to-30-year-old course of education and socialization, that part-natural, part-social sequence that we refer to as "child development" was redesigned (cf. Kessel & Siegel, 1983; Kessen, 1979).

It was hoped that systematic research in the universities would provide a scientific nucleus for the new efforts in health, education, and welfare. Practitioners want "philosophy" to guide them and to help them set goals, particularly when they try to design new services and when they intervene in a significant way in the circumstances of a child's life (Rein & White, 1982). Looking, for example, at programs in early education efforts, what we clearly see in the child study era is a period when the ideas and values propounded by traditional philosophers of early education, such as Locke and Rousseau, begin to be supplanted by a new order of empirically based "philosophers," such as G. Stanley Hall, John Dewey, and Edward L. Thorndike (White & Buka, 1987).

The active period of university-based questionnaire work lasted about a decade, from 1894 to 1904. The research was challenged because of its methodological inadequacies and overtones of zeal and sentimentality, and it then subsided. The founding of the Iowa Child Welfare Research Station in 1917 initiated a second wave of developmental inquiry.

The Child Development Movement

A movement directed towards the pursuit of studies of childhood in interdisciplinary institutes and centers reached its peak in the 1920s and 1930s. With some local support and some programmatic support from the Laura Spelman Rockefeller Foundation, 22 institutes and centers began research on child development and issues of child welfare.[1]

The Society for Research in Child Development and its journals, *Child Development Abstracts and Bibliography,* and *Child Development,* were established. The organization had its first meeting in 1934, in the midst of the Depression, and persisted with some external support until it finally became fiscally self-sufficient in 1948 (Rheingold, 1985–86). The life of the movement was intertwined with the politics of women. Women were getting PhDs, but had trouble finding employment in universities (Rosenberg, 1982). Rockefeller funding supported the centers, tried to turn their work towards parental training, and tried to use the centers as a vehicle to bring talented women into careers in parent education. The initiative was part of a broader effort to develop the behavioral and social sciences as instruments for social improvement.

Scientifically organized child rearing, the philanthropoids hoped, might serve as "preventive politics." There was a not-unfamiliar tension between grantor and grantees. The foundation pressed the institutes and centers to train women who would take positions in schools and social agencies and give scientific guidance to parents. The centers wanted to admit men and women and prepare them to do research on child development (Cahan, in press; Schlossman, 1985–86).

In this era, developmental psychology sat away from mainstream psychology. It was at least partially submerged in the interdisciplinary

---

[1] A manuscript by Lawrence K. Frank titled "CHILD RESEARCH" and dated July 8, 1932, itemizes the 22 centers as follows: (1) There are six "major centers," with "a semi-independent status in the university organization but open to all departments and schools:" Columbia, Minnesota, California, Iowa, Yale, and Merrill-Palmer; (2) There are nine programs "under the direction or control of single schools or departments:" Toronto (Department of Psychology), Michigan (School of Education), Johns Hopkins (Department of Psychology), Cincinnati (Department of Household Sciences), Western Reserve (Department of Anatomy), Chicago (Committee on Child Development of Department of Education), Harvard (School of Education), Harvard (School of Medicine), Stanford (Department of Psychology), and New York University (School of Education); (3) There are four programs in home economics divisions or departments: Cornell, Iowa State, Georgia State, and Kansas State; (4) There are three programs in women's colleges: Vassar, Smith, and Mills College.

institutes; it was female; it was "soft." The research of the movement remained conservative, directed towards efforts to establish some basic facts about children at a time when research findings were often given splashy interpretations in the media (e.g., Dennis, 1989).

The movement was dominated by a concern for "measurement," with little concern for theory.[2] Researchers tried to establish norms and extremes of various aspects of children's growth and behavior. The work was heterogeneous and wide-ranging—"stamp-collecting"—but it had its moments. Interesting observations and phenomena of development were reported in the too-little-visited journals of the era. It was at this time that the longitudinal studies were begun that today offer us our first useful data bearing on long-term change and continuity in human development.

Lawrence K. Frank managed the funding program for the Rockefeller Foundation and there exists a memo from him in 1934 reviewing the centers' work and expressing concern about their lack of theoretical focus. This concern seems to have been one reason why Rockefeller stopped funding the centers. It is curious that American researchers were so little interested in theoretical writings when, looking back, they seemed to have lived in a brilliant era. Werner wrote his *Comparative Psychology of Mental Development* in 1926. Piaget wrote *The Language and Thought of the Child, Judgment and Reasoning in the Child, The Child's Conception of the World, The Child's Conception of Physical Causality*, and *The Moral Judgment of the Child* between 1923 and 1932. In the Soviet Union, L. S. Vygotsky set forth most of his developmental psychology between 1925 and 1934, after which he died of tuberculosis. Presumably, American researchers largely ignored these theorists because they were European, philosophical, and speculative, at a time when Americans were turning away from European influences, trying to separate psychology from philosophy, and trying to establish a solid scientific base for psychological work.

Sears' (1975) history of child psychology says that World War II, effectively, closed off the child development movement. Shortly after World War II, Roger Barker described the decline of the movement in

---

[2]Before the complex, articulated philosophy of science of the Vienna Circle came along, American experimental psychology was largely governed by an informal "philosophy of science" based on the model of the physical sciences. To be scientific was to measure, do experiments, and find mathematical laws. This was the vision of science common to Titchener's (1901–1905) laboratory manuals and Thorndike's (1913–1914) educational psychology. S. S. Stevens' (1951) writing on "Mathematics, Measurement, and Psychophysics" expresses the thinking of that older psychology in an era when most psychologists had lost hope that psychology could be grounded on solid measurement and simple mathematical lawfulnesses.

terms that suggested that social support had waned. He said, in his *Annual Review* chapter, "By every index available—number of publications, number of papers presented at scientific meetings, membership in scientific societies, and establishment of research institutes— child psychology shows little life" (Barker, 1951, p. 1). Professional demands for such research remained high, but the resources were not there to meet the demand. "The fact seems to be clear that many of the important problems of child psychology require more time, staff, and resources than are now available. Some means of concentrating larger and more continuous resources upon unsolved problems of child behavior are essential" (p. 20). A few years later, Marian Radke-Yarrow and Leon Yarrow (1955), in their *Annual Review* article, reported the turning of the tide. There was a more positive climate of support and it was at this time that by far the largest and strongest surge of research on child development began to build.

Developmental Psychology

The third establishment of developmental psychology did not begin as a monolithic movement, though it came, for a while, to be dominated by Piaget's program. But the third establishment embodied a number of research programs, including an antecedent-consequent analysis of the development of children's dependency and aggression pursued by Sears and his associates; efforts by Barker, Wright, and their associates to map out a psychological ecology of child development at the University of Kansas; work in experimental child psychology seeking to establish behavior-theoretic research with children; the elaboration, at Clark University, of Werner's comparative-developmental approach to psychology, and other programmatic work.

The movement lived for the most part in psychology departments, pursuing short-term research goals and larger objectives that were quite consistent with those of other psychologists. Now the developmental theorists of the 1920s and 1930s became significant forces, joining the behavior theorists and personality theorists who entered from mainstream psychology.

Jean Piaget brought many who studied children towards a common family of research paradigms and, for a few moments at least, gave them a vision of a disciplinary enterprise made coherent by a shared theoretical framework. The vision was to fade, but there were lingering after-effects. Piaget's work introduced new flavors and depths to the developmental psychologists' experience. Some were led by his orientation towards genetic epistemology to begin thinking about what psycholo-

gists and philosophers had to say to one another. The work of developmental psychologists on long-term trends of cognitive change dove-
tailed nicely with the rising tide of work on cognitive science (Gardner,
1985)[3]. Cognitive-developmental psychology seemed to have much to
say about the War on Poverty, with its special emphasis on programs in
education. Some developmental psychologists were participants in the
formulation and evaluation of government programs for children. A
few became interested in the larger questions of social policy. In a
period of resurgent activity in developmental psychology, looking
more broadly around them, developmental psychologists could sense

---

[3]The study of child development has waxed and waned in the 20th century and the
oscillations may continue. What brings on surges of activity and what damps them? My
guess would be that social and political forces drive the waxing and waning, simply and
straightforwardly, by providing sometimes more and sometimes fewer resources for
research. (Brontenbrenner, Kessel, Kessen, & White, 1986) G. Stanley Hall's child study
movement arose in a period of significant growth of federal legislation and programs on
behalf of children, leading to the first White House Conference in 1910 and the creation
of the Children's Bureau in 1912. The child development movement of the 1920s and
1930s arose when social work was professionalized, when child guidance began, and
when many New Deal programs on behalf of children were being initiated. Contemporary
developmental psychology came to life in the 1960s, during the period of the War on
Poverty with its heavy investment in programs for children. Developmental research may
be stimulated when the social contracts need to be reconsidered and rewritten, redis-
tributing responsibilities for child rearing among families, schools, social agencies, and
various professions.

Recently, Arthur Schlesinger (1990, p. 11) has remarked: "History shows a fairly
regular alternation in American politics between private gain and public good as the
dominating motives of national policy. . . . As each conservative phase runs its course,
the republic turns at 30-year intervals to public action—Theodore Roosevelt ushering in
the Progressive era in 1901, Franklin Roosevelt the New Deal in 1933, John Kennedy the
New Frontier in 1961—until each liberal phase runs its course too."

Schlesinger's three dates—1901, 1933, 1961—fall close to the dates of peak activity in
child study, close enough to suggest that the time relationships between federal initia-
tives for children and public support for child study ought to be looked at. Schlesinger
describes the political periodicity as driven by motivation: concerns for private gain
alternating with concerns for public welfare. But the periodicity might have a structural
aspect: periods of social redesign, change, and instability alternating with periods of
equilibration, political stability, and management of the status quo. Society would
summon forth more work on child development when institutions for children were
being redesigned (and might conceivably try to dampen such work when there was a felt
need for the reassertion of stability).

This view of developmental psychology would make it a science of social design and
reconstruction; an understanding of the social meaning of the enterprise shared, in one
way or another, by G. Stanley Hall, Edward L. Thorndike, and John Dewey (White, 1991).
Of course, from a scientific perspective one might question the wisdom of the quickly
kindling, quickly dying, boom-or-bust support of research on child development that
society has offered in the past.

once again the aliveness of the connection of their enterprise with its ancestral three streams of philosophy, practice, and science.

Within psychology departments, developmental psychology became a significant part of a political "middle" bringing together a collection of research enterprises with a broad reach—extending out in various directions towards neuroscience, LISP models of cognitive processes, multivariate analyses of social phenomena, organizational behavior, the genetics of behavior, conflict resolution, and other arcane areas. The use of developmental psychology to help bring together at least elements of a diversifying field of psychology is likely to continue and, perhaps, grow in importance.

THE FOURTH ESTABLISHMENT: SOME POSSIBILITIES

The broader growth of psychology in the United States should properly be seen as the elaboration of a pluralistic enterprise embodying early-maturing and later-maturing subdisciplines. Significant changes in psychology are taking place as the balance among its constituent sub-disciplines shifts over time.

We have an unrealistically monolithic view of the history of American psychology, one that is to a considerable degree framed by Edward G. Boring's (1950) classic *A History of Experimental Psychology*. Boring said that he was writing a history of *experimental* psychology but, somehow, all the diverse groups of American psychologists have managed to live with the belief that they are children of epistemological philosophy and Wundt's brass-instruments laboratory at Leipzig. I have said that is not the case for developmental psychology. G. Stanley Hall studied with Wundt at Leipzig, but that is not where he got his child study.

Recently, O'Donnell (1979) has charged that Boring deliberately limited his history, aiming to suppress the forces of applied psychology he saw rising around him. "Beneficiaries of Boring's immense erudition, we must not remain prisoners of his perspective," O'Donnell says (p. 294). Samelson's (1980) reply seems to defend Boring's intentions and motives reasonably well. However, in his rejoinder to Boring, O'Donnell sustains a rhetorical device of the early experimental psychologists, that of placing any nonepistemological, nonexperimental psychology on lower ground by characterizing it as "applied." There is clear evidence that, in the beginning, American psychology was composed of plural scientific programs, all pursued with the most "basic" of intentions.

Textbooks in the late 19th century, recognized multiple scientific approaches to the study of mind and consciousness—Dewey's (1887/1967) *Psychology* four, James' (1890/1981) *Principles of Psychology* three. Contemporary scholarship finds evidence for the differentiations they speak about. Danziger's (1985, 1987, 1988) recent analyses of the research reports in eight psychological journals between 1879 and 1898 suggests that there were three empirical approaches which Danziger calls "the Leipzig model," "the Paris model," and "the Clark model." (As this was going to press, Danziger (1990) has published a monographic account of his important and tremendously enlightening studies of psychology's research enterprise.)

The major questions and intellectual programs of all sectors of contemporary psychology antedate the birth of the field. Not so long ago, those questions and programs lived in philosophy, not the technical philosophy of the present, but a traditional philosophy that contained within it the germs of the behavioral and social sciences—a broad consideration of human nature, governance, ethics, knowledge, manners, and morals sustained by intellectuals of men of letters of the 18th and 19th centuries. As topics in this traditional philosophy could be meaningfully connected to systematic research programs, they passed on to psychology and other behavioral and social sciences.[4]

The passage was quickest and easiest for psychologists who could use preexisting methods, methodology, and conceptions developed by the natural sciences. Boring (1951) traces a 200-year-old discussion of epistemology to Leipzig, where Wundt joined it to instruments and research paradigms gathered from European laboratories. Reproduced again and again in the United States, Wundt's laboratory could be the site of a psychology of sensation and perception. (Neither the philosophers nor the proprietors of the ancestral scientific laboratories went completely out of business and so, in time, the several parties have

---

[4]In the abstract, it seems reasonable to consider psychology as, essentially, philosophy being pursued by other means. But proponents of "the new psychology" at the turn of this century were faced with a concrete and difficult situation. They were mostly situated in philosophy departments and they wanted to separate themselves, politically and intellectually. They characterizing the philosophy all around them, and that which had come before, as "armchair." This was, in retrospect, somewhat exaggerated. The philosophers of the 19th century did appeal to scientific data, some writing copiously about it. The essential difference between the older philosophers and the newer psychologists was not so much the willingness to deal with data as the commitment to: (1) building philosophy (cooperatively), and (2) creating a dialogue between philosophy and data in research programs shared with others (White, 1977).

been rejoining in interdisciplinary programs in sensory science and cognitive science.)

Questions about the nature of human development and about the composition of human motives and powers have been the subject of other 200-year-long philosophical discussions (White, 1976, 1983; Cofer, 1986). It would take a long, slow process of discovery and fumbling before methods appropriate to such questions could be assembled to produce substantial research programs in developmental, personality, and social psychology. The later-maturing psychologies were not just slower, they were different. Wilhelm Wundt was one of a number of 19th-century German scholars who believed that experimental psychology would be insufficient for the complete development of a scientific psychology. Psychology should be bicameral, Wundt said, with experimental psychology studying simple mental processes and *ethnic psychology* studying cultural products—language, myth, and custom—to explore complex thought processes (Haeberlin, 1916). The first American psychologists managed to follow Wundt's experimental psychology and give him great honor while setting aside his larger vision (Blumenthal, 1975, 1980, 1985).

During the early years of American psychology, experimental psychology was developed, possessing laboratories and active programs, either sole proprietors or politically dominant in the laboratories and departments of psychology. Beginning in the 1930s and 1940s, research programs and institutional facilities serving the later-maturing aspects of psychology began to emerge. Personality theories came to stand beside the learning theories.

The study of human development has for some time been thought of as central for understanding the larger organizations of the human personality. As the work and interests of the later-maturing parts of psychology emerge into more prominence in psychology departments, developmental psychologists will participate more and more in the description of the person who lives and grows in nature, society, and culture. The theoretical center of developmental psychology will more and more be the study of social development, pursued in natural settings, quite often as part of practically oriented programs.

SOME SUGGESTED FOCI OF GRADUATE TRAINING

There are some contemporary signs of a waning of developmental psychology, but I do not believe that there will be something like a complete death, transfiguration, and rebirth of the research enterprise. Nevertheless, it seems worthwhile to focus this discussion on a hypothetical "fourth establishment" of developmental psychology because it is likely that the study of development will be different in the future and will sit in a different institutional context.

All the detractors and revisionists to the contrary notwithstanding, Piaget will play a large role in the intellectual life of the field for some time to come. He will not be left behind in the forward movement of the research tradition as, once, Hall was. However, it seems very unlikely that Piaget's genetic epistemology program, or any theoretical framework oriented towards cognitive development, will declare the development that developmental psychologists want to think about. Research and thinking on developmental psychology will be more and more oriented towards social development. This is not hypothetical. It is happening in the current literature.

Within pluralistic and diverging psychology departments, developmental psychology will more and more be in the "middle," holding together the biotropes and sociotropes. For those who are prone to discuss the political machinations within psychology departments, this, too, is not a particularly novel nor controversial assertion.

What might make the future quite different is the emergence of developmental, personality, and social psychology as scientifically and practically more significant entities—in psychology departments and in professional schools with or without connections to those psychology departments.

Graduate students in developmental psychology who are going to participate in the changing social milieu I have been projecting would be benefited by three shifts in emphasis in their graduate training: (1) coursework that would give them a sense of the historical development of work in developmental psychology and its meaning and justification as a part of human life in society; (2) coursework and research apprenticeship that would moderate our present almost obsessional emphasis on experimental methods and statistical inference and give students a broader, truer sense of what kinds of research methods are possible and useful for someone who wants to understand human development; and (3) a climate of graduate training that would permit and encourage each student to build for himself or herself a value-centered inquiry into human development incorporating personal concerns, issues, and ideals.

On Conveying the History and Meaning of the Enterprise

Developmental psychology is a demanding enterprise, calling for a high degree of intelligence, energy, and commitment. If we expect a young man or woman to join in our work, we have to communicate some sense of the mission of the field that is intellectually satisfying—that explains what the group does in the terms of an everyday discourse about human life in society and that says that the work of the field is valuable, worth doing. The custom of the recent past has been to say that we do Science and Science is Good. That kind of self-justification doesn't play well any more—because, for one thing, most developmental psychologists don't believe it in quite those stark and simple terms—and some more complex account is needed.

My discussion of the history of developmental psychology at the beginning of this chapter gives an indication of what I think this more complex account ought to be. Histories of origin play an important role in the lives of all social groups, explaining and justifying and interpreting what lies around in the present (White, 1978). Developmental psychologists who have for years subsisted on borrowed histories—the history of experimental psychology as given to them by Boring or the history of physics-seen-at-a-distance as given to them by the philosophers of science—have for years gone through strange cycles of elation and despair, at times almost persuaded that they are part of a company of the elect destined someday to give absolute Pythagorean truths to an unwashed world, at times almost persuaded that they will never ever be truly scientific in the truest and most beautiful sense of that word. It seems to me that a straightforward historical examination of when, where, and why work on developmental psychology came into existence in American society will give students a reasonable and coherent sense of what their training is bringing them towards. In the short term at least, such an historical account might bring some psychic peace to their instructors afflicted with some of the older myths of origin.

It has become fairly commonplace today to hear that one must observe children's development in terms of the everyday world in which children live, and seek to understand their development in a larger social and historical framework. The proposal here is simply that we must understand the activities of the developmental psychologist on the self-same ecological mappings and historical frameworks we use for a construal of children's behavior. John Dewey's writings about psychology, at the turn of the century, are an interesting attempt to undertake just that kind of understanding (White, 1991).

Diversifying Research Methods

Much has been written about the pros and cons of the present tradition of graduate training that concentrates upon experimental design and interpretations of data based upon the statistics of inference and falsificationist reasoning. What sustains the tradition is that it works; it regularly produces students who publish their papers in refereed journals, get grants and, therefore, do not perish in academia. Unhappily, the very robustness of the tradition may suggest that the problem is deep, not that it is not there. Most of the institutions of contemporary psychology were built or greatly enlarged in the period after World War II, at a time when experimental psychology dominated the several houses of psychology, so that what we face today are journals, granting agencies, and traditions of graduate training strongly oriented towards experimental definitions of what good research and science ought to look like. In that kind of academic environment, traditional research training works.

Nevertheless, it has become more and more clear that other approaches to data gathering—case studies, hermeneutic approaches, the study of children's institutions, transformational experiments, studies of group processes, and various kinds of clinical and practically oriented research—have much to say about the emotional, social, and personality development of children. These are the research methods appropriate to the later-maturing human science of developmental psychology. Many of us in graduate training now find ways to bend or bypass "the rules" to help students pursue seemingly legitimate and valuable inquiries. Sooner or later we are going to have to modify the traditional rules and customs of methodology, in the context of graduate training and in the contexts of the larger environment in which students after graduating will pursue their inquiries.

We are going to have to reconstitute our research program in the light of a theory of situations, borrowing from anthropology, sociology, and political science to help us find frameworks (White & Siegel, 1984). We will more and more have available, and use, careful descriptions of the microecologies of child development (Barker & Wright, 1954) and their connections to the larger institutions and organizations of the human environment (Bronfenbrenner, 1979). Within a larger picture of the world within which human development takes place, we will have to ask once again what our fundamental questions about children's cognitive and social development should be (Rogoff & Lave, 1984; Whiting & Edwards, 1988; Whiting & Whiting, 1972).

Developmental Psychology as a Personal Enterprise

What is the fundamental utility of developmental psychology for society at large? If we try to examine carefully the circumstances under which people call for (developmental) psychologists, we arrive at two main kinds of usage. On the one hand, developmental psychology seems to have acted as a "science of design;" people have used the findings and formulations of developmental psychologists to design programs and institutions for children—not always with complete faith and trust in the ideas, by any means, but because some ideas have to be found to design a new preschool, a new children's room in a museum, a new program in remedial intervention, or a new curriculum, and the formulations of developmental psychologists provide a helpful step in thinking about what might be done. Psychologists' knowledge about "the average child" is taken as a suggestion about the-child-in-general and, with reasonable prudence, can very often be helpful.

The tradition of developmental philosophy has historically been a liberationist tradition, concerned not only with designing institutions to fit people, but helping people to understand themselves and their personal concerns in the midst of messages and imperatives from the institutions around them. The developmental psychology that is descended from it is often used by individuals as a "science of reflection." People use the formulations and frameworks of developmental psychologists as offering useful frameworks to help formulate conceptions of themselves and their agency. Not all reflection about the self has to be taken as desperate, psychodynamically driven self-consciousness. Anyone playing a new and difficult role—parent, teacher, college freshman, professor—has to form notions of the self, one's agency, preferences, abilities, and blind spots.

The idea that one can see clearly what others do only insofar as you see yourself clearly did not originate with Freud and has been a fundamental idea for those who have sought to project a philosophy of the human sciences. For a good many years, it was taken as axiomatic that one ought to, somehow, clear out personal issues, concerns, and agendas in order to work on psychology in an unbiased and objective way. Working on topics that are a matter of deep personal concern almost guarantees that one will be tempted to dilute one's objectivity.

The view that psychological research ought to be impersonal has been slowly submerging as individuals with a variety of personal and political causes enter into work on developmental psychology with the reasonably clear intent of using the research to deal with matters of personal concern. If we are going to move towards a psychology based upon hermeneutic, interpretative methods, then we are going to have to ask for more from our graduate students than their ability to count. We are going to have to look for sensitivity in interpretation, empathy, sympathetic introspection.

The largest single difference between the human sciences and the physical sciences is that one must, in the human sciences, work with the self as an instrument. Graduate students who are going to do this work reasonably well have to confront themselves and their own questions about personal efficacy, identity, and values.

REFERENCES

Bacon, F. (1909). The New Atlantis. In The Harvard Classics (Vol. 3, pp. 153–191). New York: Collier. (Original work published 1627).

Barker, R. G. (1951). Child psychology. Annual Review of Psychology, II, 1–28.

Barker, R. G., & Wright, H. F. (1954). Midwest and its children: The psychological ecology of an American town. Evanston, IL: Row, Peterson.

Belden, E. (1965). A history of the child study movement in the United States, 1870–1920, with special reference to its scientific and educational background. Unpublished doctoral dissertation, University of California, Berkeley.

Blumenthal, A. (1975). A reappraisal of Wilhelm Wundt. American Psychologist, 30, 1081–1088.

Blumenthal, A. L. (1980). Wilhelm Wundt and early American psychology: A clash of cultures. In R. Rieber & K. Salzinger (Eds.), Psychology: Theoretical-historical perspectives. New York: Academic Press.

Blumenthal, A. L. (1985). Wilhelm Wundt: Psychology as the propaedeutic Science. In C. E. Buxton (Ed.), Points of view in the modern history of psychology (pp. 19–50). Orlando, FL: Academic Press.

Boring, E. G. (1950). A history of experimental psychology (2nd ed.). New York: Appleton-Century.

Bronfenbrenner, U. (1979). The ecology of human development: Experiments by nature and design. Cambridge, MA: Harvard University Press.

Bronfenbrenner, U., Kessel, F. S., Kessen, W., & White, J. H. (1986). Towards a critical social history of developmental psychology: A propaedeutic discussion. American Psychologist, 41, 1218–1230.

Cahan, E. (in press). Science, practice, and gender roles in early American child psychology. In F. Kessel (Ed.) The past as prologue in developmental psychology: Essays in honor of William Kessen. Hillsdale, NJ: Lawrence Erlbaum Associates.

Cofer, C. N. (1986). Human nature and social policy. In L. Friedrich-Cofer (Ed.), Human nature and public policy: Scientific views of women, children, and families (pp. 39–96). New York: Praeger.

Danziger, K. (1985). The origins of the psychological experiment as a social institution. American Psychologist, 40, 133–140.

Danziger, K. (1987). Social context and investigative practices in early twentieth-century psychology. In M. G. Ash & W. R. Woodward (Eds.), Psychology in twentieth-century thought and society (pp. 13–33). New York: Cambridge University Press.

Danziger, K. (1988). A question of identity: Who participated in psychological experiments? In J. G. Morawski (Ed.), The rise of experimentation in American psychology (pp. 35–52). New Haven, CT: Yale University Press.

Danziger, K. (1990). *Constructing the subject: Historical origins of psychological research.* New York: Cambridge University Press.

Dennis, P. M. (1989). "Johnny's a Gentleman, but Jimmie's a Mug": Press coverage during the 1930s of Myrtle McGraw's study of Johnny and Jimmy Woods. *Journal of the History of Behavioral Sciences, XXV,* 356–370.

Dewey, J. (1967). *Psychology.* (J. Boydston et al., Eds.) Carbondale and Edwardsville, IL: Southern Illinois University Press. (Original work published 1887)

Frank, L. K. (1932). *Report: "CHILD RESEARCH".* (Lawrence K. Frank Papers—Ms. C280). History of Medicine Division, National Library of Medicine, Bethesda, MD.

Frank, L. K. (1934). *Report: "PRESENT SITUATION IN CHILD RESEARCH".* Rockefeller Archives Center, North Tarrytown, NY. Archives of General Education Board, Box 369, Series 13, f. 3849.

Gardner, H. (1985). *The mind's new science: A history of the cognitive revolution.* New York: Basic Books.

Haeberlin, H. K. (1916). The theoretical foundations of Wundt's folk-psychology. *Psychological Review, 23,* 279–302.

Hall, G. S. (1904). *Adolescence: Its psychology and its relations to physiology, anthropology, sociology, sex, crime, religion and education.* New York: Appleton.

Hendricks, J. D. (1968). *The child-study movement in American education, 1890–1910: A quest for educational reform through a scientific study of the child.* Unpublished doctoral dissertation, School of Education, Indiana University.

James, W. (1981). *The principles of psychology* (F. H. Burckhardt & F. Bowers, Eds.). Cambridge, MA: Harvard University Press. (Original work published 1890)

Kessel, F. S., & Siegel, A. W. (Eds.). (1983). *The child and other cultural inventions.* New York: Praeger.

Kessen, W. (1979). The American child and other cultural inventions. *American Psychologist, 34,* 815–820.

Lovejoy, A. O. (1936). *The great chain of being.* Cambridge, MA: Harvard University Press.

O'Donnell, J. M. (1979). The crisis of experimentalism in the 1920's: E. G. Boring and his uses of history. *American Psychologist, 34,* 289–295.

Radke-Yarrow, M., & Yarrow, L. J. (1955). Child psychology. *Annual Review of Psychology, 6,* 1–28.

Rein, M., & White, S. H. (1982). Practice worries in the helping professions. *Society, 19,* 67–78.

Reynolds, W. F., Jr., & White, S. H. (1990). Psychological research at the very beginning: An analysis of secondary reports in the first year of the *American Journal of Psychology.* Paper presented at the annual meeting of the Cheiron Society, June, 1990.

Rheingold, H. L. (1985–86). The first twenty-five years of the Society for Research in Child Development. In A. B. Smuts & J. W. Hagen (Eds.), *History of research in child development* (pp. 126–140). *Monographs of the Society for Research in Child Development*, 50, Whole No. 211.

Rogoff, B., & Lave, J. (Eds.). (1984). *Everyday cognition: Its development in social context.* Cambridge, MA: Harvard University Press.

Rosenberg, R. (1982). *Beyond separate spheres: Intellectual roots of modern Feminism.* New Haven, CT: Yale University Press.

Ross, D. (1972). *G. Stanley Hall: The psychologist as prophet.* Chicago: University of Chicago Press.

Samelson, F. (1980). E. G. Boring and his history of experimental psychology. *American Psychologist, 35,* 467–469.

Schlesinger, A. M., Jr. (1990, Spring). The Liberal opportunity. *The American Prospect,* No. 1, p. 11.

Schlossman, S. (1985–86). Perils of popularization: The founding of *Parents Magazine.* In A. B. Smuts & J. W. Hagen (Eds.), *History and research in child development* (pp. 65–77). *Monographs of the Society for Research in Child Development,* 50, Whole No. 211.

Sears, R. R. (1975). *Your ancients revisited: A history of child development.* Chicago: University of Chicago Press.

Siegel, A. W., & White, S. H. (1982). The child study movement: Early growth and development of the symbolized child. *Advances in Child Behavior and Development, 17,* 233–285.

Stevens, S. S. (1951). Mathematics, measurement, and psychophysics. In S. S. Stevens (Ed.), *Handbook of experimental psychology* (pp. 1–49). New York: Wiley.

Thorndike, E. L. (1913–14). *Educational psychology* (Vols. 1–3). New York: Appleton.

Titchener, E. B. (1901–1905). *Experimental psychology: A manual of laboratory practice* (Vols. 1–4). New York: Macmillan.

White, S. H. (1976). Developmental psychology and Vico's concept of universal history. *Social Research, 43,* 659–671.

White, S. H. (1977). Social proof structures: The dialectic of method and theory in the work of psychology. In N. Datan & H. W. Reese (Eds.), *Life-span developmental psychology: Dialectical perspectives on experimental research* (pp. 59–92). New York: Academic Press.

White, S. H. (1978). Psychology in all sorts of places. In R. Kasschau & F. S. Kessel (Eds.), *Psychology and society: In search of symbiosis* (pp. 105–131). New York: Holt, Rinehart, and Winston.

White, S. H. (1983). The idea of development in developmental psychology. In R. M. Lerner (Ed.), *Developmental psychology: Historical and philosophical perspectives* (pp. 55–77). Hillsdale, NJ: Lawrence Erlbaum Associates.

White, S. H. (1985, Fall). Developmental psychology at the beginning. *Developmental Psychology Newsletter,* pp. 27–39.

White, S. H. (1990). The child study movement: 1894–1904. *Journal of the History of the Behavioral Sciences, 26,* 131–150.

White, S. H. (1991). Three visions of educational psychology. In L. Tolchinsky-Landsmann (Ed.), *Culture, schooling, and psychological development* (pp. 1–38). Norwood, NJ: Ablex.

White, S. H., & Buka, S. (1987). Early education: Programs, traditions, and policies. In E. Z. Rothkopf (Ed.), *Review of research in education* (Vol. 14, pp. 43–91). Washington, DC: American Educational Research Association.

White, S. H., & Siegel, A. W. (1984). Cognitive development in time and space. In B. Rogoff & J. Lave (Eds.), *Everyday cognition: Its development in social context* (pp. 238–277). Cambridge, MA: Harvard University Press.

Whiting, B. B., & Edwards, C. P. (1988). *Children of different worlds: The formation of social behavior.* Cambridge, MA: Harvard University Press.

Whiting, B. B., & Whiting, J. W. M. (1972) *Children of six cultures: A psychocultural analysis.* Cambridge, MA: Harvard University Press.

Wiebe, R. H. (1967). *The search for order: 1877–1920.* Westport, CT: Greenwood Press.

Wilson, L. N. (1975). *Bibliography of child study: 1898–1912.* New York: Arno.

chapter 7

Recommendations for Graduate Training in Child Psychology*

Hayne W. Reese
West Virginia University

INTRODUCTION

The purpose of this chapter is to present recommendations about graduate training in child psychology. Graduate training in a field is at least implicitly based on beliefs about the future of the field. The beliefs are likely to be "expectations" or "hopes" rather than "predictions," in that they usually have no theoretical basis and often have little or no empirical basis. Even if they are genuine predictions deduced from currently accepted theory and evidence, they can be false, either because the past and present are not necessarily good indicators of the future or, perhaps more likely, because the current theory and evidence are incomplete or inaccurate.

The likely possibility that present expectations, hopes, or predictions are false leads to my first recommendation: Train for diversity. The future of child psychology can be predicted, but the truth of the predictions is unknown, and, therefore, graduate students should be given training that will facilitate adaptiveness. Of course, the auxiliary verb *will* in the preceding sentence also reflects prediction; its basis is developed in the rest of this chapter.

* An earlier version of this chapter was presented as "Graduate Training in Child Psychology: Whither Forecasts" at the conference on Future Directions in Child Psychology, University of Iowa, Iowa City, October 1986. My attention to the statement by Robert Frost that is quoted in the text came from a presentation by Abram Amsel (1988).

As bases for further recommendations, most of which are given at the end of the chapter, I make 22 predictions about the future of psychology in general and child psychology in particular. The predictions range from trivial and obvious to, I hope, profound; but they all need to be stated in order to provide explicit bases for the recommendations. The predictions are listed in Table 7.1 in the order of their appearance in the chapter, and as can be seen in the table, the first one has already been made. Before the rest of the predictions are considered, however, a brief description of the method used to obtain them may be useful.

Alpert (1985) described three methods used in futurism, or futurology as it is also called. (This topic has both a long history of scholarly inquiry and a large literature, not only with respect to the methodology of futurism but also with respect to the future of psychology.) Alpert was referring explicitly to the future of school psychology, but distinctions between fields of psychology are not relevant in a discussion of the methods of futurism.

One futurist method is *political*: Given the political realities, predictions are based on expediency and practicality. A second futurist method is *fantastical*: The future is described as the futurist would like it to be. Alpert favored this method, but it cannot be a good basis for

Table 7.1. Predictions

1. Changes will occur, and some will be unanticipated.
2. Psychology will continue to be divided into irreconcilable camps.
3. Behaviorism will incorporate aspects of cognitive psychology.
4. Cognitive psychology will incorporate aspects of behaviorism.
5. Attempts to reconcile them will be made, but will fail.
6. Behavior analysis will increasingly deal with complex behaviors.
7. The development of "expert systems" will increase.
8. The search for system-reorganizing mechanisms may be abandoned.
9. Computer simulations will not be integrated.
10. Computer simulations will become more precise and have less scope.
11. Research on problems that have practical importance will increase.
12. Interest in naturalistic methods, the childhood/life-span connection, holism, social policy, and perhaps Soviet psychology will increase.
13. The new fads will be application, naturalistic methods, and social policy.
14. Child psychology will decline in popularity as a specialization.
15. Child psychology will become even more an *applied* specialization.
16. Theory will become more important in developmental behavior analysis.
17. Behavior analysts will become increasingly interested in philosophy.
18. Other psychologists will become less interested in philosophy.
19. Multidisciplinary research will not increase.
20. Neurophysiology will not contribute much to child psychology.
21. Students will be fewer, less dedicated, and less scholarly.
22. A sufficient number of students will be dedicated to scholarship.

predicting the future unless the futurist in question happens to have enormous power. But in that case, it is not the fantastical method, it is the political method.

The third futurist method described by Alpert is the *calculated approach*, in which demographic, economic, political, social, and psychological trends are identified and used to predict a future world, and then the adaptation of a discipline to this future world is predicted. A problem that Alpert identified in the use of this method is that relevant trends may have been ignored. Another problem is that trends can change in unpredicted ways, changing the future world to which the discipline must be adapted.

The editors of *Psychology Today* used a fourth method, which might be called the *silly approach*: They asked several Nobel laureates what they thought about the future of psychology. Whether the editors thought that the views of Nobel laureates might be interesting or only entertaining is not clear, but I found them to be neither. The editors commented, "Some laureates, of course, took the position of Samuel Beckett . . ., who told us, 'I have no views of value on the future of psychology' " ("Psychology tomorrow," 1982, p. 21). Neither did the laureates who offered their views. Perhaps neither do I, but at least my views have the credentials of my being a psychologist and of my having some relevant data.

I used a considerably modified *calculated approach*, looking only at trends within psychology. Specifically, I looked at trends in world views, theories, research, and child psychology, and I considered alternative interpretations of these trends. This survey provided the bases for the predictions listed in Table 7.1 and for the recommendations for graduate training in child psychology.

TRENDS IN WORLD VIEWS

Psychology has probably never been a unified discipline, and it very probably never will be. Most commentators have identified two camps within psychology, usually on the basis of underlying philosophy. One camp is generally held to reflect some kind of materialism, and the other some kind of idealism. In the materialist camp, forms or truths are assumed to exist only when embodied in matter, which would be brain "matter" (i.e., brain activity) in the case of "abstract" forms or truths. In the idealist camp, universal forms or absolute truths are assumed to be independent of any knower and independent of manifestation in matter. Camps of psychologists can also be identified on other bases, as will be seen in the rest of this section.

Camps Differing in World View

Commentators have labeled the camps in various ways. For example, Wheeler (1935) identified "mechanism" and "vitalism" as camps in psychology; Kozulin (1986, pp. xxi, xli) and Vygotsky (1986, p. 13) identified "naturalistic" and "mentalistic" or "idealistic" camps; and Lagerspetz (1984) identified "mechanistic" and "humanistic" camps. Lagerspetz included in the former camp "neobehaviourists, physiological psychologists, 'mechanists,' and determinists" and in the latter camp "marxists and the so called 'radical psychology,' psychoanalysts, humanists, herneneutists, phenomenologists, plus educated laymen interested in arts and culture" (pp. 25–26).

I would not classify Marxists with humanists, because I agree with Rychlak (1976) that humanism should not be confused with humanitarianism. For example, L. S. Vygotsky was a Marxist and was not a mechanist, and he seems to have been humane; but he was definitely not a humanist even though, like the humanists, he rejected spiritualism. Furthermore, as Rychlak noted, both Carl Rogers and B. F. Skinner are humanitarians but they are in different camps of psychology. The point of present concern, however, is not who follows which camp but the existence of different camps.

No precise specification of the camps is possible, because every camp that has been identified is heterogeneous. For example, all the camps identified above are heterogeneous in world view. A *world view* is a model so general that it represents every fact in the universe; such models are also called "paradigms" (Kuhn, 1962), "world hypotheses" (Pepper, 1942), and so on. In Pepper's theory, such models are based on common sense understandings; for example, in the "mechanistic" world view all facts are represented by a machine as commonly understood, not as understood in Newtonian or post-Newtonian mechanics, and in the "organic" world view all facts are represented by a growing biological organism and its developing activities, but as commonly understood rather than as understood in a biological science such as embryology. Because world views represent the universe in different ways, combining them into an eclectic view can yield only confusion— the illusion of understanding and not real understanding. (Summaries of Pepper's theory and its implications are plentiful; examples are Hayes, Hayes, & Reese, 1988; Kaye, 1977; Lerner, 1986, chap. 2; Overton, 1984; Overton & Reese, 1973; Reese, 1986a; Reese & Overton, 1970.)

Although the camps that have been identified within psychology are heterogeneous, each has a majority world view, characterized earlier as materialist and idealist. They can also be characterized as mechanistic and organic, respectively, in Pepper's senses of these terms. Given that world views cannot be usefully combined, the camps of psychology cannot be usefully integrated. Nevertheless, integrations have been foreseen. For example, Wheeler (1935) said that the two camps he identified had been alternating in dominance for hundreds of years, but he predicted that the cycle might "permanently straighten out around 1970 or later, certainly before 2000" (p. 343), with Gestalt psychology gaining hegemony. Another example is Lagerspetz's (1984) comment, "There is a good chance that the [mechanistic and humanistic] camps will in the future before integrated within psychology quite well, although this will not occur completely in the 1990's" (p. 27). (Her specific reference to the 1990s presumably reflects the fact that her article was published in a book on psychology in the 1990s.)

I doubt that the predicted integrations will be successful. Tulving (1984) said, "The idea that the two sciences [i.e., camps] are one and the fond hope that a general theory of behavior and experience is possible only testify to psychologists' respect for tradition and their love of unity and harmony in the universe" (p. 164). A stipulation that needs to be added, however, is that the "tradition" referred to is not a tradition of unity but rather a traditional desire for unity, a "desire to find one overall system of mapping, one theory" (White, 1977, p. 88). No successful integration has occurred, and none is in the offing. If any integration occurs, it will either be very confusing or very limited; physiological psychologists, for example, cannot accept phenomenological "bracketing" (Husserl, 1931) of the "real world" without abandoning their material subject matter; and Marxist psychologists cannot join the mechanistic camp without abandoning dialectical materialism.

One obstacle that will prevent full integration is world-view differences in the meanings of such basic concepts as "truth" (Pepper, 1942). These differences yield differences in the meaning of "scientific knowledge." I argued elsewhere (Reese, 1986a) that knowledge is *scientific* if it meets a methodological criterion and a theoretical criterion. The methodological criterion is that the scientific method, which is careful observation under known conditions, is used to obtain information. Ideally, this criterion would be implemented in a Baconian way: Observers would avoid any metaphysical, or world-view, presuppositions and biases that might blind them to the facts. The theoretical criterion is that information is interpreted consistently with the presuppositions of a relatively adequate world view. The effect of this criterion is on decisions about basic theoretical concepts that constrain "the choice of observation, the choice of method, the choice of analysis, and the choice of conclusion" (Kessen, 1966, p. 67). Both criteria are necessary.

As Agassi (1964) said, information that is not related to world-view issues is insignificant and has no impact. However, a currently accepted world view can be replaced by a different one. Thus, a good understanding of more than one world view may help psychologists understand and adapt to changes that occur in their field.

Any of the four world views that Pepper (1942) identified as relatively adequate—mechanism, organicism, contextualism, and formism—is an adequate basis of science, and each except perhaps formism is reflected in contemporary psychology. (For other views of adequate bases of science, see Overton, 1984, and Spiker, 1989.) Thus, at least three general camps can be identified on the basis of the world view each camp reflects—mechanistic, organic, and contextualistic. (In the contextualistic world view, all facts are represented by an act in progress in a concrete context; this world view originated in the pragmatism of Peirce, James, and Dewey.)

The Behavioral and Cognitive Camps

The behaviorism of stimulus–response learning theories is mechanistic in Pepper's sense, and the behaviorism of Skinnerian psychology is contextualistic (Hayes et al., 1988; Reese, 1986a); the cognitive psychology of computer simulation and perhaps other information-processing theories seems to be mechanistic (but this appearance is challenged later in the chapter), and Piagetian cognitive psychology is organic (Reese & Overton, 1970). Regardless of the world view reflected, however, behaviorism and cognitive psychology differ in important ways. Both behaviorists and cognitivists study behavior, but for different reasons: Behavior is the subject matter of behaviorism, and the causes of behavior are defined in terms of antecedents, which are generally environmental. In contrast, behavior is a means or vehicle for getting at the subject matter of cognitive psychology. The subject matter of cognitive psychology is the contents and operations of the mind, that is, thoughts (ideas, concepts) and thinking (e.g., "encoding," "planning," "using a problem-solving heuristic"), defined not by antecedents but by consequences. Therefore, even within the mechanistic camp, behaviorism and cognitive psychology have major differences; to extend the metaphor, these two mechanistic camps are in different fields.

Behaviorism can incorporate aspects of cognitive psychology and cognitive psychology can incorporate aspects of behaviorism. For example, Whitehurst (1977) incorporated competence variables in his behavioral account of language development; and from the other side, Siegler (1983) predicted that information-processing psychologists would reemphasize learning. I predict that such incorporations will occur; but most of them will involve reinterpretation and so might not be recognizable as incorporations. For example, Whitehurst interpreted competence in the context of learning (imitation), and information-processing psychologists are most likely to interpret learning in the context of mental operations or strategies.

The need for reinterpretation is absolute when the behavioral and cognitive camps reflect different world views. When the two camps reflect different world views, their differences are irreconcilable; and I predict that, although attempts to reconcile them will continue to arise from time to time, these attempts will, like past ones, eventually be recognized as futile and will be rejected. Knowing more than one perspective should facilitate recognition of which attempts are futile, and therefore training for breadth of perspective should benefit students and should be planned in graduate curricula (Bevan, 1980a, 1980b). However, training would need to be extremely diverse if it mapped all the camps. As already noted, neither the behavioral nor the cognitive camp is homogeneous in world view. A further complication is that these are not the only camps of this sort in psychology; the so-called Third Force is another group, most of which are in Lagerspetz's humanistic category.

TRENDS IN THEORETICAL APPROACHES

Before the 1960s, the behavioristic approach reflected in stimulus–response learning theory was dominant in American psychology. Since then, the behavioral approach reflected in behavior analysis ("Skinnerian psychology") has become more influential, but the cognitive approach reflected in information-processing theory has come to be dominant. The source of these trends is discussed in the present section, and an implication of the trends for research is discussed in the next section.

Basis for Choosing a Theoretical Approach

According to Lakatos (1978), a scientific approach, or "research program," is progressing if its theories make dramatic, unexpected predictions that are eventually confirmed, and is degenerating if its theories lag behind newly discovered facts. In his view, if one of two rival research programs is progressing and the other is degenerating, scientists tend to join the progressive one. Lakatos said:

As opposed to Popper the methodology of scientific research programmes [i.e., Lakatos's theory] does not offer instant rationality. . . . Criticism is not a Popperian quick kill, by refutation. Important criticism is always constructive: there is no refutation without a better theory. Kuhn is wrong in thinking that scientific revolutions are sudden, irrational changes in vision. The history of science refutes both Popper and Kuhn: on close inspection both Popperian crucial experiments and Kuhnian revolutions turn out to be myths: what normally happens is that progressive research programmes replace degenerating ones. (p. 6)

The decision to abandon a research program is based on rational evaluation of the program and any existing rival programs, according to Lakatos, and requires not only recognition that the program in question is degenerating but also the availability of a rival, progressive program to be adopted. No program is ever abandoned, in his view, unless it is degenerating and a rival, progressive program exists (or can be invented).

Another view is that scientists are not as rational as Lakatos and some other philosophers of science have believed. The demarcation between scientific knowledge and other kinds of knowledge has long been a concern in the philosophy of science because of a desire to make scientific knowledge *special* and therefore compelling, that is, to distinguish science from pseudoscience (Lakatos, 1978, pp. 1–7). Laudan (1977) deplored the view that science is not special. He said that science may well be only partially rational, but he considered a conclusion that it *must* be so "rather depressing" (p. 141). For better or worse, however, every research program is a "school" of knowledge, and therefore science cannot be special in the way Lakatos and Laudan wanted it to be. A school of knowledge is characterized and defined by a philosophical underpinning, a methodological justification, and an empirical grounding (Bergmann, 1956; Feyerabend, 1970; White, 1977). Basically, then, acceptance of a particular research program reflects acceptance of a particular "party line" (Feyerabend, 1970, p. 169).

Psychologically, Feyerabend's position is consistent with Pepper's and Freud's positions. According to Pepper (1942), an empirically irrefutable world view underlies the scientist's beliefs and activities, and therefore these beliefs and activities have a basis that is irrational in the sense of having no *direct* empirical justification. That is, adoption of a particular world view cannot be supported by direct evidence; therefore, even if its adoption is rational in any other sense, it is also dogmatic. Because it is dogmatic, it is not rational in Lakatos's sense. Freud's theory provides an explanation of such "irrational" behaviors, not as abnormalities but as reflections of deeply held values.

The point may need clarification: On the one hand, scientific knowledge is special because of the corroboration required to earn the designation "scientific." Consequently, scientists are special insofar as they demand that corroboration. On the other hand, scientists are not necessarily special in any other sense, and except for their insistence on corroboration, their professional behavior may be as nonspecial—it may have as much of an irrational basis—as their private behavior.

Actually, Lakatos (1978) admitted that scientists' decisions are not always entirely rational. (He apparently did not realize how deeply this admission undercut his position.) He said, "the history of science cannot be *fully* understood without mob-psychology" (footnote 2, p. 55); and in discussing a particular 19th-century research program in chemistry, he said, "some chemists became tired of the research programme and gave it up" (p. 53). Giving up a research program because it has become tiresome is not rational in Lakatos's sense of rationality.

Inferences about Trends in Theoretical Approaches

The stimulus–response learning theory approach. Consistently with Lakatos, Spiker (1977) said: "Philosophers of science have noted that a scientific theory is not discarded until it is replaced by a 'better' one. A better theory is one that predicts and explains everything that the old theory did and, in addition, correctly predicts new phenomena that the old theory did not" (p. 101). In practice, however, at least in psychology, theories get abandoned before they have been fully tested. An example is Spence's theory of discrimination learning, which, as Spiker (1977) commented, "was pronounced dead on arrival when published in 1936, again in 1937, and several times each year after that. Yet [as Spiker said], it is questionable whether it has been replaced by a better. theory, in the sense just outlined" (p. 101). Another example is mathematical learning theory, which was introduced as a rival to learning theory of the Hullian type. In this case the new theory correctly predicted new phenomena that the old theory did not, but the new theory did not deal at all with most of the old phenomena.

The behavior analytic approach. At the 1980 meeting of the Association for Behavior Analysis, Skinner (1980) commented that, in the early days of behavior analysis, exciting new facts were discovered almost every week, but that, more recently, new facts had become fewer and farther between. An obvious conclusion, though not the one Skinner reached, is that the approach is degenerating in Lakatos's sense. However, I think Skinner overstated the case; in fact, behavior analysis has been making good progress, not only in its traditional areas, such as animal learning and schedules of reinforcement, but also in such areas as concept formation, language, rule-governance, problem solving, and animal cognition (reviews can be found in Chase & Parrott, 1986; Domjan & Burkhard, 1986, chaps. 11–12; Hayes, 1989; Reese & Parrott, 1986). Many other examples could be cited, and I predict that these efforts will be continued and extended to new areas.

Behavior analysis is progressive, then, but it has not been attracting new adherents as rapidly as one might expect from Lakatos's position. Behavior analysis has received far less attention and has been far less influential in psychology than the cognitive approach. For example, Overton and Newman (1982) modified Piaget's theory to deal with performance and not only competence; but to deal with performance, they incorporated a cognitive theory (information-processing theory) rather than a behavioral theory.

The cognitive approach. Perhaps the cognitive approach is an effective rival of the behavioral approach because it is at least as progressive as the behavioral approach. However, the progress of the cognitive approach has had significant limits. For example, information-processing theory correctly predicted new phenomena that the old stimulus–response learning theories did not, but it did not deal at all with many of the old phenomena: It dealt with verbal memory, but not with traditional verbal learning; it dealt with "strategic" behavior, but not with trial-and-error behavior; it dealt with mental effects, but not with effects of motivation and reward.

Kendler (1984) said that cognitive psychology has three major problems, but one of them is not unique to cognitive psychology and the other two can be challenged. According to Kendler, the problems are: (a) parsimony, which is recognized by cognitivists to be a problem (e.g., Overton & Newman, 1982) but is shared with all approaches; (b) alliance with physiological psychology and animal experimentation, which seems to me unnecessary and unlikely; and (c) the role of affection and conation, which is not well handled in the cognitive approach, but which Siegler (1983)·considered to be not usefully studied with that approach.

The most stringent version of the cognitive approach is computer simulation of human intelligence. With respect to the role of computers, I predict a strong increase in the development of "expert systems" (Reitman, 1984, made the same prediction). However, expert systems are problem-solving devices, not simulations of human intelligence. They are often based on analysis of how human experts solve a particular kind of problem, such as airflight reservations and seat assignments; but they are used to solve the problem, not to validate the analysis (Reese, 1986b).

The future progress of the *theoretical* use of computers to simulate human intelligence seems to depend on two lines of development: (a) development of mechanisms that reorganize the *system* of operations (or "productions" in Klahr's sense, e.g., 1973, 1984) rather than ones that merely change the components of the operations, and (b) development of principles that unify the present kind of simulations, which are highly precise but very limited in scope. Siegler (1983) predicted increased efforts in the first line of development, including an increased emphasis on learning, and the prediction is being confirmed (e.g., Klahr, 1984; Klahr, Langly, & Neches, 1987). I hope the efforts continue and are successful, but the question is hard and may be abandoned.

Regarding the second line of development, in the last paragraph of their book on cognitive development, Klahr and Wallace (1976) expressed the hope that the limited theories would be integrated into some unified theory. The unification has not yet happened, and although the hope remains, I predict that it will not be fulfilled. I predict instead that the computer simulation theories will continue their past tendency to become more and more precise and more and more limited in scope. Admittedly, I am an outsider looking in, and I may be missing some key feature of the approach, but I see no reason to suppose that its future history will be different from the past history of behaviorism, which shifted from the broad early theories of Watson and Hull to increasingly narrow problem areas (Kendler & Spence, 1971b).

So far in the present subsection, I have discussed only the information-processing versions of the cognitive approach. Piaget's theory is also cognitive, but it reflects a different world view and consequently it has a different epistemology and methodology (Overton & Reese, 1973). Two of its major problems, from the view of outsiders, are that it is focused on universals rather than individuals and that it is limited to competence, using performance only as a basis for inferring competence. Consequently, context effects are largely ignored or treated as nuisances. However, as already mentioned, Overton and Newman (1982) have attempted to expand the theory to deal with performance.

Recursions of Themes

The poet Robert Frost (1915) said:

> why abandon a belief
> Merely because it ceases to be true.
> Cling to it long enough; and not a doubt
> It will turn true again, for so it goes,
> Most of the change we think we see in life
> Is due to truths being in and out of favour. (pp. 54–55)

White (1977) pointed out that themes have appeared recursively in psychological theories. He considered the shift to cognitive psychology to be a recursion, associated with a return of cognition and mind to psychology in the mid-1960s as topics worth serious consideration. However, their return does not explain the rise of cognitive psychology, because serious consideration of these topics is not at all incompatible with the stimulus–response learning theory approach, or even with the behavior analytic approach. Paivio's (1975) "neomentalism" is actually a neobehavioral psychology of mind, and Skinner has argued that the study of "private events" and "knowing" is an essential aspect of behavior analysis (1974, chaps. 2, 13).

White also cited Piaget's theory as an example of recursions:

> Piaget's theory is a grand new theory of cognitive development, quite exciting to one and all as the fruit of 40 years of scientific development in the Geneva laboratory. But much of what seems most novel and exciting in Piagetian theory is clearly foreshadowed in the turn-of-the-century writings of James Mark Baldwin. And Baldwin's evolutionary developmentalism seems related to a cascade of earlier developmentalism. (pp. 89–90)

A recursion of functionalism has been noted by several writers (e.g., Beilin, 1984; Brehmer, 1984; Nilsson, 1984). The new functionalism involves two emphases: (a) interaction between cognitive capacities and task characteristics, and (b) pragmatism in the sense of a principled truth criterion rather than mere expediency and practicality. (The pragmatic truth criterion is *principled* in the world view Pepper, 1942, called contextualism; that is, this truth criterion is entailed by the basic categories of the contextualistic world view. The pragmatic truth criterion is "successful working," Pepper, 1942, chap. 10—nothing is worth considering true, or real, unless it makes a difference in practice, Dewey, 1933, pp. 145–146; James, 1907, p. 46.)

However, unless the new functionalism is defined too broadly to be a useful label, other approaches also emphasize the role of task characteristics and other approaches are pragmatic. For example, Siegler (1983) predicted that cognitive scientists will emphasize task variables more than they have in the past; and both dialectical materialists and Skinnerians are pragmatic (although orthodox Marxists vehemently deny being pragmatic).

Another recursion, noted by Barker and Gholson (1984), is the interest in "hypotheses" as cognitive operations or strategies. The recursion is to Krechevsky's (1932) analysis.

Still other recursions are to G. Stanley Hall's vision emphasizing applied research in natural settings (White, 1980) and waxing and waning of interest in the nature–nurture issue (Overton, 1973).

Such recursions are never absolute, however. That is, they are not revivals of old schools but modern interpretations of old problems within new schools. Therefore, the recursions are generally prefixed by "new" or "neo-"; examples are "new functionalism" (Beilin, 1984), "neomentalism" (Paivio, 1975), and "neobehaviorism" (Kendler & Spence, 1971a). The recursions, in other words, are not merely more of the same old shibboleths, but reflect change.

Were the Changes Progressive?

Changes in theoretical approach could be evolutionary "problem-shifts" (Lakatos, 1978), and therefore progressive; or they could be revolutionary and not necessarily progressive—they would be progressive only if the old approach was not working. However, the old approaches in child psychology were working well enough to be considered progressive. From their own viewpoints they were making stunning new predictions and often were confirming them. Furthermore, even unexpected findings were being dealt with, for the most part, through modifications in the theories, and these modifications were being tested in further research. Finally, the revolutionary theories left many of the old anomalies unexplained and shifted attention to other phenomena. The changes, then, seem not to have reflected failure to resolve important data-theory contradictions, or abandonment of degenerating research programs in favor of progressive ones. Rather, as I will argue in more detail in the section after next, the changes seem to reflect irrationality in Lakatos's sense.

TRENDS IN RESEARCH

Trends in Rate

One concern about developmental research is that it may be declining in rate of production. Submissions to *Child Development, Developmental Psychology,* and the *Journal of Experimental Child Psychology* are down 40% or more since the late 1970s (*Child Development:* Hartup, 1986; *Developmental Psychology:* annual summary reports on journal operations, published in *American Psychologist; Journal of Experimental Child Psychology:* unpublished editor's reports). Also, submissions to the *Monographs of the Society for Research in Child Development* have declined an unspecified amount (Emde, 1986). The decrease in submissions may reflect the emergence of new developmental journals in the late 1970s, such as *Infant Behavior and Develop-*

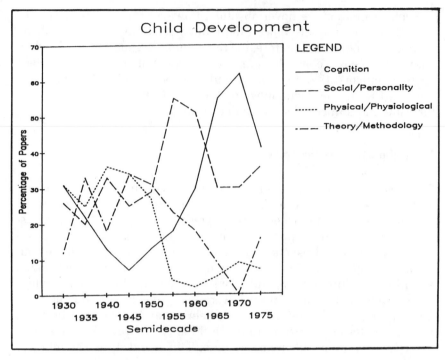

Figure 7.1.   Publication trends in *Child Development* (from data reported by Super, 1982, n.d.).

ment and the *International Journal of Behavioral Development.* However, the number of developmental psychologists (as reflected by membership in Division 7 of the American Psychological Association) has increased since then, as will be shown in the section after next, and the new journals therefore could not reasonably be assumed to have had such a large impact. The decrease in submissions is also probably not attributable to the inclusion of more experiments per submission, although the only relevant data I have are for submissions to the *Journal of Experimental Child Psychology* in 1983-1988. The annual means were 1.6, 1.5, 1.8, 1.6, 1.7, and 1.8, indicating no important increase.

Trends in Topics

Super (1982, n.d.) analyzed the topics of papers published in *Child Development* in all the semidecades between 1930 and 1979. These data are summarized in Figure 7.1. As can be seen, the hot topic was

Table 7.2. Percentage of Submissions by Topic in Various Semidecades for *Developmental Psychology* and the *Journal of Experimental Child Psychology*

Semidecade	Cogn	Lang	Learn	Memry	Percep	Read	Soc/Pers	Misc
			Developmental Psychology					
1965–1969	28		30				36	6
1970–1974	15	7	17	4	15		36	6
			Journal of Experimental Child Psychology					
1970–1974	10	9	33	17	14	1	14	2
1975–1979	18	9	24	16	11	5	13	4
1980–1984	25	10	12	17	16	9	9	2
1985–1989	22	6	12	22	15	12	7	4

Note. Some semidecades contain data from fewer than 5 years; the percentage in the last column was adjusted, when necessary, to make the row total 100. Abbreviations: Cogn = Cognition; Lang = Language; Learn = Learning; Memry = Memory; Percep = Perception; Read = Reading; Soc/Pers = Social/Personality; Misc = Miscellaneous.

Social/Personality in the 1950s and the early 1960s, then was Cognition in the late 1960s and the 1970s.

Publication rates such as those in Figure 7.1 reflect what researchers are doing after it has been filtered by the establishment—the reviewers and editors. Submission rates are better indicators of what researchers in the field are doing on their own, and are therefore more relevant for the present chapter. McCandless (1970) and McCandless and Geis (1975) reported submission rates by topic for the first 5 years of operation of *Developmental Psychology*, and the editors of the *Journal of Experimental Child Psychology* have fairly regularly compiled submission rates by topic. These data are summarized in Table 7.2. As can be seen, the data for *Developmental Psychology* indicate no change in Social/Personality, and a downward trend in Cognition and in Learning. The reason, however, seems to be in part the use of more refined categories in the later report. The data for the *Journal of Experimental Child Psychology* (JECP) indicate that Social/Personality declined; the trend in Cognition rose markedly to a peak in the 1980–1984 semidecade; and the trend in Learning was downward. Learning did not die out, however; it has been at a plateau of about one-eighth of the submissions to JECP for the last two semidecades. Other noteworthy trends are a marked increase in Reading, and a smaller increase in Perception and in Memory (Memory could have been classified with Cognition).

The trends in topics do not reflect changes within topics, in all of which interest has increased in problems that have social significance, such as learning to read, parent–infant interactions, and child abuse.

Siegler (1983) predicted, and I agree, that the trend toward social relevance will continue. Other interests that have recently advanced toward the forefront and that I predict will increase in popularity include the use of nonlaboratory, naturalistic methods; the role of childhood in life-span development; holism of all sorts (except Gestalt, contrary to Wheeler); social policy; and the theories of Soviet developmental psychologists, particularly Vygotsky, Leontyev, and Luria. The prediction about Soviet theories is very tenuous, however, because the political changes that occurred in the Soviet Union and the Eastern bloc in late 1989 and early 1990 might make these Marxist theorists unpopular in the Soviet Union and undermine their popularity in the United States.

These shifts of interests would be served well by three emphases in the training of developmental students: training in the methods used in disciplines that are traditionally naturalistic, such as anthropology; bringing back a bona fide language requirement, especially for Russian or German, perhaps, although developmental psychology is strong enough in France, Japan, Mexico, and some other countries to make learning their languages worth while; and strengthening students' training in philosophy.

Source of the Shifts in Research Topics

If a shift is based on a rational comparison of approaches, one might expect abandonment of an approach, but not necessarily abandonment of a research topic. Perhaps, then, the shifts in research topics have not been entirely rational, but rather have resulted to some extent from irrational considerations such as fads—becoming tired of the old hot topic and enamored of the new one.

But is this conclusion correct? Agassi (1964) noted that the choice of research problems is coordinated across scientists, and he suggested that it is coordinated on the basis of the prevailing world view. The world view that prevailed during the heyday of the stimulus–response learning theory approach was mechanism. In the present heyday of the cognitive approach, the world view that prevails is not necessarily mechanistic, even in the computer simulation of human intelligence. Using the computer as a simulation, or model, implies mechanism in that the computer is a machine; but reading the descriptive parts of computer simulation theories suggests that the theories are not mechanistic. No machine has at least two of the mental capacities that the theories invoke: (a) The more general theories refer to the use of heuristic strategies, but the use of heuristic strategies requires mapping presently given concrete conditions, possible actions, and possible out-comes on to abstractly specified conditions, actions, and outcomes, and these mappings are often metaphorical; (b) the use of a particular strategy is taken to be optional, implying a volitional capacity.

Clearly, several different world views are represented in current developmental psychology, yet the casual survey of research topics in the preceding subsection indicates a shift from the Social/Personality and Learning areas to the Cognitive area. If Agassi was correct, then the currently prevailing cognitive world view is the basis of this shift, *even for psychologists whose work reflects a different world view.* In fact, researchers such as Joan Cantor, Tracy Kendler, and Charles Spiker, working within the tradition of stimulus–response learning theory, shifted to cognitive issues, which they viewed as issues about media-tion and transfer. Similarly, although Chomsky (1959) said that Skin-ner's behaviorism cannot deal with language, it in fact has dealt with generative grammar issues (Guess, Sailor, Rutherford, & Baer, 1968), as well as other cognitive issues such as creativity (Goetz & Baer, 1973) and rule-governed behavior (e.g., Hayes, 1989), treating these as issues about conditioning and chaining, for example.

Finally, Piaget's theory has been criticized for not dealing with cognitive performance, which is the main issue of concern in the prevailing world view, but the work of Overton and Newman (1982) stayed within the Piagetian tradition yet was at least a beginning to-ward dealing with the competence–performance relation. Thus, even this most mentalistic version of the cognitive approach is coming to deal with the topic that characterizes the prevailing cognitive view.

In short, shifts in research topics may reflect fads, but these fads may reflect problems of significance in the world view that currently pre-vails. Researchers can shift to these faddish problems without changing the hard core of their research program. These kinds of changes are absolutely consistent with a dialectical view of the nature of scientific progress, recognizing the paradox that the contexts of discovery and justification are both contradictory *and* unitary (Reese, in press).

SOURCES OF THE TRENDS

Why do new approaches, theories, and research topics attract adher-ents, given that the choice is not always rational in Lakatos's sense? One answer can be based on an observation by Lagerspetz and Niemi (1984): "Every psychologist now in training will in the future find that his or her knowledge has become obsolete. Even worse, the very approach on which it has been based will be challenged and, most likely, overthrown by the younger generation" (p. 1). Maybe the history of psychology is like family history: The paternalistic/maternalistic establishment raises the next generation, first by spoon-feeding and gradually granting more independence, until adolescent emancipation pits the old guard's desire to conserve the tried and true against the new generation's rebellious desire to cure ills and right wrongs.

Another possibility is that ideas are borrowed from outside the discipline. According to Lagerspetz (1984), one determinant of trends in psychology is influence from other disciplines, especially biology and the social sciences. The influence of neighboring disciplines has been discussed elsewhere (Baltes & Reese, 1984; Baltes, Reese, & Lipsitt, 1980) and need not be repeated here. I will add here only the observation that sociobiology seems to be a barren field for psychologists. It is an ad hoc enterprise, and even the pragmatic truth criterion of successful working is limited therein to the meaning of successful post hoc explanation, unvalidated by successful practice. Psychology deals for the most part with behaviors acquired ontogenetically through environmental influences, rather than with phylogenetically acquired behaviors, and explanations based on environmental influences are more highly amenable to a priori empirical test than are explanations based on genetic inheritance.

Another possibility is that the choice reflects a tendency to take the fast and easy way by hopping on band wagons and leaving the hard questions behind. Unfortunately, abandoning the hard questions is not really progressive. For example, (a) both the Piagetian approach and the learning theory approach have become too far removed from performance in nonlaboratory tasks, the one because the competence–performance connection is so recalcitrant and the other because such performance is so variable, which is actually the same problem in both cases; (b) the psychometric approach has come to emphasize statistical esoterica relevant to description rather than dealing with the difficulties of prediction; and (c) the information-processing approach has abandoned some hard questions such as *why* imagery affects memory.

In reviewing a book on the concept of "psychological reactance," Peterson (1982) remarked:

> Social psychology has been criticized for following fads. Lines of research and the theories behind them are not falsified or extended so much as abandoned when a new topic captures the collective fancy of those in the field. Though not always valid, this criticism contains enough truth to explain why progress in social psychology is questioned, why the data base of the field is constantly in flux, and why theories in social psychology are overly circumscribed and short-lived. (p. 615)

Social psychologists are not the only faddists. Why were so many psychologists so willing to accept Chomsky's dictum that on logical grounds behaviorism cannot deal adequately with language? I think the answer is that the progress of behaviorism on this topic was too slow for these psychologists. Spence (1956) drew an analogy between the plight of contemporary psychology and the plight that mechanics would be in if all the knowledge of the physical sciences had been lost. He suggested that the best strategy for mechanics would be to start "measuring the time it took little balls to roll down an inclined plane" (p. 22), rediscovering the relevant laws rather than using trial-and-error methods that might accidentally provide relevant insights.

I think many psychologists are too impatient. They want the quick fix. They follow fads. A possible example is research on the "overtraining reversal effect" in rats (overtraining on a discrimination problem facilitates reversal of the discrimination). Mackintosh (1965) showed that the effect was obtained in 11 of 13 reports of *stimulus* discrimination and was obtained in only 7 of 21 reports of *position* discrimination. However, in a commentary on Mackintosh's review, Gardner (1966) pointed that an equally good split could be based on year of publication of the reports. The effect was obtained in 13 of 16 reports published in 1961 or earlier (Gardner said 14 of 16, having misclassified a study by Krechevsky and Honzik) and was obtained in only 5 of 18 reports published after 1961, and 3 of the 5 were from a single laboratory. Gardner suggested that this kind of trend could mean that the early "successes" reflected Type I statistical errors (chance rejections of the null hypothesis). The overtraining reversal effect was counterintuitive and counter to the then-accepted learning theories. Therefore, a significant effect in the other direction (overtraining interferes with reversal) would be so obviously expected that it would not be newsworthy enough to warrant publication, and a nonsignificant effect (overtraining has no significant effect) would in any case be inconclusive and not publishable, but a significant facilitative effect would warrant publication.

After the first reports of a significant facilitative effect, other investigators—especially, perhaps, young ones eager to make their mark—would be attracted to such an antiestablishment finding, would replicate the procedures, and occasionally would obtain the facilitative effect and publish a report of it. As published evidence for the facilitative effect accumulated, the more conservative, established researchers would become interested and would perform "larger and more careful studies" (Gardner, 1966, p. 417) that would generally not confirm the facilitative effect. Reports of these failures to confirm the facilitative effect would be published because of the prestige of the researchers, yielding the trend Gardner observed. The rise and fall of research on memory transfer through cannibalism in planaria is another example of this process.

The point is that some researchers follow fads. The young and restless ones want quick recognition, and they follow the new threads. Eventually, established researchers become interested and follow along to see whether the threads really lead anywhere. The catch words for the fads of the next decade are "application," "naturalistic," and "social policy."

THE PRESENT AND FUTURE OF CHILD PSYCHOLOGY

Trends in the Job Market

In order to estimate the job market for child psychologists, I looked at the trend in the membership of Division 7 (Developmental) in the American Psychological Association (APA) across the two decades between 1965 and 1985, and across the two 2-year spans of 1985–1987 and 1987–1989. For comparison, I also looked at the trends for Divisions 3 (Experimental) and 12 (Clinical). Associate members are not relevant for my purpose, and therefore I counted only fellows and members.

As can be seen in Table 7.3, the number of fellows and members of APA more than doubled across the 20-year span and grew enormously even over the 2-year spans. More relevant to the present purpose, Developmental and Experimental fared about equally in these periods, with strong growth (positive percentage change) across the 20-year span, little growth across the 1985–1987 span, and slight decline across the 1987–1989 span. Clinical fared better than Developmental and Experimental in all three periods.

On the questionable assumption that developmentalists and experimentalists are as likely as clinicians to be members of their respective divisions in APA, the percentages mean that developmental and experimental psychology have not fared as well as clinical psychology and psychology as a whole.

Nevertheless, the importance of basic knowledge about normal development has been explicitly recognized by clinical psychologists. For example, Kazdin, Bellack, and Hersen (1980) devoted almost 20% of their book *New Perspectives in Abnormal Psychology* to normal development; and Silver and Segal (1984), of the National Institute of Mental Health (NIMH), commented:

Table 7.3. American Psychological Association: Membership Trends
(Fellows and Members)

| Year | Division | | | APA total |
	Devel.	Exptl.	Clin.	
		Frequency		
1965	778	968	2,899	19,199
1985	1,214	1,472	5,418	51,620
1987	1,300	1,473	5,920	56,321
1989	1,259	1,393	5,831	60,223
		Percentage Change		
1965–1985	56.0	52.1	86.9	168.9
1985–1987	7.1	.1	9.3	9.1
1987–1989	− 3.2	− 5.4	− 1.5	6.9

Note. Compiled from frequencies reported in the 1965, 1985, 1987, and 1989 membership directories of the American Psychological Association.

Abnormal personality functioning cannot begin to be fully understood without studying the whole person in his or her environment. . . . Furthermore, the heavy investment of NIMH in basic psychological research reflects a need not only for more complete data about the parameters of abnormal behavior but also for more precise behavioral baseline data. (p. 805)

Recognition of this relationship is also seen in a 1984 NIMH initiative for support of graduate training in basic research on normal development.

The vitality of child psychology as a basic research discipline is evidenced by the large number of books devoted to reviews of this research: more than 45 volumes have been published in the two oldest series alone, *Advances in Child Development and Behavior* and the *Minnesota Symposia on Child Development*, supplemented by several more recent multivolume series and, in the 1980s alone, three major handbooks of developmental psychology—the *Handbook of Developmental Psychology* (Wolman, 1982), the *Review of Human Development* (Field, Huston, Quay, Troll, & Finley, 1982), and the massive four-volume *Handbook of Child Psychology* (Mussen, 1983). Finally, data reported by Meacham (1984) indicate that 439 articles were published in 1982 in only four of the journals devoted to research in developmental psychology (*Child Development, Developmental Psy-*

chology, *Journal of Experimental Child Psychology*, and *Journal of Gerontology*). This is only a small portion of the total number of developmental articles—some 180 journals are *regularly* searched for *Child Development Abstracts and Bibliography*. Of course, not all the articles in these journals are reports of basic research, but by far most of them are.

In spite of all this activity, a need for expansion of research training efforts is implied by the following data: The number of doctorates granted in psychology increased annually between 1965 and 1984, but was 3.9% fewer in 1987 than in 1984, and the number of academic/ research doctorates has had a downward trend since 1976. The number of developmental doctorates has remained fairly steady, and the percentage has had only a slight downward trend overall (Howard et al., 1986); but the percentage of developmental doctorates in 1982 was 17.3% less than in 1981, a considerably greater decline than for doctorates in psychology as a whole (down 5.0%). The trend is hard to interpret, because virtually all developmentalists are employed. Of 316 respondents who received the doctorate in developmental psychology in 1981 and 1982, only 6 (1.9%) were unemployed and seeking employment in those years (Stapp, Fulcher, & Wicherski, 1984); and of 87 respondents for 1983, only 3 (2.4%) were unemployed and seeking employment (Fulcher, Pion, & Stapp, 1985).

Data have not been reported separately for careers in basic developmental research and other developmental careers, but the percentage of developmental-doctorate recipients employed in academic settings has declined from 77.2% in 1975 and 66.4% in 1979 to 57.5% in 1981–1982 and 51.2% in 1983 (Howard et al., 1986; Stapp et al., 1984). If most of those in academic settings had basic interests, and most of those in other settings had applied interests, then probably no more than half of the developmental psychologists are involved in basic research.

To summarize, membership in the developmental division of APA has not been growing as much as membership in APA as a whole; the percentage of doctorates awarded in developmental psychology has declined; and interest in applied developmental psychology seems to have become more prevalent than interest in basic developmental psychology. I predict that these trends will continue, especially the greater demand for applied developmental psychology than for basic developmental psychology.

Two other trends noted by Bevan (1980a) are relevant: (a) The number of graduate students is declining. This decline reflects partly a decline in the population of persons in the modal graduate-student age range and partly a decline in the proportionate number of these persons seeking higher education. (b) The number of jobs available in higher education is declining, as reflected by increases in the proportion of tenured faculty in departments. The result is fewer academic jobs, less competition for these jobs, and less need for them.

The Basic/Applied Split

Despite the increased emphasis on application and the reduced emphasis on basic research, concern with basic knowledge about development is still strong. Its strength is seen, for example, in the increasing popularity of cognitive theories of the information-processing type, especially the subtype that involves actual computer simulation with working programs, and in what I call *developmental behavior analysis* (Reese, 1982). The latter approach to basic child psychology derives from Skinner's behaviorism, but this approach is not nearly as atheoretical as many of its practitioners believe (as noted, for example, by Shimp, 1984; Skinner, 1969, pp. vii–xii; Williams, 1984). I expect the role of theory in this approach to increase, and I expect the strength of the approach to increase as it continues its incursion into complex behaviors such as verbal behavior, social relations, individual differences, and personality (see, for example, the papers in Chase & Parrott, 1986; Lattal & Harzem, 1984; Reese & Parrott, 1986). I also expect increased recognition of the need for philosophical analysis (Marr, 1984). The need for philosophical analysis is not limited to developmental behavior analysis, and it has been recognized in the rest of child psychology. However, the trend I foresee in the rest of child psychology is, unfortunately, an increase in philosophical eclecticism.

The trend toward application in child psychology is disturbing. The trend is obvious and is expected to continue (e.g., Bevan, 1980a; Boll, 1985). However, according to the philosopher of science Larry Laudan (1977), utilitarian considerations have had little to do with the activity of scientists in any discipline, and most of the best scientific activity "is not directed at the solution of practical or socially redeeming problems" (p. 224). In the middle 1930s, Skaggs (1934) and Ross (1936) commented that *scientific* psychology had little practical value, and no one published a rebuttal (at least, not in the *Psychological Review*, in which their articles appeared). The comment has remained true.

Skaggs pointed out that "some of the less scientific psychology" had practical value (p. 576). The developmental psychology of that era might be cited as an example, in that its major focus was on preschool education and child rearing. However, this "psychology" was the province of education and home economics rather than psychology, and it was generally not accepted as a scholarly, scientific discipline in departments of psychology or even in the universities that had child development institutes (Senn, 1975).

The trend toward application is interpretable as a reflection of the shift in the American economy from production to service. The analogy is strained, but I will make it anyway: Just as the American labor force is involved less in the production of goods than in the sale of goods and other services, so child psychology is shifting from the production of knowledge to the peddling of purported knowledge. We should be rolling balls down inclined planes, not making pronouncements about public policy and other practical matters about which we have no *special* knowledge. What is needed is not social activism by child psychologists but research, especially research in basic, scientific child psychology but also—if policy pronouncements must be made— research on problems of practical importance. The trend toward the latter kind of research seems to have increased markedly beginning in the late 1970s (Bevan, 1980a, 1980b; White, 1980; Zimiles, 1980) and it is expected to continue (Lagerspetz, 1984; Siegler, 1983). It may well, however, be only the cycling of a recursion: White (1980) noted that interest in applied research in natural settings is a recursion; and Spiker (1966) mentioned a cycling of applied and basic developmental research.

Other Trends

Increased multidisciplinary research has been predicted (Hamburg, 1985; Lipsitt, 1985; McGraw, 1985), but it is difficult to do, as Hartup (1980) commented, and I expect to see lip service paid to its value more than actual implementation, continuing a long tradition in the Society for Research in Child Development (SRCD). (For documentation, see the histories of SRCD in Rheingold, 1985; Routh, 1986; Smuts, 1985. Also, according to Thelen, 1986, the number of applications to SRCD for summer institutes and study groups declined from a high of 20 in 1984 to 5 and 7 in 1985 and 1986. The intent of the program was to fund multidisciplinary institutes and study groups.)

Posner (1984) predicted progress in knowledge about mind–brain relations. Maybe so, but the breakthroughs that.have been believed to be imminent for the last quarter century or so are for the most part still believed to be imminent. Neurophysiology per se needs no apology; it has made great strides and has contributed to the understanding of child development. However, it has shed little light on basic child *psychology*, and I do not expect it to contribute much to this discipline.

Finally, none of the authors who made predictions mentioned what the students will be like. The trends I have identified lead me to predict that they will be fewer, less dedicated to basic child psychology, less driven to make scholarly contributions to their field, and more concerned with comfort—their clients' and their own. However, I predict that sufficient numbers will have the scholarly calling to keep basic child psychology alive, though not necessarily healthy—the University of Iowa, which had one of the first child development institutes, terminated its developmental psychology program in 1989, joining other universities that had already done so.

RECOMMENDATIONS FOR GRADUATE TRAINING

The 22 predictions made in this chapter lead to five recommendations about graduate training in child psychology.

1. Students should be trained for diversity. They might not have time to learn about all the camps of psychology, but they should learn about the major three (mechanistic, organic, and contextualistic), surveying well their philosophies, aims, methods, theories, and findings.

2. Students should be given a thorough grounding in philosophies of science.

3. Students should be given thorough grounding in methodology, including computer technology and naturalistic research methods, as well as laboratory research methods. Reading skill in a relevant foreign language is a highly desirable methodological tool; but a realistic recommendation is that it be encouraged rather than required.

4. Students should be given both applied and basic training.

5. Students need not be given a grounding in other disciplines, such as neurophysiology, although acquaintance with these fields would not hurt the students.

In short, a range of up-to-date contents and methods should be included in the curriculum, so that the students have enough flexibility not to spend their careers parroting their mentors. This result will come about through work in the classroom, the laboratory, and the field. Didactic training in philosophy, statistics, and computers is needed, as well as in the knowledge base of the student's specialization. However, as dialectical materialist philosophers and scientists have emphasized, the development of knowledge requires direct experience (e.g., Payne, 1968, p. 120). The point is valid whether or not the dialectical materialist rationale for it is accepted. It is the learn-by-doing dictum, endorsed by John B. Watson, for example, in a denigration of writers who have no direct experience with their subject matter (Watson, 1928; see also Cohen, 1979, pp. 249–250), and by virtually all educators, but perhaps given too little weight in most graduate training programs.

REFERENCES

Agassi, J. (1964). The nature of scientific problems and their roots in metaphysics. In M. Bunge (Ed.), The critical approach to science and philosophy: In honor of Karl R. Popper (pp. 189–211). London: Free Press of Glencoe (Collier-Macmillan).

Alpert, J. L. (1985). Change within a profession: Change, future, prevention, and school psychology. American Psychologist, 40, 1112–1121.

Amsel, A. (1988, October). What I learned about frustration at Iowa. Paper presented at the Centennial Celebration, Department of Psychology, University of Iowa, Iowa City, IA.

Baltes, P. B., & Reese, H. W. (1984). The life-span perspective in developmental psychology. In M. H. Bornstein & M. E. Lamb (Eds.), Developmental psychology: An advanced textbook (pp. 493–531). Hillsdale, NJ: Erlbaum.

Baltes, P. B., Reese, H. W., & Lipsitt, L. P. (1980). Life-span developmental psychology. Annual Review of Psychology, 31, 65–110.

Barker, P., & Gholson, B. (1984). The history of the psychology of learning as a rational process: Lakatos Versus Kuhn. In H. W. Reese (Ed.), Advances in child development and behavior (Vol. 18, pp. 227–244). New York: Academic Press.

Beilin, H. (1984). Functionalist and structuralist research programs in developmental psychology: Incommensurability or synthesis? In H. W. Reese (Ed.), Advances in child development and behavior (Vol. 18, pp. 245–257). New York: Academic Press.

Bergmann, G. (1956). The contribution of John B. Watson. Psychological Review, 63, 265–276.

Bevan, W. (1980a). Graduate education for the earthquake generation. Human Development, 23, 126–136.

Bevan, W. (1980b, Fall). Graduate education for the earthquake generation. Newsletter of the Society for Research in Child Development, pp. 4–5.

Boll, T. J. (1985). Graduate education in psychology: Time for a change? American Psychologist, 40, 1029–1030.

Brehmer, B. (1984). Brunswikian psychology for the 1990's. In K. M. J. Lagerspetz & P. Niemi (Eds.), Psychology in the 1990's: In honour of Professor Johan von Wright on his 60th birthday, March 31, 1984 (pp. 383–398). Amsterdam: North-Holland.

Chase, P. N., & Parrott, L. J. (Eds.). (1986). Psychological aspects of language: The West Virginia lectures: Springfield, IL: Charles C Thomas.

Chomsky, N. (1959). Review of Verbal Behavior by B. F. Skinner. Language, 35, 26–58.

Cohen, D. (1979). J. B. Watson: The founder of behaviorism. A biography. London: Routledge & Kegan Paul.

Dewey, J. (1933). How we think: A restatement of the relation of reflective thinking to the educative process. Boston: Heath.

Domjan, M., & Burkhard, B. (1986). The principles of learning & behavior (2nd ed.). Monterey, CA: Brooks/Cole.

Emde, R. N. (1986, Autumn). On Monographs: A new look for a revered publication. Newsletter of the Society for Research in Child Development, pp. 4–5.

Feyerabend, P. K. (1970). Classical empiricism. In R. E. Butts & J. W. Davis (Eds.), The methodological heritage of Newton (pp. 150–170). Toronto: University of Toronto Press.

Field, T. M. Huston, A., Quay, H. C., Troll, L., & Finley, G. E. (Eds.). (1982). Review of human development. New York: Wiley.

Frost, R. (1915). The black cottage. In R. Frost (Ed.), North of Boston (2nd ed., pp. 50–55). New York: Holt.

Fulcher, R., Pion, G., & Stapp, J. (1985). Preliminary report: 1983 new doctorate employment survey. Washington, DC: American Psychological Association.

Gardner, R. A. (1966). On box score methodology as illustrated by three reviews of overtraining reversal effects. Psychological Bulletin, 66, 416–418.

Goetz, E. M., & Baer, D. M. (1973). Social control of form diversity and the emergence of new forms in children's blockbuilding. Journal of Applied Behavior Analysis, 6, 209–217.

Guess, D., Sailor, W., Rutherford, G., & Baer, D. M. (1968). An experimental analysis of linguistic development: The productive use of the plural morpheme. Journal of Applied Behavior Analysis, 1, 297–306.

Hamburg, B. A. (1985). Comments on the relationship of child development to modern child health care. Newsletter of the Society for Research in Child Development (Supplement), not paginated.

Hartup, W. H. (1980, Fall). Training in child development: Old questions in modern times. Newsletter of the Society for Research in Child Development, pp. 5–6.

Hartup, W. W. (1986, Autumn). Notes from Child Development. Newsletter of the Society for Research in Child Development, p. 3.

Hayes, S. C. (Ed.). (1989). Rule-governed behavior: Cognition, contingencies, and instructional control. New York: Plenum.

Hayes, S. C., Hayes, L. J., & Reese, H. W. (1988). Finding the philosophical core: A review of Stephen C. Pepper's World hypotheses: A study in evidence. Journal of the Experimental Analysis of Behavior, 50, 97–111.

Howard, A., Pion, G. M., Gottfredson, G. D., Flattau, P. E., Oskamp, S., Pfafflin, S. M., Bray, D. W., & Burstein, A. G. (1986). The changing face of American psychology: A report from the Committee on Employment and Human Resources. American Psychologist, 41, 1311–1327.

Husserl, E. (1931). Ideas: General introduction to pure phenomenology (W. R. Boyce Gibson, trans.). New York: Macmillan. (Original work published 1913)

James, W. (1907). Pragmatism: A new name for some old ways of thinking. New York: Longmans, Green.

Kaye, H. (1977). Early experience as the basis for unity and cooperation of "differences." In N. Datan & H. W. Reese (Eds.), Life-span developmental psychology: Dialectical perspectives on experimental research (pp. 343–364). New York: Academic Press.

Kazdin, A. E., Bellack, A. S., & Hersen, M. (Eds.). (1980). *New perspectives in abnormal psychology.* New York: Oxford University Press.

Kendler, H. H. (1984). Evolutions or revolutions? In K. M. J. Lagerspetz & P. Niemi (Eds.), *Psychology in the 1990's: In honour of Professor Johan von Wright on his 60th birthday, March 31, 1984* (pp. 7–21). Amsterdam: North-Holland.

Kendler, H. H., & Spence, J. T. (Eds.). (1971a). *Essays in neobehaviorism: A memorial volume to Kenneth W. Spence.* New York: Appleton-Century-Crofts.

Kendler, H. H., & Spence, J. T. (1971b). Tenets of neobehaviorism. In H. H. Kendler & J. T. Spence (Eds.), *Essays in neobehaviorism: A memorial volume to Kenneth W. Spence* (pp. 11–40). New York: Appleton-Century-Crofts.

Kessen, W. (1966). Questions for a theory of cognitive development. In H. W. Stevenson (Ed.), *Concept of development. Monographs of the Society for Research in Child Development, 31*(5, Serial No. 107), 55–70.

Klahr, D. (1973). An information-processing approach to the study of cognitive development. In A. D. Pick (Ed.), *Minnesota symposia on child psychology* (Vol. 7, pp. 141–177). Minneapolis: University of Minnesota Press.

Klahr, D. (1984). Transition processes in quantitative development. In R. J. Sternberg (Ed.), *Mechanisms of cognitive development* (pp. 101–139). New York: Freeman.

Klahr, D., Langley, P., & Neches, R. (Eds.). (1987). *Production system models of learning and development.* Cambridge, MA: MIT Press.

Klahr, D., & Wallace, J. G. (1976). *Cognitive development: An information-processing view.* Hillsdale, NJ: Erlbaum.

Kozulin, A. (1986). Vygotsky in context. In L. Vygotsky (Ed.), *Thought and language* (pp. xi–lvi). Cambridge, MA: MIT Press.

Krechevsky, I. (1932). 'Hypotheses' in rats. *Psychological Review, 39,* 516–532.

Kuhn, T. S. (1962). *The structure of scientific revolutions.* Chicago: University of Chicago Press.

Lagerspetz, K. M. J. (1984). Psychology and its frontiers. In K. M. J. Lagerspetz & P. Niemi (Eds.), *Psychology in the 1990's: In honour of Professor Johan von Wright on his 60th birthday, March 31, 1984* (pp. 23–44). Amsterdam: North-Holland.

Lagerspetz, K. M. J., & Niemi, P. (1984). Introduction. In K. M. J. Lagerspetz, & P. Niemi (Eds.), *Psychology in the 1990's: In honour of Professor Johan von Wright on his 60th birthday, March 31, 1984* (pp. 1–3). Amsterdam: North-Holland.

Lakatos, I. (1978). *The methodology of scientific research programmes.* In I. Lakatos, *Philosophical papers* (J. Worrall & G. Currie, Eds., Vol. 1). Cambridge, UK: Cambridge University Press.

Lattal, K. A., & Harzem, P. (Guest Eds.). (1984). Special issue: Present trends and directions for the future. *Journal of the Experimental Analysis of Behavior, 42*(3).

Laudan, L. (1977). *Progress and its problems: Toward a theory of scientific growth.* Berkeley, CA: University of California Press.

Lerner, R. M. (1986). *Theories and concepts of human development* (2nd ed.). New York: Random House.

Lipsitt, L. P. (1985). Comment on relations between pediatrics and child development scholarship. *Newsletter of the Society for Research in Child Development (Supplement)*, not paginated.

Mackintosh, N. J. (1965). Selective attention in animal discrimination learning. *Psychological Bulletin, 64*, 124–150.

Marr, M. J. (1984). Conceptual approaches and issues. *Journal of the Experimental Analysis of Behavior, 42*, 353–362.

McCandless, B. R. (1970). Editorial. *Developmental Psychology, 2*, 1–4.

McCandless, B. R., & Geis, M. F. (1975). Current trends in developmental psychology. In H. W. Reese (Ed.), *Advances in child development and behavior* (Vol. 10, pp. 1–8). New York: Academic Press.

McGraw, M. (1985). Troublesome dichotomies in the study of child development. *Newsletter of the Society for Research in Child Development (Supplement)*, not paginated.

Meacham, J. A. (1984). Journal citation: The problem of size. *American Psychologist, 39*, 1200. (Comment)

Mussen, P. H. (Ed.). (1983). *Handbook of child psychology* (4th ed., 4 vols.). New York: Wiley.

Nilsson, L.-G. (1984). New functionalism in memory research. In K. M. J. Lagerspetz & P. Niemi (Eds.), *Psychology in the 1990's: In honour of Professor Johan von Wright on his 60th birthday, March 31, 1984* (pp. 185–224). Amsterdam: North-Holland.

Overton, W. F. (1973). On the assumptive base of the nature-nurture controversy: Additive versus interactive conceptions. *Human Development, 16*, 74–89.

Overton, W. F. (1984). World views and their influence on psychological theory and research: Kuhn-Lakatos-Laudan. In H. W. Reese (Ed.), *Advances in child development and behavior* (Vol. 18, pp. 191–226). New York: Academic Press.

Overton, W. F., & Newman, J. L. (1982). Cognitive development: A competence-activation/utilization approach. In T. M. Field, A. Huston, H. C. Quay, L. Troll, & G. E. Finley (Eds.), *Review of human development* (pp. 217–241). New York: Wiley.

Overton, W. F., & Reese, H. W. (1973). Models of development: Methodological implications. In J. R. Nesselroade & H. W. Reese (Eds.), *Life-span developmental psychology: Methodological issues* (pp. 65–86). New York: Academic Press.

Paivio, A. (1975). Neomentalism. *Canadian Journal of Psychology, 29*, 263–291.

Payne, T. R. (1968). *S. L. Rubinstejn and the philosophical foundations of Soviet psychology*. Dordrecht, Holland: Reidel.

Pepper, S. C. (1942). *World hypotheses: A study in evidence*. Berkeley, CA: University of California Press.

Peterson, C. (1982). Review of *Psychological reactance: A theory of freedom and control* by S. S. Brehm & J. W. Brehm. *Science, 216*, 615.

Posner, M. I. (1984). Neural systems and cognitive processes. In K. M. J. Lagerspetz & P. Niemi (Eds.), *Psychology in the 1990's: In honour of Professor Johan von Wright on his 60th birthday, March 31, 1984* (pp. 241–251). Amsterdam: North-Holland.

Psychology tomorrow: The Nobel view. (1982, December). *Psychology Today,* 16(12), 21–31.

Reese, H. W. (1982). Behavior analysis and life-span developmental psychology. *Developmental Review, 2,* 150–161.

Reese, H. W. (1986a). Behavioral and dialectical psychologies. In L. P. Lipsitt & J. H. Cantor (Eds.), *Experimental child psychologist: Essays and experiments in honor of Charles C. Spiker* (pp. 157–195). Hillsdale, NJ: Erlbaum.

Reese, H. W. (1986b, May). *Computer simulation and behavior analysis: Similarities and differences.* Paper presented at the meeting of the Association for Behavior Analysis, Milwaukee.

Reese, H. W. (in press). The data/theory dialectic: The nature of scientific progress. In S. H. Cohen & H. W. Reese (Eds.), *Life-span developmental psychology: Methodological innovations.* Hillsdale, NJ: Erlbaum.

Reese, H. W., & Overton, W. F. (1970). Models of development and theories of development. In L. R. Goulet & P. B. Baltes (Eds.), *Life-span developmental psychology: Research and theory* (pp. 115–145). New York: Academic Press.

Reese, H. W., & Parrott, L. J. (Eds.). (1986). *Behavior science: Philosophical, methodological, and empirical advances.* Hillsdale, NJ: Erlbaum.

Reitman, W. (1984). Machines, architecture, intelligence, and knowledge: Changing conceptions of the cognitive psychologist's data source. In K. M. J. Lagerspetz & P. Niemi (Eds.), *Psychology in the 1990's: In honour of Professor Johan von Wright on his 60th birthday, March 31, 1984* (pp. 111–132). Amsterdam: North-Holland.

Rheingold, H. L. (1985). The first twenty-five years of the Society for Research in Child Development. In A. B. Smuts & J. W. Hagen (Eds.), History and research in child development (pp. 126–140). *Monographs of the Society for Research in Child Development, 50*(4–5, Serial No. 211).

Ross, C. C. (1936). A needed emphasis in psychological research. *Psychological Review, 43,* 197–206.

Routh, D. K. (1986, Autumn). The Society for Behavioral Pediatrics: Retrospect and prospect. *Newsletter of the Society for Research in Child Development,* pp. 1–3.

Rychlak, J. F. (1976). A summing up. In J. F. Rychlak (Ed.), *Dialectic: Humanistic rationale for behavior and development. Contributions to human development* (Vol. 2, pp. 126–141). Basel, Switzerland: Karger.

Senn, M. J. E. (1975). Insights on the child development movement in the United States. *Monographs of the Society for Research in Child Development, 40*(3–4, Serial No. 161).

Shimp, C. P. (1984). Cognition, behavior, and the experimental analysis of behavior. *Journal of the Experimental Analysis of Behavior, 42,* 407–420.

Siegler, R. S. (1983). Information processing approaches to development. In P. H. Mussen (Ed.), & W. Kessen (Vol. Ed.), *Handbook of child psychology* (4th ed.): Vol. 1. *History, theory, and methods* (pp. 129–211). New York: Wiley.

Sigel, I. E. (1986). Mechanism: A metaphor for cognitive development? A review of Sternberg's *Mechanisms of cognitive development*. *Merrill-Palmer Quarterly, 32,* 93–101.

Silver, L. B., & Segal, J. (1984). Psychology and mental health: An enduring partnership. *American Psychologist, 39,* 804–809.

Skaggs, E. B. (1934). The limitations of scientific psychology as an applied or practical science. *Psychological Review, 41,* 572–576.

Skinner, B. F. (1969). *Contingencies of reinforcement: A theoretical analysis.* New York: Appleton-Century-Crofts.

Skinner, B. F. (1974). *About behaviorism.* New York: Knopf.

Skinner, B. F. (1980, May). Discussion. In D. F. Hake & S. Kendall (Chairs), *Some reflections on the development of behavior analysis.* Symposium conducted at the meeting of the Association for Behavior Analysis, Dearborn, MI.

Smuts, A. B. (1985). The National Research Council Committee on Child Development and the founding of the Society for Research in Child Development, 1925–1933. In A. B. Smuts & J. W. Hagen (Eds.), *History and research in child development* (pp. 108–125). *Monographs of the Society for Research in Child Development, 50*(4–5, Serial No. 211).

Spence, K. W. (1956). *Behavior theory and conditioning.* New Haven, CT: Yale University Press.

Spiker, C. C. (1966). The concept of development: Relevant and irrelevant issues. In H. W. Stevenson (Ed.), *Concept of development. Monographs of the Society for Research in Child Development, 31*(5, Serial No. 107), 40–54.

Spiker, C. C. (1977). Behaviorism, cognitive psychology, and the active organism. In N. Datan & H. W. Reese (Eds.), *Life-span developmental psychology: Dialectical perspectives on experimental research* (pp. 93–103). New York: Academic Press.

Spiker, C. C. (1989). Cognitive psychology: Mentalistic or behavioristic? In H. W. Reese (Ed.), *Advances in child development and behavior* (Vol. 21, pp. 73–90). New York: Academic Press.

Stapp, J., Fulcher, R., & Wicherski, M. (1984). The employment of 1981 and 1982 doctorate recipients in psychology. *American Psychologist, 39,* 1408–1423.

Super, C. M. (1982, Spring). Secular trends in *Child Development* and the institutionalization of professional disciplines. *Newsletter of the Society for Research in Child Development,* pp. 10–11.

Super, C. M. (n.d.). *Secular trends in Child Development and the institutionalization of professional disciplines.* Unpublished manuscript, Judge Baker Guidance Center, Boston.

Thelen, E. (1986, Autumn). Report on SRCD study groups on social and emotional development. *Newsletter of the Society for Research in Child Development*, pp. 8–9.

Tulving, E. (1984). Multiple learning and memory systems. In K. M. J. Lagerspetz & P. Niemi (Eds.), *Psychology in the 1990's: In honour of Professor Johan von Wright on his 60th birthday, March 31, 1984* (pp. 163–184). Amsterdam: North-Holland.

Vygotsky, L. (1986). *Thought and language* (A. Kozulin, Ed.). Cambridge, MA: MIT Press. (Original work published 1934)

Watson, J. B. (1928, June 16). Feed me on facts. *Saturday Review of Literature*, 4(47), 966–967.

Wheeler, R. H. (1935). Organismic vs. mechanistic logic. *Psychological Review*, 42, 335–353.

White, S. H. (1977). Social proof structures: The dialectic of method and theory in the work of psychology. In N. Datan & H. W. Reese (Eds.), *Life-span developmental psychology: Dialectical perspectives on experimental research* (pp. 59–92). New York: Academic Press.

White, S. H. (1980, Fall). Graduate training in a developing field. *Newsletter of the Society for Research in Child Development*, pp. 6–7.

Whitehurst, G. J. (1977). Imitation, response novelty, and language acquisition. In B. C. Etzel, J. M. LeBlanc, & D. M. Baer (Eds.), *New developments in behavioral research: Theory, method, and application. In honor of Sidney W. Bijou* (pp. 119–132). Hillsdale, NJ: Erlbaum.

Williams, B. A. (1984). Stimulus control and associative learning. *Journal of the Experimental Analysis of Behavior*, 42, 469–483.

Wolman, B. B. (Ed.). (1982). *Handbook of developmental psychology*. Englewood Cliffs, NJ: Prentice-Hall.

Zimiles, H. (1980, Fall). On making developmental psychology more relevant. *Newsletter of the Society for Research in Child Development*, pp. 7, 9.

chapter 8

Training in the Biology of Development: A Psychobiological Perspective*

Gene P. Sackett

University of Washington
Psychology, Regional Primate Research Center, Child Development and
  Mental Retardation Center

A SURVEY OF PSYCHOBIOLOGISTS CONCERNING THEIR TRADE

Developmental psychobiology is a fundamentally interdisciplinary field. Its potential content covers all developmental research in psychology, neurobiology, and behavior genetics. Gottlieb (1983) defines the psychobiological approach as the study of behavioral development from a broadly biological perspective. This breadth includes an interest in the physiological, biochemical, and anatomical correlates of behavior, as well as ecological and evolutionary issues.

Given this scope, it appeared as I worked on this chapter that issues concerning training in psychobiology could involve the total life sciences resources of any university. Predicting the training in this field that will be relevant for the future thus seemed beyond my level of foresight, presumption, and competence. To develop a reasonable rationale and model for psychobiology training, I polled 110 researchers who are active in this area. They were asked to respond to two questions. (a) What do you consider to be a major psychobiological research

* I thank the many psychobiologists who provided me with the often fascinating details of their own research and many thoughtful ideas that I liberally used in writing this chapter. I do, of course, take full responsibility for the form of the psychobiological philosophy expressed here. I also hope that my interpretations and biases have not misrepresented too many of the substantive issues raised and suggestions made in answer to the survey.

problem in understanding human behavioral development? (b) What training would be required for students of human behavioral development to work on this problem?

These questions must have been of interest, as they stimulated 87 replies. The answers varied from a few sentences to a six-page essay. The responses included 322 references and 108 reprints. Although some of this material represented idiosyncratic viewpoints, four themes emerged as I attempted to consolidate what I was told into a set of sensible recommendations.

MAJOR THEMES IN PSYCHOBIOLOGICAL RESEARCH

I.   A Broad Biological Perspective

Many of my respondents believe that current training in child development is deficient in that it does not provide a broad and contemporary biological perspective on behavior. As suggested by Bateson (1987), this may be due in part to equating biology with strict genetic determination of development at the expense of behavioral and environmental influences. Also, it is likely that the inability to experimentally manipulate most genetic and organismic variables in human subjects contributes to a relative neglect of biological factors in much human development research. Of greater importance, however, may be the lack of conceptual models for experimentally studying covariations of biological, environmental, and behavioral variables in a developmental context. An example of such a model has been offered by Gottlieb (1976, 1983). This model has guided my own thinking for a number of years (e.g., Sackett, Sameroff, Cairns, & Suomi, 1981). I will briefly present Gottlieb's viewpoint here, as it forms the basis for some of the ideas presented later in this chapter.

Gottlieb views the task of experimental developmental research as specifying in detail (a) the patterns of activity and sensitivity that emerge at different times in development; (b) changes in these patterns and sensitivities, including delayed effects that may not occur until well after initial emergence of a behavior or capacity; (c) periods of behavioral stability; and (d) the factors which influence these changes within individuals and differences between individuals. This epigenetic approach involves the empirical and analytic task of first describing, then explaining through experiment, transformations in the biobehavioral phenotype of individuals over time. The involvement of genes, environment, and society in development are givens, with their exact operation in any behavioral system to be understood by experiment.

Three operational concepts are offered by Gottlieb to organize the design and interpretation of these experiments, namely, induction, facilitation, and maintenance. Although he discusses these concepts in terms of the ways that experience can affect behavior, I believe that these concepts are also necessary and equally applicable to the ways in which biology can affect behavior.

Induction concerns the experiential or biological events that are necessary for a behavior to appear during development. This includes experience at critical or sensitive periods, as well as events that can induce new behaviors over a broad range of the life span. In fact, as discussed below, induction of most behaviors and capabilities probably requires the presence of both experiential and biological factors. Facilitation refers to the factors which regulate the rate of change over time in development of a behavior and achievement of typical or deviant endpoints. Maintenance refers to the experiential and biological factors necessary to preserve a developed behavior at its endpoint or steady state. Gottlieb (1983) specifies the details of these concepts and gives examples of their use in analyzing a number of developmental problems.

A major concern in developmental psychobiology is induction. With the exception of language, this has not been a great concern in human development research, perhaps because of the lack of subjects and techniques to perform the required experiments. Facilitation, especially at the level of description, has been a major part of human development research. However, this work has not often been performed in a context of relevant biological processes. It is Gottlieb's contention, and in one form or another that of many of my survey respondents, that this broad psychobiological approach is needed to understand the basics of species-typical human development and its normal variability, as well as the determinants of cultural differences, developmental risk for health and behavior problems, and realized developmental abnormalities.

II. Comparative and Evolutionary Issues in Development

A second theme concerns comparative and evolutionary approaches to problems of development. Psychobiologists uniformly believe that the experimental analysis of systems less complex than that of humans can inform us about basic process in human development (e.g., Hofer, 1981). This means that experience with animal research, knowledge about the animal literature relating to one's own specialty area, and an understanding of the strengths and limitations of animal models for solving human problems is perceived by psychobiologists as a prerequisite for human development research and theory.

Although genes by themselves can determine nothing, behavior is a property of the organism that has clearly evolved along with brain and other structure (e.g., King & Wilson, 1975). Like development itself, processes of evolution involve relationships in which environmental change can produce changes in organisms, but the altered organism may then change the environment (e.g., Plomin, Loehlin, & DeFries, 1985). At an extreme from strict genetic determinism, Gottlieb (1987) has offered the interesting proposal that nongenetic changes in species-typical development are one path leading to genetic evolutionary change. This important idea views development as both a product and a cause of evolution. Current molecular biology advances in DNA sequencing and gene manipulation provide the methodology for experimentally studying such relationships between evolution and development in animal models. It is likely that these tools will also soon be applied in altering the course of human developmental abnormalities. This suggests that methods for studying evolution, behavior genetics, and comparative animal behavior will become essential tools in future research on human behavioral development.

III. Neurobiology

The third theme concerns neurobiology. The obvious relevance of this multidisciplinary field is seen in the publication of a special section of *Child Development* devoted to neurosciences (Crnic & Pennington, 1987). Broadly defined, developmental neurobiology studies life span changes in all aspects of nervous system functioning. This includes neuroanatomy, neurochemistry, endocrinology, molecular genetics, and immunology. Most psychobiologists in my sample viewed processes involving the interdependence of these systems on environmental stimulation and behavior as the most important subject matter to be explained by developmental psychology. Thus, familiarity with the techniques and findings of the neurosciences seems an indisputable part of any future curriculum.

The role of neurobiology in understanding human development is made especially clear by work during the past 20 years concerning the effects of postnatal experience on brain development. This work addresses the central issue of the roles of genes and experience in behavioral development. The answer is that critical processes in the development of brain structure and chemistry depend on experience and behavior. Much of the work leading to this generalization is well reviewed by Greenough, Black, and Wallace (1987). However, a few examples may be useful for those unfamiliar with this area.

Research by a number of workers, including the Nobelists Hubel and Wiesel (1976), has provided information about the effects of monocular eye closure on visual development in infant cats and monkeys. If one eye is kept closed past a critical postnatal age, few neurons normally connected to that eye make contacts in the contralateral visual cortex. Instead, most of their cortical contacts are taken over by neurons connected to the open eye. This results in poor vision or blindness in the closed eye. Similar effects occur under natural conditions to children who have focusing abnormalities in one eye. This large body of research shows that visual experience is essential for the normal morphological and functional development of vision.

Other work, also reviewed by Greenough et al. (1987), shows that the pattern of neural connections in sensory areas of mature brains depends on the type and patterning of sensory stimulation experienced during the time these connections are forming. These authors present an appealing evolution-based theory concerning "experience-expectant" and "experience-dependent" information storage to explain aspects of this dependency of brain structure and function on sensory experiences of the developing individual. These results are also good examples of Gottlieb's concepts of induction of biological structure by the presence of necessary experience at a critical period.

Another example of experience effects on brain involves rearing rats in complex, enriched "playground' environments versus rearing in isolated single cages (Rosenzweig, Bennet, & Diamond, 1972; Greenough et al., 1987). These well-known studies show that the brains of enriched rats have greater neurochemical activity, more synaptic connections, and heavier weights in many cortical areas. These brain differences correlate positively with behavioral differences in exploratory behavior and performance on some learning tasks. Not so well known, but of great importance to human development, is the fact that these beneficial brain and behavior effects of enriched stimulation can be obtained in both adult and aged rats. Thus, unlike the sensory stimulation and patterning studies, the effects of general enrichment are not limited to a critical or sensitive period. In Gottlieb's terms, it is possible in rats to facilitate brain activity and behavior through enrichment across the life span.

IV.   Fetal Development

The final theme apparent in the suggestions and research of almost half of my respondents concerns continuities and discontinuities in development and the effects of early life experiences. Like most developmentalists, psychobiologists are struck, and at times perhaps dumb-founded, by the transformations in the form and function of behavior which occur over the life span. In fact, much of their research concerns the experimental analysis of how earlier processes are transformed into later behavior and function (e.g., Kucharski & Hall, 1987, Hall & Oppenheim, 1987). Thus, a complete psychobiological analysis begins with the study of embryonic and fetal behavior. This approach is based on the premise that the neuro-endocrine-behavioral organization and regulatory mechanisms induced at these stages are the foundations upon which postnatal development builds (e.g., Smotherman & Robinson, 1988). In this view, it is likely that aspects of most developmental processes have a fetal origin.

A model example is sexual differentiation, in which developmental events beginning at 8 to 12 gestational weeks are the critical determinants of many biobehavioral processes that are expressed in function many years later. Ignoring such processes eliminates the possibility of understanding the induction mechanisms that may underlie both typical and deviant postnatal development. Given recent advances in ultrasound and electrophysiological recording techniques, it is now possible to study human fetal behavior experimentally (Smotherman & Robinson, 1988) as well as perform longitudinal studies on animal subjects. This suggests that fetal behavior is a ripe and almost untouched area for future human development researchers.

The importance of studying sex differentiation and sex steroid effects on processes of fetal brain induction and facilitation is illustrated in work by Maccoby and her colleagues (Maccoby, Doering, Jacklin, & Kraemer, 1979; Jacklin, Maccoby, & Doering, 1983; Jacklin, Wilcox, & Maccoby, 1988). In this longitudinal study, umbilical blood was taken from male and female newborns and analyzed for a number of steroid hormones. Males were found to have a higher concentration of testosterone than females, and first-born males had a higher concentration than later borns. This result reveals that either induction and/or facilitation processes of male sex differentiation are altered by some aspect of maternal pregnancy biology. My personal candidate is immune sensitization by the first-born males. Such an effect could alter immune system relationships between the mother and her later born sons, while not affecting the mother–daughter system. Though highly speculative at this time, such a process could also relate to the differential vulnerability of males over females for many diseases and postnatal behavior problems (Gualtieri & Hicks, 1985).

This longitudinal study has followed the subjects into school ages, finding a number of correlations between hormone levels at birth and later social and cognitive behavior. As expected from the idea that processes induced earlier in time may have delayed facilitating effects, some of these correlations disappear with increased age, while others appear only in one sex at a later age. Thus, the 1988 article reports that higher perinatal androgen levels were associated with low spatial ability at age 6, but the correlation appeared only for girls.

RECOMMENDATIONS FOR TRAINING
IN DEVELOPMENTAL PSYCHOBIOLOGY

In an ideal intellectual world, the psychobiological component of a program in human development would include exposure to the 20 or more academic disciplines involved in the "broad biological view." Given the realities of time, core general program courses, appropriate faculty, and overall demands on the mental capacity of students, it is obvious that a compromise must be achieved. In part this could depend on the interests and needs of individual students. Given motivation, and freedom of choice, an individual can expose himself or herself to much of the broad range if it is available at a given institution.

Many of the survey respondents did agree on aspects of a core curriculum, some of which will already be part of most graduate programs. These include an emphasis on both theory and practical applications of data analysis in courses on psychometrics, computer analysis and statistical modeling, and observational research. The latter is especially important for the ethological perspective employed by most psychobiologists in describing species-typical behavior—a human development research task for which there is still much work to do. Other traditional courses include physiological psychology and behavior genetics, which may also be readily available to most students. Also available, but apparently taken less often by developmental students, would be a hands-on course in laboratory animal developmental research. The majority of respondents considered this to be a prerequisite to any real understanding of the psychobiological approach.

Complete agreement was given to the idea that every student of human development should obtain a strong background in basic biology and neuroscience. This would include evolutionary theory, genetics, immunology, biochemistry, anatomy, physiology, endocrinology, metabolism, and developmental molecular biology. Although depth is unlikely for students not actually specializing in psychobiology, exposure to these areas seems essential for understanding the significance to human development of both current and future advances in these fields. Accomplishing this goal may require the cooperation of biology and zoology departments in devising new courses meeting the needs of developmental students.

Two suggestions from my colleagues seem both practical and necessary for incorporating psychobiology into the human development curriculum. Suggestion one is that programs in human development should have a critical mass of psychobiologists on their faculty. This would automatically yield one or more courses in psychobiology, and would offer opportunities for students to perform psychobiological research. It would also provide biological expertise and stimulation to faculty interested in incorporating psychobiological variables and methods into their behavioral development studies. Finally, the presence of psychobiologists should form a natural bridge between psychology and biology departments, making joint and reciprocal course offerings more likely.

Most of what has been said here was directed toward graduate training. A second suggestion relates to the problem of lack of interest in behavioral biology by human development students and some faculty. Many psychobiologists stated that interest in this area must be fostered from undergraduate experiences. Thus, it is strongly recommended that exposure to psychobiological issues and research should begin at the undergraduate level. This is probably even more important than graduate training if human development research is to take advantage of future advances in biological theory, facts, and the application of new research technologies.

REFERENCES

Bateson, P. (1987). Biological approaches to the study of behavioural development. *International Journal of Behavioral Development, 10*, 1–22.

Crnic, L. S., & Pennington, B. F. (Eds.). (1987). Special section on developmental psychology and the neurosciences: Building a bridge. *Child Development, 58*, 533–717.

Gottlieb, G. (1976). The roles of experience in the development of behavior and the nervous system. In G. Gottlieb (Ed.), *Neural and behavioral specificity*. New York: Academic Press.

Gottlieb, G. (1983). The psychobiological approach to developmental issues. In P. Mussen (Ed.), *Handbook of developmental psychology, Vol. 2, Infancy and developmental psychobiology*. New York: Wiley.

Gottlieb, G. (1987). The developmental basis of evolutionary change. *Journal of Comparative Psychology, 101*, 262–271.

Greenough, W. T., Black, J. E., & Wallace, C. S. (1987). Experience and brain development. *Child Development, 58*, 539–559.

Gualtieri, Y., & Hicks, R. E. (1985). An immunoreactive theory of selective male affliction. *The Brain and Behavior Sciences, 8*, 427–477.

Hall, W. G., & Oppenheim, R. W. (1987). Developmental psychobiology: Prenatal, perinatal, and early postnatal aspects of behavioral development. *Annual Review of Psychology, 38,* 91–128.

Hofer, M. A. (1981). *The roots of human behavior.* New York: W. H. Freeman & Co.

Hubel, D. H., & Wiesel, T. N. (1976). Grass foundation lecture, *Society for Neuroscience,* 6th annual meeting (B.I.S. conference report No. 45). Los Angeles: Brain Information Service.

Jacklin, C. N., Maccoby, E. E., & Doering, C. H. (1983). Neonatal sex-steroid hormones and timidity in 6–18 month-old boys and girls. *Developmental Psychobiology, 16,* 163–168.

Jacklin, C. N., Wilcox, K. T., & Maccoby, E. E. (1988). Neonatal sex-steroid hormones and cognitive abilities at six years. *Developmental Psychobiology, 21,* 567–574.

King, M. C., & Wilson, A. C. (1975). Evolution at two levels in humans and chimpanzees. *Science, 188,* 107–116.

Kucharski, D., & Hall, W. G. (1987). New routes to early memories. *Science, 238,* 786–788.

Maccoby, E. E., Doering, C. H., Jacklin, C. N., & Kraemer, H. (1979). Concentrations of sex hormones in umbilical cord blood: Their relation to sex and birth order of infants. *Child Development, 50,* 632–642.

Plomin, R., Loehlin, J. C., & DeFries, J. C. (1985). Genetic and environmental components of "environmental" influences. *Developmental Psychology, 21,* 391–402.

Rosenzweig, M. R., Bennett, E. L., & Diamond, M. C. (1972). Brain changes in response to experience. *Scientific American, 226,* 22–29.

Sackett, G. P., Sameroff, A. J., Cairns, R. B., & Suomi, S. J. (1981). Continuity in behavioral development: Theoretical and behavioral issues. In G. B. Barlow, M. Main, & L. Petrinovitch (Eds.), *Behavioral development: The Bielefeld interdisciplinary project.* New York: Cambridge University Press.

Smotherman, W. P., & Robinson, S. R. (Eds.). (1988). *Behavior of the fetus.* Caldwell, NJ: The Telford Press.

chapter 9

Child Psychology—
Identity and Interaction

Winifred O. Shepard
State University of New York, College at Fredonia

The fact is that few of those who earn doctorates in child psychology will spend their professional lives doing pure research on the behavior or development of children. The problem is to adjust to that fact without compromising the continual accumulation of high quality data. This chapter explores the fact and the problem with special emphasis on their implications for the next generation of child psychologists.

The first section will discuss the present situation—numbers and activities of child psychologists—and will speculate on the origins of that situation. The second section will offer some general comments about the nature of scientific enterprises, and the third section will focus on specific training recommendations.

All the views expressed reflect my own professional experiences—training in a "hard science" orientation followed by years of teaching and advising the kind of heterogeneous population of undergraduates from which new generations of child psychologists emerge.

DEFINITION OF THE FIELD

Definitive data on numbers and current employment of child psychologists are virtually impossible to come by, in part because there is no clearly identifiable population of "child psychologists." Moreover, there is no unambiguous body of information about what those who, in one way or another, are identified with that label actually do on a day-to-day basis.

The words *child psychologist* are frequently used interchangeably with *developmental psychologist*, and neither designation has widely accepted referents, a problem clearly recognized by the APA office of Demographic, Employment and Educational Research (G. M. Pion, personal communication, September 10, 1987).

In the publication *Graduate Study in Psychology and Associated Fields* (American Psychological Association, 1986), there are no programs listed in the index for "child psychology," which "rightly or wrongly has been viewed as more of a specialty area rather than a major subfield" (G. M. Pion, personal communication, 1987). There are some programs listed as "child development" and a larger number listed as "developmental psychology," with all of the former included as a second entry in the latter category. Moreover, according to the descriptive paragraphs in the text of the volume, no department actually offers a degree called "child development," despite the index listing. All offer degrees called "developmental psychology," and these vary widely. Some emphasize the early years of life, some adulthood, and some the life span. Some focus on rigorous research, some on application, and some on all of the above.

The situation is further clouded because organizations that are viewed as the professional associations of child psychologists are actually comprised of individuals with highly diverse backgrounds. The Society for Research in Child Development is avowedly an interdisciplinary organization whose 4,000 members include "anthropologists, dentists, educators, nutritionists, pediatricians, physiologists, psychiatrists, psychologists, sociologists and statisticians" (Koek & Boyles, 1988). Even APA's Division 7 on Developmental Psychology is extremely heterogeneous. I checked biographic entries for a random sample of 223 (25%) of doctoral level entries in the "member" category of Division 7 listed in the *Directory of the American Psychological Association* (American Psychological Association, 1985). Of these, a startling 133 (60%) had received their doctorates in fields other than child or developmental, with clinical or experimental being the most frequently listed. What, then, does an individual mean when he or she self designates as a "child psychologist"?

Most parsimoniously, it appears that those who call themselves "child psychologists" are simply individuals with doctorates in psychology who have some professional interest in children, but that amorphous definition does not serve the purpose of this volume. For that purpose, I could come up with no definition that would elicit universal agreement, but decided to use the words *child psychologist* to refer to people who receive a doctorate in a psychology program primarily oriented to the study of children. In cases where the materials cited make it appropriate to use the words *developmental psychologist*, those conditions will be stated. It also should be kept in mind that, where general comments are made about *science* or *psychology*, they can be understood to apply to child psychology as well as to the larger category.

CHILD PSYCHOLOGY IN THE 1980s

Numbers. In an attempt to describe the numbers and occupations of child psychologists, I began with the reasonable assumption that the trends revealed in the APA analyses of data on doctoral recipients in psychology since 1975 apply to the subset that focuses on children as well as to the larger population.

When published, these surveys include data for 2 academic years at a time, but the trends can be shown by sampling across intervals. For the picture on numbers of new doctorates, I will discuss here the data for 1979 (Stapp & Fulcher, 1982), 1982 (Stapp, Fulcher & Wicherski, 1984), and 1985 (Pion, Bramblett, & Wicherski, 1987).

Methodologically, these surveys began by asking departmental chairs to report the number of doctorates granted for the year under consideration. Response rates by chairs have generally been excellent. For the year 1979, 91% of those contacted replied and reported 3,102 doctoral recipients, For 1982, 91% replied and reported 3,080, and for 1985, 78% replied and reported 3,151. The individuals who had been identified by the chairs were then sent questionnaires, and their replies furnished the data for subsequent analyses by subfield and field of employment. Unfortunately, response rates of doctoral recipients were, in all years, considerably lower than those of chairs. For 1979, 69% of doctoral recipients replied; for 1982, 70%; and for 1985, only 58%. Response rate by subfield was not reported in the published analyses. Indeed, in these surveys, there was no category for "child psychology" in the list from which respondents chose a self-designation. Rather there was a category called "developmental psychology." Individuals who think of themselves as child psychologists, therefore, would either have had to designate themselves as "developmental psychologists" along with an undetermined number whose primary interest was in adulthood or gerontology or life span, or they could have selected some other category that most closely resembled their field of major interest, or simply listed themselves as "other." In discussing these surveys, however, one can do nothing but deal with respondents in the field "developmental psychology," although that certainly must include many who do not deal primarily with children. Inferences about child psychologists are, therefore, suggestive at best and certainly an over-estimation. For what it's worth, in 1979, 8% of the new PhDs who responded to the survey desginated themselves as "developmental psychologist," in 1982, 7%, and in 1985, 5%. In summary, it appears that, while overall numbers of PhD graduates in psychology remain fairly stable, the numbers in the field we are here most directly concerned with are tapering off.

Job settings. The APA surveys do not provide information on employment setting broken down by field of the degree, but overall data on employment of new doctoral recipients confirm the trend that many have noted. A steady erosion of employment possibilities in traditional academic settings has been coupled with increasing employment possibilities in nonacademic settings. Various health care settings (a category which seems to include a wide array of helping services) have shown particularly high growth (Stapp & Fulcher, 1982). Nearly 50% of new PhDs in psychology are now taking full-time positions in health care settings (Howard et al., 1986), and the most frequently reported type of full-time position for the overall population of doctoral recipients is in direct human services (44.3%). Even among Ph.D.'s who are employed in academic settings, only slighting more than 50% are in departments of psychology (Stapp, Fulcher, & Wicherski, 1984).

According to the APA surveys, it was not hard, in the early years of this decade, for developmental psychologists, and, presumably, the child psychologists among them, to find jobs. In 1980, 1981, and 1982 the percentages of developmental psychologists who reported that they were unemployed and looking were 0%, (Stapp & Fulcher, 1982, 1.7%, and 2.1% (Stapp, Fulcher, & Wicherski, 1984), respectively. For the first time, however, a disturbing note emerged when the latest data available at the time of this writing were analyzed. The APA classifies developmental psychology as a "research specialty," and, for the 1985 doctoral recipients, it was found that those who earned degrees in research specialties exhibited a much lower percentage of full-time employment than those specifically trained as human services providers (Pion et al., 1987). Moreover, developmental psychologists were worse off than any of the other research specialties; a full 6% of them were unemployed and seeking work. The next highest percentage was 2.3% among experimental psychology doctorates. It is too early to tell if this is just a blip or signifies the start of a new trend.

In an effort to get more specific information on what child psychologists are doing, I returned to my sample of Division 7 members and recorded the employment of those 90 members of the sample who listed their degrees of PhD in child or developmental psychology. I counted the number whose entries indicated traditional academic activities in either psychology or educational psychology departments. Overall, 45 (50%) fell into this category; the others were scattered over a wide range of applied settings which included medical schools and hospitals, mental health clinics, developmental centers, family service agencies, and so on.

For further corroboration of this apparent trend toward applied employment, I contacted 64 of the 90 departments which, according to *Graduate Study in Psychology and Associated Fields* (American Psychological Association, 1986) offered degrees in developmental psychology. I selected American schools whose text entries suggested that their programs were primarily oriented to children. The letter I sent asked for information on the number of doctorates in child or developmental awarded over the last 10 years and the postdegree employment of the recipients. I also sought details, to be referred to later, about programs. Twenty-nine, or 45% of those I wrote to, replied, with varying degrees of completeness. Two no longer offered the degree at all. Two others did not offer the degree, but allowed students to concentrate on child psychology. Although the response rate to my inquiry was disappointingly low, the schools I heard from covered a wide range in terms of size, geographic location, and numbers of degrees awarded, and I did not see any obvious differences between them and the parent population. Collectively, they reported having granted a total of 484 doctoral degrees in child or developmental over the last 10 years, and they were able to provide a good deal of information on the postdegree employment of their graduates. One hundred and ninety of these relatively recent recipients of the PhD degree (39%) had accepted jobs in traditional academics settings, while 25 (5%) had gone on to postdoctoral study, and 197 (41%) were working in applied settings. The remaining 72 (15%) were either not seeking employment or their whereabouts were unknown.

The pattern of applied employment among recent recipients of the doctorate in child and developmental is of interest and confirms general trends already noted. Not all the responses were in classifiable form, but I was able to classify 154 of the 197 applied jobs. Overwhelmingly these recent doctoral recipients had taken "helping" jobs. Thirty-three were employed directly in hospitals or medical schools, 17 had opened private practices, and 62 were employed by public or private agencies that dealt with physical, developmental or behavioral problems. An additional 42 had taken on miscellaneous jobs including such things as director of a wilderness education program, researcher for a toy company, and legislative assistant.

Research activities. The APA classifies developmental psychology as a research specialty, but we do not know much about what that means in concrete terms, since the survey definition of research is so inclusive that it's difficult to conceive of anyone who is not in one way or another, within that definition, involved in research. "Research includes basic or applied research in any field. Includes non-faculty research positions, work in laboratory or research institute in government or private setting" (Pion et al., 1987). The regular APA surveys do not include a breakdown of research involvement by subfield or employment setting, but it is not surprising that, in a census of all psychological personnel residing in the U.S. in 1983 (Stapp, Tucker & Vanden-Bos, 1985), 82% of those with doctorates in developmental said they were "involved in research activities." Respondents who say they are doing research may be, and probably are, engaged in a great variety of activities, such as counting the number of children enrolled over a period of years in a Head Start program, doing library research relevant to a grant proposal, doing laboratory research on syntactic development, or assessing the impact of a teenage drug counseling program. We just don't know from available data. The APA surveys, while the best we have, still allow a great deal of room for interpretation on the part of respondents and a corresponding degree of latitude for readers who try to reach conclusions and, perhaps, formulate plans on the basis of the published survey data.

We not only lack a clear picture of what child psychologists mean when they say they are doing research, but we also lack information on where and how much research is underway. It's commonly assumed that research flourishes among doctoral personnel who are employed in academe. That may once have been generally true and may still be true in the large university centers, but I have observed it to be far from true in 4-year schools where teaching loads and committee responsibilities are high and there are no graduate assistants to collect data. It is certainly not generally true of community colleges, where faculties are even more burdened. I'm quite certain that at least part of the 40% drop in submissions to the major scientific child psychology journals (Hartup, 1986) reflects the fact that this cherished assumption about academe and research productivity is shaky. Many academic institutions simply do not have the economic resources necessary to provide the kind of support needed to generate a large volume of research, and, therefore, once tenure is attained, productivity often drops.

There is particular need at this juncture for a detailed study of the training, employment, and specific job-related activities of child psychologists. The in-depth study of doctoral recipients in experimental psychology programs conducted by Klatzky, Allusi, Cook, Forehand, and Howell (1985) could usefully be adapted for a similar study of child psychologists.

Trend toward application. Although each separate currently available source is flawed, the convergent findings are consistent. As compared to the 1950s and 1960s, when we were in an era of accumulating knowledge, we are now, predominantly, in an era of trying to apply it. Why?

There are several plausible explanations for the surge of interest in careers oriented toward practical application. The one most frequently cited is simply the course of development of the American academic establishment as it affected the job market. The halcyon, expansionistic days of the 1960s and 1970s played themselves out. Budgets diminished, and faculties became tenured in. Academic positions, which at least historically fostered or forced the pure research ethic, were simply no longer plentiful. Doctoral graduates had to look elsewhere for career opportunities relevant—in any measure—to their training.

Another important reason for the trend toward practical careers is seldom taken seriously enough. This is the fact that the practical problems affecting children became so numerous, various, visible, and destructive across all socioeconomic segments of our society. Americans, more than their European forebears, have always been fundamentally oriented toward direct, immediate activism rather than intellectual or philosophical analyses, and in the face of the pressing problems of childhood, this penchant was enhanced.

Most human beings have a strong feeling that children are our most precious resource. Perhaps it's because children represent a link with immortality or a channel for the protection of hard won property. Perhaps they provide an opportunity for adults to feel effective and needed and loved, or perhaps in their innocence they keep hope alive. No matter what the explanation or combination of explanations, people are moved, particularly, when children suffer, and those who trespass against children are widely perceived to be the most heinous sinners. A discipline like ours, therefore, by virtue of its subject matter, has a strong emotional factor affecting its development which is absent in many others.

It is certainly true that children have always been vulnerable—to disease, starvation, exploitation, and physical and mental abuse. Never before, however, has it been less possible for those able to help to hide from those realities. Sequestered behind garden walls, the very rich or the educated in previous centuries did not have to see young victims. Children born with or acquiring severe handicaps did not often survive to require educational services or to peer out at society from ubiquitous posters. Learning disabilities meant little in societies where only the privileged went to school and most gainful employment did not require intellectual prowess. Divorce was rare, and illegitimacy was coped

with quietly within families. Children who toiled in mines or dangerous factories were mostly invisible except to the few who set out to look
for them, and drugs and alcohol were not as significant a part of the
general culture.

To say that the situation is different today is an understatement.
Endlessly, the media flash heartrending pictures of swollen-bellied
African children onto millions of TV screens, and ignorance is impossible. Children who don't learn in school, or who drop out, are unable
to find gainful employment in a complex technological society, and
become financial and moral burdens. Drug and alcohol abuse reaches
into and devastates the rich and the middle class as well as the poor,
and unwed pregnancy and family breakup know no social distinction.
Add to this the new terrors of pollution-spawned disease and nuclear
holocaust, and there's no place to hide. The image of the dike, which
springs new leaks for every one that is mended, is inescapable.

Also inescapable is the pressure for knowledgeable people to help
the children. Some is self-generated. Consciences are activated by
awareness. I have frequently encountered students—some of our best—
who simply laughed at the thought that they would spend their time
learning abstruse statistical design when they had direct knowledge of
children who were desperately in need of immediate help. I can't
document, of course, the extent of this phenomenon, but I strongly
suspect that other undergraduate instructors have also encountered it.
A cursory glance at the statistics makes this conscience factor understandable.

The 1987 Statistical Abstract of the United States (U.S. Bureau of the
Census, 1987) includes the following information. In 1984, 1,131,300
children were reported to have been neglected or abused—up from
606,600 in 1978. In 1985, 51,402 juveniles were held in custody in
public juvenile residential facilities, up from 45,396 in 1979. Comparable figures for private facilities were 34,112 in 1985, in contrast to
28,719 in 1979. Further, in 1985, 8.6 million children between the ages
of 5 and 17, 19.4% of the population, were living below the poverty
level, as compared to 7.7 million, or 15.3%, in 1979. Again, in 1982,
27% of the population of 12- to 17-year-olds were reported to be current
users of marijuana and alcohol, as opposed to 24% in 1972. Finally, the
percent of disrupted families appears to be increasing. In 1985, 73.9%
of children under 18 lived with both parents, while in 1980 the comparable figure was 76.7%. Most of these figures, based as they are on
official reports, probably are underestimates of the actual frequencies.

There has been societal response. A huge array of institutional settings has developed to cope with these problems and, for that purpose,
to employ thousands of people who have training and/or compassion-

ate interest in working with children. In addition to the vast Federal network of helping agencies, each of the states has its own agencies and there are thousands of nongovernmental private agencies. In 1987 (U.S. Bureau of the Census, 1987) it was reported that there were 19,483 nongovernmental individual and family service organizations and 30,762 child day care services. Between 1965 and 1975 alone more than 1,000 new social programs were launched (Howard, 1985), while private practice drew large numbers of those trained in psychology. In addition there has been a controversial trend, which will be discussed later, toward the establishment of doctoral programs specifically geared to the application of child psychology (Goldstein, Wilson, & Gerstein), 1983) at the same time that pressure has increased on child psychologists to involve themselves in legislative policy making. They have been criticized for not doing so in the past: "researchers in general have not spent much time educating policy makers about the limitations as well as the potential of research knowledge" (Brim & Dustan, 1983, p. 85), and exhorted to do so in the future. Psychologists should point out the nature of the available evidence, the methods upon which research is based and the limitations and generalizability of the findings" (Miller, 1983, p.74). Masters (1984) has described some interactive details of the relationship between research and policy, as have Maccoby, Kahn, and Everett (1983), who wrote, "The impact of a piece of research depends greatly on its timing, its scope in relation to the policy issue at hand, and its concordance or discordance with political forces" (p. 83). There are fundamental differences of opinion over whether or not scientists should involve themselves in public policy, and I'll return to this later, but it's clear that the number of roles that child psychologists are assuming in society, and are being urged to assume, has exploded. Table 9.1, adapted from one presented by Goldstein et al. (1983), who were advocating applied developmental psychology programs, lists jobs child psychologists are undertaking today and settings in which they are working. It is by no means exhaustive but does illustrate that, despite frequent politically driven shifts in funding, there has been a massive institutionalization of society's commitment to children.

In summary, both available data on employment and the material contained in Table 1 support the contention that applied child psychology is currently a major force. It appears that we are now in a period of, to use George Miller's felicitous phrase, "giving Psychology away" (Miller, 1969). With this, the problem that lurks and darts and gets pushed into the background is, what do we have to give away? Can we, will we be able to, offer anything beyond sympathy, common sense, and intuition? These are not gifts to be dismissed lightly. Indeed, I suspect that, if push came to shove, most of us would choose them over

Table 9.1.   Child Psychologists: Settings and Roles

1. Schools—preschool through secondary
   a. development and evaluation of primary prevention, intervention, and mainstreaming programs
   b. consultation on curricula changes
   c. consultation with speech therapists, school psychologists, and school boards
   d. make accessible and interpret research on learning, memory, learning disabilities
2. Higher education
   a. teaching
   b. research—basic and applied, in laboratory and field
   c. supervision of graduate students
3. Health care settings—hospitals and clinics
   a. design and evaluation of prevention and health care programs for children
   b. design and conducting of research on health care issues involving children
   c. consultation with pediatricians, family practitioners, clinicians
4. Media and publishing industries
   a. research, development, and consultation on children's TV, film, books and magazines
   b. evaluation of impact of materials and advertising directed at children
   c. writing of articles for public consumption reporting on and critically evaluating research about children
5. Community
   a. conducting and disseminating research on design of schoolrooms, playgrounds and other settings for children
   b. participating in development and evaluation of community day care, after school, and parent education programs
   c. conducting research in private agencies and foundations
6. Private industry
   a. consultation on development of products for specific age groups (e.g., toys, child proof packaging, furniture, clothing)
   b. evaluate product and advertising effectiveness
7. Government
   a. conduct research in government or government sponsored agencies
   b. interpret and "translate" research for legislators concerned with policy making
   c. evaluate government sponsored programs
8. Courts
   a. consult on issues concerning children (e.g., child custody, child abuse, rights of children)

Adapted from Goldstein, D., Wilson, S.J., & Gerstein, A.I. (1983). Applied Developmental Psychology: Problems and perspectives for an emerging discipline. *Journal of Applied Developmental Psychology, 4,* 341–348. Table 1, p. 344.

any others. Still, they are unreliable and, apparently, are not enough to make a serious dent in current problems. Where does science, scientific child psychology in particular, fit in?

SCIENCE AND CHILD PSYCHOLOGY

A series of articles by Bevan (1976, 1980, 1982) on science, scientists, and social needs is particularly germane and is heavily drawn on in the paragraphs below.

Two issues are basic to a discussion of diversity in child psychology. Both of them have been far more extensively and precisely addressed in volumes on the nature of science, but require at least minimal treatment here. The first concerns the role of science as an institution in society. The second concerns the relationships among matters of fact and matters of value in the scientific enterprise.

Cultural institution. Bevan (1980) distinguishes between two opposing conceptions of science as an institution. The pure Cartesian orientation emphasizes a sacrosanct knowledge-seeking role. Science aims at "the valid conceptualization of Nature on a grand scale" (Bevan, 1980, p. 780) and requires total commitment from the scientist. It is an intrinsically worthwhile endeavor and should be immune from outside influences and ethically neutral, with the search for "Truth" taking precedence over everything else: "any scrutiny on the part of the public or its institutions is viewed as an unjustified intrusion" (p. 779). In contrast, according to Bevan (1980), the pure Baconian position stresses that "science is viewed as a social enterprise, a cooperative activity within a professional community. . .bound by a single shared altruistic commitment to the promotion of human welfare." Science has "no intrinsic social value, but gains value only as its outcomes give rise to beneficial application" (p. 781).

The position at any point in time that science occupies along this Cartesian–Baconian dimension seems to be a function of multiple aspects of the cultural context including the social status of the scientists, the technological and welfare needs of society, and the costs of doing research. The Cartesian orientation was undoubtedly considered appropriate in the days of educated kings and princes and their favored protegés, but I doubt if it ever existed in pure form except as an ideal. Even educated kings and princes faced practical problems on which they sought expert advice. Certainly pure Cartesianism does not exist today, and indeed, many think it should not. "Those of us who have been Cartesian in our view of psychology have hurt its progress not because we have been indifferent to application but because we have actively discouraged consideration of such questions on the ground that we would compromise the purity of our science" (Bevan, 1982, p. 1319). Still, I know no child psychologist today who is so opposed to application that he or she would drink to that unambiguous, although apocryphal, toast allegedly offered at a dinner for scientists at Cambridge, "To pure mathematics and may it never be of any use to anybody!" (Merton, 1973, p. 260).

The Baconian orientation flourishes in times, like those we are living through today, when social problems are numerous and well recognized and when science is heavily supported by government rather than private patronage. I doubt, however, that the Baconian orientation ever existed in pure form any more than did the Cartesian. An urge for understanding has always characterized human beings, and few "do-gooders" have ever been naive enough to believe that effective amelio-rative activities could long endure without a base of objectively "pure" knowledge.

Scientists today are deeply divided in their choices of resting places along the Cartesian–Baconian dimension we've been discussing, even though there is a clear tilt toward the Baconian pole. Indeed, the expression of preference sometimes takes the form of a rather acri-monious, potentially destructive, division.

Fact and value. The complex interactive web of relationships among fact and value in child psychology is sometimes hard to identify and its concrete manifestations harder to document. Nevertheless the possible impacts are plausible enough to merit cautious consideration. A philosophical distinction between fact and value is, with few excep-tions, not in serious question. There is, most would assert, a real world out there, there are real behavioral and emotional phenomena to study, and observations about such phenomena can, under appropriate condi-tions, be agreed upon by various scientists. Most of us believe, find it necessary to believe, in this reality. We keep this faith even while acknowledging that human beings, including very small children, per-ceive the same external reality differently, and that values systems—interests, attitudes, opinions, and feelings—affect perceptions. These last named phenomena constitute data—important data, difficult data to handle, but a part of the reality that child psychologists must study objectively.

To say that we recognize a distinction between fact and value, however, is not to say that value does not affect data collecting. It does, and to deny it flies in the face of much of what we psychologists have learned about human beings. It's not easy to attain the ideal of objective observation because data are accumulated by human beings who are affected, often in ways of which they are unaware, by personal, intel-lectual, and cultural considerations. Based on association with a wide variety of colleagues over the years, I've become convinced that the impact of values on scientists and hence on the nature of the scientific enterprise is much more significant than is generally recognized. The following paragraphs elaborate on this view.

The sociologist Merton (1973) was dealing with personal values when he wrote, "Although it is customary to think of the scientist as a dispassionate, impersonal individual, it must be remembered that the scientist in company with all other professional workers has a large emotional investment in his way of life" (p. 259). Our discipline, because of its subject matter, is, I think, particularly vulnerable here. Child psychologists were children, have children, work with them, and, for the most part, are compassionate human beings. They have strong, often unexamined, feelings about children and as much difficulty separating the emotional and professional parts of their lives as anyone else. Does this ever impact on the acquisition and dissemination of data about children? Probably. Data that support cherished personal assumptions about children, it has seemed to me, are not always subject to quite the same critical scrutiny as data that violate such assumptions. Moreover, child psychologists, like other scientists, become ego involved in their data and theoretical interpretations and may, usually unwittingly, simply ignore, discount, or suppress alternative findings. Do such personal considerations ever affect what gets accepted and rejected for professional publications? Probably.

Not only personal, emotional values, but superordinate intellectual orientations, can affect the scientific enterprise. Kimble (1984) maintains that there are two cultures, one scientific and one humanistic, in psychology, and, certainly, the design and interpretation of studies of the same domain differ depending on which culture the scientist identifies with. Child psychology today includes extreme adherents of both these intellectual cultures as well as more moderate members. Paradoxically, however, the impact of these differences is easier to detect and control for than broadly shared values among scientists. If people from different epistemological camps replicate each other's work, run reliability checks, and point out design flaws, differences attributable to that factor are likely to be brought to light. On the other hand, error due to shared values is harder to detect through replication and reexamination. Therefore, functionally, Krasner and Houts's (1984) finding that there was little difference between behavior modifiers and other randomly selected psychologists in "broad sociopolitical values," even where there were differences in scientific epistemology, should be taken seriously. It's very hard to know how much error remains because of shared intellectual orientations.

Finally, the scientific enterprise is significantly affected by changing cultural values. Some call it contextualism and some call it common sense, but it's not hard to document the contention that the choice of subject matter is often determined by cultural concerns. Writers like Wertsch and Youniss (1987) make a plausible argument that the content of child psychology has often been significantly related to cultural phenomena such as religious and racial struggles as well as to political ideology. Without passing judgment on their specific examples, their basic thesis certainly applies to much of the research in child psychology in the United States in the late 1970s and into the 1980s. The feminist movement, for example, sparked a huge number of studies on sex differences and sex roles as well as studies of the effects of maternal employment and paternal influences on child rearing. Early intervention studies mushroomed as the consequences of poverty manifested themselves in the schools, and research on teenage sexuality was at least partially a response to the soaring rate of unwed adolescent parenthood. The list could go on and on, but the message is clear.

Basic research is still done, of course, but the enormous push toward complex, socially relevant research is undeniable. The times and the personal social consciences of psychologists make it inevitable. Wertsch and Youniss (1987) adopt this point of view when they argue that "current research is embedded in a sociohistorical and cultural context." They add that "we all too readily assume that the direction of research in psychology is determined by nothing more than the intellectual interests and internal dynamics of the discipline" (p. 20). We very much need a social science of scientists, but barring that, we can at least be aware. Child psychologists of all stripes have to be vigilantly aware of the nonscientific presses on their activities and to understand the enormous variety of such presses on other child psychologists.

TRAINING CHILD PSYCHOLOGISTS

Training for diversity will have to be training about diversity—the need for it, the desirability of it, and, above all, the interdependence of those who approach the study of children from different perspectives.

A metaview. Each student needs to acquire and consciously operate with a metaview that articulates the multifaceted nature of psychology in a permanently complex society, stresses the interactions among various approaches to psychology, and locates that student's preferred niche within a complex structure. With such a metaview, the challenges of complexity can be met and psychology will benefit. Without it, I fear fragmentation into a set of competing enterprises, no one of which can alone develop fully. As educators we are faced with the formidable task of training for excellence a heterogeneous group in which variations in short-term interests obscure commonalities of long-term interests.

Separatism. One approach to training excellent child psychologists in the future focuses on the differences in short-term interest among subgroups. This approach is illustrated by the proliferation of free-standing graduate training centers—particularly designed for those headed for applied careers who felt their training requirements were not being taken seriously in the traditional university. I also suspect that, at least partially, these independent centers developed because those who aspired to applied careers were tired of being treated contemptuously. In the heady days of early success with the scientific study of childhood, there did develop a hierarchy of prestige with the scientific purists at the top. Concern for application was not really intellectually respectable, and those primarily concerned with it were, by definition, fuzzy headed. This kind of hierarchical stratification by interest is one of those intangible, but probably potent, forces which, I believe, affects the development of many scientific disciplines in ways that have not yet been adequately documented. In psychology my guess is that it has had negative consequences on curriculum content, training standards, and subsequent collegial relationships. Many have been uncomfortably aware of this for years, but it is only recently that references have appeared in print. As a case in point, Klatzky et al. (1985) report on students who spoke of the uphill struggle to train themselves for nonacademic work in the face of disdain from professors. "Many felt that their academic departments disparaged nonacademic employment instead of holding it in esteem" (p. 1036). In the face of this phenomenon, the development of free-standing schools is understandable. It's regrettable, however, not because excellent courses cannot be taught within such a setting, but because what is needed is more, not less, contact and dialogue between the "camps."

Integration. Another approach to training psychologists stresses commonalties. It can be seen in the current flurry of controversy and compromise on the topic of core curricula. Most recently the issue has been explored in the Utah National Conference on Graduate Education (Bickman, 1987). The truth is that no one can precisely specify what set of courses would best predict the ultimate long range criterion of productive careers. Indeed it would be an exceedingly difficult, if not impossible, task to empirically ferret out that relationship. What we have is a series of informed guesses and preferences. My own are as follows.

In the pursuit of effective communication, I think all child psychologists should be trained in the same or closely affiliated schools, but I don't believe there realistically can be any sizeable common core of content courses. With the explosion of knowledge in all fields and the requirements for extensive training in applied specialties, we are fast reaching the limits of what any student with a normal life expectancy can reasonably be asked to put into the formal education segment of that life.

In considering this issue I thought back to my own graduate training. In retrospect I can identify a few, a very few, courses that had lasting significance for me, many that were interesting but which, at varying rates, became obsolete, and some that I could have foregone with no discernible damage. The implication for these complex days is simply to require that all students take, and take seriously, a very small common core of courses. Standards of excellence, which are not uniquely tied to any particular content and which have been badly eroded, should be required in all aspects of training, but the core of common coursework will, of necessity, have to be very small. In my view it should be limited to those few courses which establish the multifaceted metaview referred to above and which provide the tools needed to search out and critically evaluate appropriate content as needs arise. To me this boils down to methodology, statistics, history, and systems, and some meaningful practicum experience in the other fellow's domain.

It appears that, right now, all doctoral students in child psychology are required to take at least some statistics and methodology. All 20 of the schools that provided detailed reports on their requirements in my survey indicated that that was the case. For students heading toward research careers, these courses pose no problem. Their relevance is obvious and, indeed, many future researchers voluntarily follow up the required minimum with advanced electives. Judging from the feedback I've had from more application-oriented students, however, the situation does not seem to be the same for them. They take these courses because they have to, but often resentfully, and they really don't see their relevance to their future careers. If change is needed, it is in the direction of taking the time and trouble to make explicit to those headed toward application that these scientific tool courses are as essential for them as for the research oriented, if they hope to make effective use of new data as it becomes available. Warnings about uncritical and possibly deleterious overgeneralizations have been many and eloquent. Years ago Terrell (1958) convincingly argued that we run a real danger of "getting ahead of our methodolgical resources and . . . misleading society" (p. 308). Atkinson (1977) reiterated the point when he argued that, in giving advice, "care must be taken to emphasize the limitations of the scientific evidence and to explain that there may be other tenable explanations" (p. 208). For the most part, however, these warnings have amounted to preaching to the choir. They have been printed in publications that are not widely read by those working in the field. In any case, they have certainly not been taken seriously, judging by the pronouncements I often read in the popular press, see on television, or hear from friends in child care agencies. There is great need both for the teaching of critical evaluation skills and for a practice of those skills in follow-up content courses. Reading primary sources in content courses is a must in order to promote the cautionary habit of studying the samples and peculiar research conditions of each study along with any design limitations.

For developing the metaview referred to earlier, a comprehensive history and systems course is indispensable. Unfortunately, it is seldom required. Of the 20 schools mentioned above, only two required students to take it. This course should not only thoroughly explore the major ideas and theoretical conceptions that have emerged over the years, but should attempt to relate each to the eras in which it flourished. With this background, students can come to understand the origin of their own working frames of reference, to see the modifications that have taken place in them as the intellectual and social contexts changed, and to evaluate their appropriateness to today's context. Without the intellectual perspective furnished by such background, the enormous range of current psychological points of view and activities must seem disturbingly chaotic to any thoughtful student. With that perspective, the variety makes sense. Awareness of intellectual roots can provide a base of stability in the midst of overwhelming complexity and can also go far toward instilling much needed tolerance.

An additional, not alternate, route to tolerance should be required. All doctoral students should be required to have some practicum work in areas outside of their intended specialty.

For those heading toward applied careers, this could simply take the form of requiring them to design and conduct a piece of research, whether or not it takes the form of a dissertation requirement. What's needed here is to structure this experience in such a way as to make salient for these students the relevance of this experience to their later careers. They should emerge from this requirement, not only with a clear understanding of the difficulties of doing clean research, but also with an understanding, enhancing that developed through their reading of primary sources, of the differences between the project on which they are working and the conditions they will encounter in the field. These combined experiences may be expected to deter future tendencies to uncritical overgeneralization more effectively than any academic warnings.

At the other end of the spectrum, students headed toward research, particularly laboratory research, should be required to have experience in a real world setting. As a matter of fact, the few schools that replied to my question about needed improvement in their degree programs, all indicated a need for more practicum experiences, although I suspect that they were primarily interested in employment marketability. I think, however, it should be required even for those who will never work in applied settings. Nothing could be more sobering or instructive to anyone immersed in a particular line of research, a particular theoretical orientation, than to see if it seems at all useful in a nursery school playground, a clinic, a classroom, or a family setting. Research-oriented students should emerge from such an experience, not only with a healthy respect for those who work in those settings, but with a shared, perhaps more sympathetic, understanding of the need for applicable data. I think, moreover, that, in their content courses, these students ought to spend some time brainstorming about possible potential uses of their research along with an analysis of the additional variables and conditions that would have to be incorporated before practical outcomes would seem feasible.

There's another reason for research-oriented students to have some practicum experience. It should provide another dimension to those grappling with a fundamental article of faith about human behavior that concerns thoughtful psychologists. I'm referring to the issue of ultimate explanatory unity or diversity. Some students emerge from their graduate training with a belief that, eventually, all complex behavior will be understandable in terms of a particular set of principles, be they derived from psychoanalysis, learning theory, information theory, or whatever. Others emerge believing that different forms of behavior will yield to different explanations, and that part of the task of psychology is to identify which is which. It is an important decision, whichever way it goes, and it is primarily a matter of faith, not demonstrable reality. Practical background experience with children in real settings ought to be incorporated into the decision-making process.

Whatever assumption the science-oriented student adopts on the nature of human behavior, there's another issue, alluded to earlier, to be resolved only after a mix of academic and practical experiences. This is the question of participation in public policy. Few would argue that any child psychologist should be totally unconcerned about the implications of data for social policy, but there the agreement ends. At one extreme are those who maintain that any degree of public participation corrupts or distorts the knowledge-seeking process. At the other extreme are those who hold that, since so much of the justification for science derives from its social usefulness, every scientist has an obligation to work at translating data into policy. In between are many variants of these views. Some say they simply don't have time for both kinds of activity and that we should train a group of information brokers to serve as liason between the scientific and the public decision-making communities. Still others hold that scientists must participate wherever possible in policy making because they are the ones best qualified to see that premature or misguided application is minimized, that outcome studies are appropriately designed and interpreted, and that both policy makers and the general public are educated about the scientific process. I don't think we can tell any member of the next generation of child psychologists which stance to adopt, but I do think we should insist that the issue be considered, and provide, during training, sufficient breadth of experience as to make an informed personal decision possible.

SOME GENERAL CONSIDERATIONS

What I think we are witnessing now is a meaningful transformation. When I was in graduate school some 35 years ago, Gustav Bergmann often used to mention the "a priori belief in total interactionism." He was, I'd guess, referring to the fact that many people simply held that belief as an assumption—almost an article of faith. Today when people espouse a belief in "total interactionism" they are asserting that there is abundant empirical justification for it. It is no longer being promulgated on an a priori, but rather on a factual basis.

In child psychology, Bronfenbrenner (1977) has made the most far-reaching and systematic integration of an interactionistic framework into a program for research on children, but the trend goes far beyond that.

Many connections are becoming more and more obvious—connections among subfields within disciplines, connections between science and other institutions, connections between roles that individuals play as scientists and as citizens, and connections between theoretical constructions that borrow, sometimes with other names, concepts from each other.

In this milieu there is no going back. We will not again have an environment in which developments in child psychology can go on in parallel, separate paths, often with training programs that highlight that separation and intellectual frameworks that sidestep coordination with competing ones.

There are many, from various segments of child psychology, who are not happy with the changes that have taken place. They speak wistfully of a belief that "the pendulum will swing back." I've come to believe that there is no pendulum of intellectual frameworks swinging back and forth in a vacuum between fixed oppositional poles. If any analogy is appropriate, it is rather that of a spiral of thought that moves in ever-changing contexts and in which, eventually, original forms are obliterated.

Certainly, ideas and explanatory principles reappear, but never as carbons of their original forms. In child psychology, for example, concepts of genetic determinants of behavior periodically recur but never in the simplistic form that predated the advent of recombinant gene technology. Basic principles of learning, which have never altogether disappeared, regain strength but require modification in the light of increasingly sophisticated knowledge about cognitive processes.

We live in a highly complex society comprised of many interdependent components which change rapidly. As change occurs at an accelerating pace within science, within technology, and within social and economic and political systems, both diversity and interdependence in child psychology become inevitable. "The differences among previously quite separate imperatives that stimulated advancement in science and technology on one hand, and improvement in society, on the other, are disappearing" (Holton, quoted in Bevan, 1982, p. 1304). It is no longer feasible to define scientific child psychology solely in terms of traditional nonapplied research activities. Rather, a revised conception should incorporate the view that "However much its progress may be guided by our social purposes, so long as the social science product is empirically tested and theoretically based, then we have genuine science" (Barber, 1953, p. 258). On the one hand, those who would try to keep child psychology as a bastion of pure science are, I think, doomed either to a retreat into a set of small clubs whose members "increasingly are able to talk only to themselves" (Bevan, 1982, p. 1312) or, conceivably, because of lack of public support and subsequent withdrawal of funds, to professional extinction. On the other hand, those who seek to improve the lives of children without a reliable and constantly increasing data base are doomed to failure. Child psychologists of the future, in whatever preferred niche, will need a basic understanding and constant awareness of the complex interactive web in which they work and an appreciation of the many combinations of interest and orientation and methodology of which it is composed. As biologists tell us that genetic diversity is essential for adaptation and survival of species, so, it seems, is intellectual and productive diversity necessary for the survival of child psychology.

REFERENCES

American Psychological Association. (1985). *Directory of the American Psychological Association*. Washington, DC: Author.

American Psychological Association. (1986). *Graduate study in psychology and associated fields*. Washington, DC: Author.

Atkinson, R. C. (1977). Reflections on psychology's past and concerns about its future. *American Psychologist, 32*, 205–210.

Barber, B. (1953). *Science and the social order*. London: George Allen & Unwin.

Bevan, W. (1976). The sound of the wind that's blowing. *American Psychologist, 31,* 481–491.

Bevan, W. (1980). On getting in bed with a lion. *American Psychologist, 35,* 779–789.

Bevan, W. (1982). A sermon of sorts in three plus parts. *American Psychologist, 37,* 1303-1322.

Bickman, L. (1987). Graduate education in psychology. *American Psychologist, 42,* 1041–1047.

Brim, O. G., Jr., & Dustan, J. (1983). Translating research into policy for children. The private foundation experience. *American Psychologist, 38,* 89–90.

Bronfenbrenner, U. (1977). Toward an experimental ecology of human development. *American Psychologist, 32,* 513–531.

Goldstein, D., Wilson, S. J., & Gerstein, A. I. (1983). Applied developmental psychology: Problems and perspectives for an emerging discipline. *Journal of Applied Developmental Psychology, 4,* 341–348.

Hartup. W. W. (1986, Autumn). Notes from *Child Development. Newsletter of the Society for Research in Child Development,* p. 3.

Howard, G. S. (1987). The role of values in the science of psychology. *American Psychologist, 40,* 255–265.

Howard, A., Pion, G. M., Gottfredson, G. D., Flattau, P. E., Oskamp, S., Pflafflin, S. M., Bray, D. W., & Burstein, A. G. (1986). The changing face of American Psychology: A report from the Committee on Employment and Human Resources. *American Psychologist, 40,* 1031–1037.

Kendler, H. H. (1981). *Psychology: A science in conflict.* New York: Oxford Press.

Kimble, G. A. (1984). Psychology's two cultures. *American Psychologist, 39,* 833–839.

Klatzky, R. L., Allusi, E. A., Cook, W. A., Forehand, G. A., & Howell, W. C. (1985). Experimental psychologists in industry. Perspectives of employers, employees and educators. *American Psychologist, 40,* 1031–1037.

Koek, K. E., & Boyles, C. R. (Eds.). (1988). *National organizations of the U.S.* (22nd ed.). Detroit: Gale Research Company.

Krasner, L., & Houts, A. C. (1984). A study of the value system of behavioral scientists. *American Psychologist, 39,* 840–850.

Maccoby, E. E., Kahn, A. J., & Everett, B. A. (1983). The role of psychological research in the formation of policies affecting children. *American Psychologist, 38,* 80–84.

Masters, J. C. (1984). Psychology, research and social policy. *American Psychologist, 39,* 851–862.

Merton, R. K. (1973). *The sociology of science.* Chicago: University of Chicago.

Miller, G. (1969). Psychology as a means of promoting human welfare. *American Psychologist, 24,* 1063–1075.

Miller, G. (1983). Children and the congress. A time to speak out. *American Psychologist, 38,* 70–76.

Pion, G., Bramblett, J. P., Jr., & Wicherski, M. (1987). *Preliminary report: 1985 Doctoral Employment Survey.* Washington, DC: American Psychological Association.

Stapp, J., & Fulcher, R. (1982). The employment of 1979 and 1980 doctorate recipients in psychology. *American Psychologist, 37*, 1159–1185.

Stapp, J., Fulcher, R., Nelson, S. D., Pallak, M. S., & Wicherski, M. (1981). The employment of recent doctorate recipients in psychology: 1979 through 1978. *American Psychologist, 36*, 1211–1254.

Stapp, J. Fulcher, R., & Wicherski, M. (1984). The employment of 1981 and 1982 doctorate recipients in psychology. *American Psychologist, 39*, 1408–1423.

Stapp, J., Tucker, A. M., & VandenBos, G. R. (1985). Census of psychological personnel: 1983. *American Psychologist, 40*, 1317–1351.

Terrell, G. (1958). The need for simplicity in research in child psychology. *Child Development, 29*, 303–310.

U.S. Bureau of the Census. (1987). *Statistical Abstract of the U.S.* (107th ed.). Washington, DC: U.S. Department U.S. Commerce, Bureau of the Census.

Wertsch, J. V., & Youniss, J. (1987). Contextualizing the investigator: The case of developmental psychology. *Human Development, 30*, 18–31.

chapter 10

Methodological Training:
A Guarantee for the Future

Charles C. Spiker and Joan H. Cantor

INTRODUCTION

Preliminary Considerations

In any consideration of the nature of graduate training in developmental psychology, we invariably encounter some discussion of the need for an appropriate balance between methodological and substantive knowledge. The word *methodology* means different things to different people, and its meaning varies somewhat from one context to another. Accordingly, we should begin by stating what we intend its referent to be in the context of graduate training in developmental psychology. This can be accomplished by making two important distinctions.

The first distinction is between substance and methodology. The distinction is illustrated by the statement, "We use scientific methodology in order to obtain substantive knowledge." Substantive knowledge is the empirical or factual information that has resulted from applications of the scientific method over the centuries. Methodology is the set of rules, procedures, and practices that collectively tell us "how to." If we know that (approximately) 10% of adult males are colorblind, or that (approximately) 10% of all adults are left-handed, we have substantive knowledge. If we know how to test for colorblindness or hand preference, we have methodological knowledge. A physician has vast amounts of substantive information concerning human anatomy and physiology, but conceivably may know little or nothing about the methodology by which that information was obtained.

The second important distinction is between broad and narrow methodology. Philosophers of science inform us that some methodologies are narrow and some are quite broad. In the narrow sense, methodology refers to practices that are peculiar to a subset of scientific disciplines, to a particular discipline, or even to a particular area within a given discipline. Thus, we expect to find the use of test tubes in chemistry and biological laboratories. We find the use of telescopes in astronomical observatories. Stimulus presentation devices, whether memory drums or laboratory computers, are commonly used instruments in psychological laboratories for the study of perception or other cognitive processes. These exemplify methods that are important in some disciplines but not in all.

Philosophy of science is especially concerned with issues that permeate all scientific disciplines—the broadest of methodology. For example, what is the nature of the system of logic that all scientific disciplines use? What is the common format of the definitions of scientific terms? What is the common structure of scientific laws and theories? What is the logic of scientific measurement? What is the nature of statistical inference? These are methodological questions that are pertinent to all scientific disciplines.

Methodology vs. Substance in Graduate Training

During the past several decades, the time to complete doctoral training in psychology, which at one time rarely exceeded 3–4 years, has increased to 4–6 years. This lengthening of the training program, of course, reflects in part the explosion of substantive knowledge in the field. A serious attempt to master the content of any area in psychology today requires a great deal of time, because the empirical results are available to us mainly in primary sources—that is, in scholarly journals that report the results of individual research studies. Unfortunately, the mastery of the burgeoning substantive knowledge has been achieved partly at the expense of methodological training, both broad and narrow.

What have we gained through these changes in our graduate programs, and what, if anything, has been lost? It seems to us that new PhDs today have a great deal more substantive knowledge in their own areas, much more research experience, and a far more substantial record of publication than their predecessors of yesteryear. Yet we also see them as more narrowly trained with regard to substantive knowledge in related areas, unfamiliar with major substantive findings from earlier decades, and, at least for some, inadequately equipped with methodological knowledge.

In the remainder of this chapter, we will present our perspective on the interplay of methodological and substantive knowledge in graduate training. It has been our observation that the important substantive issues in many sciences, and certainly in psychology, manifest major changes during the course of a scientific career, and that, as a result, individual scientists can easily become obsolete. How can graduate training prevent such obsolescence? The answer does not seem to us to lie in additional increases in the duration of graduate training.

Our major premise is that the key to preparing future graduate students for the long-term demands of both academic and nonacademic careers lies in extensive training in broad methodology. An individual with sound methodological training will be able to master new substantive areas without having to be retrained, and will also have the ability to maintain an historical perspective on the most important substantive knowledge in the field. It is for these reasons that we consider methodological training to be a guarantee for the future. Thus, in the discussions that follow, we will propose that graduate training emphasize (a) training in the formal aspects of methodology, including philosophy of science, probability and statistics, mathematics, and formal logic; and (b) a methodological approach to the study of current and past substantive knowledge.

COMPONENTS OF FORMAL TRAINING IN METHODOLOGY

Philosophy of Science

The philosophy of science is somewhat like the grammar of a langugage in that it is a description of the way a group of human beings behaves. Imagine an anthropologist who enters a primitive society and begins to make observations of the speech of that society. From an initial state of having no understanding of the language, this person builds up a vocabulary in, and eventually an understanding of the grammatical rules of, that language. Philosophers of science have conducted an analogous task by reading scientific works and extracting the rules that scientists seem to follow in the definitions of their concepts, the formulation of their laws, the construction of their theories, the development of their measurements, and their use of principles of probability. Not all scientists obey all these rules, and probably no scientist obeys them all the time. Just as every speaker deviates from the standard speech occasionally, every scientist deviates from the standard methodology from time to time. Nevertheless, just as the grammatical rules can quite properly be considered to describe ideal speech, the rules spelled out by philosophers of science may be considered a description of ideal scientific practices.

In the preceding paragraph, we have assigned a much more passive role to the philosopher than is characteristically the case. The major tool of the philosopher of science is analytic thought. Philosophers of science have made major contributions to the understanding of scientists by means of their analyses of certain critical problems. For example, physicists in the second half of the nineteenth century were extraordinarily confused about the results of certain experiments that dealt with the measurement of the speed of light. This confusion was subsequently shown to be the direct result of physicists' failure to follow their customary rules in defining certain terms (e.g., *nonlocal simultaneity*). Although the principles of the scientific method may not have changed much since the time of Galileo and Newton, our ability to articulate these rules has been greatly improved as a result of the efforts of philosophers of science in the last 75 years.

In major universities, courses in philosophy of science are probably best taught in departments of philosophy. Unfortunately, such courses are sometimes so highly technical that even superior graduate students in psychology do not have the background necessary to profit from them. Our friends in philosophy, however, complain about the quality of most courses that psychologists teach on the philosophy of science. Our experience with material on this topic that has been published by psychologists forces us to agree with the philosophers. Some psychologists who write methodological papers confuse with philosophy of science several topics which, though perfectly legitimate in their own right, are not methodological in character. Some of these topics are described below.

The history of science is not part of the philosophy of science. Probably it is neither possible nor desirable to teach philosophy of science without numerous references to historical material, but we should keep in mind that one who knows a good deal about the history of science may know little or nothing about scientific methodology. The history of science is important in and of itself, and for many, ourselves included, is a fascinating topic. But it is a mistake to identify it as philosophy of science. In the same light, we must be careful not to confuse or equate the philosophy of science with the history of systematic thought in our field. Courses in "history and systems" of psychology, though we view them as essential for graduate training, are not substitutes for coursework in the philosophy of science.

A sociological account of the activities of scientists belongs to the science of sociology, not to philosophy of science. The sociology of science is both interesting and intellectually important, and a certain amount of this information, properly identified, surely makes a course in philosophy of science more interesting. Nevertheless, the principles described in philosophy of science are meaningful independently of the actions, or even the existence, of any given scientist or group of scientists.

Another topic that psychologists are especially prone to mix into a discussion of philosophy of science is better labeled as the science of discovery. Characteristic ideas have included a concern about the conditions under which innovations are likely to take place, the sociological milieu in which new ideas will surface, and strategies that scientists should follow if they are to conduct successful experiments and make significant discoveries. If we only knew enough about such matters, this information would constitute a branch of psychology that would be known as the psychology of discovery. Unfortunately, we do not know a great deal about the laws of creativity and innovation. Moreover, the principles in philosophy of science are entirely mute about any such rules. Philosophy of science is description of the rules that scientists follow, not a prescription that guarantees successful research outcomes or comprehensive theories. There are no rules that guarantee successful "sciencing."

Psychologists, as a group, frequently cite Kuhn (1970) in discussions of philosophy of science. This book is a fascinating, stimulating discussion of a number of issues in science. As the author indicates in the preface, however, it is intended as a supplement to what has by now become classical philosophy of science. By its very nature, the book has a good deal to say about the psychology of discovery. It is, in fact, a competent, sociologically oriented, analytic history of science, and there is little in it that philosophers recognize as standard philosophy of science.

The philosophy of science is concerned with, in a descriptive way and using a special language, the nature of scientific deduction, both logical and mathematical. It describes the safeguards that scientists have worked out for the definition and use of technical words. It describes the fundamental format of scientific laws and distinguishes between deduction and induction. It analyzes and describes the structure that scientists refer to as theory. It analyzes scientific measurement and the probability calculus. And much more.

The philosophy of science thus provides answers to a great many questions asked by perceptive individuals, both scientists and nonscientists. What is the structure of a scientific law? How do scientists safeguard the meaningfulness of their concepts? What is the nature of logic, mathematics, and other formal systems? What is the difference between ordinary laws and statistical laws? What is the structure of scientific theories? How do scientists construct models and how do they guarantee the meaningfulness of the concepts in those models?

What is the relation between laws and theories? What are the various measurement techniques? What is the basis of the probability calculus? Clearly, precise answers to such questions are important in the training of graduate students in psychology, and it is unrealistic to expect most of them, or even most professors, for that matter, to find the answers for themselves.

Logic

Our experience has been that graduate students in psychology are typically uncertain about what constitutes the domain of logic, and that they are especially tentative about the difference between logical and empirical knowledge. Whether taken at the undergraduate or graduate level, a well-taught introductory course in symbolic logic, coupled with a course in the philosophy of science, provides answers to questions that graduate students unfortunately rarely ask.

The ancient Greeks developed functional logic (the logic of "all," "some," and "is") to a very high level. It was not until the nineteenth and twentieth centuries, however, that sentential logic (the logic of "and," "or," "if . . . then," and "if and only if") was worked out. We now understand that sentential logic is the more basic of the two in the sense that functional logic sits on top of it. Since the number system, arithmetic, and mathematics are stacked, in that order, on top of functional logic, we see that sentential logic is very basic indeed.

Although an introductory course in symbolic logic is not going to transform the student into a master debater, it will provide the student with an opportunity to grasp the nature of formal knowledge. It may also help the student to appreciate the ambiguities that reside in natural languages. Moreover, it should help the student to avoid such common logical errors as "affirming the consequent" and "denying the antecedent."

Mathematics

Until about 1940, the only area in psychology that demanded sophistication in mathematics was psychophysics. The psychological literature over the last 50 years has brought about a major escalation in the mathematical sophistication needed by psychologists. Beginning with Hull's *Principles of Behavior* (1943), the proportion of the literature that requires fairly extended mathematical training has increased steadily. Since the time when Estes (1950) published his influential statistical theory of learning, there have been a multitude of mathematical models appearing in the psychological literature. Many of these have dealt with topics in developmental psychology (e.g., Brainerd, 1983; Cantor & Spiker, 1976; Kendler, 1979; Kendler & Kendler, 1970; Spiker, 1971; Spiker & Cantor, 1973; Zeaman & House, 1963, 1974).

What level of mathematical training is desirable? Only the level of ability and the amount of time available for study should set the limit of mathematical education. Mathematics is a tool, an instrument, and the experience of our professional careers teaches us that any instrument we possess gets used. The competence–performance distinction to the contrary notwithstanding, we do what we know how to do.

In order to understand mathematical treatises in general, one must have solid training in college algebra. Substantial work in geometry and trigonometry will be found helpful later. Linear algebra will be extremely helpful in subsequent work with regression and correlation. Differential and integral calculus will permit a level of comprehension of statistics not otherwise possible. All of this coursework is available to an undergraduate student. Training in mathematics through calculus is therefore a practical goal, ideally taken as undergraduate preparation.

Probability, Statistics, and Experimental Design

As most psychologists know, probability theory and statistical analysis are very closely related. Probability theory uses the parameters and distribution forms of populations to predict distributions of the statistics from random samples. Statistical analysis uses the statistics of random samples to make inferences about the parameters and distribution forms of populations. Probability theory is entirely deductive, and the conclusions are therefore certain. Statistical analysis is primarily inductive, and the conclusion is probabilistic.

Given the close relation between probability and statistics, a course in probability theory will prove to be extremely helpful in mastering statistical inference. Perhaps the best way to state the matter is that it is possible to use statistical techniques, but it is not possible to understand statistical inference, without a good grasp of probability theory. Once more, introductory courses in probability are available at the undergraduate level.

In the late 1940s and early 1950s, when the authors were in graduate training, the introduction of the analysis of variance to experimental psychologists was relatively recent. Most of our professors had acquired the skills only within the previous 10 or 15 years. It was not unusual to hear a professor complain that the analysis of variance was not very sensitive relative to a repeated application of the t-test or critical ratio test (i.e., large sample z-test). Of course, the complaint failed to recognize that the analysis of variance is a mass test that controls for the run-away Type I error rate that occurs when all possible pairs of differences are tested, an application that often gives rise to numerous apparently reliable effects that are no more than statistical artifacts.

The tendency to ignore inflated Type I error rates is still with us today. In modern psychological laboratories controlled by computers, or in other laboratories in which batteries of psychological tests are administered, it is often the case that multiple related response measures are available on each of a large number of individuals, all of whom are organized into a given experimental design. It then becomes feasible, and often seems desirable, to conduct an analysis of variance on each of the response measures.

If an analysis of variance is conducted on each of the response measures, a problem will occur similar to that for repeated applications of a t-test or z-test—namely, a rising but indeterminate Type I error rate. The solution to this problem is multivariate analysis of variance. This technique has been available for several decades, but the computational difficulties were overwhelming prior to the advent of high-speed computers. For about 15 years, multivariate analysis of variance computer programs have been readily available to psychologists in several commercial software statistical packages.

Once again, we hear complaints that the multivariate analysis is not as sensitive as is the repeated application of univariate analysis. In this case, however, the resistance to controlling the Type I error rate is reinforced by the unfamiliarity of the method to both graduate students and professors. Understanding the procedure and correctly interpreting the results demands a reasonably good understanding of linear algebra. Even the friendliest reference books, for example, Harris (1985), despite Herculean efforts to relegate the mathematics to appendices, do not manage to exclude from the text all reference to equations in linear algebra. The deficiency in their mathematical backgrounds leads many graduate students to avoid multivariate courses, with the result that even those who do apply multivariate techniques to their data, with the aid of a statistical package, often do not fully understand what they are doing.

The increasing use of the "cookbook" approach to computer statistical packages for all types of statistical analyses should be a matter of great concern to us. A far better approach is to design graduate statistics courses so that students practice solving "miniproblems" using calculators in order to gain a full understanding of each statistical test before they learn to use the appropriate statistical packages.

Having said so much for probability and statistics, we must now emphasize the importance to methodological training of courses in experimental design. The earliest references to experimental design were from and for agricultural workers. Even in design texts written for psychologists, we find references to these earlier texts in such phrases as "split-plot" and "random block" designs. Beginning in the 1940s, textbooks on experimental design, especially published for psychological and educational research, began to appear. We now use designs that are "completely randomized," "mixed," "repeated measures," "treatment by subjects," and many others that carry psychological or educational connotations.

Within the last 15 to 20 years, reference books have been published that emphasize the general linear model as the theory underlying regression, univariate analysis of variance, and multivariate analysis of variance. Graduate students trained for future psychological research will be grounded in the theory of the general linear model, because this approach reveals regression, univariate analysis of variance, analysis of covariance, and multivariate analysis of variance to be special cases of the general model.

METHODOLOGY IN SUBSTANTIVE TRAINING

Let us return once more to the issue of substance vs. methodology in graduate training, particularly in the context of the problem we face in trying to deal with the seemingly overwhelming amount of substantive knowledge to be acquired. To begin with, we might wonder why the field of psychology finds itself in this predicament of being inundated with new information, leading to ever-increasing specialization and narrowing of training. The answer becomes clear if we compare psychology with the more mature sciences.

For an introductory course in college physics, the instructor normally selects a single text. Generally, it is a thick book, particularly if the course is to cover all of what is conventionally referred to as classical physics. The same thing is true for the textbook of an introductory course in college chemistry. Many psychologists find it quite remarkable that nearly all of the knowledge acquired over several centuries in these areas can be distilled down to a couple of books.

The state of affairs in psychology is quite different. Although the textbook for an introductory course in psychology is also a thick one, it contains only a fraction of the empirical information that psychologists have accumulated as a result of their research. Psychologists distinguish between *primary* and *secondary* sources of information. Primary sources are the descriptions of studies and experiments published in standard journals. Secondary sources are textbooks and literature reviews. A literature review typically treats a relatively narrow selected topic and is generally based on primary sources. As might be expected, secondary sources vary widely with respect to the amount and profundity of their critical evaluations of the research reported in the primary sources.

The empirically derived information in psychology is scattered through the vast psychological literature. Why cannot it be distilled into a thick book or two? The answer, of course, is that psychology is long on information and short on empirical laws at the present time. Consider the law of free fall discovered by Galileo about 400 years ago.

$$s = 16t^2$$

This law says that the distance in feet that a body will have fallen, after having been released (in a vacuum) near the surface of the earth, is given by multiplying 16 times the square of the time in seconds that the body has been falling. The discussion of this law in the introductory book will probably be limited to two or three paragraphs that explain what the formula means. Galileo may not be mentioned at all, or he may be cited in a footnote. Nothing is said of the large number of experiments he conducted using an inclined plan rather than free fall to slow the process to an observable pace, or of the leaking container that he used as a clock. As a matter of fact, Galileo should have credit for the idea of such a law and for determining that there is such a law. The credit for precision of measurement, however, belongs to later investigators.

The quantitative statement of the law of free fall, together with a small amount of explanation, summarizes all the experiments Galileo conducted as well as all those conducted by others. Students of physics need to know nothing about any of these experiments, unless they happen to have an interest in the history of physics. The same thing is true of nearly all of the areas of physics, but is true, unfortunately, of only a small number of areas in psychology. For the majority of topics, students of psychology must deal with what many refer to as a "box score" that tells in how many experiments the phenomenon was found, in how many experiments the opposite was found, and in how many experiments neither was found. Ideally, the student will examine the methodology (in the narrow sense) of the several experiments in an attempt to determine why the apparently conflicting findings were obtained. A successful resolution can be obtained only if the student is extremely skillful in the methodological analysis.

Where are students to acquire such skill and, at the same time, become familiar with the important substantive knowledge in the field? One answer lies in the manner in which substantive courses are taught. There are two extremely different ways in which graduate courses can be organized. In the first way, the instructors organize substantive courses by assembling a reading list of all the articles that they are aware of on each topic to be covered in the course, assign this list to the students for their reading, lecture on as many of the topics as time allows, and motivate the students to read the rest by examining them over both the lectures and the assigned readings.

A second, and we believe preferable, way to organize such a course uses a methodological approach to the study of content knowledge. The instructor selects as required reading on each topic a relatively small number of articles that exemplify major findings and methodologies, various types of methodological errors to which investigators have fallen victim, and important studies from earlier decades. For each selected study, the lecturer then provides a thorough methodological and substantive analysis. These lectures indicate why the investigator wanted to do the experiment; relate the study to the investigator's theory, if any; expose the experimental design of each experiment; show why it is or is not adequate to the investigator's goal; indicate how it might have been made methodologically sounder, if possible; and discuss with the students what the next experiment or study ought to be.

Clearly, this methodologically oriented approach prevents the instructor from covering a large number of articles during the course of the semester. (It does not preclude giving the students a list of additional references on each topic.) The method does, however, provide students with a critical model and exposes them to the kind of analytical thinking that outstanding scientists must be able to do. Where will the students obtain the remainder of their knowledge of the research and theory that they will ultimately need? We suggest two answers.

First, their substantive knowledge can be broadened through their own subsequent reading. The students will have the requisite analytic skills and will not need the instructor's help in separating the good studies from the poor ones. They can be expected to assimilate at least part of the necessary additional substantive information during their preparation for taking comprehensive examinations.

Second, we must make available to future graduate students good literature reviews in the form of graduate textbooks and review articles.

Just as there are two extremely different types of graduate courses, there are two extremely different types of literature reviews. The first type takes a rather broad theme and nearly exhaustively covers all the research that has ever been conducted on that theme. Because the range is so large, little can be said about any one article except for a brief statement of the problem and the findings. Some such reviews are little more than annotated bibliographies. What are needed instead are literature reviews that provide an integration of the area being reviewed and an analytical critique of the methodology for each article included. Such reviews do appear in our journals, but they are exceptions rather than the rule, and they tend to be quite narrow in scope. Graduate textbooks, on the other hand, appear to be a totally vanishing breed. We strongly believe that professors must once again be provided with incentives to write such major syntheses and critical analyses of content areas, so that future graduate students can be appropriately trained in both depth and breadth.

SUMMARY

Our major thesis is that methodological training in both the broad and narrow sense should play a key role in the graduate training of future developmental psychologists. A knowledge of philosophy of science, probability, statistics, mathematics, and formal logic provides powerful tools that are important not only during the early stages of a scientist's career, but are also particularly crucial in guiding the inevitable changes in substantive direction that characterize most careers.

We further contend that graduate students should learn how to make careful methodological and theoretical analyses of the research literature as a means of getting a grasp on important historical and current trends in the field. These analytical skills, once acquired, permit students to explore important theoretical and empirical work in greater depth and also to gain greater breadth of knowledge on their own.

Although our discussion has not really focused on training in the developmental area, we view the need for strong methodological expertise as especially crucial for developmental psychologists. The demand for breadth of knowledge is perhaps greatest for the child psychologist, who is expected to know the developmental literature in all traditional content areas of psychology including perception, cognition, learning, social development, and psychopathology. The methodological approach to substantive training would appear to provide our best hope of training future developmental psychologists who are knowledgeable about the history and current status of their field and who are also flexible enough to meet the new challenges of the future.

REFERENCES

Brainerd, C. J. (1983). Structural invariance in the developmental analysis of learning. In J. Bisanz, G. L. Bisanz, & R. Kail (Eds.), *Learning in children: Progress in cognitive development research.* New York: Springer-Verlag.

Estes, W. K. (1950). Toward a statistical theory of learning. *Psychological Review, 57,* 94–107.

Cantor, J. H., & Spiker, C. C. (1976). The effects of labeling dimensional values on the setting differences in shift performance of kindergarten children. *Memory and Cognition, 4,* 446–452.

Harris, R. J. (1985). *A primer of multivariate statistics* (2nd ed.). New York: Academic Press.

Hull, C. L. (1943) *Principles of behavior.* New York: Appleton-Century Company, Inc.

Kendler, T. S. (1979) The development of discrimination learning: A levels-of-functioning explanation. In H. W. Reese (Ed.), *Advances in child development and behavior* (Vol. 13, pp. 83–117). New York: Academic Press.

Kendler, T. S., & Kendler, H. H. (1970) An ontogeny of optional shift behavior. *Child Development, 41,* 1–27.

Kuhn, T. S. (1970) *The structure of scientific revolutions* (2nd ed.). Chicago: University of Chicago Press.

Spiker, C. C. (1971) Application of Hull-Spence theory to the discrimination learning of children. In H. W. Reese (Ed.), *Advances in child development and behavior* (Vol. 6, pp. 99–152). New York: Academic Press.

Spiker, C. C., & Cantor, J. H. (1973) Applications of Hull-Spence theory to the transfer of discrimination learning in children. In H. W. Reese (Ed.), *Advances in child development and behavior* (Vol. 8, pp. 223–288). New York: Academic Press.

Zeaman, D., & House, B. J. (1963) The role of attention in retardate discrimination learning. In N. R. Ellis (Ed.), *Handbook of mental deficiency* (pp. 159–223). New York: McGraw-Hill.

Zeaman, D., & House, B. J. (1974) Interpretations of developmental trends in discriminative transfer effects. In A. D. Pick (Ed.), *Minnesota symposia on child development* (Vol. 8, pp. 144–186). Minneapolis: University of Minnesota Press.

chapter 11

The Future of Training in Human Infant Development

Lewis P. Lipsitt
Brown University, and the American Psychological Association

PROLOGUE

A vast archive of well-founded knowledge exists in the field of human infant behavior and development today. The number of studies, journal articles, chapters in books, volumes of annual reviews, issues of abstracts, and computerized digests of results is formidable, and the task of mastering any more than a detail of that databank is even more vexing.

While progress in the acquisition and compilation of knowledge is on the face of it commendable, especially when the principal intent of scientific pursuits is precisely to enhance understanding of nature, one must lament that, virtually in defense against the seeming impossibility of learning a larger craft well, most students appear now to be learning more and more about less and less. Students in one specialty area overlap little with students in another, even as they work together in the same university departments.

*I am pleased to express my gratitude to Carolyn Rovee-Collier, my frequent colleague, for her usual perspicacity in guiding this manuscript to a state that I could not have reached by myself.

Thanks are due the National Institute of Child Health and Human Development, the National Institute of Mental Health, the W. T. Grant Foundation, the March of Dimes Birth Defects Foundation, the Mailman Family Foundation, the American Psychological Foundation (Rosen Fund), the Hasbro Corporation, the Harris Foundation, the Spencer Foundation, and Brown University. To all of these resources, for their contributions to my research on infancy over the years, I am most grateful.

Yet the knowledge explosion is irreversible and indeed, in the best of all scholarly worlds, should get worse! Our graduate training programs of the future must therefore acknowledge the reality of the student dilemma: while in the first few decades of this century it was possible for a student of psychology to learn most all the knowledge then extant in that world of scholarship, at the end of the century there is so much literature on infant behavior and development alone that a student of early language acquisition, for example, might know virtually nothing of (for other examples) conjugate reinforcement or of imitative behavior in six week olds. This parallels the professor's dilemma that there is an inherent impossibility of teaching everything to everyone.

Training for diversity in the 21st century will require graduate training administrators and teachers to assure that their students have the capacity of inquiry, and the ability to infer from, and probe constructively in, knowledge domains beyond their own specialty areas. A demonstration is attempted here to suggest that this can be done fruitfully, and perhaps best, by a method of investigation that asks a succession of questions, each based upon the answer obtained to a previous query. Each question is designed to follow up on the veracity of the previous answers obtained, and to further define the particular domain to which the statements of fact obtained thus far apply. In short, the teaching of the skills of query, and of evaluation of the veracity of answers, as distinct from both a listing of facts about nature, and sheer mastery of some technical tools which may be necessary but are never sufficient, will help assure that students become scholars and not technologists.

THE PROBLEM

The proliferation of knowledge in the field of infant behavior and development over the past few decades has been overwhelming for serious scholars. Each specialized area of investigation, such as visual perception, auditory development and sound processing, response acquisition processes as in classical and instrumental learning, psychomotor development, the ontogenetic study of language, and the exploration of attachment has evolved idiosyncratic methods, stimulus presentation tools, response recording procedures, and quantitative/ statistical operations. Infant development scholars have thus become ever more expert in increasingly restricted domains of inquiry.

It is now virtually impossible for most graduate students in child psychology to master all of the available knowledge in Mussen's (1983) four-volume Handbook of Child Psychology. Moreover, the body of researched, well-supported facts in the field of infant behavior and development, and the methods by which they were derived, have become a formidable archive (Haith & Campos, 1983; Osofsky, 1987). Difficulties inherent in studying in this area include time constraints, the struggle to obtain monetary support for one's research (Lederman, 1991), and the implicit academic mandate to publish strong effects in highly technologized areas in order to find suitable employment and to be promoted. All of these conditions and others conspire to perpetuate the already evident trend toward greater and greater specialization.

Many developmental scientists who were trained 25–40 years ago are struck by the rapid secular shift toward increased specialization and the parochialism of younger students. Carmichael's (1954) *Manual of Child Psychology*, which the Mussen volumes superceded, was formidable but not impossible to master. For the 1950s student, there was relatively little to read, for example, about sensory and learning processes of the human infant. Most specialists in the field knew their contemporaries' work, and communications among infant laboratories took place regularly. Exchanges of reprints and prepublication papers, and attendance at one another's meeting presentations were common. The escalation of research findings, the increasing use of sophisticated technology, and perhaps especially the electronic innovations in data collection, statistical analysis, and communication, all in a style hardly imaginable a generation ago, have conspired recently to put the newly trained developmental scientist at a distance from most of his or her intellectual forebears. Perhaps more sadly, some developmental psychology specialists today command domains of knowledge that are so remote intellectually from those of other specialists that one can infer that these individuals are in entirely different fields of scholarship.

What does bind scholars who have different domains of specialized expertise is the capacity, at least in principle, to understand each other's method of scientific inquiry, and to convey to one another how their respective searches for supportable factual statements were conducted. This minimal requirement of "communicative efficiency" across fields and subfields is the cornerstone of the scientific method. It is as relevant to the discipline of psychology and the study of infant behavior as to the sciences of physics, chemistry, and biology.

AN HISTORICAL NOTE

The title page of the 1925 directory of the American Psychological Association, a mere pamphlet of less than 100 pages, boasted that the organization had a membership of 471 psychologists—33 years after the founding of the association in 1892! The APA was accruing membership at this time at the rate of about 40 new members per year. Today the APA has 108,000 psychologists among its ranks, and acquires six times as many new members per year now as it took the organization 33 years to acquire in its early existence. The geometric increase in the number of psychologists, and the growth of their major association in the United States alone, are impressive indeed. The experimental psychologist cum historian, E.G. Boring, one of our "ancients" of the 1950s, was fond of reminding his colleagues that "95% of all the psychologists who have ever lived are alive today," an observation that is still true.

Perhaps more striking even than the size of "our group" in 1925 is the fact that one finds on virtually every page of the APA directories of that era someone recognizable for outstanding achievements in Psychology. Within a span of four or five pages, we find Arnold Gesell, Lillian Gilbreth, Henry Goddard, H.M. Halverson, Samuel Hayes, William Healy, Leta Hollingworth, Clark Hull, Walter S. Hunter, C.H. Judd, J.R. Kantor, C.E. Kellogg, Truman Kelley, Grace H. Kent, Helen Koch, and Samuel Kohs. Many of these psychologists were highly esteemed contributors to the literature on infancy and childhood.

Of special interest regarding this assemblage of talent are two observations: it can be confidently presumed that most of these psychologists, these forebears of ours in the empirical pursuit of psychological knowledge, knew each other, and many of them followed one another's work with great interest *despite the diversity of their respective research pursuits.* Although Walter S. Hunter was a comparative psychologist with a strong evolutionary orientation, and was quite theoretical, he knew what kind of a theoretical system Hull was working on. Hollingworth and Halverson were each engaged in quite different kinds of research work on development, the first being very descriptive and enamored of growth parameters, and the second fascinated with mechanisms and processes in eye-hand coordination and the grasping of infants. However, they shared platforms and exchanged reprints.

Most all of the aforementioned scholars could read a child psychology text of the day and find most of the general propositions and conclusions familiar. They also had close knowledge of the procedures their colleagues were using in documenting how development worked. In a funny early twist of our professional and scientific history, it can be said that these psychologists of 1925 were better *trained for diversity* than those of us trained thirty years later. Add another thirty years and we are talking about a geometric compounding of the problems inherent in training for diversity: with increasing specialization, and the proliferation of technological advances, students have sought increasingly isolated areas of empirical pursuit in which they become immensely knowledgeable without being much aware of, let alone expert in, allied domains of knowledge.

WHAT ARE WE TO DO?

What is it that our 1925 intellectual parents or grandparents had that we do not? Well, to use the vernacular, they weren't living the fast scientific life that we do! The amount of scientific literature available has increased 200 times, roughly the magnitude of increase in the American Psychological Association membership. The proliferation of meetings and conventions, the increased use of the telephone and television, the deployment of data to computers for rapid analysis, the perfection of electronic means of sending entire manuscripts to colleagues, anywhere in the world, overnight, have all increased the pace of communications appreciably.

If the 21st century student of infant behavior and development is going to find solace in training, it must be not so much through conveying particulars of *all* of the diverse domains of inquiry as through an emphasis on "inquiry methods." Surely the student must have a specialty area, such as the ontogeny of tactile sensation in all of its psychophysical, social, and intersensory aspects, but it is important for that student to be able to understand the inquiry methods of students in other areas in which he or she is *not* a specialist. Through judicious intermingling of "fact" courses with "styles of inquiry" courses, sometimes known as research methods courses, graduate students of infant development should be trained to deal as much with questions like "How do you know that about babies?" as with the question "What do you know about babies?"

Training for diversity in the future should not only acknowledge, but insist and act on the assumption, that the increasing refinement of research tools through technological advances can free the scholar to pursue ideas, hypotheses and their tests, and theoretical advances.

As indicated, knowledge about human infancy, particularly in the last two to three decades, has increased at such a rapid rate, that "infancy experts" have great difficulty remaining current not only with recently published research articles, but with "advances chapters" which critically synthesize a large amount of newly acquired empirical information.

Perhaps by looking at "the nature of babyhood," at the processes and mechanisms of behavior change in infancy, and at what it is that our child psychologist forerunners sought, we can discern what it is we seek in our advocacy of training for diversity.

What are the questions that we ask in trying to appreciate the nature of behavior and behavior development in babyhood? There appear to be three subdomains of question that one wants to address in answering overarching questions about the nature of behavior and development in infancy. The first relates to basic observation or, as one student suggested, "plain facts, as opposed to fancy facts." These are the product of simple (but sometimes not so simple) observations answering questions like "What is the baby doing?" "Can the baby see?" and "Do elements of the visual field change the direction in which the baby looks?" These questions permit empirical answers and offer the opportunity for replication and verification. The field of child development could be characterized 50 years ago as quite heavily invested in answering questions such as these. Researchers of that day were especially interested in knowing, for example, at what average age children first walked three steps unaided, or how many discernible, discriminable sounds are made by infants at each month level from 6 months to 2 years. Given that "walking three steps" and "making discriminable sounds" could be sufficiently well defined to assure that one observer could convey the definition to another, and the two could achieve interobserver reliability on the measure, a meaningful study could be performed. One can perform this type of study without addressing issues as to the antecedent conditions which may control, facilitate, or impair walking or talking in the young child.

The second type of question relates to why something takes place. Explanation questions address issues like: Why is the baby doing that? What aspect of the child's experience elicited or enhanced this behavior? Answers to such questions can often be investigated by differentially treating comparable groups of children, based upon a hypothesis as to causation, and comparing outcomes. This is by no means the only way in which to assess cause, but the experimental child psychologist frequently can confirm or refute a causative hypothesis through such tests. Critics of this method often presume that the researcher has concluded erroneously on behalf of one or another manipulated antecedent as the sole cause of the changed behavior. Selective treatment of subjects may result in powerful changes in behavior, however, without there being any implication that this is the only, or even the most powerful, antecedent of the changes investigated. Other factors mix in, and those must also be investigated empirically. A cause of behavior is not necessarily the sole cause.

The third type of question relates to what other processes or conditions prevail in controlling the behavioral or developmental phenomenon under investigation. One might ask: What general principle(s) may be operating in connection with this? Do the rules or laws by which walking is manifested developmentally have features in common with those through which talking occurs?

Why Does One Bother?

It is neither facetious nor fatuous to ask *why* we explore what we choose to understand. Every student of science must ask the question. Others will surely ask if we do not do so ourselves! Why study baby behavior?

Baby humans are intrinsically fascinating to adult humans, so there has been a history of observations of babies by adults, not all of them child psychologists. Psychologists tend to systematize their observations, and often to create a larger picture of humanity and human functioning from their observation and appreciation of particulars. Piaget, for example, tried to understand how children eventually come to be the intelligent, "scientific" thinkers and explorers which he proposed as the natural adult state of humans, by making longitudinal observations of the way infants assimilate stimulation and then utilize this information in responding to successive environmental situations. Freud inferred from his (apparently few) observations of infants that the rudiments of sexuality and aggression, not to mention orality, are there at birth, and that all the unfolding of subsequent human behavior will reveal a scenario dictated largely by what inheres in the human at birth.

Even adults with no particular training in child development are curious about babies. They often remark that infants are attractive in appearance, or "cute." Indeed, babies have been welcomed into families for eons: Adults frequently want to have babies around them!

Babies seem quite simple-minded to most adults, and it is thought that they should therefore be especially tractable. Adult humans are prone to touch these small persons, stroke their skin, speak in a falsetto voice in their presence, and express their fondness in a variety of ways, by providing the child with clothing and sustenance for extended periods of time, and speaking of what the young person "will be" when he or she "grows up." Implicit in many naturalistic and seemingly unsophisticated inquiries are questions of assessment (What is the baby like?) and of prediction (Can we tell what the future of this baby will be like from observing him or her now?).

To the scientifically oriented child psychologist, the human newborn may be cute but is not simple-minded, and can be a difficult research subject. The experimental child psychologist is likely to be interested in the mechanisms and processes involved in the functioning of the senses, the learning of new responses, the retrieval of responses learned, the acquisition of playfulness, the onset and course of irascible behavior, and the ways in which infants become indoctrinated in family constraints and socialized to other requirements of the environment.

PREPARING FOR DIVERSITY BY STUDYING INFANTS

Exploring a rather confined domain of human behavior and development can prepare one for the understanding of a wide variety of behavioral and developmental phenomena. Memory processes are never simple, in any organism, as has been revealed in the extensive programmatic studies even of one of the simplest organisms, aplysia (Kandel, 1979). If one explores carefully the basic learning processes of human infants, however, the window is opened to a whole world of infant–mother and other social relationships of the child over time, and even to a better understanding of perhaps one of the most complex of human functions and relationships, the ontogeny of attachment (Haith & Campos, 1983).

The Baby's Memory

Salient among the characteristics of infants is their capacity for altering their behavior as a consequence of environmental impingements, such as repetitions of previously sensed stimulation, or with progressive experience. Changes in behavior mediated by memory processes, or learning, are the essential cornerstones of human development, and have been fascinating to experimental child psychologists and cognitive developmentalists for as long as the field of child development has existed.

The facts of, and processes underlying, habituation, classical conditioning, and operant learning are among the most fascinating candidates for study in the young human, for it is through such mechanisms that the baby's behavior is changed as a function of specific experience. Such processes relate to the child's memory-store (the rudiments of "mind"), which is altered and capitalized upon over successive environmentally generated stimulus inputs.

We asked previously why we should be interested in whether the newborn infant is capable of classical conditioning. The answer becomes more evident if we ask, instead, why we should be interested in any of the processes whereby the behavior of very young infants is influenced by experience. Following Pavlov's systematic demonstrations in dogs of the basic associative phenomenon, classical conditioning, whereby animals can be shown to anticipate with psychophysiological reactions the onset of an accustomed stimulus before its actual presentation, early Soviet investigators became curious about the ontogeny of such behavior in humans.

The question asked was: What degree of cortical maturity is required for an organism to make such seemingly sophisticated predictions of everyday occurrences? The early Soviet investigators were principally concerned with analyzing maturational progression through the use of the classical conditioning technique (Elkonin, 1957). Numerous attempts at conditioning the human child were made at various ages within the first half year of life, as reported by Elkonin and by others, but with little success.

While common observation suggested that infants were conditionable, as when they open their mouths anticipatorily during feeding, such behavior proved more easily demonstrable in the child over six months of age than under. This prompted Krasnogorski to observe:

> In the normal newborn infant, the cortical innervations are developed to such an insignificant extent that conditioned connections cannot yet be found. In the second half of the first year, the formation of conditioned reflexes . . . is possible, but takes place more slowly than at a later age. (Krasnogorski, cited in Elkonin, 1957, and Lipsitt, 1963, p. 164)

Indeed the supposition of a classical conditioning deficit in the human newborn was echoed in Western countries by selected researchers as recently as the 1970s (e.g., Sameroff, 1971), despite the publication in 1961 of elegant conditioned head turning studies carried out by Papousek (e.g., 1959) in Czechoslovakia, combining classical and operant learning techniques. It is now apparent that more refined methodology, particularly when coupled with sophisticated technology, could have solved a number of problems inherent in the early attempts at demonstrating classical Pavlovian conditioning in human infants. As it has turned out, for example, the interval separating the conditioning (CS) from the unconditioned stimulus (UCS) is of critical importance (Rovee-Collier & Lipsitt, 1982). This feature of rudimentary classical conditioning is not so readily apparent as one observes a young child gradually open his or her mouth when the feeding source is brought progressively closer to the mouth. In this example of clear learning, the interstimulus interval (ISI) is not easily definable because both of the stimuli (the spoon CS and the food UCS) are continuous, protracted, and dynamic rather than discrete and brief as in typical classical conditioning paradigms. Early investigators of the ontogeny of mammalian learning might have been markedly aided by an appreciation of the importance of the length of the ISI and by apparatus that would enable more careful control of this aspect of the stimulus presentation procedure.

What is particularly striking is the quantum inferential leap made by Krasnogorski, from the failure of early conditioning attempts to the conclusion that the young child's level of cortical maturation is incapable of associative learning. Later Soviet investigators have retracted both the supposition that the newborn is not conditionable and, of course, the suggestion that the level of cortical immaturity of the human neonate is such as to preclude the acquisition of classically conditioned associations, since classical conditioning has been clearly demonstrated in the absence of cortex (see chapters by Woodruff-Pak; Logan; Marcus and Carew; and Thompson, in Diamond, 1991). Indeed in the Soviet Union, by 1974, Anokhin, with the benefit of modern technology, with a more sophisticated view of the structure of the human infant brain, and through the introduction of methodological niceties not previously heeded, reported that not only full-term newborns were successfully conditioned, but premature babies as well before their expected dates of birth (Anokhin, 1974).

There have been few studies of classical conditioning in the human newborn supported in the past 15 years, unfortunately, and then only when there was a clear physiological, usually neurophysiological, supposition to be investigated. The work of Blass and his colleagues (see Kehoe, 1988), investigating an opioid-release hypothesis with respect to associative learning of infant rats, and of conditioning processes by infant animals carried out by Thompson (see Diamond, 1991), may usher in a whole new interest in conditioning phenomena. Kandel's (1979) work and that of others on aplysia is also likely to illuminate the neural transmission aspects of associative processes in both the primitive aplysia and the "immature" human organism. While according to some of the finest studies in this area the order of appearance of experientially induced behavioral phenomena in aplysia is habituation, then dishabituation, then sensitization, virtually nothing is known about whether such an orderly hierarchy occurs during ontogeny in human infants. What is known is that habituation and dishabituation (Bartoshuk, 1962) and classical conditioning occur in babies under 10 days of age (Rovee-Collier, 1987).

The earliest American attempts to explore the learning potential of human newborns, and to provide evidence of neonatal conditioning, were mostly negative (see Lipsitt, 1963, for review). The investigators who were putatively best at conditioning infants were the Soviets, and they had the rather pessimistic view that the human newborn is so cortically immature that conditioning is not possible. The prevailing view was that as the torch is passed from subcortical to cortical mediation, classical and other conditioning processes are increasingly facilitated or enabled. Thus, the wisdom of the age said that the older infant, for example, at ages 2–4 months, can be conditioned, but not the newborn. Because classical conditioning is one of the basic processes through which learning takes place in older organisms, however, some of us presumed that such a process must be present at least in rudimentary form in the human newborn.

Habituation and Sensitization

The diminution of responsitivity after repeated presentations of a once-effective stimulus, called habituation, has been viewed as a means by which organisms eliminate nonessential responses to biologically irrelevant stimuli (Thompson & Spencer, 1966). Thompson and his colleagues (e.g., Groves & Thompson, 1970) have suggested that a repetitive event lacking in strong consequences, for example, a low-intensity innocuous sound, probably alters neural pathways in a way specific to that stimulus, and signals "no action required." In human infants, habituation has been demonstrated by Bartoshuk (1962) among others, along with dishabituation or recovery of the habituated response, after the passage of time greater than the interstimulus habituation interval or upon presentation of a novel stimulus.

In contrast to the foregoing basis for understanding habituation and dishabituation as change in unconditioned responses to relatively mild stimulation, Groves and Thompson contend that events with strong consequences alter a different population of neurons and produce response enhancement (sensitization). Sensitization is characteristically presumed to involve generalized enhancement of the response to a wide variety of stimuli rather than to a specific stimulus, such as the initially neutral stimulus which will become paired with the UCS in a classical conditioning setting. The sensitization phenomenon must therefore be "controlled out" as a possible determinant of response change in a classical conditioning experiment. Interestingly, in one of the most intriguing early studies of newborn classical conditioning (Wickens & Wickens, 1940), a sensitization control was introduced but it effectively precluded an interpretation of classical conditioning in the experimental group which received paired CS-UCS stimuli, even though this group appeared to have conditioned. In the Wickens' study, the CS was a buzzer sound and the UCS a shock to the foot, causing an abrupt withdrawal bilaterally of the legs. If subjects made any response to the initially "neutral" CS, they were not further studied. The ISI was about .25 sec and continued (in a delayed presentation procedure) for another .25 sec. Of the 12 infants receiving the CS-UCS in paired fashion, nine appeared to become "conditioned," showing responses during the CS-alone test period (an extinction condition) after 3 days of 12 pairings each. One control group received only an initial test with the CS and no more stimulus presentations until the test period. In this group, only 1 infant of 12 reacted to the buzzer CS. Thus, the results of this group argued against any possibility of a response change to the CS due to maturation over the 3 days of testing in the experimental group. A second control group, however, which had received only the shock for a comparable 36 trials did indeed respond to the buzzer when it was presented alone after 3 days. Eleven of these 12 infants responded, as if conditioned, without having received paired presentations of the CS and UCS. The mere presentation of an "arousing" stimulus was shown to be effective in producing conditioned-like behavior, by predisposing the subject to make responses to a previously neutral stimulus.

Such sensitization phenomena are interesting in and of themselves as they are indeed experientially induced changes in behavior to previously neutral stimuli, but they are not easily defended as instantiations of classical conditioning processes. Munn (1954, 1955) did, in fact, suggest that pseudoconditioning phenomena such as these may represent a type of conditioning, reasoning that in the Wickens study (a) the shock-stimulated controls "learned" to respond to sudden-onset stimulation, (b) the buzzer during test trials constituted such sudden stimulation, and (c) reaction to the buzzer was a generalized response from the "training" situation, in this instance the 36-trial presentation of the UCS alone. The argument Munn put forth is that a fear or startle state is induced by the shock stimulations, and this state mediates increased intensities of response to stimuli which were hitherto neutral or non-elicitors. That the CS-alone control group did not show a threshold-of-response change to the buzzer supports the argument.

The Munn interpretation perhaps begs the question of whether classical conditioning should be regarded solely as an associative change in behavior, or whether the model may incorporate threshold changes of response due to repetitive presentations of an arousal stimulus and concomitant state changes. In any event, the Wickens study suggests that sensitization appears at least as early in the newborn as apparent conditioning, and that conditioning cannot be corroborated without adequate controls for such pseudoconditioning effects. Thus we have a presumptive ordering of complexity among three experientially induced behavior processes, with habituation and dishabituation being the clearest and easiest phenomena to show, followed by sensitization, followed by classical conditioning.

Several reviews of habituation in infants exist (e.g., Clifton & Nelson, 1976; Jeffrey & Cohen, 1971) although none has appeared in the past 15 years (coincident with the decline in classical conditioning research). While some students of habituation regard it as a primitive form of *learning* (Clifton & Nelson, 1976; Stein, 1966), this position has been contrasted with the observation that after an extended interval of no stimulation with the habituated stimulus, response to that stimulus recovers, whereas conditioning effects are seen as more durable changes in behavior. Thus it may be concluded that the passage of time acts differently on a habituated response than on a classically conditioned response, suggesting that the processes underlying each are different. Further research must surely be done to illuminate the similarities and differences of classical conditioning and habituation, however, for some investigators have found habituated responses, although not in infants, to remain suppressed for long periods of time (see Rovee-Collier & Lipsitt, 1982, pp. 151–152). On the basis of present knowledge, it is fair to suggest that both habituation and sensitization have been found easier to demonstrate, historically, than classical conditioning, especially in allegedly recalcitrant organisms such as aplysia (Kandel, 1979) and the human infant (Lipsitt, 1963; Wickens & Wickens, 1940), and therefore might be viewed as more primitive experientially induced processes of behavior change.

Classical Eyelid Conditioning

The eyeblink is a protective reflex, preventing injury to the delicate eye through the defensive action of lid closure. This response can be manipulated easily and without danger through the mere presentation of an air puff to the lid of the eye or to the surrounding area. Moreover, one can readily observe that the protective eyelid response is intact at birth in normal newborns, but that the conditioned defensive lid response, part of "flinching" behavior in the older child and present throughout the later life span, is absent in the very young infant. A looming stimulus, for example, does not typically produce an anticipatory eyeblink until the infant is 1 or 2 months of age. Thus, the classically conditioned eyelid response is an attractive one for the study of ontogenetic aspects of learning processes.

Babies in the first days of life possess sensitivity to stimulation in all sensory modalities, an unconditioned repertoire of responses to some of these sensory stimuli, and a capacity for associating simultaneously presented stimuli. The human newborn is a conditionable organism. Thus a perceived but previously neutral stimulus with respect to the elicitation of some particular behavior can itself become an effective stimulus through paired associations with an effective stimulus, and may now produce a response similar to the initially effective stimulus. For such a phenomenon to occur, the organism must be capable of remembering. The duration of memory is empirically demonstrable through probes or tests with the neutral stimulus, at various time intervals following the last experience of the pairing.

Besides engaging in classical conditioning involving transfer of elicitability from an effective stimulus to a previously ineffective stimulus (or its converse, as in extinction), demonstrating that human newborns do learn, babies are also demonstrably capable habituators. They exhibit diminution of response intensity or frequency to repetitively presented, and particularly closely spaced and essentially innocuous, stimuli. Newborns also exhibit generalized sensitization to stimulation such that, when neonates are aroused, stimuli will nondiscriminatively elicit behaviors. It is thus important that appropriate controls for nonconditioning processes, which may also involve change in behavior through experience, be included in any demonstrations that purport to show the conditionability of the newborn.

SUMMARY: A LESSON IN TRAINING FOR DIVERSITY

It has been argued here that the scientific process leading to innovative findings and intellectual advances has overarching properties enabling its application to a wide variety of natural phenomena, in all areas of science. Scientific investigation involves a step-wise process which should result in accretions of knowledge that in turn will suggest further questions. Pursuit of the answers to these questions tests the mettle of the previous findings, through replication, and facilitates the discovery of larger domains of lawfulness.

The simple question of whether newborns learn and, if so, in what ways, leads to an assessment of the veracity of previous findings which, in turn, inspires further studies illuminating the processes by which learning does and does not take place.

The presumption is advanced here that the proliferation of literature, and the vast technological advances recently made in circumscribed areas of psychological investigation, virtually dictate that the training of future child developmentalists for diversity will require attention to training in the overarching modes of asking question systematically. It is argued here that much transfer of training can be obtained from one field to another, as in listening intelligently and comprehending successfully the scientific work of others, when scientists hold the rudiments of search strategies in common.

REFERENCE

Anokhin, P. K. (1974). *Biology and neurophysiology of the conditioned reflex and its role in adaptive behavior.* Oxford/New York: Pergamon Press.

Bartoshuk, A. K. (1962). Human neonatal cardiac acceleration to sound: Habituation and dishabituation. *Perceptual and Motor Skills, 15*, 15–27.

Caldwell, D. F., & Werboff, J. (1962). Classical conditioning in newborn rats. *Science, 136*, 1118–1119.

Carmichael, L. (Ed.). (1954). *Manual of child psychology* (2nd ed.). New York: Wiley.

Clifton, R. K., & Nelson, M. N. (1976). Developmental study of habituation in infants: The importance of paradigm, response system, and state. In T. J. Tighe & L. N. Leaton (Eds.), *Habituation: Perspectives from child development, animal behavior, and neurophysiology.* Hillsdale, NJ: Erlbaum.

Davis, M. (1970). Interstimulus interval and startle response habituation with a "control" for time during training. *Psychonomic Science, 20*, 39–41.

Diamond, A. (Ed.). (1991). *The development and neural bases of higher cognitive functions.* New York: The New York Academy of Sciences, and MIT Press.

Elkonin, D. B. (1957). The physiology of higher nervous system activity and child psychology. In B. Simon (Ed.), *Psychology in the Soviet Union.* London: Routledge and Kegan Paul.

Gray, P. H., Yates, A. E., & McNeal, K. (1967). The ontogeny of classical conditioning in the neonatal rat with varied CS-UCS intervals. *Psychonomic Science, 9*, 587–588.

Groves, P. M., & Thompson, R. F. (1970). Habituation: A dual-process theory. *Psychological Review, 77*, 419–450.

Haith, M. M., & Campos, J. J. (Eds.). (1983). Infancy and developmental psychobiology. Volume II of P. H. Mussen (Ed.), *Handbook of child psychology,* New York: Wiley.

Jeffrey, W. E., & Cohen, L. B. (1971). Habituation in the human infant. In H. W. Reese (Ed.), *Advances in child development and behavior* (Vol. 6). New York: Academic Press.

Kandel, E. R. (1979). *Cellular insights into behavior and learning* (The Harvey Lectures, Series 73). New York: Academic Press.

Kehoe, P. (1988). Opioids, behavior, and learning in mammalian development. In N. Adler & E. M. Blass (Eds.), *Handbook of behavioral neurobiology: Developmental psychobiology and behavioral ecology.* New York: Plenum Press.

Kimble, G. A. (1961). *Hilgard and Marquis' conditioning and learning* (2nd ed.). New York: Appleton-Century-Crofts.

Lederman, L. M. (1991). *Science: The end of the frontier?* Washington, DC: American Association for the Advancement of Science.

Lipsitt, L. P. (1963). Learning in the first year of life. In L. P. Lipsitt & C. C. Spiker (Eds.), *Advances in child development and behavior* (Vol. I). New York: Academic Press.

Lipsitt, L. P. (1969). Learning capacities of the human infant. In R. J. Robinson (Ed.), *Brain and early behavior: Development in the fetus and infant.* New York: Academic Press.

Lipsitt, L. P., & Kaye, H. (1964). Conditioned sucking in the human newborn. *Psychonomic Science, 1,* 29–30.

Lipsitt, L. P., Kaye, H., & Bosack, T. N. (1966). Enhancement of neonatal sucking through reinforcement. *Journal of Experimental Child Psychology, 4,* 163–168.

Little, A. H. (1970). *Eyelid conditioning in the human infant as a function of the interstimulus interval.* Unpublished Master's thesis, Brown University, Providence, RI.

Little, A. H. (1973). *A comparative study of trace and delay conditioning in the human infant.* Doctoral dissertation, Brown University, Providence, RI Dissertation Abstracts International, 1974, 34 (University Microfilms No. 74-3046).

Little, A. H., Lipsitt, L. P., & Rovee-Collier, C. K. (1984). Classical conditioning and retention of the infant's eyelid response: Effects of age and interstimulus interval. *Journal of Experimental Child Psychology, 37,* 512–524.

Munn, N. L. (1954). Learning in children. In L. Carmichael (Ed.), *Manual of child psychology.* New York: Wiley.

Munn, N. L. (1955). *The evolution and growth of human behavior.* Boston: Houghton Mifflin.

Osofksy, J. D. (Ed.). (1987). *Handbook of infant development* (2nd ed.). New York: Wiley.

Papousek, H. (1959). A method of studying conditioned food reflexes in young children up to the age of six months. *Pavlov Journal of Higher Nervous Activity, 9,* 136–140.

Rendle-Short, J. (1961). The puff test. *Archives of Diseases of Childhood, 36,* 50–57.

Rovee-Collier, C., & Lipsitt, L. P. (1982). Learning, adaptation, and memory in the newborn. In P. Stratton (Ed.), *Psychobiology of the human newborn.* New York: Wiley.

Rovee-Collier, C. (1987). Learning and memory in infancy. In J. D. Osofsky (Ed.), *Handbook of Infant Development* (2nd ed.). New York: Wiley.

Sameroff, A. J. (1971). Can conditioned responses be established in the newborn infant? *Developmental Psychology, 5,* 1–12.

Sameroff, A. J. (1972). Learning and adaptation in infancy: A comparison of models. In H. W. Reese (Ed.), *Advances in child development and behavior* (Vol. 7). New York: Academic Press.

Stein, L. (1966). Habituation and stimulus novelty: A model based on classical conditioning. *Psychological Review, 73,* 352–356.

Thorndike, E. L. (1898). Animal intelligence: An experimental study of associative processes in animals. *Psychological Monographs, 2*, No. 8.

Wickens, D. D. & Wickens, C. (1940). A study of conditioning in the neonate. *Journal of Experimental Psychology, 26*, 94–102.

Woodruff-Pak, D. S., & Thompson, R. F. (1989). Cerebellar correlates of classical conditioning across the life span. In P. B. Baltes, D. M. Featherman & R. M. Lerner (Eds.), *Life-span development and behavior* (Vol. 9). Hillsdale, NJ: Lawrence Erlbaum Associates.

Author Index

Subject Index